Teachers and the Law

Third Edition

Louis Fischer
University of Massachusetts

David Schimmel
University of Massachusetts

Cynthia Kelly
Loyola University of Chicago

Longman
New York & London

Teachers and the Law, Third Edition

Longman, 95 Church Street, White Plains, N.Y. 10601

Associated companies:
Longman Group Ltd., London
Longman Cheshire Pty., Melbourne
Longman Paul Pty., Auckland
Copp Clark Pitman, Toronto

Senior editor: Naomi Silverman
Production editor: Ann P. Kearns
Cover design: Anne M. Pompeo
Production supervisor: Kathleen M. Ryan

Library of Congress Cataloging-in-Publication Data

Fischer, Louis, 1924–
    Teachers and the law / Louis Fischer, David Schimmel, Cynthia
Kelly.—3rd ed.
        p. cm.
    Contents: Includes bibliographical references.
    ISBN 0-8013-0482-2
    1. Teachers—Legal status, laws, etc.—United States.
2. Teachers—Legal status, laws, etc.—United States—States.
3. Students—Legal status, laws, etc.—United States. 4. Students—
    Legal status, laws, etc.—United States—States. I. Schimmel,
David. II. Kelly, Cynthia A.
KF4175.Z9F55   1990
344.73′078—dc20
[347.30478]   90-32155
                                                       CIP

2 3 4 5 6 7 8 9 10-AL-9594939291

Contents

Topic
Overview

Preface

Americans are a litigious people. This attitude is not recent; over one hundred years ago, a sensitive French visitor, Alexis de Tocqueville, observed that in the United States all issues become "sooner or later a subject of judicial debate."

Today's schools exist and function in the midst of a complex legal environment, and it is difficult not to be aware of a wide range of legal issues that influence the lives of teachers, students, parents, and administrators. It is increasingly clear that educators ignore the law at their peril! In fact, the U.S. Supreme Court ruled in 1975 that teachers and administrators may be held personally liable in money damages for violating students' clearly established constitutional rights.

This book is about teachers and the law that affects them, law established by state and federal statutes, constitutions, and court decisions. This law will have little significance, however, unless educators know about it and make the effort to see that it is carried out.

It is not the purpose of this book to encourage teachers to go to court. Going to court is expensive—emotionally as well as economically. Litigation tends to intensify conflict and polarize the participants. Therefore, our goal is to help resolve educational conflicts without seeking out lawyers or resorting to courts. How? By helping teachers become legally literate—by providing them with information about the law that affects them, about the way the legal system works, and about the way this system can work for them in the public school. With this information, teachers can practice "preventive law." This does not mean that they will be able to be their own lawyers but rather that they will know their legal rights and responsibilities and will assume responsibility for educating other members of the school community about the law. Underlying this premise is our belief that unlawful school practices are generally not intentional but result from a misunderstanding of the law. Because most school officials are anxious to avoid lawsuits, when teachers are able to show that certain school policies are illegal, administrators usually prefer to change them voluntarily rather than as the result of a court order. In addition, we believe that students' educational experiences will be improved when all members of the school community display behavior that is consistent with basic constitutional principles such as due process of law.

Why are educators poorly informed about the law that affects schools? One reason may be that much of this law did not exist when they were students, and as a result, they learned almost nothing about this subject during their education. A second reason is that most educators have had little training in applying education law during their professional careers. This book can help fill that gap. In addition, we hope in this book to demystify the law for teachers—to break through the barrier of professional jargon and legalese that lawyers use among themselves and translate this language into everyday English.

In short, the purpose of this book is to enable teachers to constructively take the law into their own hands—to provide them with the knowledge necessary to comply with the law, assert their rights, and bring violations to the attention of administrators and colleagues.

This book is divided into two parts. Part I, "The Legal Aspects of Teaching," addresses questions related to teacher contracts, dismissals, tenure, collective bargaining, liability, child abuse, defamation, and copyright law. Part II, "Teachers' and Students' Rights," explores legal issues related to the scope and limits of personal freedom: of expression, religion and conscience, association, personal appearance, due process, and privacy. It also includes the right to be free from racial and sexual discrimination and rights related to school records, compulsory schooling, and handicapped and bilingual students. The topic overview section of this book presents questions covered in each chapter.

Most of the questions and answers are based on reported court cases. By introducing educators to the law through the use of real conflicts, we provide material that classroom teachers can personally relate to. In addition, building chapters around court cases is a more lively and effective way for teachers to approach the law than by focusing on theoretical issues or legal abstractions. At the same time, each chapter—especially in the summary—goes beyond the outcome of specific cases and identifies the underlying principles that are likely to apply to similar cases in the future.

Books about law often begin with a description of the judicial system and the court structure. For some readers, this is a helpful introduction. Others become bored with such descriptions because they do not yet care about these matters. But as readers become involved with legal questions, they begin to wonder why cases go to the federal or state courts, when a case can be appealed to the U.S. Supreme Court, and how to find a case record in the library.

Because different readers will ask these questions at different times, we have put our explanation of how the legal system works in Appendix B. Other appendixes contain relevant sections of the U.S. Constitution, excerpts from federal laws relating to education, a glossary of common legal terms, a list of legal resources, and a bibliography. For those who are using this book as a text, an *Instructor's manual* is available that includes edited Supreme Court cases as well as discussion questions, references to additional cases, suggested teaching activities, and a bibliography for each chapter.

No single volume can address all the issues involving school law; this book covers only those issues most central in the daily lives of teachers. It does not, for example, address legal issues which might be related to the use of school property, school boundaries, liabilities of school districts, school board procedures, and teacher retirement. School law is a broad and burgeoning field, and only some portions of it are directly relevant to the professional roles of most teachers.

Much of the law examined in these pages is neither simple nor unchanging. Many of the cases are as difficult to resolve for lawyers and judges as they are for educators. This is because cases involving school law often do not address simple conflicts of right against wrong but complex issues encompassing the conflicting interests of teachers, parents, administrators, and students. Moreover, education law is constantly changing. New legislation is passed, regulations are amended, school boards revise their practices, and the Supreme Court may declare a policy unconstitutional. Because of this diversity and change, our discussion of the cases and laws in each chapter is intended to be illustrative, not exhaustive. We have chosen to highlight major cases and legislation of general interest to teachers rather than focus on legal details. In addition, citations to cases are provided in a form that is most likely to be useful to teachers, as opposed to the form that is used in legal treatises and law review articles.

To summarize, this book is designed to promote legal literacy for public school teachers. It examines a wide range of constitutional, statutory, and case law that directly affects their work. Since no two cases are alike, and since the law is constantly changing, the book can neither be comprehensive nor a substitute for legal advice.

If you contemplate legal action, you should first consult with your professional association and/or a knowledgeable lawyer. But since judicial resolution of an educational dispute is often an unhappy, expensive, difficult, and time-consuming process, bringing suit should be the *last* resort. We hope this book will help you resolve disputes through discussion and negotiation rather than litigation.

We wish to acknowledge and thank those who helped us in writing this book: Naomi Silverman, Karen Philippidis, and Ann Kearns of Longman Publishing Group, who supported this effort; Meyer Weinberg, who made the resources of the Horace Mann Bond Center for Equal Education available to us; Rich Morrill, Barbara B. Fischer, Joanna Schimmel, and Barbara Morgan, who assisted us in finding and checking case citations; Kim Lambert, whose research assistance was made possible by a grant from the Illinois Bar Foundation; and Robb Cooper, who provided not only research assistance but also valuable help in editing.

PART I

The Legal Aspects of Teaching

CHAPTER 1

Do I Have a Contract?

OVERVIEW

Most school districts have written contracts with their teachers. These contracts outline both teacher and school board rights. Contract provisions can vary widely from district to district. For example, the 1989–1990 contract between the Chicago Board of Education and the Chicago Teachers Union ran to 145 pages. Contract provisions included salary schedules for teachers, maximum class size, school day length, insurance, student discipline, sick pay, transfer policies, and grievance procedures for teachers who wished to complain of contract violations. Because the contract was the result of collective bargaining negotiations, it also included a provision requiring the board to recognize the union as the bargaining agent for the teacher. (Chapter 3 gives a detailed survey of collective bargaining.)

In contrast, the 1988–1989 contract between the Lake Geneva, Wisconsin, School District and the local teachers association was only 18 pages long. This contract, too, provided for recognition of the association as the exclusive bargaining representative of the teachers, and it described teaching hours and assignments. It also outlined policies concerning leaves of absence, grievance procedures, and the teacher salary schedule.

Although length and wording may vary in teaching contracts, certain basic legal principles are common to all of them. It is these principles that we discuss in this chapter.

CREATING A CONTRACT

The *Wilson* Case[1]

On January 20, 1969, Jessie Wilson applied for a position as principal in the District of Columbia summer school program. She later received a form letter advising her that she had been selected for this position. The letter stated that the appointment was subject to full funding of the summer school program and the return of an attached acceptance form within five days. The acceptance form stipulated that the applicant's acceptance was "subject to the approval of the board of education."

Wilson returned the acceptance form within the required time. Before the board approved her appointment, however, the selection criteria for summer positions were revised, and the board decided that Wilson no longer qualified for the position as principal. After the board notified her that they could not approve her appointment, Wilson sued school officials for the loss of income resulting from their withdrawal of the offer of appointment as principal. Wilson argued that a contract was created when the summer school program received full funding and that school officials broke the contract when they refused to hire her.

The District of Columbia Court of Appeals disagreed. The court pointed out that the acceptance form specified the position was subject to approval by the District Board of Education. (The court also noted that such approval was required by law in the District of Columbia.) Since the board never gave its approval, "no binding contract of employment existed before Ms. Wilson was notified that she did not meet the criteria for appointment." Because no contract was ever created, Wilson did not have a legal right to the position as principal and was not entitled to any money from the board of education for loss of income.

When is a contract created?

As the *Wilson* case demonstrates, certain requirements must be met before a contract is legally binding on both the teacher and school officials. Like all other contracts, a teacher's contract must have

1. a meeting of the minds of both parties,
2. valid consideration,
3. legal subject matter,
4. competent parties, and
5. definite terms.

In contract law, "a meeting of the minds" refers to mutual assent to the terms of the contract. This mutual agreement is usually reached through the process of offer and acceptance. This requirement was the issue in *Wilson;* the court was asked to decide whether there was a valid offer and acceptance. The court concluded that because the board did not complete proper procedures, and did not approve Ms. Wilson's contract, there was no meeting of the minds and, thus, no contract.

"Consideration" refers to the promises bargained for and exchanged between the parties. To have valid consideration to support a contract, each party must give up something of value, or, in legal terms, "suffer some legal detriment"; that is, the parties to the contract must promise to do something they are not legally obligated to do or promise to refrain from doing something they are legally privileged to do. In the case of a teaching contract, consideration consists of the exchange of promises between the teacher and the school: the teacher promises to perform certain teaching services, and school officials promise to pay the teacher a certain salary.

"Legal subject matter" means that the contract cannot require the parties to commit a crime or act against public policy (e.g., an Illinois teacher contracted to have a student murder his principal). "Competent parties" means that the people contracting must be of legal age (21 in some states, but 18 in most) and must have the mental capacity to understand the terms of the contract. "Definite terms" means that the contract must be clear enough so that each party knows what is required by it. Like other employment contracts, a teaching contract that does not state either salary or teaching duties is too indefinite to be legally enforced. Thus, an Indiana court ruled that a contract to pay a teacher "good wages" was not valid.[2]

When does a contract become legally binding?

As Jessie Wilson discovered, a contract is not valid until the school board approves it. Because school boards act as public bodies, they cannot accept ("ratify") a contract without taking official action. Thus, one teacher's contract was not valid when the board of education did not follow the required roll-call procedure in voting on whether to offer her a teaching position.[3] In addition, state law may provide that the school board must ratify a contract before it is legally binding, as in the *Wilson* case.

EXPRESS AND IMPLIED CONTRACTS

Does a contract have to be in writing?

No. Unless state law requires that a teacher's employment contract be in writing, an oral contract that has all the necessary legal requirements is legally binding.

Does a contract contain all the relevant information regarding terms and conditions of employment?

Not necessarily. As with other contracts, a teacher's contract includes the provisions of any relevant state laws, such as those concerning teacher tenure and dismissal procedures. In addition, the contract includes any rules and regulations adopted by the school board that are in effect at the time the contract is signed. Thus, an Oregon court ruled that a teacher could be dismissed for not performing his contractual duties when he did not follow a state board of education mandate that "teachers in the public schools shall . . . inculcate in the minds of their pupils correct principles of morality and a proper regard for the laws of society."[4] In addition, where the teacher's contract contains a statement that the teacher agrees to abide by all rules and regulations adopted by school officials, or where the contract specifically states that it includes the provisions of a particular rule or regulation, the teacher's contract includes even those rules and regulations adopted after the contract has taken effect. For example, a California teacher's contract stated that the teacher was elected "under section 1609 [of the Political Code] in accordance with salary schedule adopted by the Board."[5] When a teacher challenged the school board's legal authority to lower her salary, the court ruled that this provision in her contract gave the board the power to modify the salary schedule in effect at the time she signed her teaching contract. The court noted, however, that any new schedule would have to be adopted prior to the beginning of the school year.

Can an employee handbook serve as a basis for contractual obligation?

Yes. When an employee is working without a formal employment contract, the terms of an employee handbook may be contractually binding. Although some courts reject this idea, the majority of jurisdictions recognize the contract potential of employee handbooks and manuals.[6] An employee handbook creates enforceable contractual rights if the traditional elements of contract formation (offer, acceptance, and consideration) are satisfied.[7] Different jurisdictions follow different criteria when determining if the contract elements are met. Generally, however, the handbook provisions in question must be specific and clear. The employee must be aware of the policies and believe them to be offered terms of employment; the employee must also continue to work after notification of the handbook terms, thus giving consideration.[8]

Furthermore, courts may find that an employee handbook adds terms to an existing employment contract. In a North Dakota case, the court found that a reduction-in-force policy, outlined in the employee handbook, was part of the contract between the school district and its teachers:

> Although the policy was adopted unilaterally by the District and was not a part of the negotiation process . . . an employer may be contractually bound by promises, express or implied, in employee handbooks with respect to job security and termination procedures.[9]

Once the court found the reduction-in-force policy was a contractual term, it held that the school district had properly complied with the policy, and the teacher's nonrenewal was upheld.

How long does a contract last?

The contract itself states how long it is to be in effect. Nontenured teachers generally hold their positions under annual contracts. Teachers may also be employed under "continuing contracts," which provide that they will be reemployed unless school officials give notice by a certain date that their contracts will not be renewed. Most states also allow school boards to enter into multiyear employment contracts with teachers.

Can a teacher work without a contract?

A teacher can certainly work without a contract, but may have difficulty proving that a certain amount of money is owed as compensation for teaching services. In an Illinois case, for example, the court ruled that tenured teachers did not have to sign contracts.[10] Nevertheless, when a group of tenured teachers refused to sign new contracts, the court held that they should be paid on the basis of the preceding year's salary and should be denied the benefits given to teachers who had signed the new contract. A nontenured teacher who works without a contract will have more difficulty than a tenured teacher in collecting money from school officials. The nontenured teachers may be able to recover the reasonable value of teaching services under a theory of "quasi-contract," also known as a "contract implied in law."

A quasi-contract is not a contract at all, but "an obligation imposed by law to do justice even though it is clear that no promise was ever made or intended."[11] In order for the court to impose such an obligation, the following must occur: (1) one person must confer a benefit on another, (2) the person conferring the benefit must have a reasonable expectation of compensation, (3) the person conferring the benefit must not have volunteered, and (4) the person receiving the benefit must be unjustly enriched if the person performing the service is not paid. A teacher who worked without a contract would generally meet these requirements and thus be entitled to compensation for teaching services.

BREACH OF CONTRACT

How can a contract be broken by school officials?

A contract is binding on both parties, and either party who fails to meet contractual obligations has breached (broken) the contract. For example, Bertrand Russell sued the Barnes Foundation for breach of contract when his services as a lecturer were terminated after two years.[12] Russell had entered into an oral agreement with the Barnes Foundation in which he promised to deliver lectures for five years. This agreement was confirmed in letters between the Barnes Foundation and Russell, copies of which are reprinted here:

Dear Mr. Russell:

We confirm herewith the verbal agreement made with you on August 8, 1940.

We agree to engage you as a member of the teaching staff of the Barnes Foundation at a salary of eight thousand ($8,000) dollars per year, payable in twelve (12) equal monthly installments, on the fifteenth day of each month.

The agreement is to extend for a period of five (5) years, dating from January 1, 1941. If, during the period of the aforesaid agreement, your personal affairs should make it necessary or advisable to terminate the contract, we agree that such a termination may be effected at the end of our school year; namely May 31st.

Your service to the Foundation will consist of one lecture each week during the school year, which extends from October 1st to May 31st inclusive, each lecture to be delivered in the gallery of the Barnes Foundation, at Merion, Pennsylvania.

Yours very truly,
The Barnes Foundation
Albert C. Barnes
President (Corp. Seal)
N. E. Mullen
Secretary-Treasurer

Paul Hogan, Witness
Sarah M. Cleaver, Witness

I, Bertrand Russell, hereby agree to the terms and conditions of the above agreement entered into between myself and the Barnes Foundation.

Bertrand Russell

Mary Mullen, Witness
Cynthia F. Stone, Witness[13]

After he had delivered lectures for two years, Russell was informed by the Barnes Foundation that his contract was to be terminated on December 31, 1942. Russell successfully sued the foundation for breach of contract and was able to collect damages for the money he should have received under the contract. (Chapter 4 contains a detailed discussion of damages.)

In addition to refusing to employ a teacher, a school board can breach a contract by violating one of its provisions. In Maine, for example, the school board voted to dismiss a tenured teacher who also served as a principal, citing a state law that provided the school committee could terminate a contract "when changes in local conditions warrant the elimination of the teaching position for which the contract was made."[14] The court found, however, that there was no evidence that local conditions had changed. The school officials had eliminated only the extra duty as principal, for which, in previous years, there had been a separate contract. In fact, the teacher's position was not eliminated; the teacher was merely replaced by another teacher who performed exactly the same duties. Since the school board had not followed the proper statutory procedures in dismissing the teacher, the court found that the board had breached the contract.

School officials can also breach a contract if they attempt to change the terms of a contract after it is in effect. In Oregon, for example, Mr. George, a teacher, was hired under the following three-year contract:

> THIS AGREEMENT made this 22nd day of April, 1968, by and between School District No. 8R of Umatilla County, Oregon, hereinafter referred to as the district, and Robert George, hereinafter referred to as the teacher.
>
> WITNESSETH:
> 1. The district agrees to employ the teacher for a period of 3 year(s), commencing on the first day of July, 1968, and ending on the 30th day of June, 1971, and to pay the teacher therefor an annual salary of $11,300, together with any compensation programs established by the district.
> 2. In consideration of the compensation paid hereunder, the teacher agrees to teach Secondary grades in the schools of the district during the period of the regular school year as established by the district. . . .
> 5. Additional terms of the contract are as follows:
>   Base salary 1968–69 $ 9,300
>   Extra duties: Athletics   2,000
>   Total salary 1968–69 $11,300[15]

In the middle of the first school year, the school board fired Mr. George as the football coach. In March 1969 school officials informed him that his salary for the 1969–1970 school year would be $2000 less than expected because of the elimination of his "extra duty" for football coaching. The teacher claimed that, under his contract, he was still entitled to the full salary of $11,300. School officials treated his response as a refusal to teach and hired another teacher to replace him. Mr. George sued, claiming that the school board had breached the contract. The school board defended its actions by arguing that the teacher was actually employed under two separate contracts: (1) a three-year contract to teach for $9300, plus any raises, and (2) a one-year contract to coach football for $2000. In the school board's view, Mr. George had breached his contract when he refused to teach at the $9300 salary level.

In order to resolve this dispute the court had to interpret the contract to find out what the parties actually intended their words to mean. Under the law of contracts, if a written agreement between two parties is assumed to include all the relevant information about the subject matter, the court cannot look at any prior agreements or conversations that may modify what the written contract says.[16] The court can, however, *interpret* the words of the contract, and in its efforts to find the true meaning of the words, the court can look at the circumstances surrounding the making of the contract as well as the past practices and policies of the school district concerning teaching contracts.

After examining such evidence, the Oregon court agreed with the teacher that the contract was not divisible into two parts. First, the court noted that the minutes of the school board meeting at which the teacher's contract was authorized showed that the football and basketball coaches were to be given three-year contracts. Second, after listening to testimony from a number of school officials, the court found that, although a teacher's extra-duty assignments could be changed in the middle of a contract, it was not customary for a teacher's salary to be reduced. The court therefore ruled that the school board had breached the teacher's contract by insisting that the teacher accept a $2000 salary reduction for the remaining two years of his three-year contract.

How can a teacher break a contract?

The same principles that apply to school officials also apply to teachers. A teacher who has signed an employment contract and then refuses to accept the teaching position or abandons the position in midyear has breached the contract.

A teacher who does not abide by its terms also breaches a contract. In Texas, for example, a music teacher was employed by the Mission public schools under a contract that stated that she would not teach anywhere else in Texas during the contract period.[17] When the teacher left this job to teach music and direct the band in the Cisco, Texas, public schools, the court ruled that she had breached her contract. Similarly, an Arkansas court found that a teacher had breached her employment contract when she took a leave of absence without following the procedure outlined in the school board's regulations.[18]

What are the legal consequences of breaking a contract?

When one party breaches a contract, the other party to the contract is entitled to a legal remedy that will compensate for the injury the breaching party has caused. In most situations this remedy will be an award of some amount of money, or "damages." The specific amount of money to be awarded is determined by the court according to the particular facts in each case.

In general, when a school board breaks an employment contract, the injured teacher is entitled to damages that equal the salary owed under the contract minus any money the teacher actually earned or might have earned had another teaching position been obtained. In order to understand this rule, it helps to examine a particular case.

In the case described earlier, when Bertrand Russell's teaching contract was breached, the court awarded him $20,000. To reach this figure, the court engaged in the following analysis: First, the court turned to the contract itself to determine how much money Russell would have received if he had been permitted to lecture; under the terms of the contract, the Barnes Foundation had agreed to pay $8000 a year, or $24,000 for the remaining three-year period. The court then explained that it was up to the Barnes Foundation (the defendant) "to show, in mitigation of this amount, the extent of plaintiff's [Russell's] earnings or ability to obtain other employment."[19] The evidence showed that, during the two years he was teaching for the Barnes Foundation, Russell had earned $2145.00 and $3195.68 from other sources, principally his writing and radio addresses. Russell also testified that his earning prospects from these sources for the next three years were slight, and that "his advanced age and the drastic curtailment of courses in philosophy in college curricula" made it impossible for him to obtain other employment. Given this evidence, the court found that Russell could expect to earn only $4000 from outside sources for his teaching activities during the next three years and thus ordered the Barnes Foundation to pay him $20,000 as damages for breach of contract.

In suing for breach of contract, a teacher can also collect as damages any other expenses incurred as a result of the school board's action. For example, a Montana teacher collected the value of the living quarters supplied rent free under her contract after she was wrongfully dismissed.[20] The courts have also held that teachers who are wrongfully discharged can recover expenses that they can show were incurred in seeking another teaching position.[21] Although teachers are generally not awarded money to cover attorney's fees, such expenses may be awarded as damages under state or federal laws.[22]

The same principles apply when a teacher breaks a contract: School officials are entitled to collect money damages that will cover the school's costs in hiring a replacement.* Thus, if a teacher who is under contract quits in the middle of the school year, school officials can sue the teacher for expenses incurred in finding another teacher who can assume the same responsibilities. If the district is forced to pay a higher salary to find a replacement, school officials can sue the leaving teacher for the difference between that teacher's salary and the replacement teacher's salary.

Some employment contracts include provisions that require teachers who break their contracts to pay a specific amount as damages to the school district. In North Dakota, a teacher's contract stated that a teacher who asked to be released from her contract within two weeks before she was scheduled to begin teaching was required to pay damages in the amount of 4 percent of her salary under the contract.[23] These contractual provisions are known as "liquidated damages clauses," and the courts will enforce them when it is difficult for the parties to a contract to determine the monetary value of a breach of contract. The courts will not enforce such contractual provisions when they feel that the party who breaks the contract has to pay such a large amount of money that this provision is really a penalty or punishment for breaching the contract.

In the North Dakota case, six days before she was to begin teaching, Marcia Walker notified her district superintendent that her husband was moving from the area and that she would be unable to meet her contractual obligations. The school district found a replacement before school started but maintained that Walker was still required to pay damages. Walker argued that the fixed-damages provision of her contract constituted a penalty and therefore was void under North Dakota law. The court disagreed. Although the court explained that an employer could generally recover only the costs of replacing an employee who

---

* In a time of teacher surplus, when it is relatively easy for school boards to replace teachers, money damages are apt to be minimal; the teacher is more likely to be damaged in terms of professional reputation.

breaches a contract, it noted that liquidated-damages provisions were valid when it was difficult to ascertain the exact amount of damages. The court found that teacher replacement was such a situation:

> Thus, when we consider the damages caused by a teacher's breach of an employment contract, we cannot ignore the interruption to the school system and the resultant debilitating effect such interruption has upon the learning process of students in the school system. The possibility that the replacement teacher who was obtained may be less experienced or less qualified and, thus, a less effective instructor must also be considered in the assessment of damages. It would not be possible at the time of contracting to foresee all these elements of damage that may occur. Even if known, it would be extremely difficult to evaluate these damages on a monetary basis. . . . Such damages are not legally compensable but constitute a public injury which the school district was entitled to consider.[24]

When the school board breaches a contract, must the teacher look for another teaching position to collect damages?

A teacher who is wrongfully discharged generally has the duty to look for a similar teaching position in order to "mitigate the damages." If the school board can show that other teaching jobs were available, the board can reduce the amount of money owed as damages by the salary the teacher could have earned. Nevertheless, a teacher does not have to accept a job in another locality or a job that is inferior to the denied position. A federal court found, for example, that a principal was not required to mitigate damages by accepting a position as a teacher.[25] Even though the teaching job paid as much as the principalship, the court concluded that the demotion to teacher might cast doubt on the principal's competence as an administrator and affect later career opportunities.

　　If the school board breaches a contract some time before the teacher is to start working, the teacher is not required to look for another teaching position at once. Instead, the teacher has the right to wait until the contract was to begin before looking for another job. In Michigan, for example, the court ruled that a teacher whose contract was wrongfully withdrawn over the summer did not have to abandon her vacation to seek other employment but could notify the school district that she was still prepared to teach. She could wait to look for another job until after school started in the fall.[26]

Can the court order a school board to rehire a teacher?

Yes. Although the courts generally do not order people to return to work or perform certain services, they will do so when an award of money will not adequately compensate the party who has been the victim of a breach of contract. Where a teacher has tenure, for example, the courts can order reinstatement if a teacher has been wrongfully discharged. In one instance, a university failed to follow its own regulations when dismissing a professor, and the court ordered that the professor be reinstated. The court explained: "In view of the uncertainty in measuring damages because of the indefinite duration of the contract and the importance of the status of plaintiffs in the milieu of the college teaching profession it is evident that the remedy of damages at law would not be complete or adequate. . . . The relief granted herein is appropriate to achieve equity and justice"[27]

The situation for teachers without tenure varies according to the circumstances surrounding the dismissal. If school officials failed to follow proper hearing procedures, for example, the court may merely remand for a hearing.[28] In other cases, the court may order reinstatement. For example, a federal court ordered the reinstatement of a nontenured teacher when she was improperly dismissed for exercising her constitutional rights under the First Amendment.[29]

Are other remedies available when one party breaches a contract?

Yes. The courts have the power to issue orders (known as "writs of mandamus") to force school officials to comply with the terms of a contract. When one school board was guilty of racial discrimination in refusing to renew a teacher's employment contract, the court ordered the board to renew the contract.[30] In addition, courts can issue injunctions (court orders) to require the parties to meet their contractual obligations. For example, a court issued an injunction to prevent a teacher from breaching a contractual provision that prohibited her from teaching music in any other school district in the state.[31] In another case, a court issued an injunction preventing the school board from dismissing a superintendent when the school officials had no legal power to do so.[32]

Are there other ways that a contract can end?

Yes. Under the doctrine of "impossibility of performance," a party to a contract is excused from meeting the obligations under that contract if it is impossible to do so. In Washington, for example, a teacher was discharged from his contractual obligation because of his deteriorating eyesight.[33] The court explained that when it is impossible for the teacher to meet contractual duties, the contract to teach is said to be discharged "by operation of law."

A contract can also be terminated by mutual agreement of the parties. In Kansas, a court held that a teacher's employment contract had been terminated by mutual agreement with the school board after the teacher submitted a letter of resignation and the board voted to accept her resignation.[34] Although there was some question whether the teacher had in fact resigned, the court noted that "mutual assent to abandon a contract may be inferred from the conduct of the parties and the attendant circumstances." The court found that there was sufficient evidence to indicate that both the teacher and the school board had intended to end the contract; the court thus concluded that the contract was terminated.

SUMMARY

Most teachers are employed under contracts that outline their rights and responsibilities in employment. A contract becomes effective legally when the following conditions are met: the contract has a legal subject matter, there is a meeting of the minds of both parties, there is valid consideration, the parties are competent, and the contract has definite terms. In addition, school officials must act to officially ratify a teacher's contract.

A contract is binding on both parties; either the teacher or the school officials will be legally liable if obligations under the contract are not met. A school board that breaks a contract to employ a teacher will be required to pay that teacher monetary damages to compensate for loss of salary. In such a situation, however, the teacher has the duty to mitigate these damages by attempting to secure another teaching position. In breach-of-contract situations, the teacher may be entitled to other legal remedies as well, such as reinstatement or an injunction or other order requiring the school board to fulfill its obligations under the contract.

Of course, a teacher who breaks a contract will also be liable to the school district. Under traditional contract law principles, the teacher will be liable for the school district's costs in finding a replacement and for any additional salary that might have to be paid. Today, however, teachers' contracts may describe the specific amount of damages a teacher will have to pay in this situation.

NOTES

1. *Board of Education of D. C.* v. *Wilson,* 290 A.2d 400 (D.C. App. 1972).
2. *Fairplay School Township* v. *O'Neal,* 26 N.E. 686 (Ind. 1891).
3. *Board of Education* v. *Best,* 39 N.E. 694 (Ohio 1894).
4. *Bump* v. *Union High School District No. 3,* 24 P.2d 330, 331 (Or. 1933).
5. *Rible* v. *Hughes,* 150 P.2d 455, 458 (Cal. 1944).
6. For an overview of this topic see *Duldulao* v. *Saint Mary of Nazareth Hospital,* 505 N.E.2d 314 (Ill. 1987).
7. *Id.* at 318.
8. *Id.*
9. *Law* v. *Mandan Public School Dist.,* 411 N.W.2d 375 (N.D. 1987).
10. *Davis* v. *Board of Education of Aurora Public School Dist. No. 131,* 312 N.E.2d 335 (Ill. App. 1979).
11. John D. Calamari and Joseph M. Perillo, THE LAW OF CONTRACTS 11 (St. Paul, Minn.: West, 1970).
12. *Russell* v. *Barnes Foundation,* 50 F.Supp. 174 (E.D. Pa. 1943) (establishing liability), 52 F.Supp. 827 (E.D. Pa. 1943) (awarding damages), *aff'd,* 143 F.2d 871 (3d Cir. 1944), *cert. denied,* 323 U.S. 771 (1944).
13. 50 F.Supp. at 175–176.
14. *Kenaston* v. *School Administrative District No. 40,* 317 A.2d 7, 9 (Me. 1974).

15. *George* v. *School District No. 8R of Umatilla County*, 490 P.2d 1009, 1011 (Or. App. 1971).

16. A court may find, however, that a written agreement does not contain all the relevant terms of the contract. The contract does not include all relevant terms, or is not "completely integrated," if the writing omits a consistent additional term which might naturally be omitted from the writing or which is agreed to for separate consideration. If the court finds the written agreement to be only "partially integrated," other agreements made prior to or along with the written agreement will be considered when determining the terms of the contract. *Restatement of the Law of Contracts, Second*, §§ 213 and 216 (1981).

17. *Mission Independent School District* v. *Diserens*, 188 S.W.2d 568 (Tex. 1945).

18. *Special School District of Fort Smith* v. *Lynch*, 413 S.W.2d 880 (Ark. 1967).

19. 52 F.Supp. at 829.

20. *Wyatt* v. *School District No. 104, Fergus County*, 417 P.2d 221 (Mont. 1966).

21. *Sams* v. *Board of Com'rs of Creek County*, 178 P. 668 (Okla. 1919); *McBeth* v. *Board of Ed. of DeValls Bluff School District No. 1, Ark.*, 300 F. Supp. 1270 (E.D. Ark. 1969).

22. *Ward* v. *Kelly*, 515 F.2d 908 (5th Cir. 1975); *Doyal* v. *School Board*, 415 So.2d 791 (Fla. App. 1982); *Hyde* v. *Wellpinit School District No. 49*, 648 P.2d 892 (Wash. App. 1982).

23. *Bowbells Public School District No. 14* v. *Walker*, 231 N.W.2d 173 (N.D. 1975).

24. *Id.* at 176.

25. *Williams* v. *Albemarle City Board of Education*, 508 F.2d 1242 (4th Cir. 1974).

26. *Farrell* v. *School District*, 56 N.W. 1053 (Mich. 1893).

27. *AAUP* v. *Bloomfield College*, 322 A.2d 846 (N.J. Super. 1974), *aff'd*, 346 A.2d 615, 618 (N.J. Super. 1975).

28. *Danroth* v. *Mandaree Public School District No. 36*, 320 N.W.2d 780 (N.D. 1982).

29. *Allen* v. *Autauga County Board of Education*, 685 F.2d 1302 (11th Cir. 1982).

30. *Johnson* v. *Branch*, 364 F.2d 177 (4th Cir. 1966), *cert. denied*, 385 U.S. 1003 (1967).

31. *Mission Independent School District* v. *Diserens*, 188 S.W.2d 568 (Tex. 1945).

32. *Lemasters* v. *Willman*, 281 S.W.2d 580 (Mo. App. 1955).

33. *Oneal* v. *Colton Consolidated School District No. 306*, 557 P.2d 11 (Wash. App. 1976).

34. *Brinson* v. *School District No. 431*, 576 P.2d 602 (Kan. 1978).

CHAPTER 2

How Secure Is My Employment?

OVERVIEW

Teacher tenure laws protect teachers from arbitrary actions by school officials. In the words of the Supreme Court of Pennsylvania: "Time and again our courts have stated that the purpose of the tenure provisions of the School Code is the maintenance of an adequate and competent teaching staff, free from political or arbitrary interference, whereby capable and competent teachers might feel secure, and more efficiently perform their duty of instruction."[1] Tenure laws can help maintain a good educational system by ensuring the stability and security of satisfactory teachers and by outlining orderly procedures for the dismissal of unsatisfactory teachers.

Teachers who are granted tenure can be dismissed only for a cause set out by law. However, tenured teachers do not have a right either to a particular position in a school district or to indefinite employment. Before tenured teachers can be dismissed, school boards must show cause why they are not fit to teach. Tenured teachers are also entitled to notice of these charges and a hearing where the board has the burden of proving that there is legal cause for dismissal.

In addition to these state law rights, teachers are given rights under the due process clause of the U.S. Constitution. Regardless of whether a teacher has tenure, the Supreme Court has held that teachers who have constitutionally protected interests in property or liberty are entitled to notice and a hearing prior to termination.

This chapter examines the state laws and constitutional provisions that define a teacher's right to employment. It explores such topics as how teachers acquire tenure, what rights come with tenure, and what grounds exist for dismissing tenured teachers.

ACQUIRING TENURE

The *Sindermann* Case[2]

Robert Sindermann was a teacher in the Texas state college system from 1959 to 1969. After teaching for two years at the University of Texas and for four years at San Antonio Junior College, he was employed at the Odessa Junior College for four successive years, under a series of one-year contracts.

During the 1968–1969 academic year, Sindermann was elected president of the Texas Junior College Teachers Association and became involved in public disagreements with the college's Board of Regents. In May 1969, Sindermann's one-year employment contract came to an end, and college officials did not offer him a new contract for the next academic year. They did not provide him with any stated reasons for the nonrenewal of his contract, nor did they allow him a hearing where he could challenge the nonrenewal. Sindermann brought a suit against the college authorities, arguing that their failure to provide him an opportunity for a hearing violated the Fourteenth Amendment's guarantee of procedural due process.

In considering his claim that he was entitled to a hearing, the Supreme Court examined the teacher's argument that he had a right to continued employment. The teacher alleged that, while the college had no official tenure program, it actually operated a de facto tenure program. To support his claim, Sindermann cited the following provision, which had been in the college's official faculty guide for many years:

> Teachers Tenure: Odessa College has no tenure system. The Administration of the College wishes the faculty member to feel that he has permanent tenure as long as his teaching services are satisfactory and as long as he displays a cooperative attitude toward his co-workers and his superiors, and as long as he is happy in his work.[3]

In addition, Sindermann stated, he had relied on guidelines put out by officials of the state college system, which provided that a person employed as a teacher in the system for seven years or more had a form of job tenure.

The Court explained: "A written contract with an explicit tenure provision is clearly evidence of a formal understanding that supports a teacher's claim of entitlement to continued employment unless sufficient cause is shown."[4] However, the Court went on to state that the absence of such a provision would not always foreclose the possibility that a teacher had a "property" interest in reemployment. Although the Court did not decide whether Sindermann was entitled to tenure, it did state that a teacher "who has held his position for a number of years, might be able to show from the circumstances of this service—and from other relevant facts—that he has a legitimate claim of entitlement to job tenure."[5] The Court noted that proof of such a property interest in reemployment would not automatically entitle Sindermann to reinstatement as a teacher. Nevertheless, such proof would obligate college officials to grant a hearing at his request, where he could be informed of the grounds for his nonretention and could challenge the sufficiency of these grounds.

How can teachers acquire tenure?

As the Supreme Court explained in *Sindermann*, a teacher may acquire tenure "by custom." In such a situation, a teacher's right to tenure is not formalized in a written contract but is implied from the circumstances of employment. When a teacher can prove an expectancy of continued employment, the teacher has a property interest in job tenure that is protected by the due process clause of the Fourteenth Amendment.

In most situations, however, a teacher's right to tenure is established by state law. Most states have laws that outline the requirements for tenure, and these laws generally require teachers to undergo a period of probationary service before they can become tenured or "permanent" teachers. In Virginia, for example, a teacher must teach for a probationary period of three years in the same county or city school system before attaining tenure status.[6] During the probationary period, the teacher is employed under a yearly contract and usually can be dismissed by school officials at the end of a contract period for any reason whatsoever. (See Chapter 11 for further discussion of teachers' due process rights.)

In order to acquire tenure status by law, the teacher must comply with the specific requirements of his or her state's law. In some states, tenure becomes permanent as soon as the teacher completes the required probationary period. In other states, the school board may have to take some positive action for the teacher to achieve tenure.

Whether or not the school board has to take some affirmative step to ensure that a teacher achieves tenure also depends on the nature of the teacher's employment contract. Some teachers are employed under yearly contracts. When this is the case, the board must act to renew the contract at the close of the school year before the teacher can be reemployed and thus achieve tenure status. Teachers may also be employed under continuing contracts, which are automatically renewed if the school board does not inform them by a certain date that their services will not be needed during the coming year.

Because each state has its own tenure requirements, teachers must consult the statutes and court decisions in their own state to determine what specific procedures must be followed. Nevertheless, a number of general approaches are common. First, a statute may require that the school board take affirmative action to elect a teacher to tenure status. In Texas, for example, the law reads:

> Any teacher employed by a school district who is performing his third, or where permitted fourth, consecutive year of service with the district under probationary contract, and who is elected to employment by the board of trustees of such district for the succeeding year, shall be notified in writing of his election to continuing contract status with such district. . . .[7]

The Texas tenure statute also provides that probationary teachers must be notified on or before April 1 regarding their contract renewal for the coming year.[8] In interpreting other statutes, however, the courts have ruled that school officials do not have to take any affirmative steps to award tenure status. In New York, for example, a court ruled that teachers could acquire tenure in two ways: (1) by specific award of the board of education, or (2) by acquiescence, where a teacher continued to teach beyond the probationary period and the board failed to take any action.[9]

Can a teacher be awarded tenure if school officials fail to follow required legal procedures?

It depends on the state. In Kentucky, the law specifically states that a probationary teacher will achieve tenure status if the school board fails to give the teacher the proper notice concerning reemployment for the next year.[10] A federal district court, interpreting a Michigan statute, ruled that a teacher achieved tenure as a result of the board's failure to comply with the law.[11] Similarly, a Colorado court held that a teacher who did not receive timely notice that her contract would not be renewed was automatically reemployed for a fourth year and entitled to tenure status.[12]

Other courts have not been willing to interpret tenure laws as strictly. In Illinois, for example, a court ruled that a teacher did not achieve tenure merely because the school board did not follow the proper notice procedures in attempting to dismiss her.[13] The court did agree that, without the proper notice, she was entitled to be reemployed by the school district. However, she was not automatically entitled to tenure status. In reaching its decision, the court examined the purposes of the tenure laws, noting that the probationary period of teaching was established by the legislature in order to "impose a duty upon and to provide an opportunity for school boards to observe and evaluate the actual performance of a teacher's work for two years." The court concluded that it would be inconsistent with these purposes for it to confer tenure status on a teacher. Instead, the court ruled that the teacher should be reemployed, but only as a second-year probationary teacher. Faced with a similar situation, a Tennessee court reached the same result, ordering that a probationary teacher improperly dismissed be rehired, but only under an annual contract.[14] Again the court looked to public policy considerations and concluded that the legislature did not intend that teachers should be entitled to tenure as a matter of right after completing their probationary service, but that tenure should be granted by an affirmative action of the school board based on the teacher's performance.

How else can a teacher acquire tenure?

In addition to a right to tenure under state law, a teacher may also have a right to tenure under an employment contract. The contract may specifically describe the teacher's rights to continued employment and set out detailed procedures that must be followed before a teacher can be dismissed. For example, a professor at Montana State University achieved "permanent appointment" status under the terms of his employment contract.[15] In this case, university regulations provided that the initial appointment of a professor could be for a limited term but that "reappointment after three years of service shall be deemed a permanent appointment." After teaching for six years under a series of annual contracts, the professor claimed permanent appointment status. The court agreed, finding that the university regulations were made part of the professor's contract by language in the contract that stated: "This appointment is subject to the regulations governing tenure printed on the reverse side of this sheet." Among the regulations was one granting permanent appointment after three years of service.

Can other school employees acquire tenure?

Most state laws provide that only full-time certificated employees acquire tenure. The definition of exactly which employees are required to have certification can vary from state to state. In Illinois, for example, the district employees required to be certified include superintendents, principals, and supervisors.[16] While such administrative employees may be covered by teacher tenure laws, the protection of tenure usually extends only to a teaching position, and not to an administrative post. For example, in a Wyoming case,[17] the court found that the school district was under no obligation to renew the contract of a principal who had also served as a classroom teacher. The court ruled that the principalship position was merely created under an annual contract and was not a tenured position. In addition, the court made it clear that the teacher did not lose his tenure when he was promoted to principal and, thus, even though he was not reemployed as a principal, he was entitled to be rehired as a classroom teacher. By contrast, some states also grant tenure to administrators in their administrative positions.

Similarly, a federal court held that there was no due process violation when a school district notified physical education teachers who had also served as coaches that they would be reemployed as teachers but not as coaches.[18] The court ruled that the teacher-coaches' due process rights were not violated because, since coaches were not covered under the state teacher tenure law, they had no property interest in reemployment as coaches.

Can a state do away with tenure?

Yes. When state law creates a right to tenure, it can usually take this right away. Many teachers' contracts, specifically recognizing this fact, include a provision stating that the teacher's tenure status is subject to change or termination according to any changes in the state law. Even if a teacher's contract does not include such a provision, most courts have ruled that state legislatures have the power to modify their teacher tenure laws, thus possibly depriving a teacher of tenure. In Wisconsin, for example, the court upheld the legislature's power to repeal the Teachers' Tenure Act.[19] In examining the tenure law, the court concluded that the Teachers' Tenure Act was not intended to create a statutory contract but merely to declare a public policy in favor of tenure.

In the rare situation where the state law does create a contractual right to tenure, however, the legislature cannot deprive a teacher of tenure status. In an early case, the Supreme Court held that Indiana's teacher tenure law created a contractual right to tenure and that a teacher who had attained tenure status under this law had a continuing contract that could not be broken by a new law passed by the legislature.[20] Thus the Court ruled that the teacher was entitled to maintain her tenure status even though the Indiana legislature had repealed its teacher tenure law.

RIGHTS OF TENURE

What rights does a tenured teacher have?

A teacher who achieves tenure status has the right to continued employment subject only to dismissal "for cause." The teacher does not have the right to be employed in a particular position, however. School boards retain the authority to transfer and reassign tenured teachers provided that such teachers are assigned to comparable positions, and that school officials are acting to meet the current needs of the district and are not acting arbitrarily or unreasonably.[21]

A Louisiana court, for example, ruled that a tenured teacher who taught biology at one New Orleans high school could be reassigned to another high school to teach biology.[22] The school authorities had requested that the teacher be transferred because her grading practices were at odds with those of other teachers at the high school. The court ruled that the teacher could be transferred despite her tenure status. The court noted that state law prohibited tenured teachers from being removed from office without formal charges and a hearing; nevertheless, the court explained that a teacher could not be considered "removed from office" unless

1. a reduction in salary is involved;
2. the new position requires the teaching of subjects for which the teacher is not qualified;
3. the teacher must undergo additional training, at his or her expense, in order to obtain permanent certification in the new post; and/or
4. the transfer follows a dismissal without formal charges or a hearing, and thus leaves a blot on the teacher's record.[23]

Since the teacher in this situation was assuming a similar teaching position and was being compensated at the same rate, her tenure rights were not being violated.

Courts have also ruled that tenured teachers can be reassigned as part of desegregation plans. In cases of school districts under desegregation orders, the courts have stated that school boards could not use tenure laws as an excuse to resist transferring teachers to achieve an appropriate racial balance.[24] (See Chapter 13 for a detailed discussion of school desegregation and teachers' rights.)

In addition, the courts have ruled that tenure status does not ensure that a teacher's salary can never be reduced. School boards have the authority to fix teachers' salaries, and they retain the power to reduce them. Any reductions in salary must be applied uniformly to all teachers, however, and salary schedules cannot be changed in the middle of a school year.[25]

DISMISSAL PROCEDURES

When can tenure be broken?

School officials can only dismiss a tenured teacher for "cause." Teacher tenure laws generally list specific offenses that constitute legal cause for dismissal, and school officials can dismiss a teacher only for one of these reasons. In Illinois the law provides that the school board has the power "to dismiss a teacher for incompetency, cruelty, negligence, immorality or other sufficient cause, to dismiss any teacher who fails to complete a one-year remediation plan with a 'satisfactory' or better rating and to dismiss any teacher whenever, in its opinion, he is not qualified to teach, or whenever, in its opinion, the interests of the schools require it. . . ."[26] Usually courts have held that tenured teachers can be dismissed only for a cause "which specifically relates to and affects the administration of the office, . . . something of a substantial nature directly affecting the rights and interests of the public, . . . one touching . . . his performance of his duties, showing he is not a fit or proper person to hold the office."[27] (See p. 27 for a detailed discussion of what constitutes legal cause for dismissal.)

In addition to being dismissed for cause, teachers can lose the right to tenure by their own actions. For example, a teacher may lose a tenured position by resignation. A tenured teacher in Kentucky lost his right to continued employment when he voluntarily left his teaching position to work full-time for the American Federation of Teachers.[28] Before leaving, the teacher had requested an indefinite leave of absence, but the school board had denied his request. The court ruled that "the school board was under no obligation to take the teacher back after he voluntarily absented himself from his position."

A teacher can also lose tenure status by accepting a teaching position in another school district. In California, for example, a teacher taught for two years in the Long Beach city school district and then taught for two years in the Long Beach high school district.[29] The teacher's four years of continuous teaching would have given her tenure status if she had been teaching in the same school district. However, the two school districts were separate legal entities and, by changing jobs, the teacher had no right to tenure in either district.

What procedures have to be followed before a tenured teacher can be dismissed?

Most states provide for specific procedures before tenured teachers can be dismissed. Typically these statutes require that teachers be given notice of the charges against them and an opportunity for a hearing at which they can respond to those charges. In Wisconsin, for example, the law provides that a teacher is entitled to a written statement of the charges, the right to a public hearing before the school board within 30 days of receiving this notice, and the right to be represented by counsel.[30]

Some states also provide that a tenured teacher cannot be dismissed without an opportunity to correct deficiencies that are "remediable." If, following a notice to remedy a deficiency, the teacher does not correct that deficiency within a reasonable period of time, the school district can then move for dismissal. Generally, a cause for dismissal is irremediable if damage has already been done to a student or the school, and the conduct resulting in such damage could not have been corrected had the teacher been warned. Thus, charges of inability to maintain discipline,[31] ineffective teaching techniques,[32] and a pattern of absenteeism[33] are remediable; sexual relations with a student,[34] conviction of a crime affecting fitness to teach,[35] and lying to school officials as to the reason for an absence from school[36] are irremediable. A school board that mistakenly classifies a teacher's conduct as irremediable, and thus dismisses the teacher without notice to correct deficiencies, lacks the power to dismiss the teacher for that cause, and the teacher will be entitled to reinstatement.[37]

When the state law does describe a specific procedure, it must be followed exactly. In a Pennsylvania case, a court ordered a teacher reinstated when school officials did not follow dismissal procedures required by the state's Teachers' Tenure Act.[38] The Pennsylvania law stated that a teacher could not be dismissed until the secretary of the school district had furnished "a detailed written statement of the charges upon which his or her dismissal . . . is based, together with a written notice . . . of a time and place when and where such professional employee will be given an opportunity to be heard either in person or by counsel, or both, before the Board of School Directors."[39] As it happened, the school board had merely notified the teacher that she had been dismissed and had not given her an opportunity to meet with the board. Since the board did not follow proper procedures prior to dismissal, the court ordered that the teacher be reinstated in her previous position.

What notice must be provided to a tenured teacher prior to dismissal?

The courts have stated that tenured teachers must be given clear statements of the charges against them so that they can answer those charges. Thus, a Kentucky court found that a teacher had not been given adequate notice when he was merely informed that he was guilty of "insubordination based upon fact that you refuse to co-operate with the principal of your school."[40] The court found that this statement was insufficient because it did not inform the teacher of facts on which he could reasonably formulate a defense: "It gives no date of his actions, nor does it indicate in any way the specific nature of his acts."[41] Similarly, an Alabama court ruled that a teacher could not be dismissed because the board had notified her only that her services "had been unsatisfactory and incompetent" over the past year.[42] The court concluded that "'incompetency' is a relative term which may be employed as meaning disqualification, inability or incapacity."[43] Since the board did not give the teacher any specific information about her "incompetency," she could not be dismissed. In contrast, a Kentucky court ruled that a teacher was provided with sufficient notice when the school board informed her that she would not be reemployed for the following reasons:

1. poor relationship with other teachers;
2. lack of cooperation with the principal and the guidance staff;
3. poor attitude and disruptive influence;
4. not in harmony with the educational philosophy of the school;
5. not in the best interest of the school to award a continuing contract.[44]

What kind of hearing must be provided before a tenured teacher can be dismissed?

When state laws require a hearing before a tenured teacher can be dismissed, they generally describe that hearing. In Illinois, for example, an impartial hearing officer (selected from a list provided by the state board of education) presides at a hearing that will be public at the request of either the teacher or the school board.[45] Both the teacher and the board can subpoena witnesses. The teacher also has the right to be present with counsel at the hearing, can call and cross-examine witnesses, and can present a defense to the charges. All testimony is given under oath, and the state board of education must pay a reporter to make a written record of the hearing.

Do teachers without tenure have a right to notice and a hearing prior to nonrenewal of their contracts?

State laws typically do not give nontenured teachers the right to a hearing prior to nonrenewal. Some states, however, give nontenured teachers minimal procedural rights. In Illinois, state law requires that a second-year probationary teacher be given notice of the reasons for nonrenewal.[46] In Connecticut, a nontenured teacher must make a special written request in order to receive a statement of the reasons why the board decided not to renew the contract.[47]

What constitutional protections apply in cases of teacher dismissal?

Regardless of the procedures required under the state law, the U.S. Supreme Court has ruled that teachers are entitled to notice and a hearing if their termination deprives them of "property" or "liberty" interests under the due process clause of the Fourteenth Amendment to the Constitution. In *Board of Regents* v. *Roth*[48] the Court defined these terms: "To have a property interest in a benefit, a person clearly must have more than an abstract need or desire for it. He must have more than a unilateral expectation of it. He must, instead, have a legitimate claim of entitlement to it."[49] The Court went on to explain that property interests are not created by the Constitution. "Rather, they are created and their dimensions are defined by existing rules or understandings that stem from an independent source such as state law—rules or understandings that secure certain benefits and that support claims of entitlement to those benefits."[50] In *Roth,* the teacher involved had been hired under a one-year contract, and the Court concluded that he had no such interest in reemployment as to establish a property interest that would entitle him to procedural rights under the Fourteenth Amendment.

The most obvious example of deprivation of a property interest occurs when a school board dismisses a teacher in the middle of the term of his or her contract. The courts have stated, however, that other factors may create a "property interest." In *Perry* v. *Sindermann,*[51] the Court stated that if the customary practices of the institution created a de facto tenure system, a teacher would have a property interest in reemployment and would be entitled to due process protection prior to dismissal.

In a more recent case,[52] a federal court held that a school district violated the due process rights of a coach and athletic director when it refused to renew his one-year contract. The court found that the coach had a protected property interest in his continued employment when the board had assured him that he would be employed for two years, and when he relied on this promise in leaving a job he had held for ten years. In addition, the court concluded that, since the district's action was in breach of contract, the coach was entitled to an award of damages. (This case, which was affirmed by an equally divided U.S. Supreme Court, is especially significant, because it allows public school teachers with breach of contract claims to take their cases to either federal or state court.)

In *Roth,* the U.S. Supreme Court held that teachers are also entitled to due process protection if their dismissal deprives them of a "liberty" interest under the Fourteenth Amendment. In interpreting this term, the Court included "not merely freedom from bodily restraint but also the right of the individual to contract, to engage in any of the common occupations of life."[53] In addition to actions that would foreclose a teacher's opportunities for employment, the Court stated that a liberty interest would be involved whenever the school board, in declining to rehire a teacher, made a charge that might seriously damage the teacher's standing and associations in the community (e.g., charges such as dishonesty or immorality). In the Court's words: "[W]here a person's good name, reputation, honor, or integrity is at stake because of what the government is doing to him, notice and opportunity to be heard are essential."[54] In a 1976 case[55] the Supreme Court added the requirement that "stigmatization" could occur only if statements were made publicly about an employee.

In the *Roth* case itself, the Court did not find any violation of a liberty interest. The state university had merely refused to renew Roth's one-year teaching contract; university officials did nothing that would have stigmatized Roth so as to reduce his chances of obtaining future employment. In general, the courts have found that a liberty interest is not affected when a teacher who is not rehired is free to seek another job. For example, a court held that a nontenured teacher who was not rehired because of her failure to coordinate her teaching with that of other teachers was not entitled to a hearing, even though her nonretention "unquestionably made plaintiff [the teacher] less attractive to other employers."[56] Similarly, a court ruled that no liberty interest was involved when a principal described a teacher as "anti-establishment" in a rating report.[57] In general, the courts have not required hearings when the charges against teachers have related to their inability to perform. Public charges that have been held to involve a liberty interest and entitle a teacher to a hearing prior to dismissal include allegations of manifest racism,[58] mental illness,[59] fraud,[60] and moral unfitness.[61]

In *Roth* and *Sindermann,* the Supreme Court did not describe the type of notice and hearing that must be given when a teacher is deprived of a property or liberty interest under the Fourteenth Amendment. The Court did note in *Sindermann* that the teacher must be given "an opportunity to prove the legitimacy of his claim."[62] In general, however, due process requires that a hearing must be held before an impartial body, that there be timely and specific notice of charges, and that both sides have the opportunity to present evidence and confront adverse witnesses.[63] In applying these principles in particular cases, various courts have set out more specific requirements. For example, the Fifth Circuit Court of Appeals has held that due process requires that nontenured teachers be given the names of witnesses against them.[64] The Seventh Circuit Court of Appeals has ruled that the president of a junior college was constitutionally entitled to present witnesses at a dismissal hearing.[65] In another case, where a teacher was accused of making sexual advances toward students, a federal court ruled that due process was violated when the teacher was not given prior notice of the names of his accusers or given the right to cross-examine his accusers.[66]

In still another case,[67] the Supreme Court further extended due process protections by holding that public employees with constitutionally protected property interests in employment be given "some kind of hearing" *prior* to discharge. The Court stated that the hearing "need not be elaborate" and that "something less than a full evidentiary hearing" would be sufficient, but that the hearing should be designed to determine whether there are reasonable grounds to believe that the charges against an employee are true and support dismissal. Thus, the employer must identify the grounds for dismissal and the supporting evidence, and the employee must be given an opportunity to respond before he or she is dismissed. As was true in *Roth* and *Sindermann,* the Court did not provide any further guidance about the nature of this hearing, such as who should conduct it or whether any other rights apply.

GROUNDS FOR DISMISSAL

What constitutes cause for dismissal?

State laws commonly list a number of specific reasons why teachers can be dismissed. In Illinois, for example, the board has the power to fire teachers for "incompetency, cruelty, negligence, immorality or other sufficient cause and . . . whenever, in its opinion, the interests of the schools require it."[68] The grounds for dismissal most frequently mentioned in state laws include insubordination, incompetency, immorality, and unprofessional conduct. In states that have laws listing the grounds for teacher dismissal, a teacher cannot be fired unless school officials can prove that the teacher's actions violated the state law.

When can a teacher be fired for insubordination?

Teachers cannot be dismissed for insubordination unless they willfully and deliberately defy school authorities or violate reasonable school rules. For the order to be reasonable, school officials must have the legal authority to issue it. In Wisconsin, a court ruled that a teacher could not be dismissed for insubordination because he refused to resign in person at a school board meeting.[69] The court explained that the school board had no legal power to force the teacher to submit his resignation at the meeting and concluded that the board's order was merely an unreasonable effort to save face. Teachers can also offer evidence to show that their violation of a rule was not "willful" or contemptuous of authority. For example, a court held that a teacher could not be dismissed as insubordinate when she did not return to work after being asked to change a grade of "F" that she had given a star basketball player.[70] The teacher presented medical evidence to show that she was unable to work due to stress, and that she had arranged for a substitute teacher for two days, thus showing a lack of disrespect for authority on her part.

In addition, for a rule to be reasonable, it must be clear enough for the teacher to understand. A Kentucky court held that a teacher could not be dismissed for insubordination on the grounds that he refused to "cooperate" with the principal.[71] The court stated that the school board had neither charged the teacher with violating any specific rule nor claimed that the teacher had refused to obey school authorities. Concluding that a charge of noncooperation could be asserted against almost anyone, the court declared that the school board had not proved insubordination.

Finally, teachers cannot be dismissed for failing to follow school rules that violate their constitutional rights. For example, school rules prohibiting teachers from using certain materials in the classroom may interfere with a teacher's right to academic freedom. School rules limiting what teachers can say or write may also violate their First Amendment right of free speech. (Academic freedom and First Amendment rights are discussed in detail in Chapter 8.)

In many cases, a teacher's actions speak for themselves. For example, a Utah court found a teacher to be insubordinate when he flatly refused to accept a transfer to another school, even though his contract required that he do so.[72] In less obvious cases, courts look at a teacher's pattern of behavior in order to decide whether the teacher is acting willfully. In Connecticut, a teacher's contract was terminated on the basis of insubordination when he was late to class and failed to cooperate with the administration.[73] In upholding the teacher's dismissal, the court cited a number of actions that supported its conclusion that the teacher was defiant and contemptuous of authority, among them that the teacher did not prepare the required outlines for the high school evaluation and failed to supervise his classes as the principal required. In addition, the court noted that when the principal confronted the teacher in the school office at a time when he was supposed to be in class, the teacher told the principal "to write him another letter" and said that he wouldn't return to class until he checked his mailbox and had a cup of coffee. The court concluded that this pattern of behavior threatened working relationships that were vital to maintaining school operations and thus constituted insubordination.

When can a teacher be fired for incompetency?

An incompetent teacher is one who cannot perform the duties required by the teaching contract. However, a teacher who merely has an "off day" in the classroom cannot be dismissed for incompetency. In order to fire a teacher, school officials generally have to present a number of examples of the teacher's inability to meet contractual responsibilities. For example, a Montana court recently held that a teacher was improperly dismissed for incompetence where the dismissal was based on poor performance in only four interviews in the course of a 13-year teaching career.[74] Similarly, the fact that an elementary teacher who called a student a "slob" and later in the day commented "Move over, Goodyear" to an overweight student did not provide sufficient cause for termination.[75]

The clearest example of an incompetent teacher is one who lacks knowledge about the subject he or she is supposed to teach. For example, a Louisiana third-grade teacher was dismissed for incompetency when her supervisor "noted many mistakes in her grammar and in her punctuation."[76] A Pennsylvania second-grade teacher was dismissed for incompetency after her supervisors observed that "she showed very little evidence of technical knowledge and skill . . . that she made errors in the geography lesson; that her spoken English was poor . . . and that [she] mispronounced words."[77]

Teachers may also be physically unable to teach. One principal was found to be incompetent as both a principal and a teacher when his hearing became so poor that he could not hear ordinary conversation.[78] The court noted that his defective hearing made it impossible for him to make corrections in students' recitations and prevented him from hearing the vile and obscene language being used in the classroom.

Courts have also upheld the dismissal of teachers who are mentally disabled. In a New York case, a junior high school industrial arts teacher was found to be unfit to perform his duties after psychiatrists testified that he was "unable to render consistent and effective service as a teacher."[79] In California, a court similarly upheld the dismissal of a primary school teacher hospitalized twice for mental illness.[80] The court found that the psychiatric testimony that she was unable to engage in teaching because of a schizophrenic-paranoid mental illness justified her dismissal, regardless of the fact that school authorities did not prove that her illness interfered with her work as a teacher.

Teachers are rarely found to be incompetent for one reason alone, but failure to maintain classroom discipline is one of the most commonly cited problems. Reasoning that even the best-prepared teacher cannot be effective in a chaotic classroom, the courts have emphasized that the inability to maintain discipline is a characteristic of an incompetent teacher. In Indiana, for example, the court found that a teacher had such serious discipline problems that students could not pursue their schoolwork.[81] One witness testified that "the disturbance in the room was general; the pupils doing whatever they please. . . . I went in once or twice and their conduct was something furious."[82] The court went on to note that the teacher had admitted his inability to maintain discipline in the classroom on one occasion when he had to threaten to call the police in order to regain control. Concluding that this evidence showed the teacher "wanting in practical efficiency and discipline," the court upheld his dismissal on the ground of incompetency. In a more recent case,[83] a tenured teacher of the emotionally handicapped was dismissed after witnesses documented instances of her inability to control her class and to plan and teach lessons effectively. They described the teacher as "a well-intentioned human being but one who was not capable of being a teacher." Two recent cases demonstrate how the courts generally point to a number of factors in defining incompetency. In an Alabama case,[84] the court upheld the dismissal of a teacher who smoked in front of students, left the classroom unattended, and made sexual remarks to both students and teachers. In a Pennsylvania case,[85] a school psychologist was dismissed because her reports were inadequate, her testing inadequate, her placement recommendations ill-considered, her conduct in conferences unhelpful, and her progress toward improvement imperceptible.

When can a teacher be fired for immoral conduct?

In the past, teachers were expected to teach morality through their actions, and when teachers violated community norms, they usually resigned quietly or were fired quickly. Teachers have been fired for obesity, cheating, lying, talking about sex, using "obscene" language, expressing disbelief in God, public drinking, drug use, heterosexual conduct, homosexual conduct, and rumors of an affair. Thus, what was considered immoral conduct has varied from place to place, and the definition has changed over time.

Today, teachers can still be fired for immoral conduct, but in most states such conduct must be linked to teacher effectiveness. In a Tennessee case,[86] for example, the court ruled that a tenured teacher's single drunk driving conviction was insufficient grounds for dismissal because there was no evidence that the conviction had any adverse effect upon her capacity to maintain discipline and respect in her classes. Conduct which is most likely to be upheld as immoral is that directly involving students, such as a sexual assault where a student is the victim[87] or where a male teacher told two female students about his fantasies of spanking them.[88] (Chapter 12 examines this topic in detail, including the kinds of conduct communities continue to consider immoral for teachers. It also examines the criteria courts use to determine whether such dismissals are legal or illegal.)

When can a teacher be fired for "conduct unbecoming a teacher"?

Conduct unbecoming a teacher, or "unprofessional conduct" as some states define it, is a broad reason for dismissal that can include a wide variety of actions by teachers. In general, unprofessional conduct refers to any action that violates the rules or ethical code of the teaching profession. Despite the apparent vagueness of this term, courts have ruled that it is a valid ground for dismissing teachers. The following statement by a California court is typical of the reasoning used to support the large amount of discretion school boards have when dismissing teachers: "[T]he teacher is entrusted with the custody of children and their high preparation for useful life. His habits, his speech, his good name, his cleanliness, the wisdom and propriety of his unofficial utterances, his associations, all are involved. . . . How can all of these things be provided for and offenses against them be particularly specified in a single statute?"[89]

Teachers who have attempted to use the classroom for purposes other than teaching have been found guilty of unprofessional conduct. In the California case cited above, a Sacramento high school teacher used his classroom as a forum to advocate that his students' friends and relatives support a certain candidate who was running for superintendent of schools.[90] The court ruled that the teacher could be dismissed for unprofessional conduct, reasoning that his behavior was beyond the scope of the purposes for which teachers were employed: "Such conduct certainly is in contravention not only of the spirit of the laws governing the public school system, but of that essential policy according to which the public school system should be maintained in order that it may subserve in the highest degree its purposes."[91] Teachers have also been dismissed for inappropriate use of force against students such as when a teacher used an electric cattle prod to control unruly sixth graders.[92]

Are there any other reasons why teachers can be dismissed?

Yes. Many state laws provide that teachers can be dismissed for "good and just cause." This catchall phrase gives school boards wide discretion, effectively allowing them to dismiss teachers for reasons not specifically listed under state law. Indeed, as a Massachusetts court explained, "good cause includes any ground which is put forward by the [school] committee in good faith and which is not arbitrary, irrational, unreasonable, or irrelevant to the committee's task of building up and maintaining an efficient school system."[93] Using similar reasoning, an Indiana court upheld the dismissal of a teacher-principal who had been dismissed for good and just cause when he failed to cooperate with school officials.[94] The teacher-principal had opposed a plan under which seventh- and eighth-grade students were to be taught by the high school faculty; after the plan had been in operation for a year, he had discontinued it without consulting the superintendent or county officials. In addition, he refused to fill out necessary administrative papers and catalogue the school library as required by the state's Department of Public Instruction. In upholding his dismissal, the court concluded that his actions had a negative effect on his fitness as a teacher-administrator and thus constituted good and just cause for dismissal: "A court cannot say as a matter of law that ability and willingness to co-operate are not reasonably related to the fitness or capacity of a teacher for the performance of his duties."[95]

The courts have imposed limits on school officials' power to dismiss teachers for "good and just cause." Recently, courts have emphasized that the teacher's action must bear a reasonable relationship to fitness or capacity to discharge the duties of the teaching position. For example, an Ohio court ruled that a teacher could not be fired for hitting another car and leaving the scene of the accident.[96] In interpreting the phrase "good and just cause for dismissal," the court concluded that it must refer to actions as serious as the other grounds for teacher dismissal, including "gross inefficiency or immorality." The court reasoned that the teacher's action in leaving the scene of an accident might adversely reflect upon his character and integrity, but that it was not serious enough to constitute grounds for dismissal. To constitute grounds for dismissal when only a single crime is involved, "the crime would either have to be a more serious one or involve a more serious fact situation than that here involved."[97]

Riffing: Can a teacher be dismissed for economic reasons?

When student enrollments decline in school districts, teachers may face dismissal on the grounds that a reduction in teaching staff is necessary for financial reasons, a procedure commonly known as "riffing." Such teachers are not dismissed for any adverse behavior that affects their ability to teach. Rather, in a general "reduction in force," both tenured and nontenured teachers may be dismissed in order to accommodate changing staff requirements.

Some state laws specifically provide that tenured teachers can be dismissed for economic reasons. An Alabama law states: "Cancellation of an employment contract with a teacher on continuing service status may be made for incompetency, insubordination, neglect of duty, immorality, justifiable decrease in the number of teaching positions or other good and just cause."[98] Other state laws provide more detailed guidelines about when teachers can be dismissed for economic reasons. For example, an Illinois law[99] provides that, when teachers are to be removed as a result of the school board's decision to decrease the number of teachers employed, the board shall dismiss all nontenured teachers before tenured teachers. Then, tenured teachers are to be dismissed on the basis of seniority, with those with the less seniority being dismissed first, unless an alternative procedure is established in the current collective bargaining agreement.

Even when there is no relevant state law, the courts have held that school officials have the authority to dismiss teachers for economic reasons. A Pennsylvania kindergarten teacher was dismissed when the school board recommended that the entire kindergarten department be abolished "as a matter of good school business administration and instructional efficiency."[100] The teacher argued that her tenure status prevented the board from dismissing her. The court disagreed, reasoning that the Teachers' Tenure Act was not designed to inhibit school officials from operating the schools in the most economical manner: "When an entire department is lawfully abolished for valid reasons, which may include financial ones, in the interest of a more efficient system, the teachers in that department can be dismissed. Economy is desirable in any governmental function, and we cannot so view the present legislation as to prevent the abolition of a department for this purpose."[101]

What situations commonly qualify as economic reasons for teacher dismissal?

The most common situation in which the courts have upheld the school board's right to dismiss tenured teachers for economic reasons is a decline in student enrollment. In a Pennsylvania case,[102] the court was asked to interpret the meaning of a state law that gave school authorities the power to suspend teachers whenever there was a substantial decrease in pupil enrollment in a district. Examining past, present, and projected student enrollments in one district, the school board voted to dismiss four teachers. The teachers argued that they could not be dismissed because the board's statistics actually showed a slight increase in secondary school enrollment in any two years of a six-year period. Nevertheless, the court noted that the overall trend in the statistics indicated a decrease in student enrollment and upheld the dismissals. The court emphasized that enrollment was an area in which school boards must exercise discretion and concluded that courts should not intervene unless school officials were clearly acting arbitrarily.

Courts have also ruled that teachers can be dismissed when school officials decide on curriculum reorganization for economic reasons. In Pennsylvania, for example, a tenured teacher was dismissed after the high school curriculum was reorganized.[103] Although there had been no overall decrease in student enrollment, the number of students taking this teacher's academic courses had decreased after the school had instituted a commercial course of studies. The court ruled that school authorities had the power to dismiss the teacher, emphasizing that the Teachers' Tenure Act was not intended to prohibit school officials from making administrative decisions necessary to operate the schools: "It is the administrative function of the school directors and superintendents to meet changing educational conditions through the creation of new courses, reassignment of teachers, and rearrangement of curriculum."[104] To deny the board this power "would transfer much of the discretion accorded to these administrative boards to the teachers, that they might preserve their positions in perpetuity."[105]

The courts have also stated that school officials can dismiss teachers as the result of a decision to abolish a particular position. In a New Jersey case,[106] the board of education decided to abolish the position of a full-time physical education instructor and create a new position that would require teaching both physical education and English. Because the current physical education teacher was not qualified to teach English, she was dismissed. Despite the fact that she had tenure, the court ruled that the board could dismiss her because its decision was based on "public economy" and because "the action of the local board was in good faith and not the result of prejudice or discrimination."[107] Similarly, in a more recent case, the Kansas Supreme Court held that the discontinuation of a special education cooperative program constituted good cause for the dismissal of the tenured special education teacher whose position was eliminated.[108]

Are there any limitations on a school board's power to dismiss a tenured teacher for economic reasons?

Yes. A school board has considerable discretion in deciding whether to dismiss a teacher for economic reasons, but there are limits on its power. State laws may define which teachers can be dismissed. For example, many state laws provide that probationary teachers must be dismissed before tenured teachers, and that, among tenured teachers, those teachers with less seniority be dismissed first.[109] Individual or collective bargaining contracts also may specify criteria for selecting teachers who will be dismissed in reduction-in-force situations.

Even in the absence of contractual or statutory guidelines, however, the courts have generally required that school boards give preference to tenured over nontenured teachers. For example, an Indiana court ruled that school authorities could not dismiss a tenured elementary school teacher while they retained a nontenured teacher.[110] The court concluded that to allow such a practice would make the tenure law completely ineffective:

> The principal purpose of the Act was to secure permanency in the teaching force. If a justifiable decrease in the number of teaching positions should be held to give the trustee the power to choose between tenure and nontenure teachers, both of whom are licensed to teach in the teaching position which remains, he is thereby given the power to nullify the Teachers' Tenure Act, and to discharge without cause a teacher who has, by reason of having served satisfactorily as a teacher during the specified period, secured a tenure status and an indefinite permanent contract. To countenance such an interpretation of the law would be to permit the trustee to do indirectly that which the law expressly forbids him to do directly.[111]

State laws may also limit the circumstances under which teachers may be dismissed. In Pennsylvania the state law listed four economic conditions which would be cause for dismissal of professional employees:

1. substantial decrease in pupil enrollment in the district;
2. curtailment or alteration of the educational program;
3. consolidation of schools;
4. reorganization of school districts.

The Pennsylvania Supreme Court ruled that this specific list indicated the legislature's intention to limit the school board's power to decrease staff size for economic reasons and held that the board could not dismiss a teacher solely to reduce operating expenses.[112]

Beyond these restrictions, the courts generally have stated that, in the absence of contractual or statutory guidelines, school boards can use whatever reasonable standards they wish in deciding which teachers to dismiss in reduction-in-force situations.[113] In no case, however, can a school board use a RIF procedure as a way to circumvent tenure laws or to discriminate against any individual and, if the board is acting in bad faith, the teacher who was dismissed will be entitled to reinstatement.[114] For example, a Massachusetts court found that a board had used declining enrollments as a subterfuge in a case that involved the dismissal of 39 tenured teachers; the board cited no fiscal constraints in its letter of dismissal, and then hired nontenured teachers for positions that the tenured teachers were qualified to fill.[115] As long as the school board is not acting arbitrarily or discriminating against particular individuals, however, the courts are likely to uphold a decision identifying teachers who are to be dismissed for economic reasons.

SUMMARY

Most states have passed tenure laws that give teachers the right to continued employment, subject only to dismissal for "cause." These laws describe the procedures teachers must follow to achieve tenure. They generally include the satisfactory completion of a stated number of years of probationary service. State legislatures have the power to change or repeal these laws. In addition, the courts have ruled that teachers enjoy tenure of employment and not position, leaving school boards with the authority to reassign and transfer tenured teachers.

State laws usually describe specific procedures to be followed before a tenured teacher can be dismissed. These laws make it compulsory that teachers be given notice of the charges against them and some form of hearing. The specific procedures required vary among states. In addition to these state law requirements, the U.S. Supreme Court has ruled that under the due process clause of the Fourteenth Amendment all teachers are entitled to notice and a hearing prior to dismissal whenever they are deprived of a "liberty" interest (damage to reputation) or a "property" interest (an expectation of continued employment created by a contract or the customary employment practices at an educational institution). Nontenured teachers are entitled to constitutional protections when they can demonstrate that they have been deprived of a liberty interest or a property interest. Tenured teachers have a property interest in continued employment and therefore are always entitled to due process protections prior to dismissal.

NOTES

1. *Smith* v. *School District of Township of Darby*, 130 A.2d 661, 667 (Pa. 1957). *See also Tomiak* v. *Hamtramck School Dist.*, 360 N.W.2d 257 (Mich. App. 1984).
2. *Perry* v. *Sindermann*, 408 U.S. 593 (1972).
3. *Id*. at 600.
4. *Id*. at 601.
5. *Id*. at 603.
6. VA. CODE §22.1-303 (1985).
7. TEX. EDUC. CODE ANN. § 13.106 (Vernon 1972).
8. *Id*., § 13.103.
9. *McCarthy* v. *Board of Education of Union Free School District No. 3*, 73 Misc.2d 225, 340 N.Y.S.2d 679 (1973), *aff'd*, 350 N.Y.S.2d 610 (1973).
10. KY. REV. STAT. § 161.750 (1980).
11. *Fucinari* v. *Dearborn Board of Education*, 188 N.W.2d 229 (Mich. App. 1971).
12. *Day* v. *Prowers County School Dist. RE-1*, 725 P.2d 14 (Col. App. 1986).
13. *Bessler* v. *Board of Education of Chartered School District*, 356 N.E.2d 1253 (Ill. App. 1976).
14. *Snell* v. *Brothers*, 527 S.W.2d 114 (Tenn. 1975).
15. *State* v. *Ayers*, 92 P.2d 306 (Mont. 1939).
16. ILL. STAT. ANN., ch. 122, § 24-11 (Smith-Hurd Supp. 1985).
17. *Spurlock* v. *Board of Trustees*, 699 P.2d 270 (Wyo. 1985).
18. *Smith* v. *Board of Education of Urbana School District No. 116*, 708 F.2d 258 (7th Cir. 1983).
19. *State ex rel. McKenna* v. *District No. 8*, 10 N.W.2d 155 (Wis. 1943).
20. *Indiana ex rel. Anderson* v. *Brand*, 303 U.S. 95 (1938).
21. *Proviso Council of West Suburban Teachers Union, Local 571* v. *Board of Educ. of Proviso Township High Schools, Dist. 209, Cook County*, 515 N.E.2d 996 (Ill. App. 1987).
22. *Rosenthal* v. *Orleans Parish School Board*, 214 So.2d 203 (La. App. 1968).
23. *Id*. at 207.
24. *United States* v. *Board of Education of City of Bessemer*, 396 F.2d 44 (5th Cir. 1968).
25. *Compton Community College Federation of Teachers* v. *Compton Community College District*, 211 Cal. Rptr. 231 (Cal. App. 2 Dist. 1985).
26. ILL. ANN. STAT., ch. 122, § 10-22.4 (Smith-Hurd Supp. 1985).
27. *State* v. *Board of Regents*, 261 P.2d 515, 517 (Nev. 1953).
28. *Miller* v. *Noe*, 432 S.W.2d 818 (Ky. App. 1968).

29. *Mckee* v. *Edgar*, 30 P.2d 999 (Cal. App. 1934).
30. WIS. STAT. ANN. § 118.23 (West 1973).
31. *Grissom* v. *Board of Education*, 388 N.E.2d 398 (Ill. 1979).
32. *Hanlon* v. *Board of Education of Parkway School District*, 95 S.W.2d 930 (Mo. App. 1985).
33. *Szabo* v. *Board of Education of Community Consolidated School District 54*, 454 N.E.2d 39 (Ill. App. 1983).
34. *Weissman* v. *Board of Education of Jefferson City School District*, 547 P.2d 1267 (Colo. 1976).
35. *Chicago Board of Education* v. *Payne*, 430 N.E.2d 310 (Ill. App. 1981).
36. *Bethel Park School District* v. *Krall*, 445 A.2d 1377 (Pa. Commw. 1982).
37. See *Tarquin* v. *Commission on Professional Competence*, 148 Cal. Rptr. 522 (1978); *Morris* v. *Board of Education of Chicago*, 121 N.E.2d 387 (1981).
38. *In re Swink*, 200 A. 200 (Pa. Super. 1938).
39. *Id.* at 203.
40. *Osborne* v. *Bullitt County Board of Education*, 415 S.W.2d 607 (Ky. App. 1967).
41. *Id.* at 609-610.
42. *County Board of Education of Clarke County* v. *Oliver*, 116 So.2d 566 (Ala. 1959).
43. *Id.* at 567.
44. *Sparks* v. *Board of Education of Ashland Independent School District*, 549 S.W.2d 323, 325 (Ky. App. 1977).
45. ILL. ANN. STAT., ch. 122, § 24-12 (Smith-Hurd Supp. 1985).
46. ILL. ANN. STAT., ch. 122, § 24-11 (Smith-Hurd Supp. 1985).
47. CONN. STAT. ANN. § 10-151 (West Supp. 1986).
48. 408 U.S. 564 (1972).
49. *Id.* at 577.
50. *Id.*
51. 408 U.S. 593 (1972).
52. *Vail* v. *Board of Education of Paris Union School District No. 95*, 706 F.2d 1435 (7th Cir. 1983), *aff'd*, 104 S. Ct. 2144 (1984).
53. 408 U.S. at 572.
54. *Id.* at 573 (quoting *Wisconsin* v. *Constantineau*, 400 U.S. 433, 437 (1971).
55. *Bishop* v. *Wood*, 426 U.S. 341 (1976).
56. *Shirck* v. *Thomas*, 486, F.2d 691, 693 (7th Cir. 1973).
57. *Lipp* v. *Board of Education of City of Chicago*, 470 F.2d 802 (7th Cir. 1972).
58. *Wellner* v. *Minnesota State Junior College Board*, 487 F.2d 153 (8th Cir. 1973).
59. *Lombard* v. *Board of Education of City of New York*, 502 F.2d 631 (2d Cir. 1974).
60. *Huntley* v. *North Carolina State Board of Education*, 493 F.2d 1016 (4th Cir. 1974).
61. *McGhee* v. *Draper*, 564 F.2d 902 (10th Cir. 1977).
62. 408 U.S. at 603.
63. *Goldberg* v. *Kelly*, 397 U.S. 254 (1970).
64. *Ferguson* v. *Thomas*, 430 F.2d 852 (5th Cir. 1970).
65. *Hostrop* v. *Board of Junior College District No. 515*, 471 F.2d 488 (7th Cir. 1972), *cert. denied*, 411 U.S. 967 (1973).
66. *Casada* v. *Booneville S.D. No. 65*, 686 F.Supp. 730 (W.D. Ark. 1988).
67. *Cleveland Board of Education* v. *Loudermill*, 470 U.S. 532 (1985).
68. ILL. ANN. STAT., ch. 122, § 10-22.4 (Smith-Hurd Supp. 1985).
69. *Millar* v. *Joint School District No. 2*, 86 N.W.2d 455 (Wis. 1957).

70. *Mc Ghee* v. *Milker*, 753 S.W.2d 354 (Tenn. 1988).
71. *Osborne* v. *Bullitt County Board of Education*, 415 S.W.2d 607 (Ky. Ct. App. 1967). *See also Werblo* v. *Board of School Trustees of the Hamilton Heights School Corp. et al.*, 519 N.E.2d 185 (Ind. App. 1988).
72. *Brough* v. *Board of Education of Millard County School District*, 460 P.2d 336 (Utah 1969), *reh'g denied*, 463 P.2d 567 (Utah 1970), *cert. denied*, 398 U.S. 928 (1970).
73. *Simard* v. *Board of Education*, 473 F.2d 988 (2d Cir. 1973).
74. *Trustees, Missoula County School Dist. No. 1* v. *Anderson*, 757 P.2d 1315 (Mont. 1988).
75. *Trustees of Lincoln County School Dist. No. 13, Eureka* v. *Holden*, 754 P.2d 506 (Mont. 1988).
76. *Singleton* v. *Iberville Parish School Board*, 136 So.2d 809 (La. App. 1961).
77. *Appeal of Mulhollen*, 39 A.2d 283 (Pa. Super. Ct. 1944).
78. *Alexander* v. *Manton Joint Union School District*, 255 P. 516 (Cal. Dist. Ct. App. 1927).
79. *Coriou* v. *Nyquist*, 304 N.Y.S.2d 486 (N.Y. App. Div. 1969).
80. *Alford* v. *Department of Education*, 91 Cal. Rptr. 843 (Cal. Ct. App. 1970).
81. *Biggs* v. *School City of Mt. Vernon*, 90 N.E. 105 (Ind. App. 1909).
82. *Id.* at 106.
83. *Mongitore* v. *Regan*, 520 N.Y.S.2d 194 (N.Y. App. Div. 1987).
84. *Bradshaw* v. *Alabama State Tenure Commission*, 520 So.2d 541 (Ala. Civ. App. 1988).
85. *Grant* v. *Board of School Directors*, 471 A.2d 1292 (Pa. Commw. 1984).
86. *Turk* v. *Franklin Special School District*, 640 S.W.2d 218 (Tenn. 1982).
87. *Moore* v. *Knowles*, 512 F.2d 72 (5th Cir. 1971). *See also Fisher* v. *Independent School Dist.*, 357 N.W.2d 152 (Minn. Ct. App. 1984).
88. *Penn-Delco School Dist.* v. *Urso*, 382 A.2d 162 (Pa. Commw. 1978).
89. *Goldsmith* v. *Board of Education of Sacramento City High School Dist. 66*, 225 P. 783, 787 (Cal. Dist. App. Ct. 1924); *see also Wishart* v. *McDonald*, 500 F.2d 1110 (1st Cir. 1974).
90. *Id.*
91. *Id.* at 789.
92. *Rolando* v. *Directors of Dist. No. 125*, 358 N.E.2d 945 (Ill. App. 1976).
93. *Rinaldo* v. *Dreyer*, 1 N.E.2d 37, 38 (Mass. 1936).
94. *Stiver* v. *State*, 1 N.E.2d 1006 (Ind. 1936).
95. *Id.* at 1008.
96. *Hale* v. *Board of Education, City of Lancaster*, 234 N.E.2d 583 (Ohio 1968).
97. *Id.* at 587.
98. ALA. CODE § 16-24-8 (1985).
99. ILL. ANN. STAT., ch. 122, § 24-12 (Smith-Hurd Supp. 1985).
100. *Ehret* v. *School District of Borough of Kupmont*, 5 A.2d 188 (Pa. 1939).
101. *Id.* at 193.
102. *Tressler* v. *Upper Dublin School District*, 373 A.2d 755 (Pa. Commw. 1977).
103. *Jones* v. *Holes*, 6 A.2d 102 (Pa. 1939).
104. *Id.* at 104.
105. *Id.* at 105.
106. *Weider* v. *Board of Education*, 170 A. 631 (N.J. 1934).

107. *Id.*

108. *Sells* v. *Unified School District No. 429, Doniphan County,* 644 P.2d 379 (Kan. 1982). *See also Williams* v. *Seattle School Dist.*, 643 P.2d 426 (Wash. 1982).

109. *See* CAL. EDUC. CODE § 44955 (West Supp. 1985); ILL. ANN. STAT., ch. 122, § 24-12 (Smith-Hurd Supp. 1985).

110. *Watson* v. *Burnett,* 23 N.E.2d 420 (Ind. 1939).

111. *Id.* at 423.

112. *Warwick Board of School Directors* v. *Theros,* 430 A.2d 268 (Pa. 1981).

113. *Williams* v. *Board of Education of Lamar County,* 82 So.2d 549 (Ala. 1955).

114. *See Genco* v. *Bristol Borough School Dist.*, 423 A.2d 36 (Pa. Commw. 1980); *Buchert* v. *Hamilton City Board of Educ.*, 473 N.E.2d 161 (Ohio 1984).

115. *Sherman* v. *School Committee of Whitman,* 522 N.E.2d 433 (Mass. App. Ct. 1988).

CHAPTER 3

How Does Collective Bargaining Affect Me?

OVERVIEW

The American labor union movement began in response to poor working conditions in industry but has now spread to include workers employed in the public sector. Today, over 80 percent of all public school teachers belong to the National Education Association (NEA), which has about 2 million members, or the American Federation of Teachers (AFT), which has approximately half a million members. As a result, about two-thirds of the states have passed laws outlining school boards' responsibilities in collective bargaining with these groups. This chapter examines the impact of these laws and relevant court cases that have considered such questions as: Does a teacher have a right to join a union? Can a teacher be forced to join a union? What is collective bargaining all about? What duties does a union have to perform for its members? Are teachers allowed to go on strike?

THE RIGHT TO ORGANIZE

The Norwalk Teachers' Association Case[1]

Do teachers have the right to organize?

In 1946, all but 2 of the 300 teachers in the Norwalk, Connecticut, school system were members of the Norwalk Teachers' Association (NTA). In April of that year, a dispute broke out between the NTA and the Board of Education of the City of Norwalk concerning teachers' salaries. After protracted negotiations,

230 NTA members rejected their employment contracts and refused to return to their teaching duties. After further negotiations, the NTA and the Norwalk Board of Education entered into a contract that gave the NTA the exclusive right to represent Norwalk teachers in collective bargaining over teachers' working conditions. The contract also established a grievance procedure and a salary schedule.

Even with a contract negotiated, the NTA and the board of education continued to disagree about its interpretation and about a number of state education laws that seemed to be inconsistent with the contract's provisions. Fearful of another teachers' strike, the NTA went to court to ask for an order declaring the rights of both parties to the contract. Specifically, the NTA wanted answers to the following questions:

1. Is it permitted to the plaintiff (NTA) under our laws to organize itself as a labor union for the purpose of demanding and receiving recognition and collective bargaining?
2. May the plaintiff (NTA) engage in concerted action such as a strike, work stoppage, or collective refusal to enter upon duties?

In a decision that was to be followed by courts in other states, the Connecticut court ruled that the teachers did have the right to organize a labor union. The court noted that the laws in Connecticut were completely silent on the subject of teacher unions. After pointing out that "union organization in industry is now the rule rather than the exception," the court upheld the teachers' right to organize a labor union: "In the absence of prohibitory statute or regulation, no good reason appears why public employees should not organize as a labor union." The court warned that the NTA did not have unlimited bargaining rights, however; teacher associations could only "organize and bargain collectively for the pay and working conditions which it may be in the power of the board of education to grant." The NTA's salary demands, for example, had to be subject to the board's taxation power.

Turning to the second question, the court held that the teachers had no right to strike. In reaching its decision, the court explained: "It should be the aim of every employee of the government to do his or her part to make it function as efficiently and economically as possible. The drastic remedy of the organized strike to enforce the demands of unions of government employees is in direct contravention of this principle." The court stated that government employees occupy a different status from those who work in private enterprise because they "serve the public welfare," and concluded that allowing teachers to strike would "deny the authority of government and contravene the public welfare."

Do all teachers have a right to join a union and engage in collective bargaining?

They have a constitutional right to join a union. Whether they have a right to engage in collective bargaining depends on state law. At the time *Norwalk* was decided, none of the states had passed laws permitting boards of education to engage in collective bargaining with teacher organizations, and the courts had to resolve questions that arose in this area. As of 1989, a total of 41 states have passed such laws. Only Mississippi, North Carolina, and Texas specifically prohibit collective bargaining for public school employees. Twenty-eight of the states with collective bargaining laws have also established agencies (commonly called public employee relations boards) to resolve public employee labor disputes.

The state laws vary considerably. Some states merely require boards of education to "meet and confer" with teacher organizations. In states with these general statutes, it is up to the courts to resolve any disputes concerning what are the proper subjects of collective bargaining. The Rhode Island law is an example:

> Right to organize and bargain collectively.—The certified teachers in the public school system in any city, town or regional school district, shall have the right to negotiate professionally and to bargain collectively with their respective school committees and to be represented by an association or labor organization in such negotiation or collective bargaining concerning hours, salary, working conditions and all other terms and conditions of professional employment. For purposes of this chapter, certified teachers shall mean certified teaching personnel employed in the public school systems in the state of Rhode Island engaged in teaching duties, including certified support personnel whose positions require a professional certificate issued by the state department of education. Superintendents, assistant superintendents, principals, and assistant principals (and other supervisors above the rank of assistant principal) are excluded from the provisions of this chapter.[2]

After stating that the association or organization selected by the teachers shall be the exclusive bargaining agent, the law provides:

> Obligation to bargain.—It shall be the obligation of the school committee to meet and confer in good faith with the representative or representatives of the negotiating or bargaining agent within ten (10) days after receipt of written notice from said agent of the request for a meeting for negotiating or collective bargaining purposes. This obligation shall include the duty to cause any agreement resulting from negotiations or bargaining to be reduced to a written contract; provided that no such contract shall exceed the term of three (3) years. Failure to negotiate or bargain in good faith may be complained of by either the negotiating or bargaining agent or the school committee to the state labor relations board which shall deal with such complaint in the manner provided in chapter 7 of this title.[3]

Other state laws are much more detailed and require boards of education to meet with the teachers' organizations to negotiate about specific topics. Such laws usually include more detailed procedures for resolving negotiating impasses that may arise during the bargaining process. The California law, for example, provides that the board and the teachers' representative must negotiate about health and welfare benefits, leave, transfer and reassignment policies, safety conditions, class size, evaluation procedures, grievance procedures, and the lay-off of probationary certificated school district employees.[4]

TEACHERS' RIGHTS

How are collective bargaining laws enforced?

In order to enforce collective bargaining and other laws affecting public employ-ees, many states have established labor relations boards. These boards attempt to ensure that both school officials and teachers' organizations comply with the law. For example, the Rhode Island law quoted in the preceding question provides that either party to collective bargaining negotiations can complain to the state's labor relations board if the other party fails to negotiate or bargain in good faith.

Are there any federal laws concerning teachers' unions?

There is still no federal law that specifically regulates collective bargaining for teachers.[5] In 1978, Congress did pass comprehensive legislation establishing and regulating collective bargaining rights for federal employees, and teachers who are employed in any educational institutions owned and operated by the federal government are covered by this law.[6] The vast majority of public school teach-ers, however, are employed by local school districts and must look to state laws for protection.

Is there a constitutional right to organize?

Yes. In addition to state laws giving teachers the right to join unions, the courts have ruled that the U.S. Constitution gives teachers the right to organize. In Illinois, two probationary teachers were dismissed because of their work for the American Federation of Teachers. A federal court ruled that "teachers have the right of free association, and unjustified interference with teachers' associational freedom violates the Due Process Clause of the Fourteenth Amendment."[7] An-other federal court ruled that a school board violated teachers' rights of associa-tion and free speech when the board refused to appoint teachers to supervisory positions unless they resigned from the teachers' association.[8] (For a detailed discussion of teachers' rights of association, see Chapter 10.)

Is there a constitutional right to bargain?

No. Most states have statutes that provide for collective bargaining for teachers, but, in the absence of such laws, teachers do not have a constitutional right to bargain collectively. This issue was confronted in 1974 when the North Carolina legislature passed a law abolishing collective bargaining between public employees and any state or city agency. The state education association sued to have the law declared unconstitutional, but a federal court ruled that there was no such constitutional right.[9] "The Constitution," wrote the court, does not require that the government "be compelled to talk to or contract" with any organization. Although the teachers' union "may someday persuade state government of the asserted value of collective bargaining agreements," this is a political and not a judicial matter. While the First Amendment protects the right of teachers to associate and advocate, it does not guarantee that their advocacy will be effective or that government bodies must bargain with them.

Who decides who will represent teachers in the collective bargaining process?

State laws that provide for collective bargaining for teachers generally also establish a procedure to decide who will represent the teachers in negotiations with the school board. Typically the laws state that the board must bargain with the organization that a majority of teachers in the district (or other "bargaining unit") designates as exclusive representative. This organization is usually elected. In Oklahoma, for example, the law says that teachers shall choose an employee organization to serve as their exclusive representative through the following procedure:

1. thirty-five percent or more of the employees in the bargaining unit must petition for an election to be held;
2. an election by secret ballot shall be held;
3. the local board of education shall recognize an employee organization designated by an election of the employees in an appropriate bargaining unit as the exclusive representative of all the employees in such unit;
4. if none of the choices on the ballot receives a majority of votes, a runoff election shall be held between the two choices with the largest number of votes.[10]

In addition, state laws usually define who the union will represent as part of the "bargaining unit." This unit, or group of teachers, may include all teachers in a city or school district or all teachers under the same salary schedule. Decisions about the size of such a unit and whether it is appropriate for a particular group of teachers to be represented by only one union are often made by the state's employment relations board. State laws also determine whether supervisory employees, such as principals, may be allowed in the same unit as nonsupervisory employees, such as teachers. Some statutes prohibit supervisors from participation in the same unit they supervise; other states are silent on this issue. Finally, some states prohibit superintendents from participation in a bargaining unit with teachers.

Do all teachers have to join the employee organization selected as the exclusive bargaining representative?

No. Public employees cannot be forced to join a union as a condition of their employment (the so-called union shop or closed shop). Some state laws have explicitly recognized this right. In California, for example, the law provides that, although public employees have the right to join a union, they also have the right "to refuse to join or participate in the activities of employee organizations."[11]

In addition, the U.S. Supreme Court has ruled that the First Amendment gives teachers who are not union members the right to make public comments about matters that are the subject of collective bargaining negotiations. In *Madison Joint School District* v. *Wisconsin Employment Relations Commission*,[12] Holmquist, a nonunion teacher, attended a public meeting of the board of education and spoke against a topic the union was supporting in collective bargaining negotiations. The union filed a complaint with the state's employment relations board, claiming that the board of education had violated its duty under Wisconsin law to negotiate only with the teachers' exclusive collective bargaining representative when it permitted Holmquist to speak at the board meeting.

The Court, however, ruled that the First Amendment's guarantee of freedom of speech gave Holmquist the right to express his views: "Holmquist did not seek to bargain or offer to enter into any bargain with the board, nor does it appear that he was authorized by any other teachers to enter into any agreement on their behalf. . . . Moreover, the school board meeting at which Holmquist was permitted to speak was open to the public. He addressed the school board not merely as one of its employees but also as a concerned citizen, seeking to express his views on an important decision of his government."

The Court explained that, according to its decision in *Pickering* v. *Board of Education* (see Chapter 8 for a detailed discussion of this case), teachers cannot be "compelled to relinquish the First Amendment rights they would otherwise enjoy as citizens to comment on matters of public interest in connection with the operation of the public schools in which they work," and concluded that "the mere expression of an opinion about a matter subject to collective bargaining, whether or not the speaker is a member of the bargaining unit, poses no genuine threat to the policy of exclusive representation that Wisconsin has adopted."

Can teachers who are not union members be required to pay dues to a union?

Yes. Over half of the states have passed laws that permit "agency shop" or "fair share" arrangements under which employees who are not members of a union can be required to pay union dues as a condition of their employment. Although such agreements are not likely to be upheld in the absence of such a state law, the U.S. Supreme Court has ruled that they are constitutional. In

Abood v. *Detroit Board of Education*,[13] a group of teachers challenged the validity of an agency-shop clause in a collective bargaining agreement between the Detroit Board of Education and the Detroit Federation of Teachers. Michigan law authorized a provision whereby every teacher who had not become a union member within 60 days of hire had to pay the union an amount equal to the regular dues or face discharge. The nonunion teachers stated that they were opposed to collective bargaining and that they did not approve of a number of the union's political activities unrelated to collective bargaining. They asked the Court to declare the agency-shop clause unconstitutional, arguing that it deprived them of their right to freedom of association protected by the First and Fourteenth Amendments.

The Supreme Court ruled that the agency-shop clause was constitutional. The Court noted that such arrangements had previously been upheld in labor relations in the private sector on the grounds that since the union's collective bargaining activities benefited all employees, all employees should help defray the union's expenses in these negotiations. The Court explained that a "union-shop arrangement has been thought to distribute fairly the cost of these activities among those who benefit, and it counteracts the incentive that employees might otherwise have to become 'free riders'—to refuse to contribute to the union while obtaining benefits of union representation that necessarily accrue to all employees." The Court concluded that this reasoning also made agency-shop arrangements valid for public employees:

> Public employees are not basically different from private employees; on the whole, they have the same sort of skills, the same needs, and seek the same advantages. . . . The very real differences between exclusive-agent collective bargaining in the public and private sectors are not such as to work any greater infringement upon the First Amendment interests of public employees.

Can teachers be required to support union political activities?

No. In *Abood*, the Supreme Court ruled that it was a violation of the First Amendment to require a public employee to be forced to pay dues to support a union's political activities. The Court did not attempt to define which union activities (e.g., political lobbying) need not be supported financially. Instead, the Court merely noted that there would be "difficult problems in drawing lines between collective-bargaining activities, for which contributions may be compelled, and ideological activities unrelated to collective bargaining, for which such compulsion is prohibited."

The Supreme Court provided further guidance in a 1984 case.[14] The Court was asked to decide whether a union's nonpolitical publications, conventions, and social activities incidental to meetings were sufficiently related to collective bargaining as to allow the union to charge these activities to nonunion members under an agency-shop provision. The Court said yes, reasoning that these activities were all germane to the union's work in the area of collective bargaining. The Court also found, however, that the union could not charge objecting employees for litigation expenses not involving the negotiation of agreements or settlement of grievances, or charge for general organizing efforts.

In a 1986 case,[15] the Supreme Court gave additional protection to nonunion members who are required to pay dues under an agency-shop agreement. The Court held that procedural safeguards are necessary to protect nonmembers from being compelled to subsidize political or ideological activities not germane to the collective bargaining process. Specifically, the Court ruled that the First Amendment requires that the union must provide the following: an adequate explanation of the agency fee, a reasonably prompt opportunity to challenge the amount of the fee before an impartial decision maker, and an escrow for the amounts reasonably in dispute while such challenges are pending.

What are the union's legal responsibilities as the exclusive collective bargaining representative for teachers?

The employee organization that acts as the exclusive bargaining agent also has the legal duty to represent all teachers in that bargaining unit. This "duty of fair representation" prohibits the union from discriminating against any of its members in the negotiation and administration of collective bargaining agreements. In addition, the union must represent the interests of all members of the bargaining unit—even those who are not union members—in the negotiation process. The "duty of fair representation" requires the union to be honest and fair but does not deprive it of discretion in deciding how to negotiate with the school board or how to handle teachers' grievances. Unless a union is acting out of a political, racial, or other "bad faith" reason, it is not a violation of this duty for the union to take a position that some members oppose, or to decide to settle a grievance.

The union also has the obligation to bargain with the school board in "good faith." This requires the union to meet at reasonable times to negotiate with the school board and to make a sincere effort to reach an agreement on the topics under discussion. Good faith does *not* require that the union reach an agreement with the school board, but it does mean that the union cannot merely go through the motions of meeting with school officials. The union must consider and respond to the board's proposals. Examples of "bad faith" bargaining include refusing to bargain with the designated teachers' representative, or refusing to participate in mediation required by the terms of the contract or state law.

What legal responsibilities does the school board have in the bargaining process?

The school board has the same legal duty to bargain in good faith as the union does. In addition, state law may impose certain responsibilities on the school board to inform the public about the nature of the collective bargaining process. Many states have passed "open public meeting laws," which require school boards to inform the public about educational policy decisions. The California law reads as follows: "All initial proposals of exclusive representatives and of public school employers, which relate to matters within the scope of representation, shall be presented at a public meeting of the public school employer and thereafter shall be public records."[16]

CONTRACT NEGOTIATIONS

What happens during collective bargaining?

The bargaining process can begin when either (1) the teachers' union or the school board drafts a contract proposal or (2) there is an exchange of initial proposals between the teachers' union and the school board. (If either the union or the board submits an initial proposal, the other party will submit a counter-proposal.) In either situation, after the two sides have exchanged the preliminary statements that describe their positions, they proceed to the discussion table. Each side usually appoints one spokesperson, and bargaining sessions are held to discuss each of the proposed contracts' provisions. The actual bargaining sessions involve a complicated process of give and take through which each side must evaluate the other side's demands and decide on which issues to compromise. The steps in the negotiating process vary depending on the tactics adopted by the two parties.

What do the union and the school board bargain about?

State laws determine what the union and board can bargain about, and these laws vary widely. A majority of the states require unions and school boards to bargain about "wages, hours, and other terms and conditions of employment." Other states require that the bargaining be restricted to specific subjects. The Tennessee law, for example, provides:

> The board of education and the recognized professional employees' organization shall negotiate in good faith the following conditions of employment:
>
> a. Salaries or wages
> b. Grievance procedures
> c. Insurance
> d. Fringe benefits, but not to include pensions or retirement programs of the Tennessee consolidated retirement system
> e. Working conditions
> f. Leave
> g. Student discipline procedures
> h. Payroll deductions
>
> Nothing shall prohibit the parties from agreeing to discuss other terms and conditions of employment in service, but it shall not be bad faith as set forth in this chapter to refuse to negotiate on any other terms and conditions. Either party may file a complaint in a court of record of any demands to meet on other terms and conditions and have an order of the court requiring the other

party to continue to meet in good faith on the required items of this section only.[17]

Other states include the following as mandatory items of bargaining: health and welfare benefits (California, Washington, D.C., Iowa); safety (California, Iowa, Nevada); vacations (Iowa, Nevada, Oregon); in-service training (Iowa); jury duty (Kansas); disciplinary procedures (New Jersey).[18]

When the law is not specific, the courts have had to decide the mandatory subjects for collective bargaining. Usually courts have held that those topics "directly" or "significantly" related to the teachers' working conditions are mandatory subjects of collective bargaining (e.g., salaries, sick leave, and seniority). Topics that concern educational policies that only indirectly affect teachers' working conditions and that the board must control in order to manage the schools effectively are not within the scope of bargaining (e.g., curriculum content and hiring policies).

In applying these general rules, the courts look at each individual case in light of whatever state statute may apply. As might be expected, different courts have reached different conclusions. The Alaska Supreme Court has ruled that salaries, fringe benefits, number of hours worked, and the amount of leave time are mandatory subjects for negotiation; class size, pupil-teacher ratio, school calendar, and teacher representation on school board advisory committees are not.[19] The Supreme Court of Wisconsin has held that the length of the school calendar is a mandatory subject of bargaining whereas class size is not.[20] On the other hand, the Supreme Court of Connecticut has found that the length of the school calendar is not a mandatory subject, whereas class size is.[21] Courts have also differed on whether evaluation procedures[22] and student discipline procedures[23] are mandatory subjects of bargaining.

Are there other limitations on the scope of collective bargaining?

Yes. First, the parties cannot enter into any contractual negotiations that are in violation of constitutional law. For example, the U.S. Supreme Court has ruled that nonunion teachers have the right to make comments at public meetings on issues subject to collective bargaining negotiations, and so the union and school board cannot agree to a contract that prohibits such activity. Similarly, the parties must abide by existing state and federal laws. If state laws establish certain certification requirements for teachers, the collective bargaining contract cannot set up conflicting standards. Finally, the collective bargaining contract must recognize any rights that exist under other contracts currently in effect.

What happens if the union and the school board cannot agree on a contract?

State procedures vary when the union and the school board have reached an impasse in their negotiations. As noted earlier, states with laws that merely require the school board to "meet and confer" with the union do not have any procedures for resolving a deadlock in negotiations. A majority of states, however, do make some provision for this. Some states, such as Oklahoma, give the parties the opportunity to develop a procedure for resolving impasses.[24] The most common process is mediation, in which the parties meet with a neutral third person(s) who attempts to resolve their differences through discussion and by proposing compromise provisions. The mediator has no legal power to force the parties to accept these suggestions and merely functions as a facilitator.

If the parties reject the mediator's recommendations, the next step is usually fact finding. The fact-finding process involves a more formal discussion during which each party again presents its position and supporting facts. The fact-finding body then issues its recommendations. Unlike mediation, fact-finding recommendations are generally made public, thus placing additional pressure on the parties to come to an agreement. If the parties are still at an impasse, state law may require the union and the school board to submit to arbitration. At this point, the parties agree to abide by an impartial arbitrator's decision.

The Hawaii statute incorporates all three steps.[25] The law requires mediation within 3 days of an impasse in negotiations. If the dispute continues 15 days after the date of the impasse, the Hawaii Public Employment Relations Board appoints a fact-finding panel of not more than three members from a list of qualified persons. This panel transmits its findings to the parties, and if the dispute is still unresolved 5 days later, these findings are made public. If the dispute continues 30 days after the date of the impasse, the parties may mutually agree to arbitration; if they do not, the board appoints an arbitration panel to attempt to resolve the differences. If the parties cannot agree within 50 days of the date of impasse, the arbitration panel submits its findings, which are binding on both parties.

What does a collective bargaining contract include?

Every collective bargaining contract is different, reflecting the concerns of teachers and school officials in diverse districts. Nevertheless, the provisions described below are generally part of all collective bargaining contracts:

1. *Preamble:* identifies the parties to the contract and the period for which the contract will be in effect.
2. *Recognition Clause:* identifies the union/association as the exclusive representative of the teachers in a defined bargaining unit. A typical recognition clause might state: "The Board of Trustees of Smalltown School District hereby recognizes the Smalltown Community Education Association as the exclusive representative of all teachers employed by the Smalltown Community Schools Corporation."
3. *Maintenance Clause:* provides that no changes in wages, hours, and terms and conditions of employment that are not covered in the con-

tract, but which are mandatory subjects of bargaining, shall be made without the union's agreement.

4. *Grievance Procedure:* defines "grievance" and a description of the steps to be followed if a grievance is filed. A grievance may be defined as "a claim by a teacher or by the union that there has been a violation, a misapplication, or a misinterpretation of the agreement"; a grievance may also be defined more broadly to mean "a claim by a teacher or the union that there has been a violation, a misapplication, or a misinterpretation of any policy or administrative decision affecting employees of the school district." The procedure usually defines the steps that must be taken and the time limits that apply. It may include provisions for arbitration.

5. *Teachers' Rights Clause:* provides that teachers have the right to organize for the purpose of collective negotiations and prohibits discrimination against teachers regardless of membership or nonmembership in any employee organization.

6. *Teacher Organizations' Rights Clause:* outlines union/association rights to communicate with members, including the right to use bulletin board space, place mail in teachers' mailboxes, schedule meetings with teachers, and have access to certain school board documents.

7. *Representation Clause:* describes the procedure to be followed if the school board or any employee organization wishes to challenge the union/association status as the exclusive bargaining agent.

8. *Management Rights Clause:* provides that the school board does not "waive any rights or powers granted under the laws of the state." This provision merely affirms what is already the law, that school boards cannot be required to bargain away their rights to establish educational policy.

9. *Terms of the Agreement:* describes the specific contract provisions concerning teachers' employment; it generally includes provisions concerning salaries, sick leave, pregnancy leave, other leaves of absence, insurance, vacations, transfer policy and procedures, and teaching days and hours.

STRIKES

Do teachers have the right to strike?

The situation concerning teacher strikes has changed since the *Norwalk* case was decided. Although teachers have no constitutional right to strike, about half the states have now passed laws that give teachers a limited right to strike. Generally these laws provide that teachers in a union/association are allowed to strike only after they have complied with the state's procedures for impasse resolution, and after they have notified the school board of their intent to strike. In Illinois, for example, a comprehensive law regulating educational labor relations was passed in 1984 giving educational employees the right to strike when each of the following conditions is met:

1. They are represented by an exclusive bargaining representative.
2. Mediation has been used without success.
3. At least five days have elapsed after a notice of intent to strike has been given by the exclusive bargaining representative to the educational employer, the regional superintendent, and the Illinois Educational Labor Relations Board.
4. The collective bargaining agreement between the educational employer and educational employees, if any, has expired.
5. The employer and the exclusive bargaining representative have not mutually submitted the unresolved issues to arbitration.[26]

As is the case in other states, the Illinois law also provides that if an employer believes that a strike is a clear and present danger to the health or safety of the public, the employer can ask a court for appropriate relief (such as an injunction to prohibit the strike).

What penalties can be imposed on teachers who engage in an illegal strike?

A number of state laws describe penalties that may be imposed on teachers or organization officials who engage in an illegal strike. For example, Indiana law states that a striking teachers' union/association loses its dues-deduction privilege for one year; in addition, teachers will not be paid for any school day missed as the result of a strike.[27] Nevada law provides that school officials can impose any of the following sanctions on teachers who engage in a strike:

1. Dismiss, suspend, or demote all or any employees who participate in such strike or violation.
2. Cancel the contracts of employment of all or any employees who participate in such strike or violation.
3. Withhold all or any part of the salaries or wages that would otherwise accrue to all or any employees who participate in such strike or violation.[28]

Florida law provides that a teachers' organization can be liable for damages which the school district may have suffered due to the strike and can also be fined up to $20,000 for each day of the strike.[29] Oklahoma law states that a teachers' union that engages in a strike will cease to be recognized as the representative of the teachers and that the school district is then relieved of any duty to bargain.[30]

In addition to the sanctions described in state laws, courts have ruled that school boards have certain options available to strike situations. School officials can ask the courts to issue an injunction to prohibit the strike. The union, its officers, and members can be held in contempt and fined or jailed if they remain on strike in violation of a court order to return to work.[31] The courts have ruled that the school board can fire teachers who engage in an illegal strike. In a Wisconsin case,[32] teachers went out on strike while the school board and the teachers' association were negotiating over the terms of the new contract. After sending letters to the striking teachers informing them that the strike was illegal, school officials scheduled disciplinary hearings for each striking teacher. The teachers then appeared before the school board, asking that they be treated as a group in any disciplinary proceedings. The board voted to fire all the teachers, and the Wisconsin Supreme Court upheld the board's decision.

Finally, the courts have ruled that school boards can impose economic sanctions on teachers who go on strike. A New York court upheld the constitutionality of a state law that allowed the board to make payroll deductions in the amount of twice the daily rate of pay for each day a teacher was on strike.[33] Similarly, a Florida court ruled that a school board had the authority under state law to require each striking teacher to pay $100 to the board as a condition of reemployment.[34]

SUMMARY

Over the past 30 years, collective bargaining in the public schools has become a common practice. Most states have passed laws that give teachers the right to join employee organizations, and the majority of teachers are union/association members. In addition, the courts have held that teachers have a constitutional right to organize as part of their right of free association.

Most state laws now outline procedures for teachers to follow when selecting an organization as their exclusive bargaining agent in contract negotiations with the school board. The laws vary widely from state to state but generally require school boards to bargain with teacher organizations about "wages, hours, and other terms and conditions of employment." Most states also describe the procedure to be followed when there is an impasse in collective bargaining negotiations.

Despite the support for collective bargaining in education, there are limits on teachers' rights. Teachers do not have the constitutional right to bargain with school boards, and about half the states prohibit all strikes by teachers. The trend today, however, is for states to give teachers a limited right to strike. In situations where state law prohibits strikes or teachers fail to meet the specified conditions for a strike, the courts have upheld the school board's right to dismiss striking teachers. In addition, the courts have issued injunctions against teachers who engage in illegal strikes, and upheld the board's authority to impose economic sanctions on striking teachers.

NOTES

1. *Norwalk Teachers' Association* v. *Board of Education,* 83 A.2d 482 (Conn. 1951).
2. R. I. GEN. LAWS § 28-9.3-2 (1956, Reenactment of 1979).
3. *Id.,* § 28-9.3-4.
4. "The scope of representation shall be limited to matters relating to wages, hours of employment, and other terms and conditions of employment. 'Terms and conditions of employment' mean health and welfare benefits as defined by Section 53200, leave, transfer and reassignment policies, safety conditions of employment, class size, procedures to be used for the evaluation of employees, organizational security pursuant to Section 3546, procedures for processing grievances pursuant to Sections 3548.5, 3548.6, 3548.7, and 3548.8, the layoff of probationary certified school district employees, pursuant to Section 44959.5 of the Education Code, and alternative compensation or benefits for employees adversely affected by pension limitations pursuant to Section 22515 of the Education Code, to the extent deemed reasonable and without violating the intent and purposes of Section 415 of the Internal Revenue Code. In addition, the exclusive representative of certified personnel has the right to consult on the definition of educational objectives, the determination of the content of courses and curriculum, and the selection of textbooks to the extent such matters are within the discretion of the public school employer under the law. All matters not specifically enumerated are reserved to the public school employer and may not be a subject of meeting and negotiating, provided that nothing herein may be construed to limit the right of the public school employer to consult with any employees or employee organization on any matter outside the scope of representation" CAL. GOVT. CODE § 3543.2[a] [West 1980].
5. The National Labor Relations Act of 1935 and the Taft-Hartley Act of 1977 regulate labor/management relations in private industry but do not apply to public employees, and the United States Supreme Court has ruled that the National Labor Relations Act does not cover teachers in church-related schools *(NLRB* v. *Catholic Bishop of Chicago,* 440 U.S. 490 [1979]).
6. Federal Service Labor-Management Relations Statute, 5 U.S.C. § 7101 (1980). Teachers covered by this law would include individuals who are employed overseas at schools run by the Department of Defense or at schools on Indian reservations run by the Bureau of Indian Affairs.
7. *McLaughlin* v. *Tilendis,* 398 F.2d 287 (7th Cir. 1968).
8. *Lake Park Education Association* v. *Board of Education of Lake Park,* 526 F.Supp. 710 (N.D. Ill. 1981).
9. *Winston-Salem/Forsyth County Unit of the North Carolina Association of Educators* v. *Phillips,* 381 F.Supp. 644 (M.D. N.C. 1974).
10. OKLA. STAT. ANN., Tit. 70, § 509.2 [West Supp. 1989].
11. CAL. GOV'T. CODE § 3543 (West 1980).
12. 429 U.S. 167 (1976).
13. 431 U.S. 209 (1977).
14. *Ellis* v. *Brotherhood of Railway Clerks,* 466 U.S. 435 (1984).
15. *Chicago Teachers Union, Local No. 1* v. *Hudson,* 475 U.S. 2921 (1986).
16. CAL. GOV'T CODE § 3547(a) (West 1980).
17. TENN. CODE ANN. § 49-5-611 (1980).

18. *State Statutes on School District Collective Bargaining* (Alexandria, Va.: National School Boards Association, 1987), p. 7-1.
19. *Kenai Peninsula Borough School District* v. *Kenai Peninsula Education Association,* 572 P.2d 416 (Alaska 1977).
20. *City of Beloit* v. *Wisconsin Employment Relations Commission,* 242 N.W.2d 231 (Wis. 1976).
21. *West Hartford Education Association* v. *DeCourcy,* 295 A.2d 526 (Conn. 1972).
22. Holding yes: *Board of Education* v. *Fair Lawn Education Association,* 417 A.2d 76 (N.H. Ct. App. 1980); *Northwest Community School Dist.* v. *Public Employment Relations Board,* 408 N.W.2d 46 (Iowa 1987). Holding no: *Springfield Education Association* v. *Springfield School Dist.,* 621 P.2d 547 (Or. 1980); *Wethersfield Board of Eduction* v. *Connecticut State Board of Labor Relations,* 519 A.2d 41 (Conn. 1986).
23. Holding yes: *Sutherlin Education Association* v. *School Dist.,* 548 P.2d 204 (Or. App. 1976). Holding no: *City of Beloit* v. *Wis. ERC,* 242 N.W.2d 231 (Wis. 1976).
24. OKLA. STAT. ANN., Tit. 70, §509.7 (West 1983).
25. Section 89-11 reads:

(b) A public employer shall have the power to enter into written agreement with the exclusive representative of an appropriate bargaining unit setting forth an impasse procedure culminating in a final and binding decision, to be invoked in the event of an impasse over the terms of an initial or renewed agreement. In the absence of such a procedure, either party may request the assistance of the board by submitting to the board and to the other party to the dispute a clear, concise statement of each issue on which an impasse has been reached together with a certificate as to the good faith of the statement and the contents therein. The board, on its own motion, may determine that an impasse exists on any matter in a dispute. If the board determines on its own motion that an impasse exists, it may render assistance by notifying both parties to the dispute of its intent.

The board shall render assistance to resolve the impasse according to the following schedule:

(1) Mediation. Assist the parties in a voluntary resolution of the impasse by appointing a mediator or mediators, representative of the public, from a list of qualified persons maintained by the board, within three days after the date of the impasse, which shall be deemed to be the day on which notification is received or a determination is made that an impasse exists.

(2) Fact-finding. If the dispute continues fifteen days after the date of the impasse, the board shall appoint, within three days, a fact-finding board of not more than three members, representative of the public, from a list of qualified persons maintained by the board. The fact-finding board, shall, in addition to powers delegated to it by the board, have the power to make recommendations for the resolution of the dispute. The fact-finding board, acting by a majority of its members, shall transmit its findings of fact and any recommendations for the resolution of the dispute to both parties within ten days after its appointment. If the dispute remains unresolved five days after the transmittal of the findings of fact and any recommendations, the board shall publish the findings of fact and

any recommendations for public information if the dispute is not referred to final and binding arbitration.

(3) Arbitration. If the dispute continues thirty days after the date of the impasse, the parties may mutually agree to submit the remaining differences to arbitration, which shall result in a final and binding decision. The arbitration panal shall consist of three arbitrators, one selected by each party, and the third and impartial arbitrator selected by the other two arbitrators. If either party fails to select an arbitrator or for any reason there is a delay in the naming of an arbitrator, or if the arbitrators fail to select a neutral arbitrator within the time prescribed by the board, the board shall appoint the arbitrator or arbitrators necessary to complete the panel, which shall act with the same force and effect as if the panel had been selected by the parties as described above. The arbitration panel shall take whatever actions necessary, including but not limited to inquiries, investigations, hearings, issuance of subpoenas, and administering oaths, in accordance with procedures prescribed by the board to resolve the impasse. If the dispute remains unresolved within fifty days after the date of the impasse, the arbitration panel shall transmit its findings and its final and binding decision on the dispute to both parties. The parties shall enter into an agreement or take whatever action is necessary to carry out and effectuate the decision. All items requiring any moneys for implementation shall be subject to appropriations by the appropriate legialative bodies, and the employer shall submit all such items agreed to in the course of negotiations within ten days to the appropriate legislative bodies.

The time frame prescribed in the foregoing schedule may be altered by mutual agreement of the parties, subject to the approval of the board.

The costs for mediation and fact-finding shall be borne by the board. All other costs, including that of a neutral arbitrator, shall be borne equally by the parties involved in the dispute HAWAII REV. STAT. § 58911 (1983).

26. ILL. ANN. STAT., ch. 48, § § 1701-1721, 1713 (West Supp. 1985).
27. IND. CODE ANN. § 20-7.5-1-14(a) (West 1984).
28. NEV. REV. STAT. § 25.288.260 (1983).
29. FLA. STAT. § 447.507 (1980).
30. OKLA. STAT. ANN., Tit. 70, § 509.8 (West 1983).
31. *In re Block,* 236 A.2d 589 (N.J. 1967).
32. *Hortonville Joint School District No. 1* v. *Hortonville Education Association,* 225 N.W.2d 658 (Wis. 1975), *rev'd on other grounds and remanded,* 426 U.S. 482 (1976), *aff'd,* 274 N.W.2d 697 (Wis. 1979). This case also raised the question of whether the school board violated the teachers' due process rights by both engaging in collective bargaining as agent for the school district and holding discharge hearings for striking teachers. The Wisconsin Supreme Court found a due process violation but the U.S. Supreme Court reversed the decision.
33. *Lawson* v. *Board of Education,* 307 N.Y.S.2d 333 (1970), *aff'd,* 315 N.Y.S.2d 877 (1970).
34. *National Education Association Inc.,* v. *Lee County Board of Public Instruction,* 299 F.Supp. 834 (M.D. Fla. 1969), *state question certified,* 448 F.2d 451 (5th Cir. 1971), *state question answered,* 260 So.2d 206 (Fla. 1972), *rev'd,* 467 F.2d 447 (5th Cir. 1972).

CHAPTER 4

When Am I Liable?

OVERVIEW

Many books and articles about education dwell on the dangers of being held responsible for students' injuries. They emphasize the seriousness of "personal liability," the "multiplicity of hazards" in the schools, and the "possibilities of disaster" for the teacher. The result is to portray the law as an ubiquitous monster hiding in every educational shadow and ready to ensnare every innocent teacher. There emerges a sense that teachers are in an especially dangerous profession in which the hazards are greater, liability is more personal, negligence is more likely, and the results of negligence are more disastrous than for other people. This is a seriously distorted impression.

It is true that teachers may be held personally liable for injuries that occur because of their negligence, but this is equally true of every citizen. The legal principles that apply to teachers whose negligence causes injury are the same as those that apply to anyone else. This chapter explains these principles, referred to by lawyers as the law of torts. It also considers when educators may be held personally liable for violating a student's constitutional rights.

STUDENT INJURIES

When can a teacher be required to pay damages for a student's injury?

A teacher can be held liable for damages to an injured student if, and only if, the student proves four things: (1) the teacher had a duty to be careful not to injure the student and to protect the student from being injured, (2) the teacher failed to use due care, (3) the teacher's carelessness caused the injury, and (4) the student sustained provable damages. Usually, in cases of student injury, it is easy to prove that the teacher had a duty to be careful toward his or her students and that the injuries resulted in monetary damages. Sometimes there is a question about what precisely caused the injury. In most cases, however, the critical question is whether the teacher violated his or her duty of due care and therefore was negligent.

When is a teacher negligent?

The *Sheehan* Case[1]

If a teacher fails to exercise reasonable care to protect his or her students from injury the teacher is negligent. Such negligence was involved in the case of Margaret Sheehan, an eighth-grade student at St. Peter's School who was injured one morning during recess. The injury occurred when a teacher took Margaret and 19 other girls to an athletic field where a group of eighth-grade boys were playing baseball. The teacher told the girls to sit on a log on the third-base line and then she returned to the school. About five minutes after the teacher left, some of the boys waiting their turn to bat began throwing pebbles at the girls. Although the girls protested, the stone throwing continued for several minutes, until Margaret was seriously injured by a pebble that struck her eye. Margaret's parents sued for damages on her behalf. They alleged that the school and the teacher were negligent in failing to supervise the children's recess. The evidence indicated that the teacher was absent from the athletic area from the time she brought the girls there until after the accident.

After both sides presented their case, the judge instructed the jury on the law to be applied. "It is the duty of a school," said the judge, "to use ordinary care and to protect its students from injury resulting from the conduct of other students under circumstances where such conduct would reasonably have been foreseen and could have been prevented by the use of ordinary care." The jury found that it was reasonable to foresee that a student might be hurt as a result of failure to supervise an athletic area. It therefore decided that the school was negligent. The school appealed on the grounds that there was no past proof that this activity was dangerous or that supervision would have prevented the accident. But the Supreme Court of Minnesota ruled in Margaret's favor. It noted that children have a "known proclivity to act impulsively without thought of the possibilities of danger." It is precisely this lack of mature judgment that makes supervision so vital. "The mere presence of the hand of authority," wrote the court, "normally is effective to curb this youthful exuberance and to protect the children against their own folly."

This does not mean that a teacher is expected to anticipate every situation where one child may suddenly injure another. The law does not expect a teacher to prevent an unforeseen injury that could happen quickly without warning. But this was not such a case. Here the girls protested when the pebble throwing began, and the boys continued throwing stones for several minutes before Margaret was injured. Under these circumstances, the jury concluded that a teacher using reasonable care would have put a stop to this activity and would have prevented the injury. The teacher therefore was negligent in leaving the athletic field unsupervised.

The legal principles to be applied in cases of alleged negligence are clear: Teachers have a duty to exercise reasonable care not to injure their students and to prevent them from being injured. "Reasonable care" is the degree of care a teacher of ordinary prudence would have used under the circumstances. The circumstances considered would include the age, maturity, and experience of the students, and the extent of danger involved. For example, a school board was found liable when a six-year-old student using the monkey bars swung onto a tether ball pole and was injured when she slid over a screw that protruded approximately 1 1/2 inches out of the pole.[2] The court noted that the injury occurred at 8:30 a.m., when there were between 150 and 180 children in the schoolyard under the supervision of one teacher. The teacher's duties that morning included supervising school bus unloading, patrolling the playground, and overseeing students in the school basement, a situation which made her supervisory functions "totally inadequate and virtually impossible." The court also found that the school board was negligent in placing the tether ball pole so close to the monkey bars, providing a natural incentive for a young child to try to slide down the pole.

When circumstances are more dangerous, as in shop or physical education, a teacher would be expected to exercise greater care. Failure to be more careful when dangers are greater—to provide careful instructions, clear warnings, and close supervision—would constitute negligence. For example, a shop instructor was found guilty of negligence when one student injured another student during the operation of a drill press. The student's improper operation of the press caused the drill bit to deflect and strike the assisting student in the temple, which resulted in lacerations and a skull fracture. Although the student was told to wait for the teacher's assistance, the court found the teacher negligent in giving the student the drill bit before he was ready to supervise him. The court further found the teacher liable for failing to warn the students of the dangers involved in assisting one another and for leaving the students unsupervised in a room of operational shop equipment.[3]

Are teachers required to supervise their students at all times?

Not always. According to a Minnesota court, there is generally "no requirement of constant supervision of all the movements of the pupils at all times."[4] However, a teacher would have a duty to provide constant supervision under dangerous conditions, especially among young children.

The *Mancha* Case[5]

In Chicago two teachers organized a field trip to the city's natural history museum for about fifty students, 12–15 years of age. At the museum, the students were allowed to view the exhibits without direct supervision. When he was away from the teachers, Roberto Mancha was beaten by several boys not connected with the school. Roberto's parents sued, charging that the teachers who organized the trip were negligent in not supervising their students and in failing to foresee and guard against Roberto's injury.

In discussing this question, an Illinois court observed that hindsight makes every event foreseeable. However, according to the court, a teacher's duty does not depend only on foreseeability. Judges should also consider the likelihood of the injury, the magnitude of the burden of guarding against it, and the consequences of placing that burden on teachers. The court regarded the risk that a 12-year-old boy would be assaulted in the museum as "minimal." The burden of constantly supervising children in cases such as this would be extremely heavy and would discourage teachers from planning many useful extracurricular activities. The court pointed out that even a game of hopscotch could suddenly break into a fight resulting in serious injury. And it would be practically impossible to require a teacher to watch each student at all times. Moreover, the judge noted that the museum in this case had been a "great educational enterprise," not a place of danger. Under these circumstances, the court ruled that the teachers did not have a duty to anticipate an assault or directly supervise the entire museum trip. (The court also ruled that teachers were not liable under the Illinois School Code, which imposed liability for "willful or wanton" negligence.)

Similarly, a California district was not held liable when a 12-year-old student was fatally injured playing a dangerous skateboard game at an elementary school playground at approximately 5:30 p.m. The student's parents sued the school for negligent supervision and for maintaining grounds that were not locked. The court said that schools do *not* have a duty to supervise the grounds at all times. On the contrary, the duty of supervision is limited to school-related or encouraged functions and activities that take place during school hours. "To require round-the-clock supervision or prison-tight security for school premises," wrote the court, "would impose too great a financial burden on the schools."[6]

On the other hand, the judge in the *Mancha* case did acknowledge that constant supervision would be required on some field trips (e.g., where dangerous machinery is used or where there is reason to believe an assault might take place). Similarly, it might be reasonable to require teachers to provide close supervision for students working with dangerous equipment in school. This was the ruling in an Indiana case in which Tom Peters, a ninth-grade student, lost four fingers while working with a circular saw in an industrial arts class.[7] Peters was cutting wood; one of the saw guards was broken, and his teacher was supervising another class in an adjacent room. A state appeals court found it reasonable to hold the school liable for the damage to Peters because he was allowed to use improperly guarded machinery without the personal supervision of the teacher.

Can a teacher's duty of supervision ever extend beyond school hours?

Yes. While teachers are not ordinarily liable for students' acts after school, they can be held liable if they assign or initiate dangerous activities. In a Louisiana case, for example, the court found a science teacher to be liable when a 13-year-old was injured building a model volcano in his home as part of a class science project.[8] The court found that the teacher was negligent in conducting a classroom volcano demonstration and then allowing the student to take his own volcano project home without determining exactly what chemical substances the student had used or whether the project was dangerous to himself or others.

Can teachers be held liable if a student injures another student or a teacher?

Yes. If a teacher knows or should know that a student is likely to harm another student or a teacher, the teacher has an obligation to try to prevent the injury. In a representative case from New York,[9] for example, a student who had a record of misbehavior transferred to another junior high school where she assaulted Josette Ferraro. The court noted that during her three months at the school, the student had assaulted other students on three occasions, and was "a source of constant quarrelling and aggressive behavior toward other students as well as teachers." On the day of the assault, a substitute teacher was in charge of Josette's class. The court found the school to be negligent in not informing the substitute teacher about Josette's tendency to misbehave, noting that, had it done so, steps might have been taken to prevent the assault, such as requiring the unruly student to sit in a seat directly in front of the teacher.

If teachers are careless, are they automatically liable for damages?

No. In order to recover damages, injured students must prove more than that the teacher was careless; they must also show that the teacher's failure to use due care was the cause of the injury. For example, Wilmer Nash, an elementary school student from Louisiana, was waiting for the schoolbus to take him home. He was playing with a girl when another girl struck him in the eye with a stick, leading to partial blindness. Wilmer's parents sued the school.

The court noted that the school is required to provide supervision while students are waiting for the schoolbus and that it failed to do so at the time Wilmer was injured. Nevertheless, the court did not find the school or the teachers liable because Wilmer's lawyer was not able to prove that careful supervision would have prevented the injury. "How," asked the judge, "could any teacher anticipate a situation where one child, while teasing another child, would be struck in the eye with a stick by a third child?" Even if educators can anticipate that accidents like this sometimes happen, there was no evidence that this injury could have been prevented if a teacher had been present. "As is often the case," concluded the judge, "accidents such as this involving school children at play, happen so quickly that unless there was direct supervision of every child (which we recognize as being impossible), the accident can be said to be almost impossible to prevent."[10] Thus the court did not find the school liable for damages because Wilmer failed to show a causal connection between the absence of supervision and his accident.

In New York City, Alan Kaufman was critically injured when he jumped for a basketball and bumped heads with another student. Kaufman's father sued, alleging that the school failed to properly supervise the game. But the court ruled in favor of the school.[11] According to the court, even if there was an absence of supervision and even if "such absence constituted negligence, still under the circumstances, such lack of supervision was not the proximate cause of the accident." The presence of a teacher would not have prevented the boys from bumping their heads during the basketball game. "That," wrote the court, "is one of the natural and normal possible consequences or occurrences in a game of this sort which cannot be prevented no matter how adequate the supervision."

Are there defenses against liability?

Yes. Injured students who sue teachers and administrators for damages may encounter the defenses of contributory (or comparative) negligence, assumption of risk, or governmental immunity. Of these, contributory (or comparative) negligence is the most frequent and significant defense for teachers. Assumption of risk is rarely applicable except in cases of competitive athletics. And governmental immunity may protect some school districts, but it is not a defense for individual teachers.

What is contributory negligence?

If a student's own negligence contributed to the injury, the law in many states would consider the student "guilty of contributory negligence." Unless the injured student was very young, this would usually prevent him or her from recovering damages against a negligent teacher. This principle is illustrated in the 1979 case of Jodeen Miles, a 17-year-old high school student from Nebraska. Jodeen was working on her senior project in Shop II when she attempted to remove a piece of wood from an operating machine with her hands, contrary to safe practice. As a result she severed two fingers and sued her instructor for negligent supervision.

Evidence indicated that the teacher had demonstrated the safe use of power tools, had assigned a safety booklet for students to read, had given a safety exam, and had watched Jodeen operate the machine safely. Although there was some question about whether the teacher was negligent in not directly supervising her at the time of the injury, the court ruled that Jodeen was negligent in failing to use the ordinary care that a student of her age and maturity "would have used under like circumstances." Thus the court dismissed Jodeen's claim and concluded that her contributory negligence was the "proximate cause of the injuries she sustained in this unfortunate accident."[12]

The Supreme Court of Wisconsin reached a similar finding after a high school sophomore was injured in a science class when a beaker of burning alcohol spilled on him.[13] The accident occurred when Ronald Risman and two of his friends decided to light some heated alcohol on a table during an experiment, although they had been warned not to place any flame near alcohol. Evidence indicated that the teacher was negligent in the way he attempted to put out the fire, but the court ruled that the student was also negligent and that his negligence was a substantial factor contributing to his injury.

Does a student's negligence always prevent recovery?

No. The younger the student, the more difficult it is to prove contributory negligence. In most states, courts hold that very young children are incapable of contributory negligence. This means that even if the carelessness of such students contributed to their injury, this would not prevent them from recovering damages from a negligent teacher. In about a dozen states judges have ruled that students under seven years of age cannot be barred from recovering damages because of their negligence. In other states the age has been set at four, five, or six years. For older children, usually those between the ages of seven and fourteen, there is often a "rebuttable presumption" that they are incapable of contributory negligence. With sufficient evidence concerning their intelligence, maturity, and the circumstances of the case this presumption can be rebutted and the court can find them negligent.

The most significant factor allowing negligent students to recover damages has been the trend toward adoption of "comparative negligence" statutes. In the majority of states,[14] a student's contributory negligence does not completely prevent him or her from recovering damages from a negligent teacher. Instead, comparative negligence laws permit the judge or jury to compare the relative negligence of the plaintiff and the defendant in causing the injury, and to make an appropriate damage award. Thus, where the plaintiff (student) was also responsible for causing the injury, he or she would only be entitled to a portion of the normally awarded damages. For example, in a Louisiana case involving a nine-year-old girl who broke her leg jumping off a merry-go-round, the court compared the negligence of the student with that of the school board. The court found both the school board negligent in the supervision of the student and the child negligent in jumping off the merry-go-round. Since the student was equally responsible for causing the injury, the court reduced the amount of compensation awarded to her by 50 percent.[15] (Note, however, that in many states, comparative negligence laws bar recovery if the plaintiff's negligence is equal to or greater than that of the defendant.[16])

When does a student assume the risk of being injured?

The doctrine of "assumption of risk" has been recognized as a defense against liability in activities such as competitive sports. It is based on the theory that people who know and appreciate the danger involved in an activity and voluntarily engage in it willingly expose themselves to certain predictable risks. This doctrine is illustrated by a Louisiana case in which a 17-year-old student challenged a basketball coach to a wrestling match. During the match, the student's foot got caught between two floor mats, and he fell and injured his ankle. The student filed suit against the school board for injuries sustained during the match. Although the student testified that he did not know that he could get hurt wrestling, the court stated that there are some risks that everyone must appreciate. The court held that the teenager must have known that he could be hurt from a fall while wrestling, and thus, the teacher was not liable for the student's injury.[17]

On the other hand, an 11-year-old student who sustained mouth injuries in a floor hockey game did not assume the risk of his injuries.[18] The court held that the assumption of risk was not a viable defense when the student's lack of experience, lack of information, and tender age impaired his appreciation of the dangers involved in floor hockey.

Can teachers use governmental immunity as a defense against negligence?

No. Governmental immunity is a common-law theory which holds that since the state and its agencies are sovereign, they cannot be sued without their consent and should not be held liable for the negligence of their employees. Some courts justify this practice on the grounds that public funds raised for schooling should not be legally diverted for noneducational purposes. But in recent years this doctrine has been widely condemned by legal writers, and an increasing number of state courts or legislatures have abolished governmental immunity. In other states that support the concept, the courts or legislatures have found that the purchase of liability insurance eliminates the defense to the extent of the insurance coverage, or they have created exceptions to the doctrine (such as holding schools liable for nonessential activities, such as leasing a portion of the premises). Even in states where this doctrine still can prevent negligence suits against school districts, students may sue individual teachers, who can be held personally liable for their negligence.

Does a "waiver" or "release" prevent an injured student from suing?

Generally not. Most courts that have addressed the issue[19] have found that such releases are invalid on public policy grounds. For example, the Washington Supreme Court recently held that a school district could not require parents to sign forms absolving the school of liability for sports accidents.[20] Because athletics are "part and parcel" of the educational program, the court stated, the district is obliged to participate in the dangers inherent in such programs.

Even where releases are not illegal, judges are usually extremely strict in interpreting them, and, in practice, schools are generally unsuccessful in using waivers to prohibit negligence suits. This was illustrated by a New York case in which a student, Bruce Gross, sued a parachute training school. After breaking his leg when he landed on his first jump, Gross charged that the school was negligent in failing to instruct him properly. The school tried to block the suit on the grounds that Gross signed a responsibility release that said he would "waive any and all claims" he may have against the school "for any personal injuries . . . that I may sustain or which may arise out of my learning, practice or actually jumping out of an aircraft."

Despite this release, the court allowed Gross to sue. According to the judge, such releases are "closely scrutinized and strictly construed" by the courts and will be enforced only when the limits of liability are "precisely defined" and any omissions plainly noted. In the opinion of the court, since the release did not contain any "specific provision which waives any claim for defendant's failure to instruct plaintiff properly," it did not release the school from negligence arising out of improper instruction.[21]

In the few cases where releases have been upheld, parents or guardians have generally failed to disclose important information that schools should have known about a student. For example, a court[22] upheld a release where a parent had signed a form giving permission for his son to use the swimming pool but did not inform school officials that the student could not swim.

OTHER TYPES OF LIABILITY

Are teachers liable if they fail to report child abuse?

Yes. Every one of the 50 states plus all the territories of the United States require that teachers, along with administrators and counselors, report known or suspected cases of child abuse or neglect, and those who fail to do so are subject to penalties under the law. (See Chapter 5 for an in-depth discussion of this topic.)

Can schools be held liable if students or employees with AIDS are in attendance?

That depends on the facts of the particular situation. The legal principles related to negligence would apply to a situation where AIDS was present just as to other situations. Understandably some parents as well as educators are deeply concerned about this issue in light of its seriousness and the incomplete medical knowledge surrounding it.

Most states and school districts have created policies to guide schools threatened with the virus. The concerns are equally serious for children and adults who have AIDS and are thus vulnerable to various diseases as for those who are in danger of getting the virus from infected children or adults. There are important constitutional issues related to privacy, equal protection, and due process involved in how schools handle this matter, but the protection of the community also weighs heavily on educators as they formulate and administer policies.

Typically, these guidelines follow recommendations issued by the Centers for Disease Control and the American Academy of Pediatrics. As of 1989, these groups recommend that most school-age children infected with the human immunodeficiency virus should be allowed to attend school without restrictions and with the approval of the child's physician. Infected students who pose an increased risk to others in school, such as those who lack control of body secretions, who display behavior such as biting, or have open skin sores that cannot be covered, may require a more restricted school environment. Confidential school records should be maintained, and the number of personnel aware of the child's condition should be kept to a minimum. It is generally recommended that anyone with the virus not handle food, and that school personnel be trained to deal appropriately with blood or other body fluids that might be spilled in school. It is also recommended that school districts create medical teams to examine students and/or employees who have the virus to determine whether their continued school attendance is likely to endanger others.

Schools that adopt policies reflecting current research and apply them with care are not likely to find themselves liable in a civil suit for money damages. Schools may be liable, however, if they totally exclude students or teachers with AIDS. In 1987, the U.S. Supreme Court held that a teacher's rights were violated when she was fired after testing positive for contagious tuberculosis.[23] In its decision, which can be applied to many illnesses including AIDS, the Court found that Section 504 of the 1973 Rehabilitation Act required that the teacher's case be studied to determine whether she could be accommodated safely in her employment position. The courts which have specifically addressed the issue of AIDS have followed this reasoning. In a 1987 Florida case,[24] for example, the court granted a preliminary injunction permitting three hemophiliac children who tested positive for the human immunodeficiency virus, and were thus identified as carriers of antibodies for AIDS, to attend school in a normal classroom setting. In an out-of-court settlement, the school district later agreed to pay the parents of the students $1.1 million over 30 years for preventing the children from attending classes.[25] In a more recent[26] case, the same court found that the Education for All Handicapped Children Act, P.L. 94-142, also applied to protect a student with AIDS. In that case, the school district had insisted that a mentally handicapped child with AIDS be taught at home. Her mother, however, wanted the child placed in a special class for trainable mentally retarded students. After initially ruling that the student had to be educated in a glass isolation booth to protect other students from the "theoretical possibility" that AIDS could be transmitted through tears, saliva, or urine, the court reversed itself. Following an order issued by the 11th Circuit Court of Appeals to rehear the case and decide whether there was a "significant risk" rather than a remote possibility of transmission, the court held that the child should be permitted to attend the trainable mentally handicapped class. The court concluded that it could not find "that the risk is significant enough to counterbalance the benefit and rights to this child inherent in attending school with other children."[27]

While there are still very few cases dealing with the exclusion of students or teachers with AIDS, it is clear that schools cannot exclude students or teachers without following appropriate procedures. In general, schools will not be able to exclude such students or teachers without adequate notice and a hearing to determine the nature of the disease and the extent to which other students and employees are in danger of transmission through the student's or teacher's attendance in a regular classroom. In order to make appropriate decisions, schools must maintain current medical information from a consulting physician and/or guidelines issued by the Centers for Disease Control, the U.S. Public Health Service, or state and local health departments.[28]

Can schools be held liable for failure to maintain a safe environment?

With school crime increasing, students and teachers who are injured on school premises often sue the school district for failure to maintain a safe environment. A number of courts have held that a special relationship exists between educators and students because students are required to attend school and their care is entrusted to school officials. Under this theory, the courts have held schools liable for injuries to students that are reasonably foreseeable. For example, a Florida court held that a school district was liable when a high school student was attacked and beaten by other students on school premises.[29] The student was beaten outside the cafeteria while he was using the phone after a junior varsity football team practice. The court found that the school was negligent in not providing for any supervision of the cafeteria area and that student misbehavior was a foreseeable result of such a lack of supervision.

The courts have also applied this theory to hold schools liable when students are injured by nonstudents. In a California case,[30] for example, the court found the school district liable when a student member of the wrestling team was assaulted by a nonstudent in an unsupervised restroom in the high school. The court found it reasonably foreseeable that attacks were likely to occur in an unsupervised restroom. Similarly, an Oregon court[31] held that a school district was liable for the rape of a 15-year-old high school student when a woman delivering newspapers to the school 15 days before had also been sexually assaulted on the same school property. Where the injuries to a student are not foreseeable, however, the school district will not be held liable. For example, a school will not be liable for a violent student's attack upon another student unless the school had knowledge about the aggressor's behavior that would have made the attack reasonably foreseeable.[32]

A number of states have passed statutes dealing the safe schools. The California constitution, for example, provides that all students and staff of public schools have "the inalienable right to attend campuses which are safe, secure, and peaceful."[33] A recent California Court of Appeals decision[34] held, however, that this provision merely established a general right without specifying any rules for enforcement and thus did not give a student injured at school a right to sue for damages. While at least one other court has agreed that students do not have a constitutional right to a safe school environment,[35] students may be successful in bringing claims that their constitutional rights to liberty under the due process clause are violated when they are assaulted at school. For example, a federal court[36] recently upheld students' right to bring such an action when female students alleged that they were sexually abused because the school board failed to act after it had knowledge that an employee had previously abused students but did not investigate or take other appropriate action. (See p. 68 in this chapter for further discussion of claims for deprivation of constitutional rights.)

Can schools be held liable for educational malpractice?

Probably not. Some students have brought legal actions alleging that schools should be held liable for negligent teaching that injures a student intellectually or psychologically, just as physicians and lawyers are liable to their patients and clients when they are negligent. In none of the cases have the students prevailed, however. In the first such case filed in California in 1976,[37] a high school graduate who could read only at the fifth-grade level sued the school district for failing to provide him with adequate instruction in basic skills. The court analyzed the law of negligence and concluded that the suit should have been dismissed for the following reasons: (1) There were no clear standards to determine whether the school had been negligent; (2) there was no way to determine that a teacher's negligence was the proximate cause of the student's injury; and (3) it would impose too great a financial burden on schools to hold them to an actionable duty of care in the discharge of their academic functions. Many other courts[38] have followed this decision, refusing on public policy grounds to second-guess the professional judgments of educators in selecting programs for particular students.

In a Maryland case,[39] however, parents were allowed to bring an action against school officials for intentionally and maliciously injuring their child by furnishing false information regarding the student's learning disability, altering school records to cover up their actions, and demeaning the child. The court explained that "where an individual engaged in the educational process is shown to have willfully and maliciously injured a child entrusted to his care, such outrageous conduct greatly outweighs any public policy considerations which would otherwise preclude liability to authorize recovery."[40] The significance of this decision is quite limited, however, because few parents will be able to prove that educators were acting maliciously and intentionally when a student was injured as a result of an inappropriate educational placement.

DAMAGES

What kinds of damages are awarded by the courts?

Courts can award several kinds of damages. The most common damage award is one for compensatory damages. The purpose of this award is to compensate injured persons for their actual losses—for their medical expenses, lost salary, court costs, and other expenses incurred as a result of the defendant's negligence. Damages can be awarded for monetary, physical, or psychological injury. Exemplary or punitive damages are awarded where defendants have shown malice, fraud, or reckless disregard for an injured person's safety or constitutional rights. The purpose of this award is to punish the defendants for their wrongful actions and deter similar actions in the future. Nominal damages are a small, symbolic award (e.g., one dollar), where the plaintiff has been wronged but has not been able to show actual damages.

Can school officials be held liable for violating a student's constitutional rights?

Yes. In the landmark case of *Wood* v. *Strickland,* two Arkansas students were unlawfully suspended for three months without due process, and their parents sued the school board for damages.[41] (See Chapter 11 for a detailed discussion of due process rights of students.) In this 1975 decision, the U.S. Supreme Court ruled that school officials could be held liable "if they knew or reasonably should have known that the action they took within their sphere of official responsibility would violate the constitutional rights of the students affected."[42] Public school officials who violate students' constitutional rights can be liable for damages under a federal statute that allows a suit against any person who, "under color of any statute, ordinance, regulation, custom or usage, of any State or Territory or the District of Columbia, subjects, or causes to be subjected, any citizen of the United States or any other person within the jurisdiction thereof to the deprivation of any rights, privileges, or immunities secured by the Constitution" and laws.[43] This law, referred to as Section 1983, can be used to sue local governmental officials,[44] and courts have held principals, superintendents, and school board members liable for damages to students or teachers whose rights they violated. School officials will not be liable, however, unless the actions complained about were the result of an official governmental policy or custom. In one case,[45] for example, a middle school student sued the school district, supervisory officials, and a bus driver after he was beaten by other students on a school bus, alleging that the district deprived him of liberty because its instructions to bus drivers regarding the prevention of violence were inadequate. The Fifth Circuit held that the school district was not liable because the student did not prove pervasiveness of violence or a preexisting pattern of student fights on buses which warranted an official response. Thus, there was no actionable official policy or custom. Regarding the supervisor, the student did not prove that the asserted failure to train bus drivers in a proper manner "callously disregarded" the student's constitutional rights, as required for supervisory liability.[46] In another case[47] where a student sued a school district for failure to supervise its employees, the court held that a single isolated incident by a teacher does not establish an official policy or practice sufficient to establish Section 1983 liability.

In addition, school officials may escape liability on the basis of "qualified immunity."[48] In *Wood* v. *Strickland*, the Supreme Court held that school board members "should be protected under state law for all good-faith, nonmalicious actions" taken to fulfill official duties. This definition involved both a subjective and objective test of good faith. In 1982, however, the Supreme Court modified this standard for liability in a case[49] that concerned federal officials' immunity from suits brought under the Constitution, holding that officials "generally are shielded from liability for civil damages insofar as their conduct does not violate clearly established statutory or constitutional rights of which a reasonable person would have known." This decision thus made the test for liability objective, discarding any subjective inquiry into the minds of governmental officials.

Since the Supreme Court has not decided what constitutes "clearly established" law, the courts have had to look at each case to determine the degree to which a reasonable person would have known that a certain legal principle applied. For example, when middle school students sued school officials alleging that general searches of students violated their constitutional rights under the Fourth Amendment, a federal court held that school officials were entitled to qualified immunity.[50] The court found that the legal rules applicable to this situation were not "clearly established" at the time the officials acted because the specific legal issue involved had not been addressed by the U.S. Supreme Court, the U.S. Court of Appeals for the Fourth Circuit, or the Supreme Court of Virginia. The court concluded: "While the defendants must certainly be charged with knowledge that the Fourth Amendment protects students' legitimate privacy interests, plaintiffs have not shown to the requisite level of specificity that the defendants should have known that the actions taken in this case would violate those interests."

In other cases however, courts have found that the law is "clearly established." In one such case,[51] for example, a federal court held that a teacher and principal could not raise a qualified immunity defense since they violated clearly settled substantive due process law when they tied a student to a chair for one school day and part of another, and denied her access to the bathroom. The court said that, even if there was not a case just like this one, "it suffices that [they] be aware of general, well-developed legal principles." In another case,[52] a parent sued a principal on behalf of himself and his six children for discouraging him from registering his children in public school because of the community's racial hostility. The Seventh Circuit held that the principal was not protected by qualified immunity because the law was clearly established that it was a violation of the Fourteenth Amendment to be intimidated from admission to public school because of race. In a recent case,[53] the Third Circuit held that a principal and assistant principal were not entitled to raise qualified immunity as a defense in a case where a female student alleged that they had violated her due process rights by failing to prevent her sexual harassment by the band director. The court concluded that, although the mere failure of supervisory officials to act or investigate cannot be the basis of liability, "it was clearly established law that such officials may not with impunity maintain a custom, practice or usage that communicated condonation or authorization of assaultive behavior." Since there was evidence that the administrators discouraged and minimized reports of the band director's sexual misconduct that they received from other students and teachers, the court concluded that it was possible to construe their actions as "encouraging a climate to flourish where innocent girls were victimized." (The court did not reach the question of liability, but merely sent the case to the district court for trial.)

When a student's rights are violated, how will the amount of damages be determined?

In 1978 the Supreme Court answered this question in a case involving two Chicago students who were suspended for 20 days without due process.[54] Their lawyer introduced no evidence to show that they had suffered any actual damages because of their suspension, but he argued that they should receive substantial damages simply because they had been deprived of their constitutional rights.

The Court disagreed. It ruled that when a student is deprived of his or her constitutional rights, the amount of damages should depend on the circumstances of the case. A student should be awarded substantial sums for two reasons: (1) as punitive damages to deter or punish school officials who intentionally deprive the student of his or her rights; or (2) as compensatory damages for actual injury, which can include "mental and emotional distress" as well as financial loss. When the violation is unintentional and no actual injury is shown, the student is only entitled to the award of a nominal sum of money.

In a similar case,[55] several Puerto Rican college students sued for damages when they were unlawfully suspended for up to 12 days. They were unable to prove an actual injury, such as "delay in meeting academic requirements or significant harm to plaintiff's reputation in the community or medically cognizable psychological distress." Nor were they able to show that their suspension was caused by school officials acting in bad faith or trying to harass them. Rather, the evidence indicated that the improper suspension "was nothing more than an isolated error in the administration of university discipline." Under these circumstances, the court refused to award compensatory damages for "general mental distress." Instead, the appeals court felt that the appropriate award was to grant the students nominal damages plus the costs of their attorneys' fees.

Since its pronouncements in *Carey*, the Supreme Court has amplified its remarks concerning the appropriate assessment of damages. In *Memphis Com-*

munity School District v. *Stachura,*[56] an action arising from the unwarranted discharge of a teacher, the Court cited *Carey* in support of its holding that the abstract value of a constitutional right could not serve as a basis for an award of compensatory damages in an action arising under Section 1983. In accordance with its conclusion that damages in a Section 1983 action are ordinarily determined by common-law tort principles, the Court further reaffirmed that compensatory damages might include not only verified pecuniary losses, but also payment for such subjective consequences as impairment of reputation, personal humiliation, and mental anguish and suffering. Finally, the Court observed that punitive damages in an action of this sort would be appropriate only to punish willful or malicious conduct on the part of the defendant or to deter others from similar conduct in the future.

Can teachers be awarded damages if their constitutional rights are violated?

Yes. The same legal principles that were described above determine whether a teacher can bring an action under Section 1983 and, if successful, what damages can be awarded. A 1978 federal court decision illustrated these principles in the case of a Texas teacher.[57] Jerry Burnaman was a competent, dedicated, well-qualified educator who had taught successfully in the Bay City schools for more than a decade. A new principal and superintendent (the latter considered an expert in school law) were then brought in to "shake up the school system and make substantial changes." Among the changes they wanted to make was to demote or remove Jerry Burnaman. They did this through a two-step process: They gave him the first unfavorable recommendation he had ever received and they then recommended that his year-to-year contract not be renewed. Burnaman requested a hearing in mid-April to refute the negative recommendation, but the administration delayed the hearing until late August, after which his discharge was upheld. (During this time he had further angered the administration by testifying in favor of another educator who had been fired.) As a result of these events, Burnaman sued the principal, the superintendent, and the school board, charging that they had violated his constitutional rights.

A federal judge agreed. The court found that the principal's negative evaluation was "inaccurate, nonfactual, grossly unfair," and not prepared in accordance with school policy requiring the use of objective evaluation standards. The court also found that in the evaluation the principal made statements he knew or should have known were inaccurate. The judge concluded that Burnaman's discharge violated his due process rights, was in retaliation for statements he had made that were protected by the First Amendment, and damaged his professional reputation. Therefore the jury granted him several awards: (1) compensatory damages of $16,440 for loss of wages and $17,000 "for mental anguish accompanying the termination of his employment"; (2) exemplary damages of $25,000 against the superintendent and principal for acting with malice and intentionally depriving Burnaman of his constitutional rights; and (3) fees for

Burnaman's attorney, which were incurred unnecessarily because of the "school board's unreasonable and obdurate obstinacy."

Are students or teachers who bring successful civil rights lawsuits entitled to recover their attorneys' fees?

Yes. Federal law provides that in Section 1983 lawsuits the court "may allow the prevailing party, other than the United States, a reasonable attorney's fee as part of the costs."[58] This law is intended to encourage lawyers to represent civil rights plaintiffs who may otherwise be unable to afford to hire lawyers, and courts have used it to award attorneys' fees in cases where students and teachers prevailed in lawsuits alleging violations of their rights.

In a 1989 case,[59] the Supreme Court made it even easier for students and teachers to recover legal fees. The case involved a suit by teachers who claimed that the school district's policy limiting communications with teachers concerning employee organizations violated the First Amendment. Although the teachers did not prevail on the "main thrust" of their lawsuit (to gain access to school campuses during school hours for outside representatives of employee organization), they did succeed on certain secondary issues (relating, for example, to teacher-to-teacher discussion of employee organizations during the school day). The Supreme Court ruled that even though they had not prevailed on the "central" issue in the case, the teachers were still entitled to recover attorneys' fees. In the Court's words, "If the plaintiff has succeeded on 'any significant issue in litigation which achieve[d] some of the benefit the parties sought in bringing the suit' the plaintiff has crossed the threshold to a fee award of some kind." The court therefore remanded the case to the Court of Appeals to determine what fee would be reasonable in the case.

SUMMARY

In order to hold a teacher liable for a student's injury, the student must prove the following:

The teacher owed a duty of care to the student. Teachers can only be held liable when they are legally responsible for students' care, such as during school hours or school-sponsored field trips. Ordinarily, teachers are not liable for students' after-school or off-premises injuries. Under recently passed statutes, teachers now also have a duty to report child abuse and neglect.

The teacher was negligent. Teachers have a duty to exercise reasonable care not to injure their students and to prevent them from being injured. "Reasonable care" is that degree of care that a reasonably prudent teacher would have exercised under the circumstances. The circumstances considered by the courts include the age, maturity, and experience of the students and the extent of danger involved. When conditions are more dangerous (e.g., in woodshop, a chemistry lab, or a boxing class), a reasonable teacher would be expected to be more careful—to provide closer supervision, clear warnings, and careful instructions. If teachers do not use reasonable care, there is a breach of duty, and they are negligent.

The teacher's negligence was the cause of the student's injury. To recover damages against a teacher, a student must be able to show that it was the teacher's negligence that caused the injury. Suits for educational malpractice have not been allowed because the courts have not been able to determine which of a myriad of factors actually caused a student to fail academically. In addition, the doctrines of contributory negligence or comparative negligence may identify the student as the total or partial cause of the injury, thus eliminating or reducing the amount of damages that can be recovered against a teacher.

The student was actually damaged by the teacher's negligence. Students must be able to show actual damages in order to recover from a teacher's negligence. Such damages can include monetary loss, such as medical expenses, or psychological injury. In addition, in certain cases where a teacher has acted with malice or fraud, the court may award punitive damages to deter future such actions.

In recent years, courts have also begun to hold school officials personally liable for damages if they violate the clearly established constitutional rights of students or teachers. Such awards could include compensatory damages for actual financial, physical, or psychological injury; exemplary or punitive damages for intentional violations; or nominal damages, where the violation is not intentional and no actual injuries are proven.

In sum, the law requires teachers or administrators who carelessly cause injury to pay compensation. Teachers are subject to the same law as other citizens who are held financially responsible for their negligence. Just as responsible drivers purchase liability insurance for their cars, so responsible teachers should purchase professional liability insurance to provide extra financial protection for their students and themselves.

NOTES

1. *Sheehan* v. *St. Peter's Catholic School*, 188 N.W.2d 868 (Minn. 1971).
2. *Gibbons* v. *Orleans Parish School Board*, 391 So.2d 976 (La. App. 1980).
3. *Roberts* v. *Robertson County Board of Education*, 692 S.W.2d 863 (Tenn. 1985).
4. *Sheehan* v. *St. Peter's Catholic School*, 188 N.W.2d 868 (Minn. 1971).
5. *Mancha* v. *Field Museum of Natural History*, 283 N.E.2d 899 (Ill. App. 1972).
6. *Bartell* v. *Palos Verdes Peninsula School District*, 147 Cal. Rptr. 898 (Cal. App. 1978).
7. *South Ripley Community School Corp.* v. *Peters*, 396 N.E.2d 144 (Ind. App. 1979).
8. *Simmons* v. *Beauregard Parish School Board*, 315 So.2d 883 (La. App. 1975).
9. *Ferraro* v. *Board of Education of the City of New York*, 32 Misc.2d 563, 212 N.Y.S.2d 615 (1961), *aff'd*, 14 App. Div. 2d 815, 221 N.Y.S.2d 279 (1961).
10. *Nash* v. *Rapides Parish School Board*, 188 So.2d 508 (La. App. 1966).
11. *Kaufman* v. *City of New York*, 30 Misc.2d 285, 214 N.Y.S.2d 767 (1961).
12. *Miles* v. *School District No. 138 of Cheyenne County*, 281 N.W.2d 396 (Neb. 1979).

13. *Rixmann* v. *Somerset Public Schools*, 266 N.W.2d 326 (Wis. 1978).
14. As of 1988, 44 jurisdictions have adopted some form of comparative negligence. *Prosser & Keeton on The Law of Torts*, p. 471, n. 30 (West 1988).
15. *Rollins* v. *Concordia Parish School Board*, 465 So.2d 213 (La. App. 1985).
16. 57 Am.Jur.2d *Negligence* § § 426, 431 (1971).
17. *Kluka* v. *Livingston Parish Board*, 433 So.2d 302 (La. App. 1983).
18. *Berman* v. *Philadelphia Board of Education*, 456 A.2d 545 (Pa. Super. 1983).
19. See *Porumbiansky* v. *Emory University*, 275 S.E.2d 163 (Ga. Ct. App. 1980); *Whittington* v. *Sowela Tech. Inst.*, 438 So.2d 236 (La. Ct. App. 1983).
20. *Wagenblast* v. *Odessa School Dist.*, 758 P.2d 968 (Wash. 1988).
21. *Gross* v. *Sweet*, 49 N.Y.2d 102, 424 N.Y.S.2d 365 (1979).
22. *Powell* v. *Orleans Parish School Board*, 354 So.2d 299 (La. Ct. App. 1978).
23. *School Board of Nassau County, Florida* v. *Arline*, 480 U.S. 273 (1987).
24. *Ray* v. *School Dist. of Desoto County*, 666 F.Supp. 1524 (M.D. Fla. 1987).
25. 16 *School Law News* 7 (October 13, 1988).
26. *Martinez* v. *School Board of Hillsborough County, Florida*, 711 F.Supp. 1066 (M.D. Fla. 1989).
27. 711 F. Supp. at 1071.
28. As of 1989, the best single reference for schools developing AIDS policies and procedures is *Someone at School Has AIDS* (Alexandria, Va: National Association of State Boards of Education, 1989). This book, which has been recommended as a resource by the Centers for Disease Control, includes suggested policies concerning all aspects of dealing with students with AIDS.
29. *Broward County School Board* v. *Ruiz*, 493 So.2d 474 (Fla. App. 1986).
30. *Leger* v. *Stockton Unified School Dist.*, 249 Cal.Rptr. 688 (Cal. App. 1988).
31. *Fazzolari* v. *Portland School Dist. No. 1J*, 734 P.2d 1326 (Or. 1987).
32. *McLaughlin* v. *Holy Cross High School*, 521 N.Y.S.2d 744 (N.Y. App. 1987).
33. CAL. CONST. art. I, 28, sub (C) (1982).
34. *Leger, supra* n. 30.
35. *Grubbs* v. *Aldine Independent School Dist.*, 709 F.Supp. 127 (S.D. Tex. 1989).
36. *Thelma D.* v. *Board of Education*, 669 F.Supp. 947 (E.D. Mo. 1987).
37. *Peter W.* v. *San Francisco Unified School District*, 131 Cal. Rptr. 854 (Cal. App. 1976).
38. *Hoffman* v. *Board of Education of the City of New York*, 64 A.D.2d 369, 410 N.Y.S.2d 99 (1978); *W.* v. *Fairbanks North Star Borough School District*, 628 P.2d 554 (Alaska 1981); *Tubell* v. *Dade County Public Schools*, 419 So.2d 388 (Fla. App. 1982); *Silano* v. *Tirozzi*, 651 F. Supp. 1021 (D.C. Conn. 1987).
39. *Hunter* v. *Board of Education of Montgomery County*, 425 A.2d 681 (Md. App. 1981), *aff'd in part and rev'd in part on other grounds*, 439 A.2d 582 (Md. App. 1982).
40. 439 A.2d at 587.
41. 420 U.S. 308 (1975), *reh'g denied*, 421 U.S. 921 (1975).
42. *Id.* at 322.
43. 42 U.S.C. § 1983 (West, 1988).
44. In *Will* v. *Michigan Department of State Police*, 109 S.Ct. 2304 (1989), the Supreme Court ruled that a state is not a suable person with the meeting of § 1983. Consequently, unlike a local government, a state cannot be sued in its own name under § 1983, nor can state officials be sued in their individual capacities. Local

governments can be sued directly under *Monell* v. *Department of Local Services*, 436 U.S. 658 (1978). Suits against officials in their official capacities are essentially suits against governmental units *Kentucky* v. *Graham*, 473 U.S. 159 (1985).

45. *Lopez* v. *Houston Independent School Dist.*, 817 F.2d 351 (5th Cir. 1987).

46. The court held that the student could proceed to trial in an action for negligence against the bus driver to determine whether his failure to protect the student constituted a callous disregard of his constitutional rights.

47. *De Falco by De Falco* v. *Deer Lake School Dist.*, 663 F. Supp. 1108 (W.D. Pa. 1987).

48. Qualified immunity is not a defense to a school district's liability, however, *Owen* v. *City of Independence*, 445 U.S. 622 (1980).

49. *Harlow* v. *Fitzgerald*, 457 U.S. 800, 818 (1982).

50. *Burnham* v. *West*, 681 F. Supp. 1160 (E.D. Va. 1987).

51. *Jefferson* v. *Yselta Independent School Dist.*, 817 F.2d 303 (5th Cir. 1987).

52. *Wade* v. *Hegner*, 804 F.2d 67 (7th Cir. 1986).

53. *Stoneking* v. *Bradford Area School Dist.*, 1989 U.S. App. Lexis 15771 (Aug. 16, 1989).

54. *Carey* v. *Piphus*, 435 U.S. 247 (1978).

55. *Perez* v. *Rodriguez Bou*, 575 F.2d 21 (1st Cir. 1978).

56. 477 U.S. 299 (1986).

57. *Burnaman* v. *Bay City Independent School District*, 445 F.Supp. 927 (S.D. Tex. 1978).

58. 42 U.S.C. § 1988 (West 1981).

59. *Texas State Teachers Association* v. *Garland Independent School Dist.*, 109 S. Ct. 1486 (1989).

CHAPTER 5

How Should I Deal with Child Abuse and Neglect?

OVERVIEW

Any scholarly account of the history of childhood tells us that children have been subjected to various kinds of abuse throughout the ages. Some historians trace such abuse back to biblical references, others to Greek and Roman antiquity.[1] There is ample historical evidence that, during every age, children have been grossly mistreated, abused, often whipped, sacrificed for various causes, burned, disfigured, and killed. In Western law, they were often treated as chattel, completely at the disposal of their owners. It has only been in recent years, however, that the general public has become aware and concerned about this phenomenon. One bit of evidence about the interest the general public in America has recently developed in the subject is the fact that approximately 60 million viewers watched an ABC-TV movie on the subject of child abuse when it was aired in January 1984.

We have no reliable statistics on the extent of child abuse and neglect. This uncertainty is caused by inconsistencies in definitions of abuse and neglect, variations in reporting laws from state to state, and the different methods of data collection. Nonetheless, it has been estimated that during 1982 and 1983, close to one million cases of child abuse and neglect were reported to child welfare agencies each year.[2]

Various professionals are legally responsible for reporting suspected cases of child abuse. Are teachers, therapists, and counselors among them? If yes, to whom do they report and how? What are the obligations and liabilities involved in such reporting? And just what is child abuse? These are some questions considered in this chapter.

CHILD ABUSE AND NEGLECT

What is child abuse?

There is no single, authoritative definition of child abuse. The National Committee for the Prevention of Child Abuse defines it as a nonaccidental injury or pattern of injuries to a child for which there is no "reasonable" explanation. This might be a place to start, but for our purposes it is too vague. We shall look at a definition provided by federal law as well as some variations in state laws.

In 1974, Congress enacted the National Child Abuse Prevention and Treatment Act (PL 93–247), which defines child abuse and neglect as follows:

> Physical or mental injury, sexual abuse or exploitation, negligent treatment, or maltreatment of a child under the age of eighteen or the age specified by the child protection law of the state in question, by a person who is responsible for the child's welfare, under circumstances which indicate that the child's health or welfare is harmed or threatened thereby.

Because child abuse is not a federal crime, the federal law did no more than make money available to the states that met its reporting guidelines and other qualifications, and set reporting standards. The act also provided help to local agencies concerned with child abuse and neglect and established a central registry that lists substantiated cases of child abuse.

In the Child Abuse Prevention, Adoption, and Family Services Act of 1988, Congress buttressed the federal involvement in this area by appropriating $48 million through 1991. The act also created the position of a permanent director and professional staff for the National Center on Child Abuse and Neglect, an advisory board, and an interagency task force. The center provides technical assistance as well as conducts research on the causes, prevention, and treatment of child abuse and neglect.[3]

Because child abuse is a state crime, state definitions become very important. Although there are variations among state statutory definitions, we list two that are somewhat typical:

> Child abuse or neglect means the physical injury or neglect, sexual abuse, sexual exploitation, or maltreatment of a child under the age of eighteen by a person who is responsible for the child's welfare under circumstances which indicate that the child's health or welfare is harmed or threatened. (Alaska)[4]

> "Abused or neglected child" means a child whose physical or mental health or welfare is harmed or threatened with harm by acts or omissions of his parent or other person responsible for his welfare. (Vermont)[5]

Although state laws vary, they all use a combination of two or more of the following elements in defining abuse and neglect: (1) physical injury, (2) mental or emotional injury, (3) sexual molestation or exploitation.[6]

Is it important to be able to distinguish between abuse and neglect?

No. Whereas some states define them as a single concept, others have separate definitions for them. In 1977, the U.S. Department of Health, Education, and Welfare created the Model Child Protection Act with Commentary, which does not require the reporter to know or to be certain whether it is abuse or neglect to which a child has been subjected. State laws are similar to this act in not requiring a person to know whether it is abuse or neglect that is being reported.[7]

> The time and effort spent in trying to distinguish between abuse and neglect serves no useful purpose. A child may suffer serious or permanent harm and even death as a result of neglect. Therefore, the same reasons that justify the mandatory reporting of abuse require the mandatory reporting of child neglect.[8]

STATE REPORTING REQUIREMENTS

Which states require reporting of child abuse and neglect?

All of them do, if the abuse or neglect results in physical injury. The states that do not require the reporting of emotional or mental injury are Georgia, Indiana, Iowa, Maryland, Minnesota, Oregon, and Wisconsin; those that do not explicitly require the reporting of sexual abuse are New Mexico, South Dakota, Tennessee, and Texas.[9] This picture, however, can be expected to change through the years as state legislatures amend their laws. For example, Maryland included sexual abuse in its laws in 1978; Florida so acted in 1979, also including in its broad definition the procuring or use of children in photographs, motion pictures, or other presentations depicting sexual conduct.[10] Therefore, educators must check periodically with appropriate state agencies in order to keep up-to-date with the law in their respective states.

How certain must you be that abuse or neglect is taking place?

No state requires that you be absolutely certain, before you file a report, that abuse is taking place. It is sufficient that you have "reason to believe" or "reasonable cause to believe or suspect" that a child is subject to abuse or neglect. As in many other areas of the law, the standard applied is what the reasonable person would believe under similar circumstances. Because abuse very seldom occurs in front of witnesses, and because the protection of children is the main purpose of reporting laws, the reporters are not held to unduly rigorous standards as long as they act in good faith. In fact, there are some states that even require one to report when he or she "observes the child being subjected to conditions or circumstances which would reasonably result in child abuse or neglect."[11]

SYMPTOMS OF ABUSE AND NEGLECT

What symptoms should alert you to child abuse and neglect?

There are various symptoms that should alert educators that some form of abuse or neglect is taking place. Educators in general and counselors in particular are trained observers of children. Through formal education and their work experience they have become sensitive to the range of normal behavior expected of children in their school and classes and are quick to notice deviations or exceptional behavior. They often observe the same children day after day over long periods of time; thus they are in key positions to notice signs of abuse or neglect. With a little training that focuses on the most common symptoms, they can become the most reliable reporters of such damage or danger to children.

We list, in chart form, the most common indicators of abuse or neglect (see Table 5.1). The list, however, is neither exhaustive nor definitive. Not all indicators are included in the chart, nor does the presence of a single indicator assure us that abuse or neglect exists. These are, however, some of the major indicators that should alert one to the possibility that abuse or neglect is taking place and should be investigated. Clearly, if several indicators are present, or if they occur repeatedly, the probability of maltreatment is greater.

Even in the absence of the specific symptoms or indicators listed in Table 5.1, educators might recognize some general signs of abuse and/or neglect. These can be either academic or psychological clues. Sudden changes in academic performance or sudden loss of interest in schoolwork should alert the observer to the possibility of mistreatment of a student. Studies indicate that there is a significant relationship between child abuse/neglect and learning difficulties. Delayed language development and motor development is found in high proportion among such children. Also, the emotional stress placed on families with special-needs children can bring on abuse or neglect. Educators experienced with special-needs children know that family neglect may lead to failure to provide the child with a hearing aid or glasses, which in turn impedes academic progress. Similarly, sudden changes in a child's emotional tone may be a clue to abuse or neglect. A previously outgoing, happy child who becomes angry, withdrawn, or sullen may be signaling serious changes in the child's home life. Children who are very passive and uncommunicative should alert us

TABLE 5.1. PHYSICAL AND BEHAVIORAL INDICATORS OF CHILD ABUSE AND NEGLECT (CA/N)

Type of CA/N	Physical Indicators	Behavioral Indicators
Physical abuse	Unexplained bruises and welts: —on face, lips, mouth —on torso, back, buttocks, thighs —in various stages of healing —clustered, forming regular patterns —reflecting shape of article used to inflict (electric cord, belt buckle) —on several different surface areas —regularly appear after absence, weekend, or vacation Unexplained burns: —cigar, cigarette burns, especially on soles, palms, back, or buttocks —immersion burns (sock-like, glove-like, doughnut shaped on buttocks or genitalia) —patterned like electric burner, iron, etc. —rope burns on arms, legs, neck, or torso Unexplained fractures: —to skull, nose, facial structure —in various stages of healing —multiple or spiral fractures Unexplained lacerations or abrasions: —to mouth, lips, gums, eyes —to external genitalia	Wary of adult contacts Apprehensive when other children cry Behavioral extremes: —aggressiveness, or —withdrawal Frightened of parents Afraid to go home Reports injury by parents
Physical neglect	Consistent hunger, Poor hygiene, inappropriate dress Consistent lack of supervision, especially in dangerous activities or long periods Unattended physical problems or medical needs Abandonment	Begging, stealing food Extended stays at school (early arrival and late departure) Constant fatigue, listlessness, or falling asleep in class Alcohol or drug abuse Delinquency (e.g., thefts) States there is no caretaker
Sexual abuse	Difficulty in walking or sitting Torn, stained, or bloody underclothing	Unwilling to change for gym or participate in physical education class

TABLE 5.1. (Continued)

Type of CA/N	Physical Indicators	Behavioral Indicators
	Pain or itching in genital area	Withdrawal, fantasy, or infantile behavior
	Bruises or bleeding in external genitalia, vaginal, or anal areas	Bizarre, sophisticated, or unusual sexual behavior or knowledge
	Veneral disease, especially in preteens	Poor peer relationships
	Pregnancy	Delinquent or run-away
		Reports sexual assault by caretaker
Emotional maltreatment	Speech disorders	Habit disorders (sucking, biting, rocking, etc.)
	Lags in physical development	Conduct disorders (antisocial, destructive, etc.)
	Failure to thrive	Neurotic traits (sleep disorders, inhibition of play)
		Psychoneurotic reactions (hysteria, obsession, compulsion, phobias, hypochondria)
		Behavior extremes: —compliant, passive —aggressive, demanding
		Overly adaptive behavior: —inappropriately adult —inappropriately infant
		Developmental lags (mental, emotional)
		Attempted suicide

Source: Diane D. Broadhurst, The Educator's Role in the Prevention and Treatment of Child Abuse and Neglect, National Center on Child Abuse and Neglect, U.S. Department of Health, Education, and Welfare, Publ. No. 79-30172 (1979).

to the possibility that problems exist in the life of the family. Clearly, there is not a one-to-one correlation between academic problems and abuse or neglect, but alert and knowledgeable educators can gather clues from a variety of sources in the process of identifying problems in their schools.

All these signs, of course, are only indicators that should alert reasonable educators to the *possibility* of abuse or neglect. They do not *prove* that abuse or neglect exist. Through conversations with the parents or with the child, further clues may be gathered that will confirm suspicions of abuse or neglect, or provide other satisfactory explanations for the child's condition.[12]

THE WHO AND WHAT OF REPORTING CHILD ABUSE AND NEGLECT

Do laws require educators to report child abuse and neglect?

Yes. Some state statutes explicitly name "school counselors" among the mandatory reporters of child abuse or neglect. Others include among them "educators," "other school personnel," or "employees or officials of any public or private school." Still others have catch-all provisions that require reporting by "any person" who works with children and has "reasonable cause to believe" that abuse or neglect is going on. Such general requirements would clearly include teachers, therapists, and counselors who work with children.

Is the reporter of child abuse or neglect protected from lawsuits?

Yes. Every state provides immunity by law from civil suit and criminal prosecution that might arise from the reporting of suspected child abuse or neglect. Such immunity applies to all mandatory or permissible reporters who act "in good faith." In many states, good faith is presumed; therefore, the person suing the reporter has the burden to prove that the reporter acted in bad faith. Clearly, any educator, therapist, or counselor who acts in good faith and is mandated by law to report suspected cases of abuse or neglect is immune from suit.

In order to be eligible for federal funds under the Child Abuse Prevention Adoption, and Family Service Act, states must grant immunity to reporters. All states have complied with this requirement. The expressed intent of immunity legislation is to encourage reporting without fear of civil or criminal liability.

Should counselors violate privileged communication by reporting suspected cases of abuse or neglect?

Yes, in fact they must. First of all, most states deny such privilege to counselors in any legal proceeding. Second, as a matter of public policy it is more important to require the reporting than to respect the privilege. And finally, because counselors and teachers are among those who must report, the legal requirement of reporting overrides any claim to privilege or confidential communication.

Do religious beliefs provide exemption from liability for child abuse?

Yes, in most states, although this matter continues to be a subject of controversy. Because there are some religions that believe in nonmedical spiritual healing, most states provide special laws pertaining to them. Typical is the Missouri statute, which makes the following provision:

> A child who does not receive specific medical treatment by reason of the legitimate practice of the religious belief of said child's parents, guardians, or

others legally responsible for said child, for that reason alone, shall not be considered to be an abused or neglected child.[13]

Although 44 states have similar statutes, some of them explicitly authorize courts to order medical treatment when the child's health requires it. Furthermore, courts may have such power even without explicit statutory authorization.[14]

THE MECHANICS OF REPORTING CHILD ABUSE AND NEGLECT

Is there a penalty for failure to report suspected child abuse or neglect?

Yes. At this writing, in all but six states (Idaho, Illinois, Maryland, Mississippi, Montana, and Wyoming) mandated reporters are criminally liable for failure to report a suspected case of child abuse or neglect. Failure to report is a misdemeanor in most states. The penalty might range from a 5- to 30-day jail sentence and/or a fine of $10 to $100 to as high as a fine of $1000 and a year in jail.

However, there are no *reported* cases of a criminal prosecution for failure to report a case of child abuse or neglect. Why? Because state laws usually require a "knowing" or "willful" failure to report. It is extremely difficult to prove, beyond all reasonable doubt, that someone "knowingly" or "willfully" failed to report; therefore, cases are not prosecuted. Perhaps a more likely route of enforcement is the threat of civil liability.

Some states already have enacted laws that impose civil liability (liability in money damages) for failure to report. However, different state laws require differing degrees of proof. For example, in Arkansas, Colorado, Iowa, and New York, proof of willful misconduct is required, whereas Michigan and Montana use a lesser standard for establishing liability, namely the standard of negligence.[15] Various scholars believe that civil liability for not reporting will be the trend of the future and will help increase the number of abuse and neglect cases reported.[16]

At this writing, there are no reported cases imposing civil liability on teachers or counselors for failure to report, but with the increase in the number of states imposing such liability by statute, such cases are likely to arise. Currently, the best-known cases seeking money damages for failure to report child abuse and neglect have been filed against physicians and hospitals. The landmark case of *Landeros* v. *Flood* established the principle that a physician could be held liable in money damages for failure to report a case of child abuse.[17] Reasoning by analogy, courts could hold educators, including counselors, liable for money damages for violating their mandated duty to report. Such liability will be all the more possible in states that explicitly impose liability by statute, for example, Michigan and Montana.

There are cases, however, where counselors or psychologists have been disciplined for failure to report promptly a suspected case of chlid abuse. One controversial case arose in Illinois, where Dr. Rosario C. Pesce, a tenured teacher school psychologist, was suspended without pay for 5 days and demoted from "school psychologist" to "school psychologist for the behavior disorders program." The state law required school psychologists to report *immediately* suspected cases of abuse or neglect. When information first came to Dr. Pesce about the probability of abuse, he consulted with his attorney and a psychologist and chose not to report for 10 days, at which time he became more certain of the actual abuse. The facts indicated probable sexual involvement of the student with his male teacher as well as threats of suicide. When Dr. Pesce challenged the administrative action, claiming it to violate his constitutional right to due process as well as his federal right to confidentiality, the U.S. District Court and the Court of Appeals ruled against him.[18]

How does one report child abuse or neglect?

Each state statute that mandates reporting of child abuse or neglect specifies the procedures reporters are required to follow. As indicated on the chart, most states require an oral report, within a reasonable period of time (24–72 hours, though some allow up to 7 days), followed by a more detailed written report. A number of states have set up 24-hour toll-free "hot lines" to facilitate reporting.

Most states require that the reporter include in the report, if known, the names and addresses of the child, the nature and extent of the injury or condition observed, and the reporter's name and address. The reporting form often has a general request for "any other information that the person making the report believes may be helpful in establishing the cause of the injury . . . and protecting the child." Some states and some school districts provide a reporting form in order to facilitate the making of written reports. The absence of such forms, however, does not excuse one from reporting; any piece of paper may be used as long as the required information is provided.

Is a social service agency liable for failure to protect the child after the abuse has been reported?

No, ruled a divided Supreme Court in the 1989 *DeShaney* case.[19] Joshua DeShaney was beaten by his father to the point of abuse, repeatedly, from the time he was 1 year old until the age of 4, when he landed in the hospital with life-threatening coma, and after brain surgery was expected to live as a profoundly retarded person. His father was convicted of child abuse.

Suit was filed in a federal court on behalf of Joshua and his mother alleging that the county Department of Social Services deprived him of "his liberty without due process of law" by failing to intervene to protect him after they knew or should have known of the risk of violence at his father's hands.

Although the Supreme Court acknowledged that "the facts of this case are undeniably tragic" and that the social service worker was fully cognizant of the brutality of the beatings and did not intervene except to take notes, the majority of six justices held that the Fourteenth Amendment was not violated. The purpose and the amendment, according to the majority, is to protect people from the state and not from each other or from private actors. Thus, the social worker or the Department of Social Services was under no duty to protect Joshua. If there is to be such duty placed on them, reasoned the Court, the state legislature has to create the obligation; it is not for the courts to impose it.

A minority of three justices disagreed. They would have held that once the state intervened and the Department of Social Services moved in to document and report the abuse, a duty was created to protect Joshua.

SUMMARY

Although child abuse and neglect is an age-old phenomenon, it has become a matter of concern to the general public only in recent decades. California, in 1962, was the first state to require by law the reporting of child abuse. By 1964, twenty states had followed suit. Today all states, the District of Columbia, Puerto Rico, the Virgin Islands, and American Samoa have such laws.

Laws, however much they may help, do not prevent child abuse and neglect from occurring each year. During recent years, over one million such cases per year have been brought to the attention of the National Center on Child Abuse and Neglect. This is probably only the tip of the iceberg, for it is generally believed that a very large number of child abuse and neglect cases never get reported.

Teachers, among others, are mandated by law to report cases of suspected or known abuse. If one has reasonable grounds to suspect abuse or neglect, the law requires a report under penalty of a fine and/or jail term. Furthermore, a suit for money damages may be filed against one who fails to report. States are increasingly enacting laws imposing liability for failure to report on those mandated to file child abuse reports. State laws also grant immunity for those who are mandated to report; thus individuals need not fear lawsuits for invasion of privacy, defamation, or some other cause of action.

Federal funds are available to states that meet certain requirements for reporting cases of abuse or neglect. The ultimate purpose of all these laws, federal and state, is to increase the reporting of children in danger of abuse or neglect and to provide more comprehensive services for those children and their families. Counselors and educators are in key positions to assist in these efforts and they have the duty to do so.

NOTES

1. Friedman, *Unequal and Inadequate Protection under the Law: State Child Abuse Statutes*, 50 GEO. WASH. L. REV. 243–74 (1982).

2. *See* generally U.S. DEPARTMENT OF HEALTH AND HUMAN SERVICES, REPORT BY THE NATIONAL CENTER ON CHILD ABUSE AND NEGLECT (1983).

3. For more information, *see* Child Abuse Prevention, Adoption, and Family Services Act of 1988, § § 101–401. PL-100-294, 42 U.S.C. § 5101 (1988).

4. ALASKA STAT. ch. 17 § 47.17.010

5. VT. STAT. ANN., Tit. 13, § § 1351–1356 (Supp. 1981–82).

6. Frazier, *A Glance at the Past, A Gaze at the Present, A Glimpse at the Future: A Critical Analysis of the Development of Child Abuse Reporting Statutes*, 54 CHI.-KENT L. REV. 641, 643 (1978).

7. U.S. DEPARTMENT OF HEALTH, EDUCATION AND WELFARE CHILD ABUSE & NEGLECT; STATE REPORTING LAWS (Special Report from the National Center on Child Abuse and Neglect) DHHS Publication No. (OHDS) 80-30265 at 3.

8. *Id.* at 5.

9. *Supra* note 1 at 254.

10. MD. CODE ANN. art. 27, § 35A(b)(8)(Cum. Supp. 1978); FLA. STAT. ANN. § 827.07(1)(b)(Supp. 1979).

11. Such laws are found in Arkansas, Colorado, Idaho, Maine, Utah, West Virginia, American Samoa, and the Virgin Islands. *See supra* note 7 at 3.

12. For an excellent guide to the use of such clues and interviews, see *id.* at 20–27.

13. MO. REV. STAT. § 210.115(3)(supp. 1979).

14. *See, e.g., In re* Sampson, 278 N.E.2d 919 (1972). For a list of states granting religious immunity as well as modified immunity, see *supra* note 7 at 15.

15. Aaron, *Civil Liability for Teachers' Negligent Failure to Report Suspected Child Abuse*, 28 WAYNE L. REV. 183–213 (1981).

16. *Id.*

17. *Landeros* v. *Flood*, 551 P.2d 389 (1976); *Robinson* v. *Wical*, No. 37607 (Cal. Sup. Ct.) San Louis Obispo, filed Sept. 4, 1970); *Leach* v. *Chemung*, No. 75–2652 (Chemung City Sup. Ct. N.Y., filed May 18, 1976).

18. *Pesce* v. *J. Sterling Morton High School*, 830 F.2d 789 (7th Cir. 1987).

19. *DeShaney* v. *Winnebago County Dept. of Social Services*, 57 U.S.L.W. 4218 (1989).

CHAPTER 6

What Constitutes Slander and Libel?

OVERVIEW

The law of civil defamation makes it unlawful for one person to make a false statement of fact that tends to harm another person's reputation. Statements are defamatory if they tend to expose another person to hatred, shame, disgrace, contempt, or ridicule. When such statements are spoken, they are called *slander;* when such statements are written, they are called *libel.*

Because defamation law is concerned with reputation, a statement can be defamatory only if it is communicated to a third person. For example, if a principal writes a defamatory letter to a teacher, no libel is involved unless someone besides the teacher sees the letter.

This chapter examines how the courts have applied these principles in cases involving teachers. It addresses such questions as: Can a teacher who ridicules students be found guilty of slander? Can a teacher who writes unflattering comments in a student's permanent file be guilty of libel? Can a teacher sue a principal for slander for making critical remarks about his or her teaching techniques? Can students sue teachers for giving them low grades? What constitutional considerations apply in cases of libel or slander?

DEFAMATORY STATEMENTS ABOUT TEACHERS

The *Pitka* Case[1]

How can teachers be libeled?

Elizabeth Pitka was a schoolteacher in North Pole, Alaska, a small community not far from Fairbanks. In August 1957 she resigned her position; a few days later, she withdrew the resignation with the consent of the North Pole School Board. On October 7, she wrote to the board saying that she wanted to resign "effective in thirty days from this date." On October 18, however, she received a letter advising her that the board had voted "to relieve you of your duties as head teacher and teacher as of October 18, 1957." After she ignored this letter, the board sent her another letter in which she was advised not to enter on school property. When she nonetheless returned to school, the board president had her arrested for disturbing the peace. That evening, the Fairbanks newspaper carried a front-page article describing Pitka's difficulties with the school board. The headline read "*North Pole Teacher Fights Board*," with a subheading that stated, "Territorial Police Called to Expel Fired Schoolmarm, Dispute at Outlying Community Finds Teacher Defying School Board; She Is Arrested for Disorderly Conduct." Pitka claimed that these words were false and defamatory and sued the newspaper for libel.

The Supreme Court of Alaska ruled that the newspaper headline was libelous on its face (or libelous per se). The court explained that "for a publication to be libelous per se the words used must be so unambiguous as to be reasonably susceptible of only one interpretation—that is, one which has a natural tendency to injure another's reputation [footnote omitted]. If the publication on its face shows that it is of that type, then the judge has the right to tell the jury that the words are defamatory." Examining the specific language in the newspaper headline, the court concluded that it was libelous per se: "A statement that a school teacher was engaged in a 'fight' with her employer, that she was 'fired,' that the police were called to expel her, and that she was arrested for disorderly conduct, would have a natural tendency to diminish the esteem in which she was held and to result in a lack of confidence in her professional competency."

The Supreme Court of Alaska also ruled, however, that the newspaper company should have had the opportunity to raise the defense that the statements in the headline were true. The court explained that, under the common law, truth is an absolute defense and would constitute a complete justification for the statements. Whether the teacher was involved in an actual "fight" with the school board and whether she had actually been "fired" were questions of fact that ought to have been submitted to the jury for their decision. If the jury found that the statements were true, the newspaper would not be liable.

Is truth always an absolute defense to a defamation action?

No. This rule, relied on by the court in *Pitka*, was the standard under the English common law and was followed by the overwhelming majority of jurisdictions in the United States. About a dozen states, however, have modified this common law rule, either by statute or judicial decision. Now, in some states, truth is a defense unless the defamation was published with "malicious motives"; in others there is a requirement of a "justifiable purpose." [2]

What kinds of statements are defamatory?

As the court pointed out in *Pitka,* some statements are automatically assumed to be defamatory. Historically, words have been held to be clearly defamatory on their face if they

1. impute a criminal offense;
2. impute a loathsome disease (e.g., venereal disease, tuberculosis);
3. disparage professional competency (as in *Pitka); or*
4. impute unchastity or immorality of a woman (e.g., a charge of adultery or incest).

Statements that do not fall into one of these four categories also can be defamatory. Such statements are not defamatory on their face, however, but require additional information to show that they injured someone's reputation. For example, a New York school principal sued a newspaper publisher for an article that appeared months after the principal had transferred to another school. [3] The article stated that at the school where the principal had formerly taught, a new principal had "brought harmony out of chaos," the "teachers would do anything in the world for him," and from 150 to 200 boys "used to come late to school and now the average is not more than seven or eight." Although these statements were not defamatory on their face, the former principal argued that anyone who knew he had previously been in charge of the school would interpret these statements to mean that he had lacked administrative ability.

The court did not agree that these additional facts made the statement libelous. The court concluded that no particular charge was made against the former principal, and there was no reason why readers should assume that the charges of chaos and disharmony referred to him. In addition, the court stated that there was no reason to assume that the principal was responsible for the tardiness of the boys: "He may have materially improved conditions during his administration of the school, and the parents or guardians of the pupils may have been responsible for their tardiness."

Courts in some states treat slander and libel differently. Reasoning that written statements are more likely to cause harm because they are permanent, some courts have not required that a written statement fall into one of the four categories listed above in order to be found defamatory on its face. In these states, any written words that expose a person to hatred, ridicule, or abuse are defamatory on their face; spoken words are actionable on their face only if they fall into one of the four listed categories.

What is the significance of finding that a statement is "defamatory on its face"?

If a statement is defamatory on its face, the law assumes that an individual's reputation has been injured. An individual who can prove that such a statement was made falsely will be awarded damages automatically. This individual is not required to show how he or she was injured by the false statements. The amount of the damages can vary, however, according to whether or not the statements were made maliciously.

If the false statements are not defamatory on their face, the injured party can collect monetary damages only by showing that he or she was directly harmed in some way by these statements. Examples of such harm could include physical or mental illness or loss of salary.

What are some examples of statements about teachers that have been found to be defamatory on their face?

The courts have ruled that any statements that falsely disparage a teacher's professional competence are defamatory on their face. In an early Ohio case,[4] for example, the court found the following statement about a teacher, made by the president of the board of education, was defamatory on its face: "He is not a fit person to teach in any school. He is no good as a teacher and he will not get the school another year. He plays for dances and then goes to sleep in the school room during school hours." In addition, courts have held all the following charges defamatory on their face: a newspaper article that described a college professor as "illiterate, uncultivated, coarse, and vulgar" and that also conveyed the impression that he made himself ridiculous "both in his method of instruction and by his public lectures";[5] a statement before the school board that a teacher was so "intoxicated at the public dinner at Bundick's creek. . . that it was necessary that [he] be brought to the table";[6] and a teacher's statement that a principal allowed students to "pet" in the hallways without taking any disciplinary action.[7] In addition, statements falsely charging teachers with criminal activity have been held to be defamatory on their face, as when an Indiana newspaper printed an article headlined "A School Child Killed in Pike County by a Teacher."[8]

In order to be defamatory, however, the false statements must relate to the teacher's professional performance. For example, an Iowa court ruled that a letter from a finance company to a school superintendent stating that a teacher in his district owed money on a debt was not defamatory on its face.[9] The court concluded that a statement that a teacher owed an unpaid debt did not reflect on professional ability or qualifications: "The statements allegedly made of plaintiff [teacher] do not impute insolvency or that plaintiff has failed to pay the debt from dishonest motives and from a desire to defraud the creditor. They do not relate to her profession."

When an individual is slandered or libeled, how is the amount of damages determined?

In a suit for libel or slander, the jury has the responsibility to listen to the evidence and decide if the plaintiff is entitled to any damages and, if so, how much. As noted in earlier questions, the jury can assume damage to the plaintiff's reputation when the defendant has made a statement that is defamatory on its face. The amount of damages awarded to the plaintiff will vary, however, according to how seriously the jury feels the plaintiff's reputation has been harmed. In making a decision, the jury can consider such factors as the plaintiff's general character and reputation in the community, the nature of the statements made, and the number of people who heard or read these statements. Quantifying damage to reputation is obviously a difficult task, and the size of the awards varies considerably.

For example, a South Dakota jury awarded only one dollar to a secretary after his employer falsely told others that he was a crook, that he had stolen a carpet, and that he belonged in the penitentiary.[10] A New York jury awarded an attorney damages of $100 after a woman remarked within earshot of his wife and some of his neighbors: "You're no lawyer. You're a crook. You took graft."[11] A principal and vice principal in West Virginia were each awarded $7000 after the school superintendent charged them with willful neglect of duty at a meeting of the county board of education.[12]

In addition to injury to reputation, damage awards may include compensation for mental or physical injury or for other financial losses suffered as a result of defamatory statements. A Louisiana court awarded a customer $3250 after she had been falsely accused of shoplifting in a clothing store.[13] Convinced that she was shoplifting, a store employee had grabbed Levy after she left a dressing room and stopped her from leaving the store. In order to establish her innocence, Levy emptied her purse on the floor and raised her blouse and lowered her slacks; these activities occurred in front of between 40 and 60 people. The jury awarded Levy $2500 to compensate her for the humiliation and embarrassment she suffered; it also awarded her $750 for mental pain and suffering. A District of Columbia jury awarded an attorney $15,000 in damages to compensate him for mental anguish and the business he lost after one of his clients was falsely informed that he had acted fraudulently in the past, practiced bigotry, and should be sued for malpractice.[14]

Finally, if the defendant has acted maliciously or with reckless disregard for the truth, the jury can award punitive damages. These damages are imposed to punish the defendant and deter such further behavior. In Georgia, for example, the court awarded $200,000 to a former university student after the head of the chemistry department falsely accused him of forging paychecks.[15] The award of punitive damages was based on the fact that the university professor made defamatory remarks about the student to many people not involved in the criminal investigation and that he continued to claim that the student was guilty long after the university investigation had disclosed that the discrepancy in the accounts had been caused by an embezzler in the professor's department.

Can teachers sue administrators for defamatory statements made in letters of recommendation or on evaluation forms?

The courts have ruled that school administrators generally have what is known as a "qualified privilege" to comment on matters concerning the operation of the school. Under this qualified privilege, school administrators will not be liable for defamatory statements even if false if administrators are under a duty to comment and are acting in good faith. This privilege extends to comments made in letters of recommendation.

For example, a Wisconsin court ruled that a school superintendent could not be sued for libel when he wrote a negative letter of recommendation about a teacher formerly employed as a speech therapist in his school district.[16] The teacher, Hett, had applied for a job at another school and had listed the superintendent as a reference. In writing a letter in reply to a request for information, the superintendent made the following statements: "I, personally, feel that Mr. Hett does not belong in the teaching field. He has a rather odd personality, and it is rather difficult for him to gain the confidence of his fellow workers and the boys and girls with whom he works." The court ruled that the superintendent's statements were made in good faith and as part of his official responsibilities, thus Hett could not sue him for libel: "The background of the relationship of Hett and Ploetz [the superintendent] satisfactorily demonstrates that the latter's negative recommendation was grounded on the record and not upon malice. Ploetz was not an intermeddler; he had a proper interest in connection with the letter he wrote."

Similarly, a Kentucky court ruled that a college president's letter to a student's father was privileged.[17] The college president had written two letters to the student's father describing how the student had indecently exposed himself "at the open window of his room in such way as persons traveling the street saw his nude form and were embarrassed thereby," and asking the student to withdraw from the college. In a suit for libel brought against the president by the student's father, the court found the statement to be protected by a qualified privilege. The court concluded that in writing the letter, the president was acting both out of duty and in good faith:

> [T]he president of the school, being in charge of the student body, owed a duty to the father and family of young Baskett [the student], which he could not discharge except by faithfully, fully, and accurately reporting to the father and family the progress and deportment of the student. . . . In this case Dr. Crossfield [the president] appears to have done only what his duty required of him. He gently and rather apologetically wrote and sent to the father of the student the two letters of which complaint is made. That these letters were

written in the utmost good faith and for the good of the father and the dismissed student is beyond cavil. [18]

School officials can lose this qualified privilege if they act in bad faith or without regard for whether the statements are true. For example, the president of a Texas commercial college incorrectly wrote a letter to a student's prospective employer stating that the student "was arrested and put in jail for stealing a typewriter." [19] Evidence showed that the president later discovered that this charge was false but did not correct it because he wanted the job filled by a graduate of the college. The court ruled that his statements in the letter were not privileged.

In some situations, however, courts have ruled that school officials' statements are "absolutely privileged," and an administrator cannot be found liable for defamation even in cases where he or she acted maliciously or in bad faith. For example, a Missouri teacher sued a school superintendent for slander, claiming that, in response to her request for the reasons for her not being reemployed, she was defamed when he falsely stated at a school board meeting: "that plaintiff [teacher] had disobeyed school rules and regulations; that plaintiff was insubordinate; and that plaintiff was insufficient and inadequate with her students." [20] In reaching its decision, the court first noted that whether a statement is subject to an absolute or a qualified privilege depends on "the occasion or circumstances surrounding the utterance of the alleged slander." The court concluded that the superintendent's statements were absolutely privileged because they were made in response to the teacher's request: "[T]he publication of false and defamatory matter of another is *absolutely* privileged if the other consents thereto." When the teacher asked the superintendent why she was not going to be reemployed the following school year, the superintendent was "absolutely protected in his explanation" and was not liable for slander. Similarly, a Pennsylvania court[21] held that an absolute privilege protected a principal who made negative comments in a letter to a teacher explaining that the teacher's services would no longer be required because of his failure to follow administrative policies.

Courts have also held that statements made by public officials during judicial, legislative, or official executive proceedings are absolutely privileged. Thus, where school officials have made comments about teachers as part of their administrative duties, some courts have ruled that these statements are also absolutely privileged. An Illinois court dismissed a suit for slander against a superintendent of schools who made statements to the board of education that a teacher's performance in the classroom was poor, that he had done poorly in certain college courses, and that he had left his room unattended. [22] The court explained that "all communications, either verbal or written, passing between public officials pertaining to their duties and in the conduct of public business are of necessity absolutely privileged and such matters cannot be made the basis of recovery in a suit at law." Finding that the superintendent was carrying out an official duty when making these comments, the court dismissed the suit against him.

In general, then, statements by school officials are subject to a qualified privilege when they are made in good faith and about matters concerning school administration. School officials are not liable for defamatory statements that fall under this qualified privilege even if such statements turn out to be false. School officials are liable if they act maliciously or with reckless disregard for the truth of their statements, or if their statements concern matters outside the scope of their official duties.

Some statements by school officials, however, are held to be absolutely privileged; in those situations, school officials can never be held liable for defamatory statements. An absolute privilege can extend to statements to which the other party consents or invites, or statements made in the course of judicial, legislative, or administrative proceedings.

DEFAMATORY STATEMENTS ABOUT STUDENTS

Can students sue teachers for written statements in students' files?

The Family Educational Rights and Privacy Act of 1974 guarantees students' rights to privacy in their educational records.[23] In general it provides that in schools receiving federal funds, students and their parents must have access to permanent school records. This right becomes the student's exclusively when she or he becomes 18 years old or is attending an institution of postsecondary education. Under the act, teachers can make notes about students for their own personal use. As long as a teacher does not show these notes to any person except a substitute teacher, students and their parents have no right to see them. In addition, the act provides that students can give up their rights to have access to certain papers. (See Chapter 16 for a more detailed discussion of this act.)

Teachers can be sued for defamatory statements published in students' permanent records. In an early case in Oklahoma, a teacher was found to have libeled a student after he made a note in the school register that the student was "ruined by tobacco and whisky."[24] In order to avoid being sued for defamation, teachers should be careful to accurately describe relevant, observable behavior rather than make derogatory remarks about students.

Can teachers be sued for ridiculing students in classrooms or in the teachers' lounge?

If teachers knowingly spread false gossip that harms a student's reputation, they can be found guilty of slander. Nevertheless, some court decisions suggest that a teacher's statements are subject to a qualified privilege if they are made as part of the teacher's professional responsibilities. For example, a Georgia court held that a college president's statements charging a student with theft were conditionally privileged when made during an investigation of the crime.[25] The president had accused the student of theft during a meeting with the student and the college chaplain. The court ruled that such statements were conditionally privileged because they were made by the president as part of his official responsibility to "inquire into and regulate the behavior of members of the student body." Although the state supreme court later found that there was no slander because the student had not proved that the chaplain actually heard this statement, the court discussed the privilege question.[26] This reasoning was not essential in reaching its decision, but the Supreme Court of Georgia agreed with the lower court that such statements would be conditionally privileged, invoking the concept of *in loco parentis* as support:

> This case can not be justly decided if the fact that it involves the relationship, standards and duties of a college faculty and the students is lost sight of. Does a father slander his child when he accuses it of wrong in the presence of its mother? The parent-child relationship very closely parallels that of a college faculty and students in matters of discipline, discovering misconduct and punishing therefor. Any legal restraint of either parent or faculty in the reasonable discharge of duty, not only would not be beneficial to the child or student but might well be disastrous to them.[27]

Following this reasoning, a teacher's statements may be conditionally privileged if they are made as part of the disciplinary process or his or her administrative responsibilities.

Can students sue teachers for negative statements made in letters of recommendation?

The Family Educational Rights and Privacy Act provides that parents and students do not have the right to see letters of recommendation to colleges or prospective employers placed in students' records prior to January 1, 1975. In addition, the act states that a student can waive the right to see such letters if the student, upon request, is notified of the names of all persons making such recommendations and if the recommendations are used solely for the purpose for which they were specifically intended.

Again, however, if students gain access to these letters, teachers can be sued for any defamatory statements they may have made. The same general principles outlined regarding administrators' liability in suits by teachers apply here: A teacher's statements about a student will be at least conditionally privileged when a student lists a teacher as a reference and the teacher responds to such a request for information about the student's competence and character. Thus, unless a teacher acts maliciously by making statements he or she knows are untrue, the teacher will not be liable for any negative statements made in such letters.

Can students sue teachers for giving them low grades?

Low grades certainly may expose students to shame or ridicule, but the courts have not found that giving low grades is libelous. The courts have reasoned that they do not have the expertise to evaluate the accuracy of a teacher's grading decision and will not intervene in grading unless it can be shown that school officials acted in bad faith.

This philosophy was illustrated in an early Massachusetts case where the court ruled that it was not proper for a jury even to examine the question whether a high school student had been properly dismissed for failure to attain an adequate standard of scholarship.[28] The court explained: "So long as the school committee act in good faith, their conduct in formulating and applying standards and making decisions touching this matter is not subject to review by any other tribunal. . . . It is an educational question, the final determination of which is vested by law in the public officers charged with the performance of that important duty." In effect, this position prohibits any libel suit by students because the courts refuse to consider the "truth" or "falsity" of the grade.

A federal district court in Vermont applied the same reasoning in a more recent case in which a medical student sued the state college of medicine claiming that he should not have been dismissed for failing to attain a proper standard of scholarship.[29] The third-year medical student failed the pediatrics-obstetrics course and was not allowed to advance to the fourth year because of a college of medicine rule stating that no student could continue who had failed 25 percent or more of the third-year courses. The student's petition to repeat his third-year work was denied, and he was dismissed from school. He then sued school officials, claiming that his work was of passing quality and that he should not have been dismissed.

The court ruled that school authorities had "absolute discretion in determining whether a student [had] been delinquent in his studies" and that the court would only consider cases where the student could show that his dismissal was motivated by "arbitrariness, capriciousness or bad faith." The court explained: "The reason for this rule is that in matters of scholarship, the school authorities are uniquely qualified by training and experience to judge the qualifications of a student, and efficiency of instruction depends in no small degree upon the school faculty's freedom from interference from other noneducational tribunals. It is only when the school authorities abuse this discretion that a court may interfere with their decision."

PUBLIC OFFICIALS

Do any constitutional considerations apply in slander or libel cases?

Yes. In *New York Times* v. *Sullivan,* the Supreme Court ruled that the First Amendment guarantees of freedom of speech and press require that public officials cannot be awarded damages for libel or slander unless they can prove that such statements were made with actual malice.[30] "Actual malice" means that the defendant made the libelous or slanderous statements either knowing that they were false or with a reckless disregard for the truth of the statements. Sullivan, an elected official in Montgomery, Alabama, sued the *New York Times,* alleging that he had been libeled by an advertisement in that paper that included false statements about police brutality and harassment directed against students who had participated in a civil rights demonstration. Since Sullivan's duties included supervision of the police department, he claimed that these statements referred to him and were libelous.

The Alabama trial court instructed the jury that such statements were "libelous per se" since they concerned Sullivan's execution of his public duties and that injury to his reputation was assumed under the law. In a landmark decision, the U.S. Supreme Court disagreed. The Court ruled that the First and Fourteenth Amendments required that public officials must meet a higher standard of proof in defamation suits. The Court first noted that the First Amendment embodied "a profound national commitment to the principle that debate on public issues should be uninhibited, robust, and wide-open, and that it may well include vehement, caustic, and sometimes unpleasantly sharp attacks on government and public officials." A rule that would require a critic of official conduct to guarantee the truth of all factual assertions or risk a suit for defamation would be inconsistent with this principle; it would make people afraid to voice their criticism, thus dampening the vigor and limiting the variety of political debate. The Court therefore protected individuals who criticized public officials by holding that such individuals would not be liable for defamation unless they acted with "actual malice."

Can teachers or students be considered "public officials"?

Yes. The *New York Times* standard would apply to any teacher or student serving as a duly elected public official. For example, an elected member of a board of education would be considered a public official.[31] This standard would also apply to an individual appointed as a member of such a public body.[32]

An Arizona court has held that elected student government representatives can be public officials.[33] The court reasoned that it would be inappropriate that there be "one law of libel in this state for 'public officials' off the campuses of our state universities and another law of libel applicable to the student government officers upon such campuses, when the systems of politics and news media are so obviously patterned after the situation off campus, and when the publication is primarily addressed in the 'interested community.'" The court therefore ruled that a law student who was a duly elected member of the Student Senate of the University of Arizona qualified as a public official under *New York Times* v. *Sullivan.*

Whether other teachers or school officials will be considered public officials varies from state to state. The United States Supreme Court has not yet decided this issue, and courts have reached different conclusions depending on the role of the educator. For example, one court[34] has held that an elementary school principal should be considered a public official in a case where the president of the parent-teacher association made negative statements about the principal's performance. Other courts have held that superintendents are public officials.[35] Reasoning that a teacher-coach is in a position to influence important policies concerning athletics, at least one court has held that a coach is a public official.[36] Most courts have concluded, however, that classroom teachers are not public officials.[37]

Does the *New York Times* standard apply to all defamatory statements made about public officials?

No. The *New York Times* standard applies only when the defamatory statements relate to "official conduct." For example, a New York court held that this standard applied in a libel suit brought by a member of a board of education when a newspaper made charges that she was pressuring her son's math teacher to raise his grade.[38] While conceding that she was a public official, the school board member argued that the *New York Times* standard should not apply because the defamatory statements concerned private rather than official conduct. The court agreed that the *New York Times* rule would not apply to statements about conduct as a private citizen and mother. However, since these charges stated that she had used the power of her office for personal gain, the court found that they related to her duties as a public official and that the newspaper would not be liable unless she could show that the statements were made with actual malice.

Can the New *York Times* standard be applied to others besides public officials?

Yes. The Supreme Court has extended the *New York Times* standard to public figures. A "public figure" is one who either (1) achieves general fame or notoriety in the community or (2) "voluntarily injects himself or is drawn into a particular controversy and thereby becomes a public figure for a limited range of issues. In either case such persons assume special prominence in the resolution of public questions."[39]

Depending on the circumstances, administrators, teachers, and students could all qualify as public figures. For example, a Texas court held that a university professor was a public figure after he led an anti-Vietnam war demonstration "which aroused a considerable amount of interest and comment in the city of El Paso."[40] A Maryland court found that a high school principal fell within the "public figure-public official" classification.[41] In that case, the local newspaper had published an article entitled "Our High School Principals: How Good Are They?" When Dunn, a principal, was given an "unsuited" rating in this article, he brought a libel action against the paper. On the grounds that his suitability for the position was "a matter of public or general interest or concern," the court ruled that the *New York Times* standard applied. Similarly, a

New York Court[42] concluded that a school district's superintendent of buildings and grounds was a public figure in the context of a controversy over his appointment.

Do constitutional principles apply to damage awards?

Yes. In *Gertz* v. *Robert Welch, Inc.*,[43] the Supreme Court held that the First Amendment restricted the damages that a private individual could obtain from a publisher for a libel that involved a matter of public concern. The Court stated that in these circumstances the First Amendment prohibited awards of presumed and punitive damages for false and defamatory statements unless the plaintiff shows "actual malice."

To prove actual malice, the plaintiff must show that the defendant made the objectionable statements either with knowledge that they were false or with reckless disregard of whether or not they were false. In attempting to meet this test, the plaintiff is allowed to inquire into the defendant's state of mind at the time the statements were made and to gather other evidence to show that the defendant knew the statements were false when he or she made them.[44] A Louisiana court, for example, concluded that a doctor had proved that a grocery store owner falsely accused him of being a communist when he was a candidate for public office.[45] After the store owner testified that, on an earlier occasion, he had defended the doctor when someone else accused him of being a communist, the trial court stated that it "was not greatly impressed with the defendant's testimony or his defense as a whole," that much of what he said was "poppycock," and concluded that his remarks about the doctor were completely untrue and were meant to harm, belittle, and malign the doctor.

A black high school principal did not prove actual malice when he sued a black citizens' group that published a pamphlet criticizing his supervision of the school.[46] The pamphlet called the principal "an Uncle Tom, a traitor to his race, a stooge, a stool pigeon, an informer and a betrayer of his people." Although the defendants testified that it was their intention to have the principal removed from his position at the school, the court ruled that this ill will did not constitute actual malice. Since the principal offered no evidence that the defendants knew the statements were false or that they were made with reckless disregard for whether they were false, he did not meet his burden of proving actual malice, and the suit was dismissed.

In a 1985 case,[47] the Supreme Court limited the application of the *Gertz* decision. At issue in the case was an inaccurate Dun & Bradstreet credit report that had been circulated to five subscribers. A plurality of the Court held that the "actual malice" standard did not apply in determining the award of damages in this case. The Court found that the credit report was not a public matter but was "speech solely in the individual interest of the speaker and its specific business audience," and concluded that "speech on matters of purely private concern is of less First Amendment concern." The Court ruled that awards for presumed and punitive damages could be made in such cases even in the absence of showing "actual malice."

SUMMARY

Both teachers and administrators who make false statements that harm teachers' and students' reputations are liable for defamation. A written comment in a student's school record can lead to a libel suit. A gossip session in the teachers' lounge can support a charge of slander.

In many situations, however, teachers and administrators are protected in making statements about other teachers' and students' character and ability. The courts have ruled that educators who are acting in good faith have a "qualified privilege" to comment on matters that are within their scope of authority. For example, an educator can explain to a parent why a student was disciplined without being liable for defamation. Even if these statements actually turn out to be false, the teacher is not liable for defamation unless found to be acting maliciously (knowing that these statements were false when he or she made them) or from some improper purpose (lying to the parent because of personal animosity toward the student). This conditional privilege also protects teachers and administrators who write negative evaluations or letters of recommendation.

In some situations, the courts have also ruled that educators' statements are absolutely privileged and that they cannot be held liable even if their comments were made maliciously. An absolute privilege could apply, for example, to an administrator who presents the reasons for a teacher's dismissal at a board of education meeting.

Of course, teachers can also sue individuals who defame them. When teachers are falsely charged with matters relating to their professional competence, they can collect damages to compensate for injury to their reputation. If such statements are clearly related to a teacher's professional competence (e.g., a charge of brutality against students), the courts automatically assume that a teacher has been injured and is entitled to some amount of damages. In other situations, a teacher may have to prove that the comments actually did harm his or her reputation in order to be awarded damages. In addition to collecting damages for injury to reputation, teachers can also be awarded monetary damages to compensate them for mental or physical injury or financial loss. Punitive damages can be awarded when false statements are made maliciously.

Teachers and administrators found to be either public officials or public figures have a higher burden of proof in defamation suits. In *New York Times* v. *Sullivan* the Supreme Court ruled that public officials/public figures can be awarded damages for libel or slander only if they can prove that the defendant made defamatory statements with actual malice. To prove actual malice, the plaintiff must show that the defendant made the statement either knowing that it was false or with reckless disregard for whether it was true or false.

NOTES

1. *Fairbanks Publishing Company* v. *Pitka,* 376 P.2d 190 (Alaska 1962).
2. Barbara Dill, *The Journalist's Handbook on Libel and Privacy* (New York: The Free Press, 1986), p. 5-3.
3. *Barringer* v. *Sun Printing and Publishing Ass'n,* 160 App. Div. 691, 145 N.Y.S. 776 (1914).
4. *Mulcahy* v. *Deitrick,* 176 N.E. 481 (Ohio App. 1931).
5. *Triggs* v. *Sun Printing and Publishing Ass'n,* 71 N.E. 739, 742 (N.Y. App. 1904).
6. *Ford* v. *Jeane,* 106 So. 558, 558-559 (La. 1925).
7. *Larive* v. *Willitt,* 315 P.2d 732 (Cal. App. 1957).
8. *Doan* v. *Kelley,* 23 N.E. 266 (Ind. 1890); *Joseph* v. *Elam,* 709 S.W.2d 517 (Mo. App. 1986).
9. *Ragland* v. *Household Finance Corporation,* 119 N.W.2d 788 (Iowa 1963).
10. *Walkon Carpet Corporation* v. *Klapprodt,* 231 N.W.2d 370 (S.D. 1975).
11. *Kruglak* v. *Landre,* 23 A.D.2d 758, 258 N.Y.S.2d 550 (1965).
12. *Chambers* v. *Smith,* 198 S.E.2d 806 (W. Va. 1973).
13. *Levy* v. *Duclaux,* 324 So.2d 1 (La. App. 1975).
14. *Collins* v. *Brown,* 268 F.Supp. 198 (D.C. 1967).
15. *Melton* v. *Bow,* 247 S.E.2d 100 (Ga. 1978).
16. *Hett* v. *Ploetz,* 121 N.W.2d 270 (Wis. 1963).
17. *Baskett* v. *Crossfield,* 228 S.W. 673 (Ky. 1920).
18. *Id.* at 675-676.
19. *Lattimore* v. *Tyler Commercial College,* 24 S.W.2d 361, 362 (Tex. Ct. App. 1930).
20. *Williams* v. *School District of Springfield R-12,* 447 S.W.2d 256, 267 (Mo. 1969).
21. *Sobel* v. *Wingard,* 531 A.2d 520 (Pa.Super. 1987); *see also, Webster* v. Byrd, 494 S.2d 31 (Ala. 1986) and *Sullivan* v. *Board of Education of Eastchester Union Free School Dist.,* 517 N.Y.S.2d 197 (N.Y.A.D. 2 Dept. 1987).
22. *McLaughlin* v. *Tilendis,* 253 N.E.2d 85 (Ill. App. 1969).
23. 20 U.S.C. § 1232(g) (West 1978 and Supp. 1985).
24. *Dawkins* v. *Billingsley,* 172 P. 69 (Okla. 1918).
25. *Davidson* v. *Walter,* 91 S.E.2d 520 (Ga. App. 1956).
26. *Walter* v. *Davidson,* 102 S.E.2d 686 (Ga. App. 1958), *rev'd,* 104 S.E.2d 113 (Ga. 1958).
27. *Id.* at 115.
28. *Barnard* v. *Inhabitants of Shelburne,* 102 N.E. 1095, 1096 (Mass. 1913).
29. *Connelly* v. *University of Vermont and State Agricultural College,* 244 F.Supp. 156 (D. Vt. 1965).
30. 376 U.S. 254 (1964).
31. *Cabin* v. *Community Newspapers, Inc.,* 50 Misc.2d 574, 270 N.Y.S.2d 913 (1966), *aff'd,* 27 A.D.2d 543, 275 N.Y.S.2d 396 (1966).
32. *Henry* v. *Collins,* 380 U.S. 356 (1965).
33. *Klahr* v. *Winterble,* 418 P.2d 404 (Ariz. App. 1966).
34. *Stevens* v. *Tillman,* 855 F.2d 394 (7th Cir. 1988).
35. *State* v. *Defley,* 395 So.2d 759 (La. 1981); *Scott* v. *News-Herald,* 496 N.E.2d 699 (Ohio 1986).
36. *Basarich* v. *Rodeghero,* 321 N.E.2d 739 (Ill. App. 1974).
37. *Poe* v. *San Antonio Express News Corp.,* 590 S.W.2d 537 (Tex. Civ. App. 1979);

McCutcheon v. *Moran*, 425 N.E.2d 1130 (1981); *True* v. *Ladner*, 513 A.2d 257 (Me. 1986); *Richmond Newspapers, Inc.* v. *Lipscomb*, 362 S.E.2d 32 (Va. 1987).

38. *Cabin* v. *Community Newspapers, Inc.*, 50 Misc.2d 574, 270 N.Y.S.2d 913 (1966), *aff'd*, 27 A.D.2d 543, 275 N.Y.S.2d 396 (1966).
39. *Gertz* v. *Robert Welch, Inc.*, 418 U.S. 323, 351 (1974).
40. *El Paso Times, Inc.* v. *Trexler*, 447 S.W.2d 403, 404 (Tex. 1969).
41. *Kapiloff* v. *Dunn*, 343 A.2d 251 (Md. App. 1975).
42. *DiBernardo* v. *Tonawanda Pub. Corp.*, 499 N.Y.S.2d 553 (N.Y.A.D. 4 Dept. 1986).
43. 418 U.S. 323 (1974).
44. *Herbert* v. *Lando*, 441 U.S. 153 (1979).
45. *Sas Jaworsky* v. *Padfield*, 211 So.2d 122 (La. App. 1968).
46. *Reaves* v. *Foster*, 200 So.2d 453 (Miss. 1967).
47. *Dun & Bradstreet, Inc.* v. *Greenmoss Builders, Inc.*, 472 U.S. 74a (1985).

CHAPTER 7

How Does Copyright Law Affect Me?

OVERVIEW

Copyright law is designed to give authors and artists the right to own their creative works. Under principles of state law adopted from the law in England, an author has the right to publish his or her writings first. In addition to this common-law "right of first publication," federal law also provides protection, giving authors the exclusive right to control who can make copies of their work. A comprehensive law[1] that became effective on January 1, 1978, describes the procedures that must be followed to obtain a federal copyright. This chapter describes that law, answering such questions as: What materials can be copyrighted? How long does a copyright last? Can teachers copyright their own teaching materials? Can teachers make photocopies of published materials without violating copyright laws? What are the penalties for violating copyright laws?

INTRODUCTION TO COPYRIGHT LAW

Copyright law is a branch of property law which protects the creative works of authors. For the purposes of copyright law, "authors" are not only those individuals who produce written works, but also those who produce musical, dramatic, or other pictorial or graphic works. Almost any type of original work can be copyrighted; the only exceptions are inventions that deal with machines, which are covered by patent law, and symbols used to identify businesses, which are covered by trademark law.

The purpose of a copyright is to give the author the right to establish ownership of a creative work, and to prevent anyone else from copying it or using it in any other way without the author's permission. A copyright gives the author the exclusive right to reproduce copies, prepare derivative works, distribute copies, and publicly display the copyrighted work. It also gives the author the power to transfer these rights to others.

Our current law can be traced to Renaissance Italy, when the Italian city-states gave authors and architects exclusive rights over their works, and to sixteenth-century England, when the law protected the printer but not the author. In the United States, a copyright clause was included in the U.S. Constitution, giving Congress the enumerated power to pass laws "[t]o promote the progress of science and useful arts, by securing for limited times to authors and inventors the exclusive right to their respective writings and discoveries."[2] Congress acted in 1790 to pass the first federal copyright law.

In addition to this federal legislation, there is a common law of copyright. Common law refers to the rules of law that developed over time from decisions made by courts in individual cases in the various states. Prior to 1978, this common law of copyright existed along with various revisions of the federal copyright statute. As of January 1, 1978, however, a new copyright law[3] went into effect that is so comprehensive as to supersede most rules under the common law. This chapter will examine this federal law. Because so many works currently in existence were created prior to 1978, however, a brief discussion of the common law is also included.

MATERIALS COVERED BY COPYRIGHT

The *Williams* Case[4]

Do teachers have a copyright on their own materials?

Operating a business known as Class Notes, Edwin Weisser published and sold outlines and notes from various courses at the University of California at Los Angeles (UCLA). Weisser obtained these materials by paying UCLA students to attend classes and turn over copies of their notes to him. In 1965 Weisser paid Karen Allen to attend Dr. Williams's class in Anthropology I and provide him with typed copies of notes from the lectures. After Allen delivered her notes, Weisser put a copyright notice on them in the name of Class Notes and sold them to other students. When Dr. Williams discovered that notes from his lectures were being offered for sale by Class Notes, he sued Weisser. Dr. Williams claimed that the lecture notes were his property and that they were protected by a common-law copyright. He asked the court to prohibit Weisser from publishing the notes and to award him a sum of money as damages.

The California court agreed with Dr. Williams. First, the court found that the lectures were indeed protected by a common-law copyright. Weisser argued that the lectures were "merely lightly embellished and thinly disguised paraphrasings of the works of others, both as to form and content. . . [and were] wholly in the public domain." The court, however, found that the lectures were created by Dr. Williams and were therefore covered by the common-law copyright law that gave the author the first right to publish the notes.

The court also rejected Weisser's argument that Dr. Williams lost his common-law copyright protection when he delivered his lectures. The court recognized that an author loses a copyright under common law after the materials have been made generally available but concluded that Dr. Williams was not making a "general" publication when he delivered his lectures: "[W]here the persons present at a lecture are not the general public, but a limited class of the public, selected and admitted for the sole and special purpose of receiving individual instruction, they may make any use they can of the lecture, to the extent of taking it down in shorthand, for their own information and improvement, but cannot publish it."

Finally, the court considered the question whether the university owned the copyright on Dr. Williams's lecture notes. The court noted that while the common law gives the copyright to the creator of an intellectual/artistic work, employers own the copyright on materials their employees produce as part of their job. Under this doctrine of "work for hire," the employer owns the copyright only when the materials are created as part of the employee's duties and when the employer has control over the employee's work product. In the case of a university professor, the court concluded that this doctrine did not apply and that Dr. Williams owned the copyright on his lectures. As the court explained: "A university's obligation to its students is to make the subject matter covered by a course available for study by various methods, including classroom presentation. . . . As far as the teacher is concerned, neither the record in this case nor any custom known to us suggests that the university can prescribe his way of expressing the ideas he puts before his students."

Finding that Weisser had indeed violated Dr. Williams's common-law copyright in his lecture notes, the court ordered Weisser to pay him $1500 as damages.

What material can be covered by a copyright?

As the court explained in *Williams,* a common-law copyright protects all intellectual products before publication, including writings, drawings, photographs, and musical scores. A copyright does not cover everything, however. The basic rule of copyright is that expression is protected, but that ideas are not. A teacher can copyright his or her lecture notes in a math class, for example, but no one can copyright a mathematical formula.

In determining what constitutes "publication," the courts have held that a common-law copyright applies up to the point of *general* publication. Thus the common law protected Williams's limited publication of his lecture notes. The common law did not protect another university employee, however, who submitted a grant proposal through the university administration to the federal government. The court in that case stated that a limited publication is one directed "to a definitely selected group and for a limited purpose, and without the right of diffusion, reproduction, distribution, or sale,"[5] and that the university employee had engaged in a general publication when the grant proposal was so widely distributed.

The Copyright Act of 1976 supersedes this common law protection, however, providing that federal copyright law covers all works that "are fixed in a tangible medium of expression."[6] Federal copyright therefore applies as soon as an author uses a pen or a typewriter to put ideas on paper, or as soon as an artist puts paint on a canvas. In addition, federal law covers such other "fixed" works as sound recordings and computer programs. In fact, almost the only creative works not covered by federal copyright law are extemporaneous performances such as dances or musical compositions. In those situations, state law still applies to protect the creator's ownership of the artistic product.

What is the significance of having a copyright under federal law?

Any author who has a federal copyright has, in effect, a monopoly on the materials created; the author has the right to control how the materials are to be distributed to the general public. Under the copyright act, the copyright owner has the exclusive right to reproduce the work, prepare derivative works, distribute copies by sale or other transfer, and display the work publicly. Under this law, copying includes fixing a work in any form through which it can be "perceived, reproduced, or otherwise communicated, either directly or with the aid of a machine or device"[7] and therefore includes copying a work on paper or onto a magnetic tape or other recording device. Protection under federal copyright law enables the copyright owner to go to federal court to sue anyone who reproduces, distributes, or displays copies of the owner's work without permission.

How can one obtain a copyright?

As explained above, federal law gives authors and artists the right to own their creative works as soon as they are "fixed" in a tangible form.

Under the Copyright Act of 1976, an author or artist was required to put a copyright "notice" on all copies of the work. The notice had to include:

1. the symbol © or the works "copyright" or "copr.,"
2. the year of first publication of the work, and
3. the name of the owner of the copyright.[8] The notice also had to be placed in such manner and location as to give reasonable notice of the claim of copyright.[9]

While failure to affix a notice did not destroy a copyright, it meant that anyone who used the materials before the notice was given would not be liable for damages, and could only be enjoined from further infringing use.[10]

However, in 1988 this law changed when Congress passed the Berne Convention Implementation Act, which made the United States a party to the Convention for the Protection of Literary and Artistic Works. The Berne Convention has been in effect for over 100 years, and over 70 other countries participate. Our participation made it easier to have access to courts in other countries to enforce copyright violations. The act went into effect on March 1, 1989, and after that date authors and artists are no longer required to place a copyright notice on their works. Affixing such a notice, however, prohibits anyone from raising a defense that they "innocently" infringed a copyright and thus are not liable for the full amount of actual or statutory damages.[11]

An author who wishes to be fully protected, however, must register the copyright and deposit two copies of the work with the copyright office within three months after the work is published. A registration fee of $10 is also required.[12] An author who does not register a copyright will not be able to maintain a suit against anyone who makes unauthorized copies. Registration and deposit are also necessary before a court can take certain actions against those who violate a copyright.

Where a copyright notice is required, is a copyright lost if the author does not follow these procedures?

Under common law, the copyright was lost as soon as there was a general publication of the work. After the work had been distributed to the public, the author had to turn to federal law for copyright protection. Under prior federal law, an author who distributed a work without complying with copyright notice provisions lost exclusive rights to copy and distribute it. At this point, the work was said to "fall into the public domain," and anyone was free to copy, distribute, or perform it.

The situation is different today. For works produced prior to March 1, 1989, that are required to have a copyright, the law provides that a copyright is not lost when an author omits the copyright notice from only a "relatively small number"[13] of copies distributed to the public. In addition, the act states that even an author who distributes copies without a copyright notice will retain the copyright if he or she registers the work with the copyright office within five years of publication *and* if a "reasonable effort"[14] is made to add the copyright notice to all copies distributed to the public after the omission was discovered. To date, there are no cases defining what a "relatively small number" of copies is, nor is it clear what would be a "reasonable effort" to correct an omission. The courts will be required to interpret these terms on a case-by-case basis. Given these generous and somewhat vague standards, it is difficult to determine at any particular time whether or not a work is in the public domain.

How long does a copyright last?

The "right of first publication" that existed under common law existed indefinitely. Federal law now states that all works created on or after January 1, 1978, have copyrights that last until 50 years after the death of the author. If there is more than one author, the 50-year term begins only after the death of the last surviving author.[15]

Can an author sell a copyright?

Yes. Some confusion has arisen in the law because a copyright—the right to make or distribute copies of a work—can be sold separately from the work itself. For example, an artist may own an original painting, while another person owns the right to make and sell copies of the painting.

In earlier decisions under both state and federal laws, the courts established rules to determine who owned the creative object and who owned the copyright. The new federal law has attempted to simplify matters by providing that the owner of a copyright can transfer this right to someone else. Merely transferring the physical object itself is not sufficient to transfer the copyright, however; the copyright owner must clearly state in writing that he or she is giving someone else the right to make copies of the work. After such transfer is made, federal law gives the new copyright owner the power to sue for violation of the exclusive right to make and distribute copies of the original work.

Who owns the copyright when there is more than one author?

When two or more authors collaborate on a "joint work," they will both (all) own a right to the entire work. Although the authors can agree among themselves to any other type of division of rights to the work, the law gives each of them the right to transfer his or her interest in the work without asking permission from any of the others.

In many cases, it is easy to determine what is a joint work. As the federal copyright law provides, a joint work is a work "prepared by two or more authors with the intention that their contributions be merged into inseparable or interdependent parts of a unitary whole."[16] When two authors agree to write a book together and carry out that agreement, the work is clearly a joint work. A question can arise, however, when a work is not "inseparable or interdependent," as in the case of an author and a photographer who collaborate on a picture book. In such a case, whether the work is a joint work will depend on the intent of the author and the photographer when each made his or her contribution.

Does an employee own a copyright on works produced on the job?

Teachers and many other employees produce original works while they are employed. Teachers may create lesson plans, books, and other teaching materials that they wish to copyright. Under a rule known as "work made for hire," however, the author of the work is considered to be the employer; the employee who actually created the work does not own the copyright. Thus, the copyright to any materials that a teacher produces within the scope of his or her employment is owned by the school district (or other employer).

In 1989 the U.S. Supreme Court decided a case[17] that provided additional guidance as to what constitutes a "work prepared by an employee within the scope of his or her employment." In that case, the Community for Creative Non-Violence (CCNV), an organization dedicated to eliminating homelessness, decided to sponsor a Christmas display that would dramatize the plight of the homeless. One of CCNV's trustees contacted James Earl Reid, a sculptor, and Reid agreed to sculpt three human beings along with a shopping cart. CCNV hired others to produce additional parts of the display, including the pedestal. Neither CCNV nor Reid discussed who would own the copyright, but when Reid later objected to CCNV's plan to take the sculpture on tour, Reid and CCNV both filed applications for copyright registration. CCNV claimed that Reid was their "employee" because CCNV had conceived of and directed the project and that the sculpture was a work made for hire.

The U.S. Supreme Court disagreed. The Court looked at the history behind the Copyright Act and concluded the Congress had intended to adopt the common law distinction between employees and independent contractors. Under these common law principles, one party's right to control the manner and means by which the product is accomplished is only one of the factors to consider; others include:

> the skill required; the source of the instrumentalities and tools; the location of the work; the duration of the relationship between the parties; whether the hiring party has the right to assign additional projects to the hired party; the extent of the hired party's discretion over when and how long to work; the method of payment; the hired party's role in hiring paying assistants; whether the work is part of the regular business of the hiring party; whether the hiring party is in business; the provision of employee benefits; and the tax treatment of the hired party. No one of these factors is determinative.[18]

Applying these factors the Court held that Reid was not an employee of CCNV but an independent contractor. Although CCNV directed Reid's work, all other factors weighed against finding an employment relationship (Reid supplied his own tools, worked in his own studio, was retained for a short period of time, and had absolute freedom to decide when and how long to work). The Court left open the question of whether CCNV could be considered a joint author of the sculpture; if so, CCNV and Reid would be co-owners of the copyright in the work.

Under the reasoning of this case, a teacher who acts as an "independent contractor" can obtain a copyright. A reading teacher might agree, for example, to produce materials for the school district. If the district relies on the teacher's expertise, specially compensates the teacher for this project, requests that the teacher use his or her own equipment and resources, and otherwise gives the teacher complete freedom as to how to structure the materials, the teacher could be considered an independent contractor and not subject to the work for hire doctrine. A teacher could also avoid the application of this doctrine by signing a contract with the employer limiting the employer's rights in two ways. First, the contract could specify that certain types of activities, for example, any materials presented at national professional meetings, will not be considered within the scope of employment. Second, the contract could give the teacher rights other than ownership of the copyright. For example, under such terms, the employer, who still owns the copyright, could give the teacher the right to reproduce or distribute curriculum materials.

FAIR USE

Is it ever possible to make copies of an author's copyrighted work without first securing permission?

Yes. Under a doctrine known as "fair use," courts have ruled that it is in the public interest to allow certain uses of copyrighted materials. Generally, it is not a violation of a copyright to use the "idea" or "system" developed by an author. Although an author has a monopoly on the particular form of expression created, the author has no exclusive right to control dissemination of the theory developed. Another author can quote Einstein's theory of relativity, for example, without violating any copyright held by Einstein. In addition, the courts have held that it is a fair use of copyrighted material to make copies in newsreporting, criticism, or scholarly research. For example, a scholar who as part of doing research copies a short quotation from an earlier writer in the field does not violate the copyright laws.

What is "fair use"?

The doctrine of fair use is an exception to the general rules of copyright law which allows use of copyrighted material in a reasonable manner without securing the copyright owner's consent. The fair use doctrine is designed to balance the exclusive rights of the copyright owner against the public's interest in dissemination of information of universal concern. There are no clear rules to define "fair use." Nevertheless, the new federal copyright act lists four criteria for the courts to consider in cases involving fair use:

1. the purpose and character of the use, including whether such use is of a commercial nature or is for nonprofit educational purpose;
2. the nature of the copyrighted work;
3. the amount and substantiality of the portion used in relation to the copyrighted work as a whole;
4. the effect of the use upon the potential market for or value of the copyrighted work.[19]

An example of what the U.S. Supreme Court considered not to be fair use occurred in a case where Harper & Row had been given the exclusive right to license prepublication of President Ford's memoirs.[20] Harper & Row agreed to let *Time* magazine publish a 7500 word excerpt from the memoirs, but, shortly before the excerpt was to appear in *Time,* an unauthorized source sent a copy of the manuscript to the *Nation.* The *Nation* then published a 2250 word article, using between 300 and 400 words of the copyrighted material. As a result, *Time* decided not to publish its scheduled article and refused to pay the $12,500 it still owed Harper & Row.

The Supreme Court examined the four factors listed in the federal law defining fair use, and held that the *Nation's* use was not fair. First, the Court found the fact that the subject matter was news was not determinative; the *Nation* was publishing for commercial purposes and tried to exploit the headline value of its infringement. Second, even though the nature of the work was fact and not fiction, the *Nation's* publication went far beyond what was necessary to disseminate the facts. Third, although the quotes from the copyrighted material were only a small portion of the total, they constituted the essence of Ford's distinctive expression. The Court also looked at the fourth factor, the effect of the use on the potential market, and stated that this factor is undoubtedly "the single most important element of fair use." The Court found that *Time's* cancellation of its projected serialization and its refusal to pay the $12,500 owed to Harper & Row were the direct effect of the infringement and that this case presented "clear cut evidence of actual damage." Finally, the Court went on to clarify the burden of proof in this area, explaining that once a copyright holder establishes a causal connection between the infringement and loss of revenue, the burden shifts to the infringer to show that the damage would have occurred had there been no infringement of the copyright. To negate a claim of fair use, it is only necessary to show that if the challenged use should become widespread, it would adversely affect the potential market for the copyrighted work.

By way of contrast, a New York court[21] found that it was fair use for a physician to present a medical syllabus at a nuclear medicine review course. The physician was a collaborator and joint author with another physician, who had previously served as a resident under him and who had presented the same syllabus at another conference two years earlier. After concluding that the physicians were joint authors, and thus each entitled to license work without the other's consent, the court went on to explain that even if they were not joint authors such a publication would be fair use. The court reached its conclusion by applying the factors described above in *Harper & Row* as follows: (1) the use was entirely noncommercial and for nonprofit educational purposes (the physician neither profited nor stood to profit from any publication); (2) the nature of the work was factual and scientific in nature and already published by the plaintiff; (3) the entire syllabus was copied, and the content virtually in its entirety had been published by both authors; (4) the use of the syllabus would not impair its market value at all, and dissemination of results and research at any institution would in all likelihood only increase the "marketability" of a paper emanating from that department.

Are there any "fair use" exceptions for teachers?

Although members of Congress did not agree on standards for educational copying, they did endorse guidelines developed by the Ad Hoc Committee of Educational Institutions and Organizations on Copyright Law Revision, the Author's League of America, Inc., and the Association of American Publishers, Inc. These guidelines are included in the official comments on the statute[22] and list a number of specific exceptions for teachers. First, teachers are permitted to make *single* copies of the following copyrighted works for their own use in scholarly research or classroom preparation:

1. a chapter from a book;
2. an article from a periodical or newspaper;
3. a short story, short essay, or short poem;
4. a chart, graph, diagram, drawing, cartoon, or picture from a book, newspaper, or periodical.

In addition, a teacher can make multiple copies of the following copyrighted works for use in the classroom (with the number of copies not to exceed one copy per student in the class), provided that copying meets certain tests of brevity, spontaneity, and cumulative effect, and that each copy includes a notice of copyright. The definition of *brevity* is

1. a complete poem, if it is less than 250 words and printed on not more than two pages;
2. an excerpt from a longer poem, if it is not more than 250 words;
3. a complete article, story, or essay if it is less than 2500 words;
4. an excerpt from a prose work, if it is less than 1000 words or 10 percent of the work, whichever is less; or
5. one chart, diagram, cartoon, or picture per book or periodical.

The definition of *spontaneity* is when

1. the copying is at the instance and inspiration of the individual teacher, *and*
2. the inspiration and decision to use the work and the moment of its use for maximum teaching effectiveness are so close in time that it would be unreasonable to expect a timely reply to a request for permission.

The definition of *cumulative effect* is when

1. the copying of the material is for only one course in the school in which the copies are made;
2. not more than one short poem, article, story, essay, or two excerpts are

copied from the same author, or more than three from the same collective work or periodical volume during one class term;

3. there are not more than nine instances of such multiple copying for one course during one class term.*

In addition, teachers cannot make copies of "consumable" materials such as workbooks or answer sheets to standardized tests. Finally, teachers are prohibited from making a copy of works to take the place of an anthology.

In addition to the exceptions for copying, the act also exempts certain public performances. For example, the performance of a copyrighted dramatic work by students and teachers in the classroom is not a copyright violation. If students give a "public performance" of a copyrighted work, however, they will be protected from copyright violation only when there is no admission charge and no compensation paid to any performer or promoter. Even when students perform without pay, if the school charges admission to the performance, the copyright owner has the right to prohibit the performance by giving proper notice.[23]

Are there any "fair use" exceptions for libraries?

Yes. These federal copyright law exceptions apply only in cases where the following standards are met:[24]

1. the library is making a reproduction without any purpose of commercial advantage;
2. the library collection is open to the public;
3. the library reproduces no more than one copy of a work;
4. the reproduction includes a notice of copyright.

A library complying with these requirements is permitted to make copies in the following situations:

1. to preserve in facsimile form an unpublished work currently in the library or for another library (such as putting a copy of a doctoral dissertation on microfiche);
2. to replace in facsimile form a published work that is damaged, lost, or stolen if the library has, after reasonable effort, determined that an unused replacement cannot be obtained at a fair price;
3. in response to a request by a user or by another library on behalf of a user. (This exemption only applies if the copy becomes the property of

---

* Numbers 2 and 3 above do not apply to current news periodicals and newspapers.

the user, the library has no reason to believe that it will be used for purposes other than private study or research, and the library displays a copyright warning notice.)

In addition, the law provides that a library shall not be liable for copyright infringement by its patrons where it displays on its copying equipment a notice that the making of a copy may be subject to the copyright law.[25]

Is it "fair use" to copy computer software for educational purposes?

No. Computer programs are eligible for copyright.[26] Neither the federal copyright law nor the guidelines mentioned above apply to copying computer software, and such copying is not fair use. The federal law was amended in 1980, however, to provide that the owner of a copy of a copyrighted program does not infringe the copyright if the "new copy or adaptation is created as an essential step in the utilization of the program in conjunction with a machine" or if the new copy or adaptation is for archival (backup) purposes only.[27] Thus, teachers who load a copyrighted program onto a classroom terminal or make a backup copy of a program are not infringing a copyright, but a teacher who makes copies of software for students or who uses the original program in one terminal while a student uses the backup copy is. Whether it is a violation to "down load" a computer program onto multiple terminals is unclear.

Another unresolved legal question in this area concerns exactly what components of a computer program should be protected under a copyright. Since a copyright only protects expression and not ideas, courts have been required to determine how this legal rule applies to computer programs. The few courts that have addressed this issue have decided that a copyright protects both the source code of a program (the part of the program written in a computer language such as BASIC) and the object code (the part of the program read by the machine).[28]

Is it "fair use" to videotape for educational purposes?

The federal law only allows libraries or archives to tape an audiovisual news program.[29] As in the case of educational photocopying, the law did not include specific rules for educational videotaping. To deal with this issue, in 1979 the House Judiciary Committee formed a committee consisting of representatives of education organizations, copyright proprietors, and creative guilds and unions to develop appropriate guidelines.[30] The committee submitted guidelines that applied to off-air recording by nonprofit educational institutions. In general, these guidelines provide that nonprofit educational institutions may videotape copyrighted television programs but may only keep the tape for 45 days (unless they obtain a license). At the end of 45 days, the tape must be erased or destroyed. During the first 10 consecutive school days after taping, teachers may use the tapes for instructional purposes, but teachers may only repeat such use once for purposes of instructional reinforcement. After this 10-day period, the tape may only be used for purposes of evaluating its educational usefulness.

There have been a number of court cases involving the question of whether videotaping constitutes fair use. In a New York case,[31] a federal district court found that a nonprofit educational service agency was guilty of copyright violations. The service agency had routinely copied all daytime programs broadcast by the local public television station, as well as some evening programs on commercial stations, and had maintained a library of 4300 videotapes that were available for distribution to teachers at over 100 schools. The court stated that the "massive and systematic videotape copying"[32] and the highly sophisticated methods used by the defendants could not be considered fair use.

In 1984 the U.S. Supreme Court decided a videotaping case that, while not directly involving education, does establish a standard for fair use in videotaping.[33] The issue in the case was whether Sony Corporation's sale of videotaping equipment (VTRs) to the general public constituted an infringement of copyright. The plaintiffs argued that Sony was liable for copyright infringement because it supplied the means for infringement.

The Supreme Court held that Sony's VTR sales were not contributory infringement. The Court examined the four factors listed in the federal law concerning fair use, and discussed two of them. First, the Court noted that private, home use time-shifting was a noncommercial, nonprofit use. Second, the Court did not find any harm to the television market. The Court concluded that the VTR is capable of many noninfringing uses, and that Sony's sale of it was not contributory infringement.

Although the case seems to establish a fairly broad definition of fair use, it is important to note what the Supreme Court opinion did not address. First, it did not state that all home videotaping constitutes fair use. Second, the Court did not address the issue of whether it is a copyright violation to retain copies of videotaped programs. Until the courts do decide these issues, educators are probably best advised to follow the federal guidelines described above.

How can an individual get permission to photocopy or videotape in cases where there is no fair use exception?

Teachers who believe that their photocopying or videotaping goes beyond fair use should get written permission to copy or tape from the copyright owner. In requesting permission, the teacher should specify the following: the exact material to be copied, the number of copies, and the proposed use of these materials.

COPYRIGHT VIOLATION

Are all schools liable for damages when charged with copyright violations?

According to at least two courts, no. Two federal courts[34] have held that in copyright suits the Eleventh Amendment affords immunity for liability to state universities and university officials acting in their official capacities. Although states can waive this immunity, such as when a state seeks a benefit under a federal law that requires the receiver of the benefit to surrender Eleventh Amendment immunity, these courts concluded that no such waiver could be implied under the Copyright Act. In some states, public school systems are considered state bodies and, under these decisions, would also be immune from suit.

The U.S. Supreme Court has declined to hear either of these cases and, in response, bills have been introduced in Congress[35] that would strip state schools and colleges of their immunity to copyright-infringement lawsuits. Whether or not Congress has the power to abrogate the states' Eleventh Amendment immunity is unclear, however, and, if passed, such a law will certainly be challenged. In the meantime schools can best protect themselves by abiding by the law and developing written policies regarding photocopying of printed materials and library use, work for hire, procedures for seeking permission in situations beyond fair use, and securing appropriate releases to use materials for school purposes.

What are the penalties for violating a copyright?

The Copyright Act of 1976 provides that the owner of a copyright can sue anyone who "infringes" his or her exclusive right to control the distribution of literary or artistic property.[36]

In a suit for copyright infringement, a court has the power to issue an injunction to prevent people from making or distributing further copies of a work. A court may also impound all copies claimed to have been made in violation of the owner's copyright. If the court later finds that there has been a copyright violation, it can order that all illegal copies be destroyed or otherwise disposed of. The copyright act also states that the copyright owner can collect *either* of the following monetary awards:

1. any actual damages the copyright owner has sustained, as well as any profits the copyright infringer has made; or
2. an amount of money to be determined by the court, which can range from $500 to $20,000 for an infringement of any one work. If the court finds that the infringer has acted willfully, the court can increase the award to $100,000; if the infringer was unaware that he or she was violating someone else's copyright, the court can award as little as $200.[37]

Thus, even when the copyright owner cannot show that he or she was damaged in any specific way (such as through a loss of sales of the work), the court can still make a monetary award. For example, one author's copyright was violated when two commercial book companies published and sold copies of his book without his permission.[38] Although both publishing companies lost money on the book, and the author could not show that he had suffered any damages, the court still awarded the author ten cents for every copy that was sold. In addition, as the copyright act allows, the court made an award to cover the costs of the author's attorney's fees in bringing the suit.

The act also provides that "any person who infringes a copyright willfully and for purposes of commercial advantage or private financial gain" shall be fined not more than $25,000 or imprisoned for not more than one year, or both.[39] Infringers who make a large number of copies[40] of phonorecords or audiovisual works in a 180-day period incur even heavier penalties: a fine of $250,000, imprisonment up to five years, or both. Moreover, any person who knowingly puts a false notice of copyright on a copyrighted work, can be fined up to $2500.[41]

SUMMARY

Copyright law gives authors property rights in their work. Under the common law, they have the right of first publication. Once an author publishes or distributes a creative work, however, this protection under the common law is lost and the author must look to federal law to protect his or her right to control distribution of the work. Federal law now protects all literary and artistic works from the moment that they are "fixed" in some form, whether in writing or on a floppy disk.

To establish a copyright under federal law, an author or artist merely places the proper copyright notice on all copies of the work. In order to maintain a suit for copyright infringement, however, the copyright owner must also register and deposit copies of the work with the Copyright Office. Federal law provides various remedies for copyright infringement, including the owner's right to monetary damages and criminal sanctions against the perpetrator in cases of willful infringement.

NOTES

1. Copyright Act of 1976, 17 U.S.C. § § 101-914 (West 1977 and Supp. 1989).
2. U.S. CONST. art. I, § 8, cl 8.
3. *See* 17 U.S.C. § § 101-914 (West 1977 and Supp. 1989).
4. *Williams* v. *Weisser,* 78 Cal. Rptr. 542 (Cal. App. 1969).
5. *White* v. *Kimmel,* 193 F.2d 744, 746 (9th Cir. 1952), *cert. denied,* 343 U.S. 957 (1952).
6. 17 U.S.C. § § 101-914 (West 1977 and Supp. 1985).
7. *Id.,* § 101.
8. *Id.,* § 401(a)&(b).
9. *Id.,* § 401(c).
10. *Id.,* § 405(b).
11. *Id.,* § 401(d) (West Supp. 1989).

12. For information on how to register, write to: Register of Copyrights, Library of Congress, Washington, D.C. 20559.

13. *Id.*, § 405(a)(1).

14. *Id.*, § 405(a)(2).

15. *Id.*, § 302.

16. *Id.*, § 101.

17. *Community for Creative Non-Violence* v. *Reid*, 109 S.Ct. 2166 (1989).

18. *Id.*, at 2178–79.

19. *Id.*, § 107.

20. *Harper & Row Publishers, Inc.* v. *Nation Enterprises*, 471 U.S. 539 (1985).

21. *Weissmann* v. *Freeman*, 684 F. Supp. 1248 (S.D.N.Y. 1988).

22. NOTES OF COMMITTEE ON THE JUDICIARY, H.R. No. 94-1476, 94th Cong., 201 Sess. 68-70 (1976).

23. *Id.*, § 110(1); *Id.*, § 110(4)(B).

24. *Id.*, § 108.

25. *Id.*, § 108(f)(1).

26. *Id.*, § § 102(a) and 117.

27. *Id.*, § 117.

28. *Apple Computer, Inc.* v. *Formula International, Inc.*, 725 F.2d 521 (C.A. Cal. 1984); *Apple Computer, Inc.* v. *Franklin Computer Corporation*, 714 F.2d 1240 (3d Cir. 1983), *cert. denied*, 464 U.S. 1033 (1984).

29. 17 U.S.C. § 108(f)(3).

30. GUIDELINES FOR OFF-AIR RECORDING OF BROADCAST PROGRAMMING FOR EDUCATIONAL PURPOSES, CONG. REC. § E4751 (October 14, 1981).

31. *Encyclopedia Britannica Educational Corporation* v. *Crooks*, 542 F.Supp. 1156 (W.D. N.Y. 1982).

32. *Id.*, at 1181.

33. *Sony Corporation of America* v. *Universal City Studios, Inc.*, 464 U.S. 417 (1984).

34. *Richard Anderson Photography* v. *Radford University*, 633 F. Supp. 1154 (W.D. Va. 1986); *BV Engineering* v. *University of California, Los Angeles*, 858 F.2d 1394 (9th Cir. 1988).

35. H.R. 1131 is known as the Copyright Remedy Clarification Act. The Senate is considering a similar bill (S. 497).

36. 17 U.S.C. § 501(b).

37. *Id.*, § 504 (West Supp. 1989).

38. *Robinson* v. *Bantam Books, Inc.*, 339 F.Supp. 150 (S.D. N.Y. 1972).

39. 18 U.S.C. § 2319(b) (West Supp. 1989).

40. Reproduction or distribution of at least 1,000 phonorecords or at least 65 copies of audiovisual works.

41. 17 U.S.C. § 506(d).

PART II

Teachers' and Students' Rights

CHAPTER 8

When Can Schools Restrict Freedom of Expression?

OVERVIEW

During the first half of this century, the Bill of Rights was rarely referred to when teachers or students challenged the constitutionality of school rules. Courts generally used the "reasonableness" test to judge school policies. If there was any reasonable relationship between the rule and the goals of the school, the rule would be upheld even if most judges believed it was unwise, unnecessary, or restricted constitutional rights. Courts felt that school boards should have wide discretion and that judges should not substitute their judgment for that of school officials, who were presumed to be experts in educational matters.

In 1969 the U.S. Supreme Court handed down a historic decision that challenged the reasonableness test. In *Tinker* v. *Des Moines,* the Court ruled that neither teachers nor students lose their constitutional rights to freedom of expression when they enter the public schools. The fact that the Constitution now applies to schooling, of course, does not mean that teachers and students can say or write anything they wish.

When conflicts arise between the rights of teachers or students and the authority of school administrators, it is the job of the courts to balance the legitimate rights in conflict and determine when to protect and when to limit freedom of expression. In resolving these conflicts, the courts establish legal principles that apply to similar cases. Based on these cases and principles, this chapter explains when the Constitution protects teachers' freedom to criticize school policy, engage in partisan activities on controversial issues, and alter teaching methods; and when students' freedom of speech, academic freedom, and freedom of the press are protected.

In this chapter, and throughout Part II, we have not separated teachers' and students' rights but have put related issues concerning both in the same chapter.

CRITICIZING SCHOOL POLICY OR PERSONNEL

An employee of a private business who is discharged for publicly "blasting" the boss has no constitutional right to be reemployed. Should a public school teacher have more freedom than an employee in private industry? Or should a teacher have a duty of loyalty to superiors, an obligation to go through prescribed channels before making criticism public, and a greater responsibility than the average citizen to speak carefully and accurately about educational matters? If a teacher fails to exercise this responsibility, what disciplinary actions can a school board take?

The *Pickering* Case[1]

Marvin Pickering was a high school teacher from Will County, Illinois, who published a long, sarcastic letter in the local newspaper about the way his superintendent and school board raised and spent school funds. Pickering's letter detailed his objection to the "excessive" athletic expenditures by school officials who were then allegedly unable to pay teachers' salaries. He also wrote that "taxpayers were really taken to the cleaners" by those who built one of the local schools. And he criticized the "totalitarianism teachers live in" at the high school.

Angered by the publication of the letter, the board of education charged that it contained false and misleading statements, "damaged the professional reputations" of school administrators and the board, and was "detrimental to the efficient operation and administration of the schools." Pickering argued that his letter should be protected by his right of free speech, but an Illinois court ruled against him. Since Pickering held a position as teacher, the state court wrote that he "is no more entitled to harm the schools by speech than by incompetency."

Pickering still believed his letter was protected by the First Amendment, so he appealed to the U.S. Supreme Court. On behalf of the Court, Justice Thurgood Marshall wrote that the problem in this case is "to arrive at a balance between the interests of the teacher, as citizen, in commenting upon matters of public concern, and the interests of the state, as an employer, in promoting the efficiency of the public services it performs through its employees." The Court's examination of the issues in this case are outlined in the questions that follow.

Can a teacher be dismissed for publicly criticizing school policy?

The Court found that Pickering's letter consisted mainly of criticism of the school board's allocation of funds and of both the board's and the superintendent's method of informing (or not informing) the taxpayers of the real reasons why additional funds were sought. Since such statements were not directed toward people Pickering normally worked with, they raised no question of maintaining discipline by immediate superiors or harmony among co-workers. Pickering's relationships with the board and superintendent, wrote the Court, "are not the kind of close working relationships for which it can persuasively be claimed that personal loyalty and confidence are necessary." Thus the Court "unequivocally" rejected the board's position that critical public comments by a teacher on matters of public concern may furnish grounds for dismissal.

The question whether a school system requires additional funds is a matter of legitimate public concern. On such an issue, wrote the Court, "free and open debate is vital to informed decision making by the electorate. Teachers are, as a class, the members of a community most likely to have informed and definite opinions as to how funds allocated to the operation of the schools should be spent. Accordingly, it is essential that they be able to speak out freely on such questions without fear of retaliatory dismissal."

Can a teacher be dismissed for making public statements that are not accurate?

Pickering's inaccurate statements mainly consisted of exaggerated cost claims for the athletic program, the erroneous suggestion that teachers had not been paid on occasion, and a false statement regarding the cost of transporting athletes. The Court found no evidence that these inaccurate statements were intentional or that they damaged the professional reputations of the board and the superintendent. In fact, wrote the Court, "Pickering's letter was greeted by everyone but its main target, the board, with massive apathy."

According to Justice Marshall, the accusation that administrators are spending too much money on athletics cannot be regarded as "detrimental to the district's schools." Such an accusation, wrote the Court, reflects "a difference of opinion between Pickering and the board as to the preferable manner of operating the school system, a difference of opinion that clearly concerns an issue of general public interest."

In sum, Pickering unintentionally made several incorrect statements on current issues that were critical of his employer but did not impede his teaching or interfere with the regular operation of the schools. The Court therefore concluded that "absent proof of false statements knowingly or recklessly made by him, a teacher's exercise of his right to speak on issues of public importance may not furnish the basis for his dismissal from public employment."

Can a teacher be transferred for publicly criticizing a school program?

The decision in *Pickering* protected a teacher from being fired, but what about a teacher who is simply transferred with no loss of pay or status? In Arizona, a guidance counselor publicly opposed the way Mexican-American children were placed in classes for the mentally retarded because they were tested in English rather than Spanish. After the teacher suggested that parents could sue to stop this practice, she was transferred to a wealthy school with very few Mexican-American children. She felt the transfer violated her rights, however, and a federal appeals court agreed.[2] The court acknowledged that she had no right initially to be assigned to work with Mexican-American children. But once she was given such an assignment, officials could not constitutionally transfer her because of her public criticism. The court concluded that the school's interest in being free from criticism "cannot outweigh the right of a sincere educational counselor to speak out against a policy she believes to be both harmful and unlawful."

Can a school board ever restrict teachers' rights to publicize their views?

Yes. In *Pickering,* Justice Marshall wrote: "It is possible to conceive of some positions in public employment in which the need for confidentiality is so great that even completely correct public statements might furnish a permissible ground for dismissal." Such a situation might occur, for example, if a teacher publicly played a tape recording of a confidential student interview or published personal information from student files without permission.

Similarly, unprofessional disclosures within the school may not be protected by the First Amendment. Thus, an Ohio guidance counselor was disciplined for telling a school secretary that two of the students she was counseling were homosexual. In supporting the disciplinary action, an appeals court wrote that this disclosure "was a serious breach of confidence which reflected seriously on the [counselor's] judgment and qualifications" and were "sufficient reason to suspend or reassign her."[3]

A related Alabama case involved James Swilley, a teacher who disseminated charges about a local principal's negligence to the news media.[4] The school board reprimanded the teacher because he refused to wait until the board's investigation was complete before publicizing his allegations. Swilley then charged the board with violating his freedom of speech. A federal judge, however, ruled in favor of the board. The court wrote that this case was not like *Pickering:* The possible removal of a principal is not a matter of public policy to be resolved by majority vote; it is a personnel decision of the board. The court concluded that when such problems are made public before they are investigated, they can indeed "interfere with the orderly operation of the school system."

In New Jersey, the president of a local teachers' association was dismissed as a result of a speech she gave at an orientation for new teachers. In her speech she described the district as a "snakepit for young teachers" and characterized the superintendent as a "villain" who was "intimately embroiled" in local politics. A state appeals court ruled that her speech was not protected by the First Amendment, that free speech does "not endow a teacher. . . with a license to vilify superiors publicly."[5] Unlike *Pickering*, the court found that this teacher did not speak directly about issues of public concern "but distorted them into a vehicle to bring scorn and abuse" on the school administration.

Can teachers be disciplined for publicly criticizing their immediate superiors?

This would depend on the circumstances. In *Pickering*, Justice Marshall wrote that "certain forms of public criticism of the superior by the subordinate would seriously undermine the effectiveness of the working relationship between them" and thus justify appropriate discipline. In an Alaska case, for example, the court upheld the dismissal of two teachers for publishing an "open letter" to the school board that contained a series of false charges against their immediate superior.[6] Unlike Pickering's letter, these false allegations "were not consistent with good faith and were made in reckless disregard of the truth." (For a discussion of teacher liability for slander and libel, see Chapter 6.)

On the other hand, a federal court protected Haywood Lusk, a Texas teacher, after his critical statements received wide media coverage and seriously injured his relationship with his principal.[7] The teacher was dismissed after he testified before the school board and city council that his principal and co-workers were "mentally and sociologically unqualified to deal with modern, complex, multiracial student bodies." He also charged that students in his school "learn to disobey authority, run, lie, cheat and steal" in order to survive. In rejecting Lusk's dismissal, a federal court wrote that his criticism concerned "matters of vital interest to every citizen of Dallas" and that they were properly brought to the attention "of the governing bodies who had the power to act" on them. In this case the court concluded that "society's interest in information concerning the operation of its schools far outweighs any strain on the teacher-principal relationship."

Can teachers always be punished if their statements cause disruption in the school?

Not necessarily. It depends on the facts of the case. In Arkansas, Bob Bowman, an assistant football coach, publicly criticized the head coach, Jimmy Walker, for using excessive corporal punishment. The criticism led to extensive press coverage, intense public debate, and "turmoil in the community." As a result, Walker apologized and kept his job. Bowman, however, was transferred to a less desirable school; he sued, claiming that the transfer violated his rights.

In this case, the court balanced the interests of the teacher against the interests of the school board by considering several factors: (1) the need for harmony in the schools, (2) whether the criticism injured the working relationships, (3) the time, manner, place, and context of the speech, (4) the degree of public interest involved, and (5) the effect of the speech on the teacher's ability to work effectively.[8]

The judge noted that two of the factors clearly favored the school board: (1) Bowman's speech contributed to turmoil in the community, and (2) destroyed his working relationship with Coach Walker. On the other hand, several factors favored Bowman: (1) there was intense public interest in the physical mistreatment of students, (2) Bowman's comments were made at school board meetings and other appropriate places, and (3) there was no evidence that the controversy affected Bowman's ability to work with students—only that Walker refused to work with him.

After weighing these competing factors, the court ruled that Bowman's speech was protected. "In our minds," wrote Judge Ross, "the public's need to know whether children are being mistreated in school outweighs the other legitimate concerns of the government."

Would the *Pickering* decision always protect teachers who make unintentional false public statements?

Generally, but not always. In Hartford, Connecticut, for example, a tenured high school teacher was dismissed for distributing leaflets that contained a number of false statements about her principal.[9] Prepared by a radical student group at a time of racial tension, the leaflets charged the principal with imposing a "reign of terror" at the school and falsely alleged that he had refused to reinstate a militant student despite a court order and had used "military riot gas" against demonstrating students at another school. The teacher testified that she did not know the charges were false at the time she distributed them. A federal court ruled that her distribution of these leaflets was not protected by the First Amendment because their basic purpose was to cause dissension; and they contained serious, damaging, and incorrect accusations that had an immediate and harmful impact on the school.

Is private criticism protected?

It depends on the circumstances. Bessie Givhan, an English teacher, was dismissed after a series of private encounters with her principal. The principal alleged that Givhan made "petty and unreasonable demands" in an "insulting, loud and hostile" manner. The trial court found that her demands were not petty or unreasonable since they involved practices she felt were racially discriminatory. But a court of appeals ruled for the school on the grounds that private complaints were not protected by the Constitution. The Supreme Court disagreed and extended the *Pickering* ruling to apply to private as well as public criticism.[10]

The Court rejected the notion that the First Amendment does not protect criticism of a principal simply because of the close working relationship between principal and teacher. The Court emphasized that freedom of speech is not lost when a teacher "arranges to communicate privately with his employer rather than to spread his views before the public." On the other hand, a teacher's criticism might not be protected when it specifically impedes classroom duties or the operation of the schools. In personal confrontations between an educator and an immediate superior, the Court noted that judges may also consider the "manner, time, and place" of confrontations when balancing the rights in conflict.

In contrast, a federal appeals court ruled that a tenured teacher, Evelyn Anderson, could be dismissed for telling her black principal and assistant principal, "I hate all black folks."[11] Unlike the *Pickering* case, Anderson's remarks created tension between the teacher and her principals, they caused an adverse reaction among co-workers, and they "cast serious doubt on her judgment and general competence as a teacher" in a school district where most students were black. Under these circumstances, the court ruled that the school board's interest in maintaining an efficient system and in employing effective teachers outweighed Anderson's free speech interest and, therefore, that her dismissal was not unconstitutional.

Can teachers be required to go through the chain of command?

Not about matters of public concern. In Oregon, for example, a coach was suppended for mailing a letter about the athletic program directly to the school board and not sending it through proper channels. In ruling against the board, the judge barred the enforcement of "any policy which prohibits direct communication by teachers on matters of public concern with the members of the District School Board."[12]

In Arkansas, the contracts of several teachers were not renewed because they wrote to the State Department of Education complaining of a colleague's deficiencies in implementing the special education law. The district said the teachers' letter should not be protected because it was merely an "internal grievance over employment" and made the school "look bad." But a federal judge ruled for the teachers who, he wrote, "were exercising their rights as citizens regarding a matter of public concern with respect to the quality of education and observance of federal policy" regarding handicapped children.[13]

Are personal complaints protected by the First Amendment?

No. In 1983, the U.S. Supreme Court ruled in *Connick* v. *Myers* that "when a public employee speaks not as a citizen upon matters of public concern, but instead as an employee upon matters only of personal interest. . . a federal court is not the appropriate forum in which to review the wisdom" of the public agency's personnel decision.[14]

Are all personnel matters excluded from First Amendment protection?

Not necessarily. Most personnel issues are considered matters of private, not public concern; but this is not always true. It depends on the "content, form, and context" of the statements in dispute.

The case of a North Carolina teacher, Edwin Piver, illustrates when controversial statements about a personnel controversy were protected by the courts. After Piver spoke in favor of renewing his principal's contract at a school board meeting and later urged the board to reverse its nonrenewal decision, he was transferred to a less desirable assignment. The board argued that the dispute was not protected by the First Amendment since it was an internal personnel matter. But a federal appeals court disagreed.[15] Piver's speech to the board was protected because there is community interest in "frank and open discussion of agenda items at public meetings." Furthermore, Piver had "particular expertise" concerning his principal's performance, and "the public has a need to hear from those who know" about the performance of public officials.

Are all activities in schools and government offices matters of public concern?

No. In a 1988 decision, a federal appeals court ruled that a series of "sarcastic, unprofessional, and insulting" memoranda written by an Illinois teacher to various school officials were not protected by the First Amendment.[16] This is because the teacher "was not attempting to speak out as a citizen concerned with problems facing the school district, but was instead attempting to articulate his own private disagreement with policies and procedures which he had either failed to apply or refused to follow."

Similarly, a federal court ruled that teacher complaints about classroom materials were not protected. Otherwise, the judge explained, complaints about innumerable other school conditions would also be protected, such as "the number of teacher aides, the tightness of class scheduling, the size of blackboards, or the adequacy of laboratory equipment."[17] According to the court, questions of this sort are best resolved by school administrators, not judges. "To hold otherwise," wrote the court, "would be to transform every personal grievance into protected speech."

How is the *Connick* decision being applied to teachers?

A Florida controversy illustrates how some courts are applying *Connick* in schools. The case involved Lawrence Ferrara, a high school history teacher, whose class assignments were changed in retaliation for his outspoken criticism of administrative policy.[18] Ferrara strongly and repeatedly objected to allowing students to choose their teachers, to using coaches as social studies teachers, and to his change of assignment. After reviewing the entire record, the court ruled against the teacher. According to Judge Gonzales, Ferrara's speech "while tangentially related to matters of public concern, constitutes nothing more than a series of grievances with school administrators over internal school policies." The judge observed that Ferrara's "flag-raising first amendment claims" are simply "a smokescreen to camouflage" his disagreements with school administrators. "In the wake of *Connick*," wrote Judge Gonzales, "the federal courts have substantially broadened the employer's rights to control employee speech activities that *relate to his employment.*"

In several similar cases, courts have ruled against teachers who claimed that their public criticism should be protected by the First Amendment. In St. Louis, a teacher alleged that his contract was not renewed due to his public criticism about the quality of education and discipline in the high school. But a federal court ruled against the teacher when the school showed that the teacher's "inability to work harmoniously with the administration and his fellow teachers," plus his "abrasive relationship" with students were the primary reasons that his contract was not renewed.[19] In Alabama, Cheryl Renfroe, a nontenured teacher, was not rehired because she filed a grievance about an administration's request that she share her job with another teacher for budgetary reasons. A federal appeals court ruled that Renfroe's grievance about her job was primarily "personal in nature" and not a matter of public concern.[20]

On the other hand, a federal court protected a New Jersey teacher, Arthur Wichert, against being discharged for making derogatory public statements about his board of education.[21] In answer to a reporter's question, Wichert had criticized the board's transfer of a fellow teacher as a "ridiculous, stupid, and obvious political move." Wichert was then charged with "insubordination" and "unbecoming conduct" because of his intentionally "reckless," "false," and "misleading" statements. But the court ruled that an employee's statements are matters of public concern when they seek "to bring light on actual or potential wrongdoing. . . by government officials." "What distinguishes a democratic state from a totalitarian one," noted the judge, "is the freedom to speak and criticize the government. . . without fear of government retaliation."[22]

However, a federal appeals court ruled that the First Amendment did not protect an Indiana teacher who was not rehired because of a controversial newspaper interview concerning his termination as basketball coach.[23] According to this 1988 decision, a teacher's personal grievance is not transformed into a matter of public concern simply because there is a story about it in the newspaper.

How do courts rule when some of a teacher's speech is protected and some is not?

In these complex situations, the courts follow a four-step analysis. This process was illustrated by a case from Peoria, Illinois, involving Terry Knapp, a tenured high school teacher and coach who was reprimanded, relieved of his coaching duties, and transferred because of his repeated complaints to his principal and school board.[24] His complaints concerned his classroom assignment, his evaluations, the district's grievance procedure, the inequitable mileage allowance for coaches, and the inadequate liability insurance for coaches and parents who drove athletes to games.

The first step in the court's four-step analysis was to decide whether Knapp's complaints involved matters of public concern. The appeals court ruled that some did and some did not. According to Judge Coffey, classroom assignments and evaluations "are clearly personal matters relating solely to Knapp's employment." Therefore, the teacher's complaints about these issues are simply disagreements with "internal decisions made by his immediate superiors" and are not protected by the First Amendment.

The court ruled differently about Knapp's other complaints. The teacher's criticism of inequitable mileage allowances, wrote the judge, "enlightened the public" about the unequal expenditures and "involves not only Knapp but all of the coaches." The complaints about inadequate liability insurance, also, are about a matter of public concern in "today's litigious society." And the grievance procedure was an issue about which the school board requested teacher comments and was of concern to taxpayers who have a financial interest in the settlement of school disputes.

Since the court found that some of the teacher's complaints involved matters of public concern, the second step was to apply the Pickering test—balancing Knapp's interest as a citizen in discussing public issues against the board's interest as an employer in promoting efficiency. Since Knapp's complaints did not interfere with his teaching, did not cause disruption or destroy morale, and were directed at policies not individuals, the court ruled that the teacher's right to discuss public matters outweighed the interests of the administration and were protected by the First Amendment.

The third step was to ask, Was Knapp's protected speech a "substantial or motivating factor" in the board's action against him? Since the evidence indicated it was, the final issue to be decided was, Would the board have reached the same decision "even in the absence of the protected conduct?" The evidence indicated it would not. Therefore, Knapp was awarded compensatory damages and reassigned to his teaching and coaching jobs.

Do teachers have the right to circulate controversial petitions on school premises?

According to the California Supreme Court, they do.[25] In Los Angeles, the school board prohibited the circulation of a teachers' union petition to public officials protesting cutbacks in education funds and calling for an overhaul of the tax structure. The board prohibited the petition because it was controversial and would cause teachers to take opposing political positions, thereby creating discord. However, the liberal California court strongly defended the right of teachers to petition for redress of grievances.

The court pointed out that "tolerance of the unrest intrinsic to the expression of controversial ideas is constitutionally required even in the school." According to the court: "It cannot seriously be argued that school officials may demand a teaching faculty composed . . . of thinking individuals sworn never to share their ideas with one another for fear they may disagree." The court concluded: "Absent a showing of a clear and substantial threat to order and efficiency in the school, such proposed First Amendment activity should not be stifled."

Can a school prohibit distribution of potentially disruptive union material?

It depends on the circumstances. In Mobile, Alabama, when the school board proposed a teacher competency test, the union objected. Administrators allowed the distribution of letters supporting the board's position, but prohibited circulation of the union's views because of their "possible disruptive effect." A federal judge ruled that the board's action was unconstitutional since he found no difference in the "possible disruptive effect" of the communications of the board and the union.[26] While a school policy can prohibit distribution of disruptive material, the policy cannot permit the "unbridled discretion" that was used in this case to interfere with the "rights of teachers to communicate with each other."

When discussing a contract at an open meeting, can a school board prohibit nonunion members from speaking?

No. During contract negotiations in Madison, Wisconsin, a nonunion teacher was allowed to address the school board concerning a controversial contract provision over the objection of the union. The union claimed this constituted unauthorized negotiations, and the Wisconsin courts agreed. But the U.S. Supreme Court rejected the notion that nonunion statements were "negotiations." The Court wrote, "When the State has opened a forum for direct citizen involvement, it is difficult to find justification for excluding teachers . . . who are most vitally concerned." Whatever its duties as an employer, when a school board sits in public meetings to hear the views of citizens, it cannot be required to discriminate against speakers who are not members of the union.[27] (For a discussion of other collective bargaining issues see Chapter 3.)

Are teachers at private schools that receive state funds protected by the First Amendment?

Probably not. This was the ruling of the U.S. Supreme Court in a case concerning teachers who were dismissed from a private school for publicly opposing polices of the administration and publishing a letter protesting the school's picketing policy.[28] Although the state paid over 90 percent of the school's budget, the Court ruled that the acts of the school in dismissing the teachers did not become acts of the government since the government did not influence those actions. Thus, the First Amendment did not apply to this case since the discharge of the teachers was not a state action.

Do whistleblowing statutes protect teachers?

Yes. As of 1989, 35 states had passed whistleblowing laws that cover teachers and other employees who in good faith report a violation of law, gross waste of public funds, or specific dangers to public health, safety, or welfare.* These statutes protect teachers who make such reports against discharge, coercion, or discrimination and thus supplement rights protected by the First Amendment.[29]

CONTROVERSIAL ISSUES AND ACADEMIC FREEDOM

What is academic freedom?

Academic freedom includes the right of teachers to speak freely about their subjects, to experiment with new ideas, and to select appropriate teaching materials and methods. Courts have held that academic freedom is based on the First Amendment and is fundamental to our democratic society. It protects a teacher's right to evaluate and criticize existing values and practices in order to allow for political, social, economic, and scientific progress. Academic freedom is not absolute, and courts try to balance it against competing educational values.

Does academic freedom protect the assignment of controversial materials?

It may if the material is relevant to the subject, appropriate to the age and maturity of the students, and does not cause disruption. In Montgomery, Alabama, Marilyn Parducci assigned her eleventh-grade class a satire by Kurt Vonnegut, Jr., entitled "Welcome to the Monkey House." The next day her principal and associate superintendent advised her not to teach the story again. They described the story as "literary garbage," which condoned "the killing off of elderly people and free sex." Parducci considered the story a good literary piece and believed she had a professional obligation to teach it. Because she refused the advice of her principal and assigned "disruptive" material, she was dismissed. Parducci felt her dismissal violated her right to academic freedom.

A federal court agreed.[30] In considering the case, Judge Johnson first summarized the constitutional principles involved. The Supreme Court, he wrote, "has on numerous occasions" emphasized that academic freedom—the right to teach, to evaluate, and to experiment with new ideas—is "fundamental to a democratic society." On the other hand, academic freedom, like all other constitutional rights, is not absolute, and must be balanced against competing interests. According to Judge Johnson, school officials cannot restrict First Amendment rights unless they first demonstrate that "the forbidden conduct would *materially* and *substantially* interfere" with school discipline.

Applying these principles to this case, the court found that the school board

---

* States with whistleblowing statutes include Alaska, Arizona, Arkansas, California, Colorado, Connecticut, Delaware, Florida, Hawaii, Illinois, Indiana, Iowa, Kansas, Kentucky, Louisiana, Maine, Maryland, Michigan, Minnesota, Missouri, Nebraska, New Hampshire, New Jersey, New York, North Carolina, Ohio, Oregon, Pennsylvania, Rhode Island, South Carolina, Texas, Utah, Washington, West Virginia, and Wisconsin.

"failed to show either that the assignment was inappropriate reading for high school juniors or that it created a significant disruption to the educational process." Therefore, this liberal decision held that Parducci's dismissal "constituted an unwarranted invasion of her First Amendment right to academic freedom."

Can a school board require or prohibit the use of textbooks?

Yes. School boards usually have the authority to select or eliminate texts, even if teachers disagree with the board's decision. In Colorado, for example, a board approved a broad, diverse list of 1285 books for use in elective high school literature courses; however, they banned from the list 10 books that teachers had used. The teachers argued that this prohibition violated their rights. A federal appeals court disagreed.[31]

The court recognized that teachers do have "rights to freedom of expression in the classroom" and "cannot be made to simply read from a script prepared or approved by the board." In addition, the board probably cannot "prohibit mention of these books in class" or their brief discussion. State law, however, gives control of instruction to local school boards. Since these boards can eliminate an elective course completely, they can eliminate certain books from being assigned if their decisions are not arbitrary. The court distinguished this case from *Parducci*, since in that case the "school authorities acted in the absence of a general policy" and "after the fact." Thus, when teachers and school boards have a legitimate disagreement about what texts to use, the boards have the ultimate authority to make these decisions in elective as well as in required courses.

Can schools remove literary classics from the curriculum?

Yes. In Florida, a school board removed Aristophanes' *Lysistrata* and Chaucer's *The Miller's Tale* from the curriculum of an optional high school Humanities course because of their "sexuality and excessively vulgar language." A federal appeals court ruled that the board's action was not unconstitutional since it was reasonably related to legitimate educational concerns about the "exceptional sexual explicitness" in these books.[32]

This 1989 case illustrates the difference between what courts think is unlawful and unwise. Thus, the judges emphasized that they did "not endorse the Board's decision"; they only ruled that the books' removal was not unconstitutional. In fact, the judges wrote: "We seriously question how young persons just below the age of majority can be harmed by these masterpieces of Western Literature."

Can school boards reject texts for any reason?

No. A 1989 California decision explained that a school board's discretion to remove books must be exercised in a constitutional manner. Thus, a board's decision would be impermissible if it were based: (1) "upon disagreement with the constitutionally protected ideas contained in the books" or (2) "upon the board's desire to impose upon the students a religious [or political] orthodoxy."[33] Similarly, a federal appeals court held that a Minnesota school board could not constitutionally ban *The Lottery* from its American Literature course because a majority of the board "object to the film's religious and ideological content and wish to prevent the ideas contained in the material from being expressed in the school."[34] Furthermore, decisions cannot be based on a desire to promote a particular religious viewpoint by prohibiting texts that teach evolution or by requiring texts that teach "creation science."[35]

Nor do boards have the discretion to reject texts based on racially discriminatory motives. Thus, a federal court ruled that a decision to reject a controversial history book by a Mississippi textbook selection committee based on "an intent to perpetuate ideas of segregation and discrimination" was unconstitutional.[36]

Can social studies teachers be prohibited from discussing controversial issues?

No, it would probably be unconstitutional for a school official to order teachers of civics, history, or current events not to discuss any controversial questions. This was the ruling of a federal court in a case that arose in Stafford, Texas.[37] Parents objected to the way Henry Sterzing, a civics teacher, taught a unit on race relations and to his response to a question that indicated he did not oppose interracial marriage. As a result, the principal and the school board told him to teach his course "within the text and not discuss controversial issues." After Sterzing replied that it was impossible to teach current events to high school seniors and avoid controversial questions, he was dismissed for insubordination. But the court ruled that he could not be fired for discussing controversial issues. The judge acknowledged that a teacher has a duty to be "fair and objective in presenting his personally held opinions" and to ensure that different views are presented. In this case, however, the court held that Sterzing's classroom methods were "conducted within the ambit of professional standards" and that his statements in class neither interfered with discipline nor subjected students to unfair indoctrination.

In a related case, another Texas teacher, Janet Cooper, got into trouble for using a controversial "sunshine simulation" to teach about American history after the Civil War. The technique involved role playing by high school students and evoked strong feelings about racial issues. As a result, a number of parents complained to the school board, and Cooper was advised "not to discuss Blacks in American History." Because of her use of the simulation, Cooper's contract was not renewed. But she argued that her classroom discussions were protected by the First Amendment. A federal appeals court agreed, reinstated Cooper, and awarded her back pay and attorney's fees.[38]

In a third Texas case, a high school psychology teacher in a conservative community was fired for using a masculinity survey from *Psychology Today*.

But a federal district court ruled that the school violated her constitutional right "to engage in a teaching method of her choosing even though the subject matter may be controversial" without showing that it caused substantial disruption or that there was a clear, prior prohibition against it.[39]

Do teachers have the right to preach their religious beliefs in school?

No. In New York an art teacher was dismissed for recruiting students for her religious organization under the guise of guidance and for using classroom facilities during schooltime to preach about her religion. Since the teacher failed to stop discussing her beliefs and recruiting for her faith in school, a state court ruled that her actions were not protected.[40]

Does academic freedom allow teachers to disregard the text and syllabus?

No. A federal court considered this question when a biology teacher was not rehired for overemphasizing sex in his health course.[41] The teacher explained that his students "wanted sex education and mental health emphasized," and he agreed to "only touch on the other topics covered by the assigned text and course syllabus." In rejecting the teacher's contention that his First Amendment rights had been violated, the court ruled that he had no constitutional right "to override the . . . judgment of his superiors and fellow faculty members as to the proper content of the required health course." The court concluded that academic freedom is not "a license for uncontrolled expression at variance with established curricular content." Furthermore, an Alaska decision upheld the right of a school district to discipline a teacher for using a supplementary text that had not been approved in advance as clearly required by school policy.[42]

Can a teacher be punished for allowing a class to discuss personnel issues?

Usually, but not always. In 1987, a federal court ruled in favor of a high school social studies teacher who was punished after he allowed students to discuss their principal's contract renewal and to circulate a petition in his support in class.[43] The court acknowledged that teachers should not communicate their "personal prejudices" about controversial issues, but in this case it found no evidence that the teacher "tried to propagandize his views." Instead, he "merely allowed the students to discuss the issue and to use class time to organize their own petition drive." According to this liberal decision, "these factors add up to an exercise of First Amendment rights."

Can teachers be punished for discussing topics or distributing materials that are not relevant?

Yes. Academic freedom does not protect materials, discussions, or comments that are not relevant to the assigned subject. A federal case from Cook County, Illinois, illustrated this point when it upheld the dismissal of three eighth-grade teachers for distributing movie brochures about the 1969 rock festival "Woodstock."[44] These contained various pictures, articles, and poems that included positive views on drugs, sexual freedom, and vulgar language. The three teachers taught French, industrial arts, and language arts. The brochures were distributed to any student who wanted them ("to promote rapport"), but the teachers did not relate the brochures to what the students were studying. In addition to being irrelevant, the court found that the brochures were inappropriate for eighth-grade students and promoted a viewpoint on drug use that was contrary to what state law required students to be taught about the "harmful effects of narcotics."

Similarly a court upheld the dismissal of a St. Louis teacher who told his math class that army recruiters had no right to be at their high school and that the students could push the recruiters, throw apples at them, make them feel unwanted, and get them off campus. The teacher argued that he should not be dismissed because his comments did not cause substantial disruption and therefore were protected by the First Amendment. But the court ruled that his statements were not protected since they were "completely irrelevant" to his math class and "diverted the time and attention of both students and teacher from the prescribed curriculum."[45]

Can a teacher be punished if his use of approved materials causes substantial disruption in the community?

Probably not. In Michigan, the teaching of an approved unit on human reproduction in a seventh-grade life science class led to an uproar in the community. It also resulted in widely publicized charges against the teacher that were false, his suspension without a fair hearing, and a large jury verdict in his favor. An appeals court said that the school board's actions were irresponsible, violated the teacher's academic freedom, and injured his professional career. However, the court ruled that the citizen who organized the protests against the teacher's course should not be held liable since her charges to the school board were protected by her First Amendment right to petition the government.

The trial court had awarded three types of damages: (1) to compensate the teacher for actual harm done (e.g., medical or emotional injury), (2) to punish school officials for malicious conduct, and (3) to compensate the teacher for damages based on the importance of his constitutional rights. The U.S. Supreme Court reversed the trial court on the issue of constitutional damages. The Court did not question the legitimacy of the compensatory or punitive damages, but it ruled that an individual could not be compensated for the "abstract value" of his constitutional rights.[46]

Can a teacher be punished for showing an R-rated film to students?

Probably, although it may depend on the students, the movie, and how it is shown. An example of how not to do it is provided by the case of Jacqueline Fowler, a tenured Kentucky teacher, who was fired for showing an

R-rated film, *Pink Floyd—The Wall*, to students in grades nine through eleven. The movie was shown at the request of students on the "noninstructional" last day of school while Fowler was completing grade cards. She had not seen the film, did not discuss it with the class, but asked one of the students to "edit out" any parts that were unsuitable for viewing in school. He attempted to do this by holding a 8½ × 11-inch file folder in front of the 25-inch screen.

Fowler argued that the film contained "important, socially valuable messages." But a federal appeals court held that in this case it was not a constitutionally protected educational activity.[47] The judge concluded that by introducing a "controversial and sexually explicit movie into a classroom of adolescents without preview, preparation, or discussion," Fowler "abdicated her function as an educator" and demonstrated a "blatant lack of judgement" that constituted "conduct unbecoming a teacher."

The *Keefe* Case[48]

Robert Keefe, a high school English teacher from Ipswich, Massachusetts, wanted to expose his students to provocative contemporary writing. He gave each member of his class a recent issue of the *Atlantic Monthly* magazine and assigned the lead article, which discussed dissent, protest, and revolt. Entitled "The Young and the Old," the article contained the term *motherfucker*, which was repeated a number of times.

Although there was no evidence of negative student reaction to the article, a number of parents found the "dirty" word offensive and protested to the school committee. Members of the committee asked Keefe if he would agree not to use the word again in class. But Keefe refused to agree (as a matter of conscience) and was dismissed. His case raises a number of issues about controversial speech and illustrates how one federal appeals court treated them.

Can teachers assign articles with vulgar words?

It depends on the quality of the article and the way in which the language is used. In this case, the judge read the article and found it "scholarly, thoughtful, and thought-provoking." The court said it was not possible to read this article as an "incitement to libidinous conduct." If it raised the concept of incest, wrote the judge, "it was not to suggest it but to condemn it," for the word was used "as a superlative of opprobrium."

Assuming the article had merit, couldn't the teacher have discussed it without using the controversial word?

Not in this case. Here the offending word was not artificially introduced but was important to the thesis and conclusions of the author. Therefore, no proper study of the article could avoid considering the controversial word.

Can schools prohibit offensive language?

Usually they can. But it might depend on the specific situation—the age of the students, the word used, and the purpose of its use. In this instance the word was used for educational purposes among high school seniors. Under these circumstances, the judge doubted that quoting a "dirty" word in current use would be a shock to these students or that they needed to be "protected from such exposure." In a frequently quoted conclusion, the court wrote that the sensibilities of offended parents "are not the full measure of what is proper in education."

Does a teacher have the right to use "any" language in the classroom?

No. In fact, the court acknowledged that "some measure of public regulation of classroom speech is inherent in every provision of public education." But the judge ruled that the application of such a regulation in the *Keefe* case "demeans any proper concept of education."

TEACHING METHODS

Can a teacher be punished for using a controversial teaching method that is not clearly prohibited?

Not usually. If a teacher does not know that a certain method is prohibited, it would probably be a violation of due process for the teacher to be punished for using that method unless it had no recognized educational purpose. (The concept of due process for teachers is discussed more fully in Chapter 11.)

In Lawrence, Massachusetts, an eleventh-grade English teacher, Roger Mailloux, was discussing a novel about conservative customs in rural Kentucky when a student said that the custom of seating boys and girls on opposite sides of the classroom was ridiculous. Mailloux said that some current attitudes are just as ridiculous. As an example he introduced the subject of taboo words and wrote the word *fuck* on the blackboard. He then "asked the class in general for an explanation. After a couple of minutes, a boy volunteered the word meant 'sexual intercourse.' Plaintiff [Mailloux], without using the word orally, said: 'We have two words, sexual intercourse, and this word on the board; one is accepted by society, the other is not accepted. It is a taboo word.' " After a few minutes of discussion, Mailloux went on to other matters.

As a result of this incident, a parent complained and an investigation took place; Mailloux was dismissed and took his case to court. The court found that Mailloux's method did not disturb the students, that the topic of taboo words was relevant to the subject, and that the word *fuck* was relevant to the topic of taboo words.[49] ("Its impact," wrote the judge, "effectively illustrates how taboo words function.") The court also found that educational experts were in conflict about Mailloux's method: Some thought the way he used the word was reasonable and appropriate; others did not.

With these facts in mind, the judge discussed the law in such cases. The *Keefe* case, wrote the court, upheld two kinds of academic freedom: the "substantive" right of a teacher to choose a teaching method that serves a "demonstrated" educational purpose and the "procedural" right of a teacher not to be discharged for the use of a teaching method not prohibited by clear regulation. This procedural protection is afforded a teacher because he is engaged in the exercise of "vital First Amendment rights," and he should not be required to "guess what conduct or utterance may lose him his position." Since Mailloux did not know that his conduct was prohibited, the court ruled that it was a violation of due process for the school committee to discharge him.

In a related California case, Eileen Olicker, a young reading teacher, was dismissed for distributing students' writings containing vulgar descriptions of sexual organs and the sex act. The material was written as part of a class assignment for poor readers, who were told that they could write about anything they chose and that their stories would be shared with the class. Olicker was dismissed after a student she had disciplined left a copy of the material in the principal's box a month after the incident.

In a 2–1 decision, a state appeals court ruled in Olicker's favor.[50] The court noted that she had been an unusually sensitive, dedicated, and effective teacher and that this one incident did not cause "any disruption or impairment of discipline." Moreover, two experts testified that Olicker's method of having students write about subjects that interested them was "a sound educational approach," although they would not have reproduced the materials. The majority concluded that teachers should not be disciplined "merely because they made a reasonable, good faith, professional judgment in the course of their employment with which higher authorities later disagreed."

When are controversial methods not protected?

When methods are inappropriate, when they are not supported by any significant professional opinion, or when they are clearly prohibited by reasonable school policy, they are not likely to be protected by academic freedom. The following cases indicate when two courts were unwilling to protect controversial methods and why.

Allen Celestine, a fifth-grade teacher from Louisiana, became increasingly concerned about the vulgar language used by his students. Therefore, when two girls in his class used the word *fuck,* he required them to write it 1000 times. As a result, he was dismissed for incompetence. Celestine claimed that his academic freedom should protect his choice of punishment, but no educational experts defended Celestine's method, and a state court ruled against him.[51] It wrote that the First Amendment does not entitle a teacher to require young students to use vulgar words "particularly when no academic or educational purpose can possibly be served."

Frances Ahern, a high school economics teacher, attended a summer institute that led her to change her teaching methods and allow students to determine course topics and materials. She also began spending substantial time discussing classroom rules and school conflicts and policies. The principal directed her to stop discussing school politics, to teach economics, and to use more conventional teaching methods. When Ahern ignored the warning, she was dismissed. The teacher defended her action in the interest of "guarding her academic freedom to select the method of teaching to be employed in the classroom." But a federal appeals court ruled that the Constitution does not give a teacher the right to use methods which violate valid administrative requirements.[52]

Is it legal for a school to refuse to rehire a teacher because of basic disagreement over teaching methods and philosophy?

Probably. For example, Phyllis Hetrick was not rehired as an English instructor at a college in Kentucky. The college expected instructors "to teach on a basic level, to stress fundamentals, and to follow conventional teaching patterns." Hetrick emphasized student freedom and choice and failed to cover the material she had been told to teach. The issue in this case, wrote a federal court, is not which educational philosophy has greater merit but whether a school "has the right to require some conformity" to its educational philosophy and whether it may decline to hire a teacher whose methods are not conducive "to the achievement of the academic goals they espoused." In ruling for the administration, the court wrote that academic freedom "does not encompass the right of a non-tenured teacher to have her teaching methods insulated from review."[53] Similarly, the Washington Supreme Court ruled that requiring high school history teachers to teach in a conventional manner contrary to their teaching philosophy did not violate their academic freedom.[54]

Is academic freedom the same in public schools and in colleges?

No. While academic freedom applies to all teachers employed by the state, the scope of this freedom is usually broader in colleges and universities than in public schools. In *Mailloux*, Judge Wyzanski explained that this is so because in secondary schools "the faculty does not have the independent traditions, the broad discretion as to teaching methods, nor usually the intellectual qualifications, of university professors. . . . Some teachers and most students have limited intellectual and emotional maturity. . . . While secondary schools are not rigid disciplinary institutions, neither are they open forums in which mature adults, already habituated to social restraints, exchange ideas on a level of parity. Moreover . . . a secondary school student, unlike most college students, is usually required to attend school classes, and may have no choice as to his teacher."[55]

STUDENTS AND FREE SPEECH

The *Wooster* Case[56]

Earl Wooster was expelled from a California high school because he refused to apologize for a controversial speech he made during a school assembly. The speech was highly critical of the Fresno School Board for "compelling" students to use "unsafe" facilities, and it included caustic comments about some of the board's policies. School officials called Wooster's talk a "breach of school discipline" that was intended to discredit the board in the eyes of the students. A state court agreed and wrote that Wooster's refusal to apologize not only "accentuated his misconduct" but also "made it necessary" to expel him to maintain school discipline.

The *Wooster* case was decided in 1915. Wooster's lawyer didn't even raise the possibility that his client's speech might be protected by the Constitution. How would the case be decided today? Even if students have freedom of speech in public schools, can't schools restrict that freedom? Can administrators, for example, limit student speech if they fear it will lead to disruption or if they know it will offend other students? Some of these questions are confronted by the Supreme Court in the following controversy.

The *Tinker* Case[57]

Does freedom of speech apply to students in the classroom?

In 1965, when the debate over American involvement in the Vietnam war was becoming heated, a group of students in Des Moines, Iowa, decided to publicize their antiwar views by wearing black armbands. On learning of the plan, principals of the Des Moines schools established a policy prohibiting armbands in order to prevent any possible disturbance. Although they knew about the policy, several students wore armbands to school, refused to remove them, and were suspended. Although a federal judge ruled that the anti-armband policy was reasonable, the students appealed their case to the Supreme Court, presenting it as a conflict between their rights and the rules of the school.

First, the Court outlined the legal principles to be applied. While it recognized that school officials must have authority to control student conduct, it held that neither students nor teachers "shed their constitutional rights to freedom of speech or expression at the schoolhouse gate." To support this ruling, Justice Fortas noted that since school boards "are educating the young for citizenship," they should scrupulously protect the "constitutional freedoms of the individual, if we are not to strangle the free mind at its source and teach youth to discount important principles of our government as mere platitudes."

Concerning this particular case, the Court wrote that the First Amendment protects symbolic speech as well as pure speech. The wearing of an armband to express certain views is the kind of symbolic act protected by that amendment. After reviewing the facts, the Court found "no evidence whatsoever" that wearing armbands interfered "with the school's work or with the rights of other students to be secure or to be left alone." School officials might have honestly feared that the armbands would lead to a disturbance, but the Court said that this fear was not sufficient to violate student rights. "In our system," wrote the Court, "undifferentiated fear or apprehension of disturbance is not enough to overcome the right to freedom of expression."

While the Court recognized that free speech in the schools may cause problems, it noted that "any word spoken in class, in the lunchroom, or on the campus that deviates from the views of another person may start an argument or cause a disturbance. But our Constitution says we must take this risk: and our history says that it is this sort of hazardous freedom—this kind of openness— that is the basis of our national strength and of the independence and vigor of Americans who grow up and live in this relatively permissive, often disputatious society."

In a provocative comment about education and freedom, the Court wrote: "In our system, state operated schools may not be enclaves of totalitarianism. . . . Students in schools as well as out of school are possessed of fundamental rights which the State must respect, just as they themselves must respect their obligations to the State. In our system, students may not be regarded as closed-circuit recipients of only that which the State chooses to communicate."

In sum, the *Tinker* case held that school officials cannot prohibit a particular opinion merely "to avoid the discomfort and unpleasantness that always accompany an unpopular viewpoint." On the contrary, unless there is evidence that the forbidden expression would "materially and substantially" interfere with the work of the school, such a prohibition is unconstitutional.

Does the *Tinker* decision apply only to the classroom?

No. The Court ruled that the principles of this case are not confined to the curriculum or to classroom hours. On the contrary, a student's right to freedom of expression applies equally "in the cafeteria, or on the playing field" and in other school activities.

Can schools legally limit student expression or symbolic speech?

Yes. There are limits to all constitutional rights. In *Tinker,* the Court stated that any student conduct which "materially disrupts classwork or involves substantial disorder or invasion of the rights of others is, of course, not immunized by the Constitutional guarantee of freedom of speech." Thus, a federal appeals court upheld the rule of a Cleveland high school forbidding all buttons and badges because the wearing of some symbols had led to fighting between black students and white students.[58] Evidence indicated that if all symbols were permitted, racial tensions would be intensified and the educational process would be "significantly and substantially disrupted."

Must officials wait until a disruption has occurred?

No. In a case involving a student demonstration inside a high school, a federal judge ruled that the First Amendment does not require school officials to wait until actual disruption takes place before they may act.[59] The judge explained that an official may take reasonable action to restrict student expression when there is significant evidence to conclude that there is a "reasonable likelihood of substantial disorder."

A federal court reached a similar conclusion in an Indiana case in which several high school students were suspended for distributing leaflets calling for a "School Walkout." Since the leaflets did not cause a substantial disruption (only four students walked out), the suspended students claimed their leaflets should be protected. But the judge disagreed. He pointed out that student expression is not protected where school officials "can demonstrate any facts" which might reasonably lead them "to forecast substantial disruption" of school activities. Since fifty-four students had disrupted classes when they participated in a walk-out the day before, and since the administrators had reason to believe that the leaflets would prompt another substantial disruption, they met their burden of justifying a "reasonable forecast" of material disruption in light of the specific circumstances of this case.[60]

Can officials always restrict symbols that might lead to disruption?

Not according to a Texas case where officials prohibited armbands because they expected those who opposed the armbands to cause disruption.[61] Since no one thought the armband wearers would cause trouble, the court ruled that the expectation of disruption by others was not enough to suspend the students' right of symbolic speech. What more was required? To justify the school's action, administrators should determine "based on fact, not intuition" that disruption would probably result from wearing the armbands. In addition, officials should make an effort to bring leaders of different student factions together to agree on mutual respect for each other's constitutional rights. If actions such as these had been tried and failed, this failure might have justified restricting the armbands.

Can administrators change a school's symbol against the wishes of most students?

Yes. For years, the symbol of Virginia's Fairfax High School Rebels was "Johnny Reb." The principal eliminated the symbol after receiving complaints that it offended black students, and he allowed students to choose a new symbol unrelated to the Confederacy. But many students protested the elimination of their traditional symbol and claimed that the principal censored their expression. However, a federal judge disagreed. He explained that educators might have to tolerate students' symbolic speech, but have no obligation to sponsor it.[62] Since a school symbol "bears the stamp of approval" of the institution, administrators "are free to disassociate the school from such a symbol" because of the educational concerns that prompted the principal's decision.

Can demonstrations be prohibited near the school?

If they interfere with schoolwork, they can. The Supreme Court upheld the conviction of a high school student who violated a law prohibiting demonstrations on or near school grounds that disturbed classes.[63] In upholding the law, Justice Marshall noted that the constitutionality of a restriction may depend on what is being regulated and where. Making a speech in a public park might be protected, while making the same speech in a public library might not be. "The crucial question," wrote the Court, "is whether the manner of expression is basically incompatible with the normal activity of a particular place at a particular time." Just as *Tinker* made clear that free speech is not off limits in the schools, so Marshall emphasized that "the public sidewalk adjacent to school grounds may not be declared off-limits for expressive activity." Thus a federal judge recently ruled that a school policy broadly prohibiting "distribution of any materials" on a public sidewalk in front of an Illinois high school violated the First Amendment rights of a citizen who wanted to peacefully pass out Bibles there.[64] However, protected expression may be prohibited if it "materially disrupts classwork."

Are "fighting words" protected?

No. In a Pennsylvania case, a high school senior was punished when he loudly commented to a friend off campus that his teacher was "a prick."[65] The court said that the student's conduct involved an invasion of the right of the teacher "to be free from being loudly insulted in a public place." The judge concluded that the use of "fighting words—those which by their very utterance inflict injury"—is not protected by the constitutional guarantee of freedom of speech.

Can school officials punish lewd and offensive speech?

Yes. In a 1986 decision, the U.S. Supreme Court held that school officials have broad authority to punish students for using "offensively lewd and indecent speech" in school-sponsored educational activities. The case arose in Bethel, Washington, when a high school senior, Matthew Fraser, gave a nominating speech at a school assembly that referred to his candidate using terms of "an elaborate, graphic, and explicit sexual metaphor."[66] The Court ruled that such speech could be punished even if it was not legally obscene and did not cause substantial disruption. Furthermore, *Fraser* held that school officials have discretion to determine "what manner of speech" is vulgar and offensive in classrooms and assemblies. However, the *Fraser* decision does not apply to speech about political, religious, educational, or other controversial public policy issues that is not indecent. Such speech is still protected by the First Amendment unless it causes substantial disruption or interferes with the rights of others.*

Can a student be punished for "discourteous" remarks at a school assembly?

According to some federal appellate judges, he can. The case arose in Tennessee when Dean Poling, a candidate for president of his high school council, gave a speech which included "discourteous" statements about the administration and the vice principal. As a result, he was disqualified as a candidate and went to court.

A majority of the judges ruled against Poling. Although they acknowledged that the school administration may have overreacted to the speech (which contained no vulgar language), the court wrote that such a "judgment call is best left to the locally elected school board, not to a distant, life-tenured judiciary."[67] Since the election assembly was a school-sponsored educational activity, the actions of the administration should be upheld if related to "legitimate pedagogical concerns." According to the majority, "the art of stating one's views . . . without unnecessarily hurting the feelings of others surely has a legitimate place in any high school curriculum."

In a strong dissenting opinion, Judge Merritt wrote: "If the school administration can silence a student criticizing it for being narrow-minded and authoritarian, how can students engage in political dialogue with their educators about their education?"

Can states make it a crime to insult teachers?

Probably not. In 1985, state courts in Kentucky and Washington held that statutes that made it a crime for anyone to "insult or abuse any teacher in the public schools" were unconstitutionally vague and overbroad and, consequently, in violation of the First Amendment. This does not mean that schools cannot punish students for insulting and abusing teachers; it only means that criminal statutes that apply to all citizens and restrict speech must be more precise and narrow in scope.[68]

Do students have a right to remain silent?

Yes. Closely related to the right to speak is the right to remain silent—especially in relation to matters of conscience. (A detailed discussion of students' rights under freedom of conscience can be found in Chapter 9.) Thus, students cannot be compelled to say the Pledge of Allegiance or salute the flag. Similarly, a court ruled in favor of a New Jersey student who refused to stand during the Pledge.[69] The judge wrote that the state cannot require a student to

---

* For more information on this topic, see David Schimmel," Lewd Language Not Protected: *Bethel v. Fraser*," 33 Ed. Law Rep., 999 (1986).

engage in "implicit expression" by standing at attention while the flag is being saluted. A requirement that students engage in a form of symbolic speech is unconstitutional and interferes with the students' right "not to participate" in the flag ceremony.

Do students have a right to academic freedom?

No. Although student choice in courses, curriculum materials, assignments, teachers, and schools is increasing in some school districts, this is a matter of educational policy and not a constitutional right. Courts have not ruled that students have a right to determine courses, texts, or teaching methods. Thus a federal appeals court held that students have no constitutional right to challenge a school board's decision to eliminate a popular course or remove certain books from the curriculum.[70]

Can schools remove controversial books from a school library?

The answer depends on the facts of the case. After obtaining a list of "objectionable" books from a conservative parents' organization, a New York school board removed 10 books from their school libraries because they were "anti-American, anti-Christian, anti-Semitic and just plain filthy." But a group of students and parents claimed that the board's action was unconstitutional, and a majority of the U.S. Supreme Court agreed.[71] Justice Brennan emphasized that students' First Amendment rights are applicable to the school library, and that a school board's discretion "may not be exercised in a narrowly partisan or political manner" because "our Constitution does not permit the official suppression of ideas."

If board members "intended by their removal decision" to deny students "access to ideas" with which the board disagreed and if this intent was "the decisive factor" in the board's decision, then the board's action was unconstitutional. On the other hand, Justice Brennan indicated several legitimate motivations for removing library books, including pervasive vulgarity, educational suitability, "good taste," "relevance," and "appropriateness to age and grade level."

In sum, to avoid violating the First Amendment, "boards may not remove books from school library shelves simply because they dislike the ideas contained in those books." Rather, they should establish and follow constitutional criteria and reasonable procedures before removing controversial material.[72] (The related issue of a student's right to hear controversial speakers is considered in Chapter 10.)

Under some state laws, judges have gone further than the U.S. Supreme Court in protecting students' and teachers' First Amendment rights. Thus, in 1989, a California appeals court ruled that a school district could not remove five books of award-winning author Richard Brautigan from a high school library because they were not "socially acceptable" and contained offensive language. The court's liberal majority concluded that under California law "the

Board did not have the authority to remove the Brautigan books from the school library based on their perceived offensive content.[73]

STUDENT PUBLICATIONS

Can schools regulate student publications?

The answer depends on whether the publication is sponsored by the school as part of the curriculum. If it is, educators have substantial control over its contents and style. However, underground student newspapers that are written and published off campus are protected by the First Amendment according to the principles of the *Tinker* decision. The following cases examine the scope and limits of school authority to regulate different types of student publications.

The *Hazelwood* Case: School-Sponsored Publications

Can educators control publications sponsored by the school?

Yes. The Supreme Court explained the scope of such control in a case that arose in Missouri's Hazelwood High School. The controversy concerned two stories that were deleted by principal Robert Reynolds from *Spectrum*, a newspaper published by the Journalism II class. The first described three students' experiences with pregnancy. Although the article used false names, Reynolds was concerned that the students still might be identifiable and that references to sexuality were inappropriate for younger students. Reynolds objected to the second article about divorce because one student complained about her father's behavior without giving the father an opportunity to respond.

Staff members of *Spectrum* charged that the principal violated their First Amendment rights, but a majority of the Supreme Court disagreed.[74] The Court ruled that educators can exercise substantial control over school-sponsored activities such as student publications or plays that are part of the curriculum, "whether or not they occur in a traditional classroom setting."

Can educators regulate the contents of school-sponsored publications or plays even if they do not cause disruption?

Yes. This is because the school, as publisher of a newspaper or producer of a play, may "refuse to lend its name and resources" to student expression that does not meet its "high standards." Thus, educators have broad discretion to prohibit articles that are "ungrammatical, poorly written, inadequately researched, biased or prejudiced, vulgar or profane, or unsuitable for immature audiences." Furthermore, schools may refuse to sponsor student expression that may "advocate drug or alcohol use, irresponsible sex" or associate the school with a controversial political position. The Court held that educators do not violate the First Amendment by "exercising editorial control over the style and content of student speech in school-sponsored expressive activities so long as their actions are reasonably related to legitimate pedagogical concerns." Thus, in *Hazelwood*, the Court ruled that the principal acted reasonably in removing the articles about pregnancy and divorce because of concern about protecting student anonymity and the privacy interests of the father, as well as protecting younger students from the "frank talk" about sex.

Are there limits to administrative control over school-sponsored publications or plays?

Yes. According to the Court, educators do not have unlimited discretion "to censor a school-sponsored publication" or theatrical production. Such censorship would violate the Constitution if it had "no valid educational purpose" or was "unreasonable." For example, if schools permitted articles or editorials about political or social issues, it would probably be unconstitutional to censor student views simply because administrators, parents, or other students disagreed.

Does *Hazelwood* require educators to control the contents of school-sponsored publications?

No. *Hazelwood* only ruled that schools *may* control school-sponsored publications. Such regulation is not required. In fact, state laws or school board policies may prohibit broad administrative control over student publications.

In California, for example, the Education Code states that "students of the public school shall have the right to exercise freedom of speech and of the press . . .in official publications . . . supported financially by the school."[75] Thus, in a case concerning an allegedly defamatory article in a faculty-supervised school newspaper, a California judge wrote: "The broad power to censor expression in school-sponsored publications for pedagogical purposes recognized in [*Hazelwood* v.] *Kuhlmeier* is not available to this state's educators."[76] The judge noted that administrators "may censor expression from official school publications which . . . contain actionable defamation, but not as a matter of taste or pedagogy." Similarly, a Massachusetts law protects the right of students "to write, publish, and disseminate their views" in the public schools "provided that such right shall not cause any disruption."[77]

Underground Publications

Does the *Hazelwood* decision apply to student publications that are not sponsored by the school?

No. *Hazelwood* does not give educators control over the style and content of "underground" student periodicals that are published without school sponsorship or support and are not part of the curriculum. Instead, the *Tinker* case governs underground publications, which usually cannot be restricted unless they are libelous or obscene or are likely to cause substantial disruption or interfere with the rights of others.

Can an underground newspaper be banned for discussing controversial or unpopular topics?

No. In a case involving a high school underground paper, a federal appeals court wrote: "It should be axiomatic at this point in our nation's history that in a democracy 'controversy' is, as a matter of constitutional law, never sufficient in and of itself to stifle the views of any citizen."[78] The controversial subjects in the student publication included a statement about the injustice of current drug laws and an offer of information about birth control, venereal disease, and drug counseling. The court seemed surprised that an educational institution "would boggle at controversy" to such an extent that it would restrict a student publication merely because it urged students to become informed about these widely discussed and significant issues. The court commented that "our recollection of the learning process is that the purpose of education is to spread, not to stifle, ideas and views. Ideas must be freed from despotic dispensation by all men, be they robed as academicians or judges or citizen members of a board of education."[79]

Can an underground publication be prohibited from criticizing school officials?

No, such criticism is protected by the First Amendment. In a Texas case, school officials defended their ban of a student newspaper because of its "negative attitude" and its criticism of the administration.[80] In rejecting this defense, the court explained that "aversion to criticism" is not a constitutional justification for restricting student expression. The Bill of Rights, wrote the court, protects freedom of the press precisely because those regulated "should have the right and even the responsibility" of commenting upon the actions of their regulators.

In a related Illinois case, a student was suspended for writing an editorial in an underground paper that criticized the senior dean and indicated that in the student's opinion one of the dean's statements was "the product of a sick mind."[81] The court acknowledged that the editorial reflected a "disrespectful and tasteless attitude toward authority." Nevertheless, it ruled that the statement itself did not justify suspending the student. As *Tinker* pointed out, schools cannot punish students merely because they express feelings that officials do not want to confront.

Can an underground newspaper be prohibited from criticizing school policies?

No. Mere criticism of school rules and policies is not enough to allow officials to ban student publications or punish the writers. To support such action, officials would have to show that the publications caused or would probably cause substantial and material disruption.

In the Illinois case mentioned in the previous question, the student editorial had strongly criticized some school procedures as "utterly idiotic and asinine" and called the school's detention policy "despicable and disgusting." The court ruled that this did not justify suspending the student responsible for the editorial. Moreover, the court noted that "prudent criticism" by high school students may be socially valuable because they possess a unique perspective on matters of school policy.

Do schools have any control over the distribution of underground publications?

Yes. Officials can enforce reasonable regulations concerning the place and the manner in which student publications are distributed, but the rules cannot be so restrictive that they have the effect of preventing the distribution of student views. This means that administrators could probably not prohibit all "in-school" distribution or distribution "while any class is being conducted" since such rules are broader than necessary for safety or to prevent disruption of school activities.[82] Examples of appropriate restrictions might include prohibiting distribution in laboratories, on stairways, or in narrow corridors and establishing rules aimed at minimizing litter on campus.

Can schools ever restrict the content of underground publications?

Yes. School officials may restrict the distribution of material that is libelous, obscene, or substantially disruptive. Officials cannot restrict an underground publication simply on the basis of their "fear," "intuition," or "belief" that it will cause disruption; their judgment must be supported by significant facts and evidence.

Libel is a false written statement that injures a person's reputation. A person who is libeled can sue for damages. If the person is a public figure, he or she must prove that the writer knew or should have known that the statement was untrue. Writing falsely that the principal stole $1000 would probably be libelous; an editorial alleging that "some teachers" in a school district are incompetent probably is not. (For more on libel, see Chapter 6.)

Is a publication obscene if it contains offensive, vulgar, or "dirty" language?

No. Many parents and teachers equate obscenity with offensive four-letter words, but this is not what lawyers and judges mean. To be legally obscene, material must violate three tests developed by the U.S. Supreme Court: (1) it must appeal to the prurient or lustful interest of minors, (2) it must describe sexual conduct in a way that is "patently offensive" to community standards, *and* (3) taken as a whole, it "must lack serious literary, artistic, political or scientific value."[83]

Parents, teachers, and administrators may be offended by student use of profanity in their writing; however, most controversial articles about social, political, or educational issues in underground newspapers, even though they may use offensive language, do not violate the three Supreme Court tests.

However, judges are less likely to protect student publications with vulgar offensive language and more likely to protect controversial political ideas.

Are policies that require administrative approval of underground publications unconstitutional?

Some courts believe they are. Their position is illustrated by a 1988 case that arose when five students at Washington's Lindbergh High School distributed 350 copies of an underground student newspaper, *Bad Astra*, at a senior class barbecue. The paper, which was printed off campus, included a mock teacher evaluation poll and articles that were critical of administrative policy. The students were censured for violating a school rule which required all student-written material to be submitted to the administration for approval before distribution on school property. However, the Ninth Circuit Court of Appeals held the rule unconstitutional.[84]

Since *Bad Astra* was not school-sponsored, the administration did not have authority to control its contents, and it should not have been targeted "for review for censorship." According to the court, "student distribution of non-school-sponsored material under the Supreme Court's decisions in *Tinker* and *Hazelwood* cannot be subjected to regulation on the basis of undifferentiated fears of possible disturbances or embarrassment." Since the school acknowledged that is would have approved the distribution of the paper after review, the judge noted that "no more than undifferentiated fear appears" as the basis for punishment in this case. The court concluded that there was no justification for Lindbergh's broad prior review policy "of unlimited scope and duration."

Similarly, an earlier decision by the Seventh Circuit Court of Appeals held that a rule requiring advance approval of student publications by the superintendent was "unconstitutional as a prior restraint in violation of the First Amendment."[85] The court indicated that schools could punish students who distribute literature that is obscene, libelous, or causes substantial disruption, but it ruled that schools could not require that all student publications be submitted to the administration for approval before distribution.

Do courts permit schools to require that underground publications be reviewed prior to distribution?

The federal courts are divided on this issue. As noted above, two appeals courts appear to hold that prior review policies are unconstitutional. But most circuit courts do not.[86] In 1987, for example, the Eighth Circuit Court of Appeals considered a Minnesota high school's guidelines requiring administrative review before the distribution of "unofficial written material on school premises."[87] Students who wanted to distribute an underground paper, *Tour de Farce*, claimed the guidelines violated their rights. However, the court ruled that the school's policy is "not unconstitutional merely because it asserts a right of prior review." Furthermore, the court approved the guidelines that prohibit material that is obscene, libelous, or disruptive or is "pervasively indecent or vulgar." Nevertheless, the judge reminded school officials that "criticism of established policies, even in vigorous or abrasive terms, is not be to equated with disruptiveness," and educators "are not at liberty to suppress or punish speech simply because they disagree with it."

What procedures and standards are necessary before schools can require prior review of student publications?

Some courts have held prior review procedures unconstitutional because they lacked either clear standards or due process safeguards. In a Maryland case, for example, a judge wrote that rules requiring prior review "must contain narrow, objective, and reasonable standards" by which the material will be judged.[88] Such standards are required so that those who enforce the rules are not given "impermissible power to judge the material on an ad hoc and subjective basis." The court emphasized that legal terms such as "libelous" or "obscene" used without explanation "are not sufficiently precise or understandable by high school students and administrators untutored in the law" to be acceptable criteria of what is prohibited. Therefore, prior review policies must contain "precise criteria sufficiently spelling out what is forbidden" so that students may clearly know what they may or may not write.

In another federal case, an appeals court declared a Texas school's prior review requirement unconstitutional because it lacked due process safe-guards.[89] There was no provision for an appeal if the principal prohibited distribution, nor did the rules state how long the principal could take to make her decision. Delays in reviewing newspapers, wrote the court, "carry the inherent danger that the exercise of speech might be chilled altogether during the period of its importance." Therefore, the court held that any requirement for screening student publications before distribution must clearly state (1) how students are to submit proposed materials to the administration, (2) a brief period of time during which the administration must make its decision, (3) a clear and reasonable method of appeal, and (4) a brief time during which the appeal must be decided. Due process should also provide for some kind of informal hearing for the students affected. Because the regulations challenged in this case provided none of these procedures and violated the students' First Amendment rights, the court commented that "it would be well if those entrusted to administer the teaching of American history and government to our students began their efforts by practicing the document on which that history and government are based."

Can administrators suppress student publications without written guidelines?

Sometimes. In a New York high school, for example, the principal seized all copies of a student newspaper because of a "threatening" letter falsely attributed to the lacrosse team and a "libelous" letter about the vice president of the student government. The student editors claimed that the principal could not legally suppress their paper because there were no specific school policies giving him that authority. A federal court disagreed, however.

The judge acknowledged that suppression of a publication by school officials must be "scrutinized more carefully" in the absence of guidelines. Nevertheless, Judge Pratt ruled that school officials have the power to prevent distribution within the school of material which is "libelous, obscene, . . . likely to create substantial disorder or which invades the rights of others," even if the school has no written policies on the subject.[90]

Can schools ban the sale of underground publications on campus?

Probably not. An Indiana case held that a rule prohibiting the sale of all publications except those benefiting the school was unconstitutional.[91] School officials had argued that newspaper sales and other commercial activities are "unnecessary distractions" that are "inherently disruptive." The judge acknowledged that administrators have a legitimate interest in limiting commercial activities on campus by nonstudents. But he pointed out that the reason the students sold the newspaper in this case was only to raise the money needed to publish their paper. The court noted that administrators have ample authority to regulate the time, place, and manner of newspaper sales to maintain order and avoid littering or interference with others without restricting First Amendment rights. In a related California case, the state supreme court wrote: "We fail to see how the *sale* of newspapers on the school premises will necessarily disrupt the work and discipline of the school, whereas their distribution free of charge will not."[92]

Can schools prohibit the distribution of material not written by a student or school employee?

Probably not. In the Indiana case mentioned in the preceding question, the court wrote that such a rule would prohibit use of materials by all sorts of people "whose views might be thought by the students to be worthy of circulation." And the judge indicated that he had "no doubt" that such a rule violated the students' First Amendment rights.[93]

Can schools prohibit the distribution of anonymous articles?

Not according to a federal judge who noted that historically anonymous publications have been an important vehicle for criticizing oppressive practices and laws and that anonymous student publications can perform a similar function in schools. "Without anonymity," wrote the judge, "fear of reprisal may deter peaceful discussion of controversial but important school rules and policies."[94] The problem with this prohibition, the court explained, is that it is not limited to potentially libelous, obscene, or disruptive material but applies equally to thoughtful, responsible criticism.

Can administrators ban the distribution of underground newspapers that contain advertisements for drug paraphernalia?

Yes. In a Maryland case, a federal appeals court upheld the authority of a high school principal to seize an "underground" publication because it contained an advertisement for a waterpipe used to smoke marijuana and hashish.[95] Student publishers of the nonschool-sponsored newspaper claimed the seizure violated their rights since the ad would not substantially disrupt school activities. The court rejected this argument, however.

Substantial disruption, wrote the judge, "is merely one justification for school authorities to restrain distribution," not the "sole justification." The judge noted that "advertisements encouraging the use of drugs" can endanger students' health. Therefore, the court ruled that the First Amendment rights of students "must yield to the superior interest of the school" in prohibiting the distribution of publications "that encourage actions which endanger the health or safety of students."

Can schools regulate off-campus publications?

Not according to Judge Irving Kaufman. The case concerned several high school students from a small, rural New York community who produced *Hard Times,* a satirical publication addressed to the school community. The language in the publication was considered "indecent," but it was not legally obscene. *Hard Times* was written, sold, and printed off campus. But when the president of the local school board learned about the publication, she urged administrative action. As a result, the school penalized the student publishers, and they took their case to court.

According to the court: "We may not permit school administrators to seek approval of the community-at-large by punishing students for expression that took place off school property. Nor may courts endorse such punishment because the populace would approve."[96] Despite the good intentions of school officials, Judge Kaufman said they must be restrained in moving against student expression since they act "as both a prosecutor and a judge" and since their desire to preserve decorum gives them "a vested interest in suppressing controversy." In addition, they are "generally unversed in difficult constitutional concepts such as libel and obscenity." For these reasons, the court concluded that the First Amendment "forbids public school administrators and teachers from regulating the material to which a child is exposed after he leaves school each afternoon."

Could officials ban *Hard Times* if students tried to distribute it on campus? In a concurring opinion, Judge Newman said yes. Even though the publication was not obscene, the judge felt that schools should be able to prohibit it since "by contemporary standards" it was "indecent and vulgar for school age children." The publication described itself as "vulgar." And this description, wrote Judge Newman, "was not false advertising." He believed that school authorities could regulate indecent language because "its circulation on school grounds undermines their responsibility to try to promote standards of decency" among students.

SUMMARY

For most of this century, the Constitution did not protect students or teachers when they spoke out on controversial issues. In 1969, however, the U.S. Supreme Court ruled that neither teachers nor students lose their right to freedom of expression when they enter the public schools. But freedom of expression, like most constitutional rights, is not absolute; it can be limited when it conflicts with other basic values.

To decide when a teacher's controversial out-of-class statements are protected, judges usually balance "the interests of the teacher, as citizen, in commenting on matters of public concern and the interests of the state, as employer, in promoting the efficiency of the schools." In the *Pickering* case, the Court emphasized that voters should be able to hear the informed opinions of teachers about public educational issues and that teachers should not be punished merely for expressing their views on controversial topics. If teachers' statements are constitutionally protected, they cannot be reprimanded, transferred, or otherwise disciplined for making them. On the other hand, courts have held that the First Amendment does not protect a teacher's false and reckless accusations, statements to the press about a personnel matter under investigation, scornful and abusive personal attacks on school officials, repeated criticism of teaching assignments and evaluations, or public disclosure of confidential information. Furthermore, the Supreme Court had ruled that if a teacher speaks, not as a citizen about matters of public concern, but as an employee about matters of personal interest, such views are not protected.

When teachers allege that they are unconstitutionally punished because of their statements, recent court decisions suggest a four-step analysis. (1) Do the statements involve matters of public concern? If so, (2) Does the teacher's right to discuss public matters outweigh the school's interest in promoting efficiency? If the court answers these questions in the affirmative, the teacher's statements would be protected by the First Amendment. But before judges order schools to rescind the punishment, they also ask, (3) Was the teacher's speech a substantial or motivating factor in the action against him? If so, (4) Did the administration prove that it would have taken the same action even in the absence of the protected conduct? If not, courts should find the punishment unconstitutional and perhaps award damages. Since judges have differing notions of what constitutes "a matter of public concern," and since they weight the rights of the teachers and the interests of the schools differently, the outcome of a close case may vary from one court to another.

In deciding whether to protect controversial teaching methods and materials, most courts use a "balancing test," a case-by-case inquiry that balances the teacher's right to academic freedom against the legitimate interests of the community. When judging academic freedom cases, courts give special consideration to the following factors: whether the controversial language or publication was relevant to the curriculum, whether it was appropriate to the age and maturity of the students, the quality of the teaching material and its effect on the students. According to most courts, even when schools can prohibit certain methods or materials, teachers should not be disciplined for using them unless teachers know they are prohibited.

In sum, teachers who are punished for using controversial materials that are relevant, appropriate, and nondisruptive are likely to be protected by the courts—especially if such materials were not clearly prohibited. Academic freedom, however, does not give teachers the right to refuse to use required texts or to ignore the established curriculum; nor does it protect incompetent teaching or religious or political indoctrination.[97]

Courts now recognize that the First Amendment applies to students as well as teachers. In *Tinker*, the Supreme Court held that it is unconstitutional to restrict student expression unless it would "materially and substantially interfere" with school activities. According to some courts, an "expectation of disruption" is not enough to justify suspending student rights unless (1) such an expectation is based on fact, not intuition, and (2) school officials first make an honest effort to restrain those who might cause the disruption. Schools can restrict symbolic expression when such symbols have caused material disruption in the past or when there is evidence that they would probably cause substantial disorder. Although officials may not suppress student access to ideas for political or religious reasons, they may remove library books which are pervasively vulgar or educationally unsuitable. Furthermore, the Supreme Court has ruled that students can be punished for using "vulgar and offensive" language in classes, assemblies, and other school-sponsored educational activities.

In the 1988 *Hazelwood* case, the Supreme Court held that educators had broad discretion to regulate the style and content of student expression in curriculum-related publications or plays. As a result, courts will probably uphold any regulation of school-sponsored publications or plays if the regulation is reasonable unless state laws protect student freedom of expression. *Hazelwood*, however, does not allow schools to control the contents of "underground" student periodicals that are written and published off campus without school support. Instead, *Tinker* governs such publications, which usually cannot be restricted unless they are libelous or obscene, or are likely to cause substantial disruption or interfere with the rights of others. Thus, underground student newspapers cannot be censored by school officials because they discuss unpopular or controversial topics, or criticize administrators, teachers, or school policies.

Schools have the right to establish reasonable rules regulating the time, place, and manner for distributing all student publications. Moreover, most courts allow schools to screen student publications prior to distribution if they have issued clear, objective standards and have procedural safeguards for the review process. And one court has ruled that even without written policies, officials can suppress a student publication that is libelous, obscene, or likely to create substantial disorder.

NOTES

1. *Pickering* v. *Board of Education,* 225 N.E.2d 1 (1967); 391 U.S. 563 (1968). For a more recent application of *Pickering,* see *Anderson* v. *Central Point School District No. 6,* 746 F.2d 505 (9th Cir. 1984).
2. *Bernasconi* v. *Tempe Elementary School District, No. 3,* 548 F.2d 857 (9th Cir. 1977).
3. *Rowland* v. *Mad River Local School District, Montgomery County,* 730 F.2d 444 (6th Cir. 1984). For other aspects of this case, see Chapter 12, p. 237.
4. *Swilley* v. *Alexander,* 448 F.Supp. 702 (S.D. Ala. 1978).
5. *Pietrunti* v. *Board of Education of Brick Township,* 319 A.2d 262 (N.J. 1974).
6. *Watts* v. *Seward School Board,* 454 P.2d 732 (Alaska 1969).
7. *Lusk* v. *Estes,* 361 F.Supp. 653 (N.D. Tex. 1973).
8. *Bowman* v. *Pulaski County Special School District,* 723 F.2d 640 (8th Cir. 1983).
9. *Gilbertson* v. *McAlister,* 403 F.Supp. 1 (D. Conn. 1975).
10. *Givhan* v. *Western Line Consolidated School District,* 439 U.S. 410 (1979); see also *Ayers* v. *Western Line Consolidated School District* 691 F.2d 766 (5th Cir. 1982).
11. *Anderson* v. *Evans,* 660 F.2d 153 (6th Cir. 1981).
12. *Anderson* v. *Central Point School District No. 6,* 746 F.2d 505 (9th Cir. 1984).
13. *Southside Public Schools* v. *Hill,* 827 F.2d 270 (8th Cir. 1987).
14. *Connick* v. *Myers,* 461 U.S. 138 (1983).
15. *Piver* v. *Pender County Board of Education,* 835 F.2d 1076 (4th Cir. 1987).
16. *Hesse* v. *Board of Education of Township High School District 211,* 848 F.2d 748 (7th Cir. 1988).
17. *Daniels* v. *Quinn,* 801 F.2d 687 (4th Cir. 1986).
18. *Ferrara* v. *Mills,* 596 F.Supp. 1069 (S.D. Fla. 1984), 761 F.2d 1508 (11th Cir. 1986).
19. *Derrickson* v. *Board of Education of the City of St. Louis,* 738 F.2d 351 (8th Cir. 1984).
20. *Renfroe* v. *Kirkpatrick,* 722 F.2d 714 (11th Cir. 1984), *cert. denied,* 469 U.S. 823 (1984).
21. *Wichert* v. *Walter,* 606 F.Supp. 1516 (D. N.J. 1985).
22. *Id.*
23. *Vukadinovich* v. *Bartels,* 853 F.2d 1387 (7th Cir. 1988).
24. *Knapp* v. *Whitaker,* 757 F.2d 827 (7th Cir. 1985).
25. *Los Angeles Teachers Union* v. *Los Angeles City Board of Education,* 455 P.2d 827 (Cal. 1969).
26. *Hall* v. *Board of School Commissioners of Mobile County, Alabama,* 681 F.2d 965 (5th Cir. 1982).
27. *City of Madison Joint School District No. 8* v. *Wisconsin Employment Relations Commission,* 429 U.S. 167 (1976).

28. *Rendell-Baker* v. *Kohn*, 457 U.S. 830 (1982).

29. Louise Ebeling, "Whistleblowing in the Public Schools," paper presented at the NOLPE Convention, San Francisco, November 18, 1989.

30. *Parducci* v. *Rutland*, 316 F.Supp. 352 (N.D. Ala. 1970).

31. *Cary* v. *Board of Education, Adams-Arapahoe School District*, 598 F.2d 535 (10th Cir. 1979).

32. *Virgil* v. *School Board of Columbia County, Florida*, 862 F.2d 1517 (11th Cir. 1989).

33. *McCarthy* v. *Fletcher*, 254 Cal. Rptr. 714 (Cal. App. 1989).

34. *Pratt* v. *Independent School District No. 831, Forest Lake*, 670 F.2d 771 (8th Cir. 1982).

35. *Epperson* v. *Arkansas*, 393 U.S. 97 (1968).

36. *Loewen* v. *Turnipseed*, 488 F.Supp. 1138 (N.D. Miss. 1980).

37. *Sterzing* v. *Ft. Bend Independent School District*, 376 F.Supp. 657 (S.D. Tex. 1972), 496 F.2d 92 (5th Cir. 1974).

38. *Kingsville Independent School District* v. *Cooper*, 611 F.2d 1109 (5th Cir. 1980).

39. *Dean* v. *Timpson Independent School District*, 486 F.Supp. 302 (E.D. Tex. 1979).

40. *La Rocca* v. *Board of Education of Rye City School District*, 406 N.Y.S.2d 348 (1978).

41. *Clark* v. *Holmes*, 474 F.2d 928 (7th Cir. 1972), *cert. denied*, 411 U.S. 972 (1973).

42. *Fisher* v. *Fairbanks North Star Borough School District*, 704 P.2d 213 (Alaska 1985).

43. *Piver* v. *Pender County Board of Education*, 835 F.2d 1076 (4th Cir. 1987).

44. *Brubaker* v. *Board of Education, School District 149, Cook County, Illinois*, 502 F.2d 973 (7th Cir. 1974).

45. *Birdwell* v. *Hazelwood School District*, 491 F.2d 490 (8th Cir. 1974).

46. *Stachura* v. *Truszkowski*, 763 F.2d 211 (6th Cir. 1985), *Memphis Community School District* v. *Stachura*, 477 U.S. 299 (1986).

47. *Fowler* v. *Board of Education of Lincoln County, Kentucky*, 819 F.2d 657 (6th Cir. 1987), *cert. denied*, 484 U.S. 986 (1987).

48. *Keefe* v. *Geanakos*, 418 F.2d 359 (1st Cir. 1969).

49. *Mailloux* v. *Kiley*, 323 F.Supp. 1387 (D. Mass. 1971), 448 F.2d 1242 (1st Cir. 1971).

50. *Oakland Unified School District* v. *Olicker*, 25 C.A.3d 1098 (1972).

51. *Celestine* v. *Lafayette Parish School Board*, 284 So.2d 650 (La. 1973).

52. *Ahern* v. *Board of Education of School District of Grand Island*, 456 F.2d 399 (8th Cir. 1972).

53. *Hetrick* v. *Martin*, 480 F.2d 705 (6th Cir. 1973).

54. *Millikan* v. *Board of Directors of Everett School District*, 611 P.2d 414 (Wash. 1980).

55. *Mailloux* v. *Kiley*, 323 F.Supp. 1387 (D. Mass. 1971).

56. *Wooster* v. *Sunderland*, 148 P. 959 (1915).

57. *Tinker* v. *Des Moines Independent School District*, 393 U.S. 503 (1969).

58. *Guzick* v. *Debras*, 431 F.2d 594 (6th Cir. 1970), *cert. denied*, 401 U.S. 948 (1971).

59. *Karp* v. *Becken*, 477 F.2d 171 (9th Cir. 1973).

60. *Dodd* v. *Rambis*, 535 F.Supp. 23 (S.D. Ind. 1981).

61. *Butts* v. *Dallas Independent School District*, 436 F.2d 728 (5th Cir. 1971).

62. *Crosby by Crosby* v. *Holsinger*, 852 F.2d 801 (4th Cir. 1988).
63. *Grayned* v. *City of Rockford*, 408 U.S. 104 (1972).
64. *Bacon* v. *Bradley-Bourbonnais High School District No. 307*, 707 F.Supp. 1005 (C.D. Ill. 1989).
65. *Fenton* v. *Stear*, 423 F.Supp. 767 (W.D. Penn. 1976).
66. The following excerpts are illustrative of Fraser's six sentence nominating speech: "I know a man who is firm—he's firm in his pants . . . his character is firm . . . he's a man who takes his point and pounds it in. . . . He doesn't attack things in spurts—he drives hard, pushing and pushing until finally he succeeds. Jeff is a man who will go to the very end—even the climax, for each and every one of you. . . ." *Bethel School District No. 403* v. *Fraser*, 478 U.S. 675 (1986).
67. *Poling* v. *Murphy*, 872 F.2d 757 (6th Cir. 1989).
68. *State* v. *Reyes*, 700 P.2d 1155 (Wash. 1985); *Commonwealth* v. *Ashcraft*, 691 S.W.2d 229 (Ky. App. 1985).
69. *Lipp* v. *Morris*, 579 F.2d 834 (3d Cir. 1978).
70. *Zykan* v. *Warsaw Community School Corporation*, 631 F.2d 1300 (7th Cir. 1980).
71. *Board of Education, Island Trees Union Free School District No. 26* v. *Pico*, 457 U.S. 853 (1982).
72. For more on this topic, see David Schimmel, "The Limits of School Board Discretion: Board of Education v. Pico," 6 ED. LAW REP., 285 (1983).
73. *Wexner* v. *Anderson Union High School District*, 258 Cal. Rptr. 26 (Cal. App. 1989).
74. *Hazelwood School District* v. *Kuhlmeier*, 484 U.S. 260 (1988).
75. *Leeb* v. *DeLong*, 243 Cal. Rptr. 494 (Cal. App. 1988).
76. *Id.* at 498.
77. Massachusetts General Laws, Chapter 71, Section 82 (1989).
78. *Shanley* v. *Northeast Independent School District*, 462 F.2d 960 (5th Cir. 1972).
79. *Id.*
80. *Id.*
81. *Scoville* v. *Board of Education of Joliet Township*, 425 F.2d 10 (7th Cir. 1970).
82. *Jacobs* v. *Board of School Commissioners*, 490 F.2d 601 (7th Cir. 1973).
83. *Miller* v. *California*, 413 U.S. 15 (1973).
84. *Burch* v. *Barker*, 861 F.2d 1149 (9th Cir. 1988).
85. *Fujishima* v. *Board of Education*, 460 F.2d 1355 (7th Cir. 1972).
86. For example, the Second Circuit allowed broad prior review in *Eisner* v. *Stamford Board of Education*, 440 F.2d 803 (1971), and the Fifth Circuit held that a policy of prior review was not unconstitutional "per se" in *Shanley, supra* Similarly, the First Circuit in *Riseman* v. *School Committee of Quincy*, 439 F.2d 148 (1971) and the Fourth Circuit in *Baughman* v. *Freienmuth*, 478 F.2d 1345 (1973) indicated that a narrowly drawn set of prior review guidelines would be constitutional.
87. *Bystrom* v. *Fidley High School Independent School District 14*, 822 F.2d 747 (8th Cir. 1987).
88. *Baughman* v. *Freienmuth*, 478 F.2d 1345 (4th Cir. 1973).
89. *Shanley, supra.*
90. *Frasca* v. *Andrews*, 463 F.Supp. 1043 (E.D. N.Y. 1979).
91. *Jacobs* v. *Board of School Commissioners*, 490 F.2d 601 (7th Cir. 1973).
92. *Bright* v. *Los Angeles Unified School District*, 134 Cal. Rptr. 639 (1976).
93. *Jacobs, supra.*

94. *Id.*
95. *Williams* v. *Spencer*, 622 F.2d 1200 (4th Cir. 1980).
96. *Thomas* v. *Board of Education, Granville Central School District*, 607 F.2d 1043 (2d Cir. 1979).
97. For more on this topic, see Jennifer Turner-Egner, *Teachers' Discretion in Selecting Instructional Materials and Methods*, 53 ED. LAW REP. 365 (1989).

CHAPTER 9

When Can Schools Limit Religious Freedom?

OVERVIEW

Controversies concerning the appropriate place, if any, of religion in the schools have occurred periodically since the early days of the Republic. Though the First Amendment states that "Congress shall make no law respecting the establishment of religion, or prohibiting the free exercise thereof," the interpretation of these general provisions and their application to public schools have been problematic. Religion tends to be so important in the lives of people, and so surrounded by powerful emotions, that many want to use the schools to maintain and spread their religious beliefs at the same time that others insist on the complete exclusion of religion from public schools.

Some of the most bitter controversies that have embroiled America's schools have involved questions related to religion. This chapter addresses only those questions concerning religion and public education that are of greatest relevance to teachers and students. For example, must teachers and students salute the flag or follow the curriculum if it violates their religious beliefs? Are prayers permitted in the public schools? What about silent meditation? Are students exempt from compulsory schooling or from certain courses in the curriculum on religious grounds? Can voluntary student religious groups meet in school facilities before or after school? Can creationism be taught in public schools?

TEACHERS' FREEDOM OF CONSCIENCE

In recent decades, although attention has focused on issues related to religion and public education, the attention of the courts and media has been primarily on students: their right and/or obligation to read the Bible in school, to pray, to salute the flag, to be exempt from objectionable parts of the curriculum, and other issues. But teachers, too, have religious beliefs and commitments. There are various important differences between teachers and students, the most salient being that teachers are adults and are paid employees hired to accomplish certain objectives for the community. Students are minors and are compelled by law to attend school. Should these differences lead to different applications of the Constitution for teachers and for students? We must look to court cases for our answers.

Can teachers be excused from saluting the flag?

Yes, they can, if their objections are based on either religion or conscience. When a New York high school art teacher refused to participate in the daily flag ceremony, she was dismissed from her job. A federal circuit court upheld her right not to participate in such a ceremony and the Supreme Court denied a request to review the decision, allowing the ruling of the lower court to stand.[1] The nonparticipating teacher stood silently and respectfully while another instructor conducted the program. The teacher's objections were held a matter of conscience and not necessarily disloyal. In the words of the court of appeals, "we ought not impugn the loyalty of a citizen . . . merely for refusing to pledge allegiance, any more than we ought necessarily to praise the loyalty of a citizen who without conviction or meaning, and with mental reservation, recites the pledge by rote each morning."

What if state law requires a daily flag salute?

State law requiring a flag salute is superseded by the First Amendment of the Constitution. Many states mandate daily flag salutes and other patriotic exercises. For example, a Massachusetts law passed in 1977 provides that "each teacher at the commencement of the first class of each day in all public schools shall lead the class in a group recitation of the Pledge of Allegiance to the Flag."

The state supreme court advised the governor that the law violated the First Amendment rights of teachers.[2] The court based its opinion on the U.S. Supreme Court ruling in the *Barnette* case (see page 166), indicating that the reasons used to excuse students from saluting the flag apply equally to teachers. According to the Massachusetts court, "any attempt by a governmental authority to induce belief in an ideological conviction by forcing an individual to identify himself with that conviction through compelled expression of it is prohibited by the First Amendment."

Can a teacher refuse to follow the curriculum if the refusal is based on religious objections?

No. This question was raised in the Chicago public schools when Joethelia Palmer, a probationary kindergarten teacher and a member of Jehovah's Witnesses, informed her principal that because of her religion she would not be able "to teach any subjects having to do with love of country, the flag or other patriotic matters in the prescribed curriculum." For example, she considered it "to be promoting idolatry . . . to teach . . . about President Lincoln and why we observe his birthday." School officials insisted that these matters were part of the regular curriculum; although *she* did not have to salute the flag, provisions should be made for students to do so. Moreover, students were to follow the prescribed curriculum, which included holiday observances, songs, and patriotic exercises.

The U.S. Court of Appeals ruled in favor of the school board, and the Supreme Court upheld the ruling.[3] The court commented that "the First Amendment was not a teacher license for uncontrolled expression at variance with established curricular content." Furthermore, "there is a compelling state interest in the choice and adherence to a suitable curriculum for the benefit of our young citizens and society." While Palmer's right to her beliefs must be respected, she has no "right to require others to submit to her views and to forgo a portion of their education they would otherwise be entitled to enjoy."

Are teachers who belong to Jehovah's Witnesses unqualified to teach in public schools?

Not necessarily. Their qualifications depend on their willingness to provide the prescribed curriculum for children in their classes. For example, Bein, a New York kindergarten teacher, told the parents of her students that she could no longer lead certain activities or participate in certain projects because these were "religiously oriented" according to her newly acquired faith of Jehovah's Witnesses. She could not decorate the classroom for holidays, coordinate gift exchange during the Christmas season, sing "Happy Birthday," or recite the Pledge of Allegiance. When some parents and school officials wanted to dismiss her, the teacher insisted that she was competent to teach and that the First Amendment protected her from participating in activities forbidden by her religion. The important difference between this case and the one discussed in the previous question was that Bein made arrangements to provide the children with all the curricular activities she could not conduct. With the cooperation of parents, older students, and other teachers, all activities specified in the curriculum were conducted. Thus, Bein's religious views were not imposed on the children, and the school's objectives in connection with patriotic exercises and holiday celebrations were satisfied. The New York State Commissioner of Education ruled in Bein's favor and held that her dismissal violated the religious freedom provisions of the First Amendment.[4]

RELIGIOUS HOLIDAYS

Can teachers take religious holiday leaves?

Yes, if they don't take too many leaves. State laws or local district policies usually allow teachers to be absent from school for the major holidays of recognized religions. Nevertheless, problems have arisen over questions of pay for religious holidays, as well as over the taking of an excessive number of days off for religious reasons.

Must schools pay teachers for religious holiday leaves?

No, they don't have to pay for such days. Payment for religious holiday leaves is within the discretion of the local school district. This question arose in California when a high school teacher requested a "personal necessity leave" to observe Rosh Hashanah, a Jewish holiday. Like many other states, California provides a certain number of paid days a year for "personal necessity leave" for teachers. It is up to local school authorities to adopt rules controlling the use of such leaves.

The teacher, Waldman, claimed that under the First Amendment she had a right to a leave for a major religious holiday and that it should be a paid leave under the personal necessity leave policy of the state and the district. The courts ruled against her, holding that it was within the discretion of the school board to decide when to consider a leave a personal necessity.[5] If courts imposed such a rule on schools, said the court, "the results would be chaotic. Every school teacher belonging to every sect, whether a legitimate religious group or not, would forthwith be entitled to six days of paid holidays. It appears reasonable, therefore, to limit the definition of personal necessity in a way which allows for effective supervision."

A federal appeals court reached the same conclusion when a teacher brought suit under Title VII, which requires reasonable accommodation to religious beliefs. The teacher claimed that a school policy that allowed only two days "special leave" violated the First Amendment. The court, holding that the policy was reasonable, ruled that school districts are not required to enact policies so broad as to accommodate each and every religious preference. The loss of a day's pay for time not worked does not amount to a significant infringement on First Amendment rights and "does not constitute substantial pressure on a teacher to modify his or her behavior."[6]

By contrast, the United States Court of Appeals for the Second Circuit ruled in favor of a teacher who wanted to use paid leave time to observe religious holidays that fell on school days. In this case, Ronald Philbrook, a member of the Worldwide Church of God in Connecticut, wanted to use six school days for religious observance. The collective bargaining contract between the school board and the teachers granted only three days paid leave for religious purposes and specified that personal business leave must be used for secular purposes. When Philbrook challenged this arrangement and lost at the district court level, he appealed. On appeal the circuit court, interpreting Title VII,[7] held that an employer must make reasonable accommodations to employees' religious needs, unless such accommodations will cause "undue hardship on the conduct of the employer's business." Furthermore, held the court, if both the employer and the employee propose reasonable accommodations, "Title VII requires the employer to accept the proposal the employee prefers unless the accommodation causes undue hardship on the employer's conduct of the business."[8] In light of such conflicts in court decisions, state laws and constitutions should also be consulted. There will be no uniform law on this issue until the Supreme Court rules on it.

Can teachers take unpaid religious holidays at will?

Within limits, teachers' freedom of religion will be protected even if the number of special holidays taken seems excessive to some school officials. This issue arose in California, and the judges were closely divided in their attempts to balance the rights of the individual to the free exercise of his religion and the legitimate interest of the state to provide effective schooling for all children.[9] Byars was a competent teacher employed by his school district in 1969. He joined the Worldwide Church of God in 1971 and requested certain days off for religious holidays. Despite the fact that his request was denied, between 1971 and 1975 he was absent from work for 31 days to observe religious holidays. School officials notified him in 1973 that his absences were not approved and that if he continued them, he would be dismissed for "persistant failure to abide by the rules of the District." Byars, insisting that he had a constitutional right to practice his religion, continued to observe the religious holidays of his church and missed more classes. When the school board dismissed him, Byars went to court.

The school board claimed that continuity of instruction was very important and that the repeated use of substitutes would diminish the educational benefits of the students. The court ruled in favor of the board; recognizing the clash of interests between the individual and society, the court observed: "While the free exercise clause prevents any governmental regulation of religious beliefs, in this case we are concerned not with . . . [the teacher's] beliefs but only with his practice in leaving his teaching duties for the purpose of religious observances while under contract with the district."

Nevertheless, the Supreme Court of California, by a vote of 4-3, reversed the decision and ruled in favor of the teacher. The court based its ruling on the California Constitution's provision protecting freedom of religion. The court was influenced by the fact that the total number of days Byars was absent was approximately the same as the mandatory number of paid leave days provided for teachers by the state. Thus the majority held that this teacher's religious beliefs must be accommodated, despite the inconvenience and disruption it might entail for the schools.[10] The U.S. Supreme Court dismissed an appeal "for want of a substantial federal question."

In a related case also involving a member of the Worldwide Church of God, plaintiff H. claimed that she was not hired because of religious discrimination. The facts indicated that her attendance would have been quite unpredictable because it would be influenced by "the moon and stars," according to her religious beliefs. The court ruled in favor of the school board and held that it may choose not to hire a person on the basis of nondiscriminatory reasons such as a preference for teachers without attendance problems. Thus, school boards have some discretion when considering the religious preferences of teachers in the process of hiring.[11]

Can teachers wear distinctively religious clothing in public schools?

Probably not, although there is no uniform law on this question applicable to the entire nation. Objections have arisen to Catholic nuns teaching in religious garb. When there was no evidence that the nuns injected religious views into their teaching, some courts did not prohibit them from wearing their religious clothing.[12] Other courts, however, even forbade nuns from teaching in public schools, on the grounds that their lives are dedicated to religion and their constant presence in the classroom violates the "establishment clause" of the First Amendment.[13] There are no recent cases on this issue, but it is probable that today nuns or ministers may teach secular subjects in public schools if they do not wear religious garb or other sectarian symbols. The fact that they may contribute their earnings to a church is their own personal and private business.[14] This principle would apply with equal force to members of, say, the Hare Krishna sect, as well as to more traditional religions.

When the issue of teaching in religious garb has arisen, most states have passed laws against the practice or forbidden it by administrative regulation. Such laws and regulations have been upheld by the courts.[15] A majority of educators and judges today hold the view that the wearing of religious garb introduces a sectarian influence that should not be present in the public schools. Such garb also gives the impression, particularly to less mature students, that the school supports the particular religion. In sum, the teacher's religious *beliefs* are always protected; *actions* based on religious beliefs may be limited when a compelling state interest is at stake.

STUDENTS' FREEDOM OF CONSCIENCE

"If there is any fixed star in our constitutional constellation, it is that no official, high or petty, can prescribe what shall be orthodox in politics, nationalism, religion, or other matters of opinion or force citizens to confess by word or act their faith therein. If there are any circumstances which permit an exception, they do not now occur to us."[16] As this quote suggests, certain social issues or conflicts are never completely resolved; they are perennial. The specific substance of the issues may change over time, but the general substance and form remain the same. They all relate to two basic principles of the First Amendment, one of which guarantees the free *exercise of religion,* while the other orders government officials not to *establish* any religion. But what do these principles mean in the daily lives of students in public schools?

Must students salute the flag?

No, they do not have to salute the flag if they have a genuine religious objection to such an act. However, most schools still require children to recite the Pledge of Allegiance at the start of each school day by virtue of state law or by policy of the school board. In the 1940s, children of the Jehovah's Witnesses faith refused to participate in the official pledge and offered, instead, to recite their own religious pledge. When school officials insisted on their reciting the official pledge, the students went to court. Their refusal eventually led to a Supreme Court ruling in favor of the children.[17] In the words of the Court: "We think the action of the local authorities in compelling the flag salute and pledge transcends constitutional limitations on their power and invades the sphere of intellect and spirit which it is the purpose of the First Amendment to reserve from all official control."

The Court overruled an earlier case that did not consider saluting the flag to be a significant enough religious act to merit constitutional protection. Many people, perhaps most, do not consider flag salutes or other patriotic exercises to be religious activities; therefore they cannot understand why anyone should have religious objections to them. Nevertheless, the Court held that school administrators or other officials may not determine for a religious group whether such activities are allowed or proscribed by their religion. There is to be no official orthodoxy under the Constitution. Majority vote, or the vote of a legislature, cannot resolve this question, said the Court. "The very purpose of a Bill of Rights was to withdraw certain subjects from the vicissitudes of political controversy, to place them beyond the reach of majorities and officials and to establish them as legal principles to be applied by the courts. One's right to life, liberty, and property, to free speech, a free press, freedom of worship and assembly, and other fundamental rights may not be submitted to vote; they depend on the outcome of no elections."

The majority of the Court considered freedom of religion to be a *fundamental* or *preferred freedom.* Such freedoms can be abridged only if the state shows it has a *compelling* need to do so. This is in contrast to *ordinary freedoms,* such as the freedom to drive a car, which can be restricted or regulated if the government has some legitimate reason to do so (e.g., to reduce pollution or congestion). There was no compelling state interest requiring Jehovah's Witnesses to salute the flag since no major public interest was threatened by their refusal; thus their fundamental religious freedom prevailed. There have been instances of religious freedom being outweighed by a powerful public interest, however. For example, mandatory polio immunization of all schoolchildren has been upheld, despite the religious objections of some parents.

Is religion the only basis for not saluting the flag?

No. There are students, as well as people in general, who object to saluting the flag as a matter of conscience. Courts have held that a sincerely held conscientious objection to the flag salute receives the same protection from the Constitution as an objection based on religious beliefs.

A student at Coral Gables High School in Florida had a deeply felt objection to the flag salute and did not even want to stand while the salute was being conducted. A board policy allowed him not to participate but required that nonparticipating students stand quietly during the salute. The student claimed that such a requirement violated his right of free speech, and a federal district court upheld this contention.[18] The court noted that "standing is an integral portion of the pledge ceremony and is no less a gesture of acceptance and respect than is the salute or the utterance of the words of allegiance."

A federal appeals court ruled similarly in the case of a New York honors student, president of his class, who refused to pledge allegiance to the flag because he believed "that there [isn't] liberty and justice for all in the United States." The school board offered the student the option of leaving the room or standing silently. The student wished instead to remain seated. The court, citing *West Virginia* v. *Barnette,* held that the state may not compel students to affirm their loyalty "by word or act." In this case, the act of standing was itself part of the pledge and a gesture of respect similar to the salute. "Therefore, the alternative offered plaintiff of standing in silence is an act that cannot be compelled over his deeply held convictions. It can no more be required than the pledge itself."[19]

In a similar case, New York students challenged the rule that nonparticipating students must leave the room and wait in the hall. They considered such treatment to be a punishment for the exercise of a constitutional right. The New York court agreed with the students and upheld their right not to participate in the flag salute for reasons of conscience, as well as their right to remain quietly in the room.[20] What if the refusal becomes contagious and other students also refuse to salute the flag? The New York case noted that "the First Amendment protects successful dissent as well as ineffective protest."

Can public schools start the day with prayers?

No. Historically, many public schools began each day with a required prayer, Bible reading, or both. In 1959 Pennsylvania enacted a law requiring daily Bible reading in the schools but exempting children who had written requests for exemption from their parents. The Schempp children, who were Unitarians, challenged the law. Their case eventually reached the Supreme Court, which ruled in their favor.[21]

The Court held that state-required Bible reading or prayer violates the establishment clause of the First Amendment when it is part of the curriculum in schools children are required to attend: "They [prayers] are held in the school buildings under the supervision and with the participation of teachers employed in those schools . . . such as opening exercises in a religious ceremony." The fact that students may be excused from the exercises does not change the fact that schools, which are arms of the state, are involved.

Can there be prayers at graduation ceremonies?

The answer may depend on the language used in the invocation and/or benediction. A federal district court in Iowa found the practice to be unconstitutional since its purpose and primary effect were religious.[22] A district court in Michigan recognized a secular purpose as well as a religious one in such a practice, and thus upheld it pursuant to a Supreme Court case where the Court recognized a dual purpose served by a nativity scene.[23] However, the Michigan case, *Stein* v. *Painwell Community Schools*, was reversed on appeal due to the religious language used.[24]

Invocations and benedictions at graduation exercises can serve a "solemnizing" function. As Justice O'Connor said in 1983, some governmental acknowledgment of religion, as in legislative prayers, "In God We Trust" on coins, and opening court sessions with "God save the United States and this honorable court" serve ". . . the legitimate secular purpose of solemnizing public occasions, expressing confidence in the future, and encouraging the recognition of what is worthy of appreciation in society." Ceremonial invocations and benedictions serve such purposes, and the public nature of the occasion and the usual presence of parents act as buffers against religious coercion. Thus, such ceremonials do not violate the First Amendment unless the language used in them is unacceptable. Such language was found in the *Stein* case in Michigan, where the language of Christian theology and prayer was employed, including the name of Jesus as the Saviour. This was held to be inconsistent with America's "civil religion" and a violation of the establishment clause.[25]

A novel situation found its way to the federal courts in the *Guidry* case,[26] in which Angela Guidry in Sam Houston High Shcool in Moss Bluff, Louisiana, was scheduled to deliver a valedictorian speech at graduation exercises. Following the practice of previewing such speeches, the principal found it to be a thoroughly Christian, personal statement of the importance of God, the Bible, and Jesus in the life of Angela, who urged all other students to ". . . give your heart and your life to Him so you can live forever in Heaven with Him." When the principal requested the deletion of all personal religious beliefs from the speech and the student refused to do so, her speech was deleted from the graduation proceedings.

Guidry went to court claiming that her freedom of speech was restricted because of its content. In the final analysis the federal district court ruled in favor of the school administration, holding that the primary effect of permitting the speech would have been to communicate "a message of governmental endorsement . . . of religion." Even if there were no actual support or endorsement by the school, concluded the court, there is the danger of public perception of such endorsement, therefore the principal's action was a reasonable attempt to avoid such appearances.

Are invocations at school athletic events constitutional?

Not according to a 1989 federal appeals court decision. The case concerned Doug Jager, a member of a Georgia high school marching band, who objected to invocations before home football games. The invocations had been organized by local Protestant ministers and frequently closed with the words "in Jesus' name, we pray." The court found this practice unconstitutional.[27]

Because of the controversy surrounding the clergy-led invocations, the school then proposed an "equal access plan" that involved the random selection of invocation speakers from among student, parent, or school staff volunteers. The school argued that the purpose of the plan was to provide "inspirational speeches about sportsmanship, safety and the values of teamwork and competition." However, a federal appeals court found that the school could have achieved all of these purposes by providing "wholly secular" inspirational speeches and that the school's real purpose was to provide invocations "that publicly express support for Protestant Christianity." These invocations, ruled the court, "violate the Establishment Clause of the First Amendment."

Must religion be completely excluded from schools?

The Supreme Court never mandated such exclusion. In fact, the *Schempp* case, which declared prayers and Bible reading unconstitutional, made it clear that studying *about* religion is perfectly legitimate, whether it be through comparative religion; the history of religion; art, music, and religion; or other approaches. Religious exercises, rituals, and celebrations, however, are against the law, whether compulsory or voluntary.

In 1981 the Supreme Court in a 5–4 decision declared unconstitutional a Kentucky statute that required posting a copy of the Ten Commandments, purchased with private contributions, on the wall of each classroom in the public schools of the state. After the state courts upheld the law, the Supreme Court applied its three-part *Lemon* test: (1) a statute must have a secular legislative purpose, (2) its principal or primary effect must be one that neither advances nor inhibits religion, and (3) the statute must not foster an excessive government entanglement with religion.[28] The Court struck down the law concluding that it served a religious rather than a secular purpose.

Certain school practices and a school board policy related to Christmas programs in public schools were challenged in Sioux Falls, South Dakota, in 1979. In short, the courts ruled that schools may teach about religion as a significant aspect of our culture and our history. Religious ceremonies must not be performed in schools "under the guise of 'study,'" yet the performance of religious art, literature, or music does not necessarily invalidate the activity if the primary purpose served is secular and not religious. Schools should be sensitive to the "religious beliefs and disbeliefs of their constituents and should attempt to avoid conflict," according to the court, "but they need not and should not sacrifice the quality of the students' education."[29]

Christmas programs in schools have led to controversies and lawsuits in many communities. "Balancing" Christmas celebrations with Hanukkah celebrations does not resolve the legal problem, for if one such activity violates the establishment clause of the First Amendment, a double violation is not the right remedy. Whether or not some children or parents object to the practice is not the key issue. *Religious* celebrations have no place in public schools, while teaching *about* religion is acceptable. Thus, the challenge to educators is how to incorporate such activities into school programs in ways consistent with their educational mission and deemphasize or eliminate their religious flavor. Recent Supreme Court cases related to the display of nativity scenes, along with other Christmas and patriotic symbols, would support this analysis.[30]

In these cases, one of which had a display in the Pittsburgh County Courthouse that was exclusively religious, while in the City-County Building one block away stood a display that contained a huge decorated Christmas tree, a large menorah (a Hanukkah candelabrum), a large sign from the mayor, "Salute to Liberty," with an additional message from the mayor.

In the final analysis, the Supreme Court in a 5–4 decision struck down the first display and upheld the second one. According to the majority the "principal and primary effect" of displaying the creche is to advance religion and thus violate the establishment clause. A divided majority upheld the other display as one that sends "a message of pluralism and freedom to choose one's own beliefs" along with support for patriotism. Thus, the overall impression created is secular and not religious. The strong dissenting opinions of four justices indicates that the Court is seriously divided on this issue and that we can anticipate further cases that might revise the three-prong test that developed in the *Lemon* case, noted in the next section.

Can students receive religious instruction during school hours?

Yes. The instruction must take place away from school, however, not on school grounds, and must be conducted by teachers or religious figures independent of the school and not paid by the school. This "released time" religious education is used in some communities in the country, and the Supreme Court has ruled that the arrangement does not violate the Constitution.[31]

A very different situation arose in Lubbock, Texas, where pursuant to school board policy students could gather before or after school hours, under school supervision, for voluntary moral, religious, or ethical activities led by students. When the policy and practice were challenged, the court of appeals also applied the three-pronged *Lemon* test:

1. Does the policy or practice have a secular purpose?
2. Is the primary effect of the policy or practice one which neither advances nor inhibits religion?
3. Does the policy or practice avoid an excessive entanglement with religion?[32]

To satisfy the Constitution, the answer must be in the affirmative for *each* of these questions. In the *Lubbock* case, the policy and practice failed on all three grounds. The facts showed the purpose to be clearly to advance religion and that its primary effect would do the same. Furthermore, school supervision of the activities is precisely the kind of entanglement that is impermissible under constitutional precedents.[33]

The *Lemon* test, however, is undergoing reexamination by the Court. This is clear from a careful reading of *Wallace* v. *Jaffree*,[34] a 1985 case that declared an Alabama statute providing for silent prayer in schools unconstitutional. The Court ruled that the statute violated the Establishment Clause because it had no secular purpose and was a government "endorsement" of prayer. However, a strong dissent by Justice Rehnquist indicates his readiness to abandon the *Lemon* test and the idea of "separation of church and state." His views along with those of Justices O'Connor, Scalia, Kennedy, and White, gleaned from several cases, lead us to believe that the Court is moving toward "accommodation" between church and state, a position different from a view previously dominant and embodied in the *Lemon* test. A clear, authoritative statement of the new, evolving doctrine is yet to be announced.

Are silent meditations allowed?

Maybe. It depends on the wording of the statute or policy and the intentions behind it.

Massachusetts passed a law that required public schools to observe a minute of silence "for meditation or prayer." The law was challenged by students and parents who claimed that it was a violation of the establishment clause of the First Amendment. The word "or" saved the law from being declared unconstitutional, however. According to the court, meditation refers to a silent reflection on any subject, religious or secular. Thus, since mediation can be on a secular subject, and the law used the disjunctive "or," there is no necessary prayer involved—only a moment of silence.[35]

Other cases, however, reached different conclusions. A Louisiana statute authorizing a brief period of silent meditation was also challenged by students. The statute, in addition to its provision for silent meditation, authorized teachers to ask students whether they wished to pray. If no students chose to pray, the teacher was permitted to pray for a period of up to five minutes. Although there was no compulsion for students to participate or even to be present, the courts ruled the statute unconstitutional. The federal appeals court held that the principles of *Schempp* applied and that the voluntary nature of the activity is "no defense to a claim of unconstitutionality under the Establishment Clause."[36]

In Alabama, three students challenged a state law that provided for a one-minute period for meditation or voluntary prayer in public schools and that permitted teachers to lead their classes in prayer. The district court recognized that the Alabama statute violated the establishment clause as construed by the Supreme Court. Nevertheless, the district court ruled "that the United States Supreme Court has erred." On appeal, the Supreme Court held that the district court was obligated to follow procedures established by the Supreme Court and that the state statute was unconstitutional.[37] In their written opinions the majority of the justices indicated that a period of meditation, provided for a secular purpose, would be constitutionally acceptable. Whether it is necessary to legislate such a period of silence, or whether it is educationally desirable, is not for courts to decide.

A variation on this issue arose in New Mexico, where a statute authorized school boards to permit one minute of silence at the beginning of school days. The schools claimed that the purpose of the statute was to enhance discipline and instill "intellectual composure" in the students. Furthermore, the schools claimed that "meditation," as used by the statute, indicated a neutral purpose. The district court considered the statutory language, statements of its legislative sponsors, and the historical context in which it was enacted and concluded that the legislative purpose was nonsecular, that is, "to establish prayer in public schools."[38]

In light of the foregoing cases Massachusetts changed its law in 1985 and completely excluded any mention of prayer in its new legislation. The new law reads: "At the commencement of the first class of each day in all grades in all public schools the teacher in charge of the room in which each such class is held shall announce that a period of silence not to exceed one minute in duration shall be observed for personal thoughts, and during any such period, silence shall be maintained and no other activity engaged in."[39]

Is Transcendental Meditation allowed in schools?

No, it is not, ruled a federal court in New Jersey after schools introduced a course in Transcendental Meditation (TM), claiming that it would reduce stress and produce a variety of beneficial physical effects. Some parents believed that TM was a religion and, as such, had no place in public schools. Although there was conflicting testimony on whether or not the course was religious, the judge ruled that it was.[40] A *mantra,* a special word repeated regularly by the meditating person, and a special textbook were assigned to each student at an out-of-school religious ceremony. In the estimate of the judge, the goals of TM may have been secular, but the means used were religious and therefore violated the First Amendment.

Must children attend public schools?

No, they and their parents may choose among several alternatives that include public schools, private religious or secular schools, or private military schools. (See Chapter 17 for a detailed discussion of schooling and parents' rights.) The Supreme Court established this principle in 1925 when an Oregon law that required every child between the ages of eight and sixteen to attend public schools was challenged by a Catholic religious order. The Court ruled in their favor.[41]

The Court recognized the right of states to require that all children of certain ages attend school and the right of states to provide reasonable regulations for all schools, public and private, related to school buildings, teachers, and the curriculum. Nevertheless, to require that all educating be done in public schools was considered arbitrary and unreasonable. In a famous quote the Court warned against the standardization of children and recognized the parents' right to guide and nurture the young:

> The fundamental theory of liberty upon which all governments in this Union repose excludes any general power of the state to standardize its children by forcing them to accept instruction from public teachers only. The child is not the mere creature of the state; those who nurture him and direct his destiny have the right, coupled with the high duty, to recognize and prepare him for additional obligations.

Can children attend church school at home?

They can only if the "home school" qualifies under the requirements of the particular state. (See Chapter 17 for a detailed discussion of home schooling.) In most states this would mean that the parents or other adults teaching the children would have to be qualified in the eyes of the court and would have to present an acceptable educational program for the children. That a school claims to be a religious school does not exempt it from reasonable state regulation.

A court in Florida ruled on a case involving a church "school" in a home where the mother was the only teacher.[42] The parents claimed that their religious beliefs forbade "race mixing as practiced in the public schools" as "sinful." The mother was not certified to teach, nor did she meet state regulations for private tutors, and the church to which they claimed to belong was not a regularly established church in Florida. Thus the court held that the home arrangement was unacceptable and the children had to attend either the local public school or some acceptable private school.

Can children avoid school attendance altogether for religious reasons?

In general, they cannot, although special circumstances may lead to some exemptions. A child who lives in a state that requires school attendance must attend *some* acceptable school during the years of compulsory education. What if the family has religious objections? This question was raised by some Amish children in Wisconsin, and the Supreme Court provided some exceptions to the general rule stated above.[43] Wisconsin required school attendance until the age of 16. The Amish believed that the curriculum of the high school, particularly its emphasis on intellectual and scientific achievement, competition, worldly success, and social life, was inconsistent with their religious beliefs. They accepted the need for basic literacy but were convinced that schooling beyond the eighth grade would destroy their close-knit rural, religion-centered way of life. They insisted that after eighth grade, their youth should learn the skills relevant to the Amish way of life on their farms and in their homes. The state, on the other hand, insisted that the compulsory laws applied to all children, without exception.

After reviewing all the evidence and arguments, the Court exempted the Amish children from high school attendance. The Court was impressed by the fact that this religion-based, self-sufficient community has existed successfully for over two hundred years. In effect, the Amish way of life was an "alternative to formal secondary school education" and enabled the Amish to live peacefully and to successfully fulfill their economic, social, and political responsibilities without becoming burdens on the larger society. After balancing the interests of the state against the Amish interest in the preservation and practice of their religion, the Court reached a decision on behalf of religious freedom. As the Court recognized, the case involved "the fundamental interest of parents, as contrasted with that of the State, to guide the religious future and education of their children" and the primary role of parents in the upbringing of their children "is now established beyond debate as an enduring American tradition."

Courts are unlikely to extend the ruling regarding the Amish to other religious groups that object to school attendance. The Court made it clear that the long history of the Amish religious way of life was important to its decision and groups "claiming to have recently discovered some 'progressive'" or other enlightened way of rearing children for a modern life will not qualify for similar exemption. Since the law is always growing and changing, however, only time will tell whether some other groups will find ways to successfully challenge state compulsory education laws.

An attempt by other parents in Wisconsin illustrates this point. When the Kasuboski parents did not send their eight children to public schools, they claimed an exemption for religious reasons. They were members of the Basic Bible Church and alleged that the schools' teaching of racial equity, humanism, and "one-world government," together with the influence of communists and Jews, was offensive to their religion. Evidence showed that the particular church was not opposed to education and that some of its members sent their children to public schools. The court ruled that the Kasuboski children could not be exempt because their parents' objection was based on philosophic and ideological grounds and not on religious ones.[44] The Amish case could not be used as a precedent by them. "A personal, philosophic choice by parents, rather than a religious choice, does not rise to the level of a First Amendment claim of religious expression." (A related question appears on page 349.)

Can students be exempt from certain courses for religious reasons?

That depends on the state law. Religious objections have been raised by parents and students to various parts of the curriculum. The most often heard objection is to sex education courses whether labeled family life education, human development, human sexuality, or some other title. The course itself does not violate freedom of religion, ruled a California court, particularly if the state law permits children to be excused from participating in such classes.[45] Schools usually make such courses voluntary, but the New Jersey Commissioner of Education ruled that even a required course on family living, in which some sex education was included, does not violate freedom of religion.[46]

Religious objections have also been raised against dancing in physical education classes, and courts have long protected students who have genuine religious objections from participating in dancing.[47] Similarly, courts would uphold a student's religious objection to watching movies in schools or playing with cards, though such activities were part of the curriculum. A federal appeals court also ruled in favor of a high school student who objected to ROTC training on grounds of religious freedom.[48] In his high school, ROTC was part of a required physical education course, and the court held that the student need not "choose between following his religious beliefs and forfeiting his diploma, on the one hand, and abandoning his religious beliefs and receiving his diploma on the other hand."

In 1985 a federal circuit court ruled on a case involving a parental request to remove a book from the curriculum on the grounds that it violated their religious beliefs. Cassie Grove, a sophomore, together with her mother, claimed that *The Learning Tree* by Gordon Parks offended their religious views and advanced secular humanism, thus violating both religious clauses of the First Amendment.

The court inquired into: (1) the extent of the burden upon the free exercise of religion, (2) the existence of a compelling state interest to justify that burden, and (3) the extent to which accommodating the student would impede the state's objectives.

Since the student was assigned an alternate book and could absent herself during discussions of *The Learning Tree*, the burden on her was minimal. At the same time, the state's compelling interest in providing a well-rounded education would be critically impeded by accommodating the plaintiff's wishes, for by the same logic the schools should eliminate everything objectionable to any other religious views. In the court's opinion this would "leave public education in shreds." The court also found that the book served a secular educational function since it shared a working-class black family's perspective of racism. Thus, its use did not constitute establishment of religion or of an antireligion.[49]

In *Mozert* v. *Hawkins County Public Schools*, a federal district court in

Tennessee ruled that students may "opt out" of reading books objectionable to their religion. The case involved fundamentalist Christian families who objected to stories such as the *Wizard of Oz, Rumpelstiltskin, Macbeth,* and the Holt Rinehart & Winston series. They objected to materials that expose children to feminism, witchcraft, pacifism, vegetarianism, and situational ethics.

However, in 1987 the Sixth Circuit Court of Appeals reversed this decision.[50] Although the appeals court was unanimous in reversing the lower court, the judges each had different reasons for their conclusions. The basic conflict in the *Mozert* case is between students' right to free exercise of religion on the one hand and the state's compelling interest in educating children on the other. In all likelihood, public schools can expect students to particiapte in the required parts of the curriculum if they can show those parts essential to the achievement of some compelling state interest, for example competence in the 3R's and in citizenship. This is particularly the case if there aren't easily applied practical alternatives to achieving the same educational objectives.

Can the state regulate private religious schools?

Yes, provided it has an important reason to do so and the regulations are not vague or overly broad. Members and officers of fundamentalist Christian churches in Maine brought suit against the State of Maine and its Department of Educational and Cultural Services, claiming that the state law related to compulsory attendance violated their First Amendment right to free exercise of religion. The state law excused from attendance in public school students who obtained "equivalent instruction in private school. . . if the equivalent instruction is approved by the commissioner." The state statute empowers public officials to prescribe courses of study and to scrutinize school programs prior to authorizing the schools' curricula.

The court found the regulations valid in that the state of Maine has a compelling interest in the education of all children between the ages specified by state law. Its regulations must be reasonable and not too vague. Furthermore, the court found that the regulations did not reach "a substantial amount of constitutionally protected conduct," that is, they did not interfere with the free exercise of religion in any substantial manner.[51]

By contrast, the Court of Appeals for the Sixth Circuit struck down the state of Ohio's efforts to investigate a religious school when charges of sexual discrimination were made against the school. A state statute forbids discrimination in employment and housing based on sex, among other attributes.[52] When the church schools objected to a state agency investigating them, the district court upheld the right of the state to investigate the charges of discrimination. This, however, was overruled by the circuit court on the grounds that the controls exercised by the civil rights commission would place an undue burden on the schools' exercise of freedom of religion and require the kind of continuous supervision that would lead to excessive entanglement between church and state.[53]

Can public school teachers do remedial work in religious schools?

No. The Supreme Court ruled in two separate cases that such arrangements involve "excesssive entanglement" between government and religion.

In a case from New York that involved the sending of public school teachers into private and parochial schools to teach remedial classes to economically disadvantaged children under a federal Title I program, the Court struck down this arrangement in a close vote (5-4). The majority was concerned that, in such a program, the public school teachers as well as the religious institutions in which they work must be subjected to "comprehensive, discriminating and continuing surveillance . . . This itself is a constitutionally excessive entanglement of church and state."[54]

A case in Grand Rapids, Michigan, involved a shared-time program authorized by Michigan law, under which public school teachers performed remedial work in religious schools. In Michigan, as in New York, all religious symbols were removed from the classrooms used for such remedial instruction. The Grand Rapids district also employed parochial school teachers on a part-time basis to teach "community education" courses, after school hours, on the premises of the religious schools.

The Supreme Court, with an identical close vote (5–4), struck down both of the arrangements as violative of the establishment clause of the First Amendment. The majority was concerned that these arrangements: (1) created a danger that teachers would engage in religious teaching, (2) created a "symbolic union of church and state," and (3) subsidized religious functions in the church school by taking over portions of their responsibility to teach secular subjects.[55]

Can student religious groups use school facilities?

We cannot answer with certainty right now. Both congressional action and case law must be analyzed in attempting to answer this question. The Equal Access Act,[56] passed by Congress in 1984, provides that it shall be unlawful for any public secondary school receiving federal funds and which has a limited open forum* to deny equal access or a fair opportunity to, or discriminate against, any students who wish to conduct a meeting in that forum. The Act applies to "noninstructional time," that is, before or after regular school hours. The student group must be voluntary and student-initiated. The school or its employees may not sponsor the meetings and employees may be present only as nonparticipants. Such meetings may not interfere with the conduct of educational activities, and persons not associated with the school may not direct, conduct, control, or regularly attend such meetings.

The Equal Access Act seems to answer our question in the affirmative; however, there are serious questions regarding its constitutionality. Four federal

---

* A school has a limited open forum if noncurriculum-related student groups may meet on school premises during noninstructional time.

circuit courts have ruled such meetings unconstitutional as violative of the establishment clause and the Supreme Court has agreed to review one such case, *Bender* v. *Williamsport*. This case involved the "Petros" (The Rock), a small, voluntary group of students who sought permission to form a "nondenominational prayer fellowship" open to all students in the school for the purpose of promoting "spiritual growth and positive attitudes in the lives of its members."[57]

The superintendent and the school board denied their request upon advice from the school district's attorney. They based their denial on their conviction that to allow the formation of the fellowship in the school would violate the establishment clause. The students claimed that a denial would violate their First Amendment right to free speech. The district court ruled in favor of the students, but on appeal the circuit court found that, although the Petros had a secular purpose, permitting them to meet would have the primary effect of advancing religion and thus violate the establishment clause. The court held that, on balance, the school's interest in preventing the establishment of religion outweighed the students' interest in free speech. The Supreme Court has ruled on a similar "equal access" case before, but that arose at the college level.[58] In the *Widmar* case, the Court indicated that "religious worship and discussion. . . are forms of speech and association protected by the First Amendment." School policies or rules that would forbid them must be "necessary to serve a compelling state interest" and "narrowly drawn to achieve that end." The Supreme Court, however, on March 28, 1986, dismissed the *Bender* case on procedural grounds. In a 5–4 decision, the Court ruled that the appeals court erred when it allowed a single member of the Williamsport School Board to appeal the district court's ruling.[59] Thus, for the time being, the district court's ruling is reinstated and the students of Williamsport may meet in student-initiated prayer groups during extracurricular periods. Other circuit court cases, however, in the second, fifth, tenth, and eleventh circuits have forbidden the practice. Courts are concerned that impressionable high school students will believe that schools support the religious groups and this would violate the posture of neutrality schools should maintain.

Two recent cases reached seemingly inconsistent results. Students in Westside High School, in Omaha, Nebraska, attempted to form a Christian Bible Study Club, a voluntary, student-run club with no adults involved. The students were not requesting a faculty sponsor, unless one was required by school policy and then only for "custodial purposes." School administrators and the School Board denied the request as a violation of the establishment clause. The students brought suit, alleging violation of their freedom of speech, assembly, and association and their free exercise of religion, as guaranteed by the First and Fourteenth Amendments, the Nebraska Constitution, and the Equal Access Act (20 U.S.C. § 4071-4074).[60] (This is known as the *Mergens* case.)

The District Court ruled in favor of the school administration on the grounds that Westside High School had no limited open forum because all of its clubs were curriculum-related. Since the Equal Access Act applies only to public secondary schools with limited open forums, and since a Bible Club would not be curriculum-related, argued the administrators, the act does not apply to their school.

On appeal, the U.S. Court of Appeals for the Eighth Circuit, reversed the decision and ruled in favor of the student request. The appeals court examined the meaning of "limited open forum" and found that the school officials placed too restrictive a meaning on it. For example, they approved the Chess Club as curriculum-related for it allegedly fosters critical thinking and logic; a scuba diving club for its alleged relation to physical education; and two service clubs for their relationship to sociology and psychology. The appeals court concluded that allowing such broad interpretation of "curriculum-related" would make the Equal Access Act meaningless. It would allow administration near arbitrary power to decide what is or is not curriculum-related, a result Congress sought to prohibit by enacting the EAA. The appeals court, in its analysis, presented excerpts from congressional discussions to establish the intent behind the EAA and further ruled that the EAA itself is constitutional. The court noted that the EAA codifies the Supreme Court's decision in the *Widmar* case (a college level case) and extends that holding to public secondary schools.

In contrast, the Ninth Circuit Court of Appeals ruled against the request of students from Lindbergh High School, Renton School District, in the state of Washington.[61] Students there requested the use of a classroom for "weekday morning meetings of their non-denominational Christian student group." The request was denied because the school policy explicitly stated that the district "does not offer a limited open forum," and all its clubs were "cocurricular" and related to specific courses or programs. In the opinion of the administrators, the proposed Bible study and prayer group would not qualify as cocurricular and granting it permission would violate the establishment clause. The court also emphasized the difference between high school and college students and would not extend the holding of *Widmar* down to high school. It noted that the potential for undue influence is much greater at the high school level, where students must attend and they are younger, than with more mature college students who voluntarily enroll in courses. This distinction warrants a difference in constitutional results.

On June 4, 1990, however, the Supreme Court in an 8–1 decision upheld the constitutionality of the Equal Access Act and extended the *Widmar* principle down to high schools, ruling in favor of the student group in the *Mergens* case (reported in the *New York Times*, June 5, 1990).

Can "creationism" be taught in public schools?

It could probably be taught in social studies classes as describing a belief held by certain segments of the population. However, state laws that require the teaching of "creationism" or "scientific creationism" in courses that also teach about the theory of evolution have been declared unconstitutional. The leading case declaring such laws to be efforts to advance religion was the 1982 *McLean* case in Arkansas.[62]

Later cases reached similar conclusions and the majority of the Supreme Court declared the Louisiana Creationism Act unconstitutional becuse it lacked a clear secular purpose.[63] The federal appeals court reasoned that: "The Act's intended effect is to discredit evolution by counterbalancing its teaching at every turn with the teaching of creationism, a religious belief." While the majority of the Court agreed with the appeals court, declaring the Louisiana law unconstitutional, Chief Justice Rehnquist along with Scalia would uphold it if it had *any* secular purpose.

SUMMARY

Throughout the history of public schooling, disagreements concerning the appropriate relationship between religion and public education have resulted in spirited controversies that have had to be resolved by our courts. Although controversies still abound, there are some guiding principles for the conduct of daily schooling.

It is clear today that teachers and students may be exempt from saluting the flag if they have objections based either on religion or conscience. Teachers or students so exempt may remain in the classroom and sit or stand respectfully while others participate in the ceremony. Teachers may not, however, refuse to follow a curriculum, properly adopted by a school board, even though they may have personal religious objections to it. If parts of the curriculum are objectionable to them, they must provide acceptable alternative ways for the students to learn the materials.

Teachers may take personal leave for religious holidays, but it is up to the local school district whether to pay them for such personal leaves. When school officials consider such leaves to be excessive and thus an interference with the continuity of instruction, provisions of the state law or state constitution must be consulted. In one such case a teacher was protected by the California Constitution, and the U.S. Supreme Court rejected an appeal on the grounds that no "substantial federal question" was involved.

A teacher who brought suit under Title VII of the Civil Rights Act of 1964 prevailed in a case where a federal appeals court required school boards to make reasonable accommodations to the teacher's religion as long as no undue hardship accrues to the employer. But another appeals court ruled to the contrary in a similar case under Title VII. Such divergent rulings are likely to continue until the Supreme Court rules on this question sometime in the future.

Courts have ruled that prayers or Bible reading must be excluded from public schools as violations of the establishment clause of the First Amendment. This is the case whether such practices are mandatory or voluntary, and whether led by faculty or students. Studying *about* religion is legal, however, and so is released-time religious instruction as long as it takes place away from school facilities and does not involve school personnel or other support from the schools. Provisions for a period of silent meditation may or may not violate the

Constitution, depending on the wording of the statute or policy as well as the intent behind its creation. If it is clear from the legislative history that the intent of the statute or policy is to further religion, courts will strike them down as violative of the establishment clause of the First Amendment. A court ruled similarly on the inclusion of Transcendental Meditation in the curriculum. On the other hand, a simple provision of a brief period of silence at the start of the school day is likely to be upheld.

The right of high school students to form voluntary student-initiated and student-led prayer groups that meet on school property outside regular school hours was decided by the Supreme Court in June 1990. This kind of extracurricular activity has been ruled acceptable at the college level, but courts often distinguish secondary schooling from college because of the age and maturity differences of the students, and because secondary school attendance is mandatory, while college attendance is voluntary. Congress authorized student-initiated religious meetings in its Equal Access Act, and, due to inconsistent rulings by federal appeals courts, the constitutionality of this law was decided by the Supreme Court, and the act was upheld.

Students have the right to attend either private or public schools, and state compulsory attendance laws may be satisfied by attending religious or secular schools. In at least one case, some students were exempt from attending school beyond the eighth grade when they could show that the high school curriculum would violate their religious beliefs and religiously based way of life. Other attempts at "home schooling" based on religious grounds succeeded only if the state requirements for such alternatives were satisfied. State law may also specify whether students may be exempt from certain parts of the curriculum. For example, courses related to sex education are often made elective, though some courts have upheld their inclusion in the curriculum even when they were required. Students have been exempt from participating in ancillary parts of the curriculum such as dancing in physical education classes when they could show genuine religious objections to the activities.

Thus, while controversies still abound surrounding the issue of religion and public education, careful examination shows that both students and teachers have made significant gains in asserting their right to free exercise of religion on the one hand and being free from the states' efforts to use the schools to "establish" religion on the other. It is likely that with recent changes in the Supreme Court we may expect new interpretations of the First Amendment's clauses related to religion.

NOTES

1. *Russo* v. *Central School District No. 1*, 469 F.2d 623 (2d Cir. 1972), *cert. denied*, 411 U.S. 932 (1973).
2. *Opinions of the Justices to the Governor*, 363 N.E.2d 251 (Mass. 1977).

3. *Palmer* v. *Board of Education of City of Chicago,* 603 F.2d 1271 (7th Cir. 1979), *cert. denied,* 44 U.S. 1026 (1980).
4. MATTER OF BEIN, 15 EDUC. DEP. REP. 407, N.Y. Comm'r. Dec. No. 9226 (1976).
5. *California Teachers Association* v. *Board of Trustees,* 138 Cal. Rptr. 817 (Cal. App. 1977).
6. *Pinkster* v. *Joint District Number 283,* 735 F.2d 388 (10th Cir. 1984).
7. 42 U.S.C. 2000e(i).
8. *Philbrook* v. *Ansonia Board of Education,* 37 F.E.P. Cases 404 (March 7, 1985).
9. *Rankins* v. *Commission on Professional Competence of Ducor Union School District,* 142 Cal. Rptr. 101 (Cal. App. 1977).
10. *Rankins* v. *Commission on Professional Competence of Ducor Union School District,* 154 Cal. Rptr. 907 (Cal. App. 1979), *appeal dismissed,* 100 S.Ct. 515 (1979).
11. *Ruby Williams* v. *Van Buren School District, No. 82-1169,* slip op. (6th Cir. Aug. 3, 1984).
12. *Rawlings* v. *Butler,* 290 S.W.2d 801 (Ky. 1956); *New Haven* v. *Torrington,* 43 A.2d 455 (Conn. 1945).
13. *Harfst* v. *Hoegen,* 163 S.W.2d 609 (Mo. 1942).
14. *Gerhardt* v. *Heidt,* 267 N.W. 127 (N.D. 1936).
15. *Commonwealth* v. *Herr,* 78 A. 68 (Pa. 1910); *Zellers* v. *Huff,* 236 P.2d 949 (N.M. 1951).
16. *West Virginia* v. *Barnette,* 319 U.S. 624; 642 (1943), Justice Jackson.
17. *Id.*
18. *Banks* v. *Board of Public Instruction of Dade County,* 314 F.Supp. 285 (S.D. Fla. 1970).
19. *Goetz* v. *Ansell,* 477 F.2d 636 (2d. Cir. 1973); the same result was reached in *Lipp* v. *Morris,* 579 F.2d 834, 836 (3d. Cir. 1978).
20. *Frain* v. *Barron,* 307 F.Supp. 27 (E.D. N.Y. 1969).
21. *Abington School District* v. *Schempp,* 374 U.S. 203 (1963).
22. *Graham* v. *Central Community School District,* 608 F.Supp. 531 (S.D. Iowa 1985).
23. *Marsh* v. *Chambers,* 463 U.S. F83 (1983).
24. *Stein* v. *Plainwell Community Schools,* 822 F.2d 1406 (6th Cir. 1987).
25. *Id.*
26. *Guidry* v. *Calasieu Parish School Board, et al.,* Civil Action No. 87-2122-LC (W.D. La. Feb 22, 1989).
27. *Jager* v. *Douglas County School District,* 862 F.2d 824 (11th Cir. 1989).
28. *Stone* v. *Graham,* 449 U.S. 39 (1981).
29. *Florey* v. *Sioux Falls School District,* 49-5, 619 F.2d 1311 (1980), *cert. denied,* 449 U.S. 897 (1980).
30. *County of Allegheny* v. *American Civil Liberties Union Greater Pittsburgh Chapter; City of Pittsburgh* v. *American Civil Liberties Union Great Pittsburgh Chapter,* 57 LW 5045 (July 3, 1989).
31. *Zorach* v. *Clausen,* 343 U.S. 306 (1952).
32. *Lemon* v. *Kurtzman,* 403 U.S. 602 (1971).
33. *Lubbock Civil Liberties* v. *Lubbock Independent School District,* 669 F.2d 1038 (5th Cir. 1984).
34. 427 U.S. 38 (1985).
35. *Gaines* v. *Anderson,* 421 F.Supp. 337 (D. Mass. 1976).

36. *Karen B.* v. *Treen,* 653 F.2d 897 (5th Cir. 1981), *aff'd on appeal,* 455 U.S. 913 (1982).

37. *Jaffree et al.* v. *Board of School Commissioners of Mobile County,* 459 U.S. 1314 (1983).

38. *Duffy* v. *Las Cruces Public Schools,* 557 F.Supp. 1013 (D. New Mexico 1983); *see also, May* v. *Cooperman,* 572 F.Supp. 1561 (D. New Jersey 1983).

39. Chapter 690, General Laws of Massachusetts, 1985.

40. *Malnak* v. *Yogi,* 440 F.Supp. 1284 (D. N.J. 1977), *aff'd,* 592 F.2d 197 (3d. Cir. 1979).

41. *Pierce* v. *Society of Sisters,* 268 U.S. 510 (1925).

42. *T.A.F and E.M.E.* v. *Duval County,* 237 S.2d 15 (Fla. 1973).

43. *Wisconsin* v. *Yoder,* 406 U.S. 205 (1972).

44. *State* v. *Kasuboski,* 275 N.W.2d. 101 (Wis. Ct. App. 1978).

45. *Citizens for Parental Rights* v. *San Mateo City Board of Education,* 124 Cal. Rptr. 68 (Cal. App. 1975).

46. *"J.B." and "B.B." as Guardians and Natural Parents of "P.B." and "J.B."* v. *Dumont Board of Education,* Dec. of N.J. Comm'r of Education (1977).

47. *Hardwick* v. *Board of Trustees,* 205 P. 49 (1921).

48. *Spence* v. *Bailey,* 465 F.2d 797 (6th Cir. 1972).

49. *Grove* v. *Mead School District No. 354,* 753 F.2d 1528 (9th Cir. 1985).

50. 827 F.2d 1058 (6th Cir. 1987); *cert. denied* 108 S. Ct. 1029 (Feb. 22, 1988).

51. *Bangor Baptist Church* v. *State of Maine, Department of Educational and Cultural Services,* 549 F.Supp. 1208 (D. Maine 1982).

52. Ohio Rev. Code Ch. 4112.

53. *Dayton Christian Schools* v. *Ohio Civil Rights Commission,* No. 84-3124, slip. op. (6th Cir. 1985), 54 U.S.L.W. 2034 (July 16, 1985).

54. *Aguilar* v. *Felton,* 105 S.Ct. 3232 (July 1, 1985).

55. *Grand Rapids* v. *Ball,* 534 L.W. 3430 (July 2, 1985).

56. Equal Access Act, Pub. L. No. 98-377, sec. 801 et seq., 1984 U.S. CODE CONG. & AD. NEWS (98 Stat.) 1267, 1302. 20 U.S.C., sec. 4071.

57. *Bender* v. *Williamsport Area School District,* 741 F.2d 538 (3d Cir. 1984), *cert. granted,* 105 S.Ct. 1167 (February 19, 1985).

58. *Widmar* v. *Vincent,* 454 U.S. 263 (1981).

59. *Bender* v. *Williamsport Area School District,* 54 L.W. 4307 (1986).

60. *Mergens* v. *Board of Education of Westside Community Schools,* 867 F.2d 1076 (8th Cir. 1989);—U.S.—June 4, 1990.

61. *Garnett* v. *Renton School District No. 403,* 865 F.2d 1121 (9th Cir. 1989).

62. *McLean* v. *Arkansas Board of Education,* 529 F.Supp. 1255 (E.D. Ark. 1982).

63. *Edwards* v. *Aquillard,* 482 U.S. 578 (1987).

CHAPTER 10

When Can Schools Limit Freedom of Association?

OVERVIEW

Citizens often judge teachers and students by the company they keep and the organizations they join. In the past, teachers have been fired for being members of groups considered subversive by their community or even for being active in partisan politics. Students have been prohibited from organizing radical groups on campus if the aims of the groups were controversial or seemed to conflict with the goals of their school. Some teachers and students believed they were victims of guilt by association and that restrictions on their organizational activity violated their freedom of association. But many administrators argued that teachers and students were in a special class and that their associational freedom should not be as broad as that of other citizens.

On the other hand, increasing numbers of teachers and students are rejecting the notion that their rights should be less or their obligations should be more than those of other people. Teachers object to the practice of penalizing them for failure to sign loyalty oaths, for membership in unpopular or radical organizations, or for taking an active part in partisan politics. Students want to be able to organize fraternal, religious, or political groups in school and to organize demonstrations and hear controversial speakers.

The scope and limits of teachers' and students' freedom of association is the focus of this chapter. The court cases discussed indicate how judges have been resolving conflicts on these issues.

OATHS OF LOYALTY

What are the goals of loyalty oaths?

The goals of loyalty oaths have varied according to the times and the legislatures that enacted them. In the 1950s, when half the states passed such oaths, their focus was to ensure that teachers were loyal to the American form of government and that schools were free from the influence of subversive teachers. In upholding a New Jersey loyalty oath, a judge noted: "A teacher who is bereft of the essential quality of loyalty and devotion to his government and the fundamentals of our democratic society is lacking in a basic qualification for teaching."[1] Some oaths sought to promote "reverence for law and order" or "faithful" job performance. Others had procedures for investigating and firing disloyal teachers. While educators have debated whether these oaths are a good way to ensure loyal teachers, courts have considered whether they are constitutional.

Can teachers be required to swear that they will promote "respect for the flag," "reverence for law and order," and "undivided allegiance" to the government?

No. The state of Washington required its teachers to swear to the above until the U.S. Supreme Court declared the oath unconstitutionally vague, ambiguous, and overly broad.[2] The Court wondered about the institutions for which the teacher is expected to "promote respect." Do they include those institutions to which most Americans are loyal? If so, the oath might prevent a teacher from criticizing his state's judicial system, the Supreme Court, or the FBI. Would a teacher who refused to say the Pledge of Allegiance because of religious beliefs be charged with breaking his or her promise to promote respect for the flag? "It would not be unreasonable," wrote Justice White, "for the serious-minded oath taker to conclude that he should dispense with lectures voicing far-reaching criticism of any old or new [government] policy" lest he be accused of violating his oath to "promote undivided allegiance" to the U.S. government. The result of these uncertainties is that teachers who are conscientious about their "solemn oath" and sensitive to the dangers posed by the oath's indefinite language can avoid risk "only by restricting their conduct to that which is unquestionably safe." Free speech, wrote the Court, "may not be so inhibited." Whenever statutes place limits on First Amendment freedoms, they must be "narrowly drawn," and the conduct prohibited must be "defined specifically" so that the teachers affected remain secure in their rights to engage in constitutionally protected activity.

Can teachers be required to swear that they are not subversive and do not teach others to overthrow the government by force or revolution?

No. In two related cases, the Supreme Court held that "negative" oaths that prohibit "subversive activities" are unconstitutional. In the first case, the Court noted that it was not clear what "subversive" or "revolutionary" activity includes.[3] Does revolution include altering the government through any rapid or fundamental change? If so, any person supporting or teaching peaceful but far-reaching constitutional amendments might be engaged in subversive activity. In the second case, a Maryland loyalty oath law provided for the discharge of subversive persons and called for perjury action against those who violated the oath.[4] The Court wrote that "the continuing surveillance which this type of law places on teachers is hostile to academic freedom," and its "over-breadth" makes possible "oppressive or capricious applications as regimes change." Here, concluded the Court, "we have another classic example of the need for 'narrowly drawn' legislation in this important First Amendment area."

Can teachers be required to swear that they will uphold the federal and state constitutions?

Yes. A group of Denver teachers argued that such an oath was unconstitutional, but a federal court disagreed.[5] According to the court, the oath is simply a recognition of our system of constitutional law. It is not overly broad and is not an improper invasion of a teacher's freedom of expression. On the contrary, the judge wrote that "support for the constitutions and laws of the nation and state does not call for blind subservience." This oath, explained the court, has roots as deep as the Constitution, which requires that government officials swear to uphold it. Thus the writers of the Constitution thought a positive loyalty oath was worth whatever minor deprivation of freedom of conscience might be involved.

Is an oath that teachers will "faithfully perform" their duties constitutional?

Yes. Again, Denver teachers argued that this oath was unconstitutionally vague, and again the court disagreed.[6] It held that a state can reasonably ask teachers in public schools to subscribe to professional competence and dedication. "It is certain," wrote the court, "that there is no right to be unfaithful in the performance of duties."

Is a loyalty oath unconstitutional if it applies to teachers and not to other state employees?

No. Teachers claimed that such an oath deprived them of equal protection by arbitrarily requiring educators but not all state employees to take it. The court replied that an oath to uphold the federal and state constitutions is "an almost universal requirement of all public officials, including lawyers and judges, and it cannot be truthfully said that teachers are being picked on."[7] As long as the oath is reasonable as applied to teachers, who work in an influential area, there is no constitutional requirement that it be applied to all public employees.

Can teachers be required to swear to "oppose the overthrow" of the government by any "illegal or unconstitutional method"?

Yes. Opponents of this Massachusetts oath said it raised the specter of "vague, undefinable responsibilities actively to combat a potential overthrow of the government." However, Chief Justice Burger rejected such "literal notions." On behalf of the Court, he wrote that the purpose of the oath was not to create specific responsibilities but "to assure that those in positions of public trust were willing to commit themselves to live by the constitutional process of our system," and not to use illegal force to change it.[8] The Chief Justice indicated his hope that these oaths and the intense controversy they cause might someday disappear. "The time may come," he wrote, "when the value of oaths in routine public employment will be thought not worth the candle." The Court concluded that those who fear the oath may lead to the prosecution of innocent people should bear in mind that such dire consequences will "not occur while this Court sits."

POLITICAL AND SOCIAL AFFILIATIONS

Can a teacher be fired for belonging to a communist, Nazi, or revolutionary organization?

No. A teacher cannot be punished merely for being a member of such an organization. This was the ruling of the U.S. Supreme Court in the case of a New York instructor Harry Keyishian.[9] To comply with state law, Keyishian was asked to sign a certificate stating that he was not a communist. The law disqualified any New York public school teacher or administrator who belonged to an organization that advocated the overthrow of the government by illegal means. When Keyishian refused to sign the certificate, his contract was not renewed. Administrators explained that to preserve our democracy, it was reasonable not to employ teachers who belonged to subversive orgarizations.

The Supreme Court disagreed. On behalf of the Court, Justice Brennan wrote: "Under our traditions, beliefs are personal and not a matter of mere association, and men in adhering to a political party or other organization do not subscribe unqualifiedly to all of its platforms or asserted principles. A law which applies to membership, without the specific intent to further the illegal aims of the organization, infringes unnecessarily on protected freedoms. It rests on the doctrine of guilt by association which has no place here."

The Court believed that the New York law would "cast a pall of orthodoxy over the classroom," encourage suspicion and distrust, and restrict academic freedom in the schools. Thus, it would have a damaging effect on educators and the nation. "Teachers and students," wrote Justice Brennan, "must always remain free to inquire, to study, and to evaluate, to gain new maturity and understanding; otherwise our civilization will stagnate and die." According to the Court, those who join an organization but do not share its unlawful purposes and do not participate in its unlawful activities pose no threat, either as citizens or as teachers. Therefore, mere membership in the Communist party or any other subversive organization, without a specific intent to further the unlawful aims of the organization, is not a constitutional basis for excluding an individual from his teaching position.

Does the *Keyishian* case automatically void similar state laws prohibiting membership in subversive organizations?

No. When the Supreme Court declares a state law unconstitutional, similar statutes in other states are not automatically voided. They remain "on the books" and are sometimes enforced unless the state legislature repeals them or a court specifically holds that they are unconstitutional. This was the situation in Arkansas when a professor who taught his course from a Marxist perspective and advocated "revolutionary change" was fired under a state law which prohibited any "member of a Nazi, Fascist, or Communist" organization being employed by the state. The Supreme Court of Arkansas reluctantly ruled that the law was unconstitutional.[10] After considering *Keyishian* and related decisions of the U.S. Supreme Court, the Arkansas court indicated that it had "no choice but to follow these decisions of the Court which is the final arbiter when constitutional interpretation is in dispute." In a subsequent federal case, the court upheld the professor's right to inform his students of his Marxist views; however, the court did not indicate whether the same expression by a high school teacher would also be protected.[11]

A similar situation occurred in California in 1980 when Marvin Schmid applied for a teaching position and was required to sign a non-Communist loyalty oath pursuant to state law. Most school districts realized the requirement was unconstitutional and did not enforce it. Schmid's district, however, said it had to enforce the law, so the teacher went to court. The state judge ruled that the law was clearly "repugnant to both the United States and California constitutions," and he ordered the state to inform all schools of its unconstitutionality and to prohibit its enforcement.[12]

Do teachers have a right to advocate, organize, and join a union?

Yes. According to the federal courts, the First Amendment protects the right of teachers to promote and organize a union. It also protects the rights of teachers' associations "to engage in advocacy on behalf of their members."[13] Furthermore, state legislatures may not pass laws that discriminate against teachers' unions because of their politically unpopular proposals.[14] (For more on teachers' unions and collective bargaining, see Chapter 3.)

On the other hand, the Mississippi Supreme Court upheld a school board decision not to reemploy the president of the local teachers' association mostly because of her insubordination and partly because of her criticism of the administration.[15] The court did not reinstate the teacher since her insubordination was a "substantial and credible" reason for her nonreemployment and since the district would have taken the same action even if she had not participated in the union activity. (For more on the scope and limits of teacher freedom of expression, see Chapter 8.)

Can teachers be prohibited from sending their children to private, segregated schools?

The answer depends on the circumstances. In the 1975 *Cook* case, a federal appeals court supported such a prohibition.[16] The case involved several Mississippi teachers who were not rehired when they sent their children to private, segregated academies in violation of school board policy. The policy was designed to ensure faculty support for the desegregated public schools. The court upheld the policy because of evidence that students in desegregated classes are "likely to perceive rejection . . . from a teacher whose own children attend a nearby racially segregated school." Because of the importance of desegregation, the court concluded that in this case the board can restrict the exercise of these teachers' associational rights that conflict with their effectiveness and job performance.

In two subsequent cases, however, federal appeals courts have given greater weight to the rights of teachers. In a 1983 Mississippi case, the court ruled that a school employee's interest in controlling the education of her child "takes precedence over the school board's interests" unless the enrollment of her son in a private school "materially and substantially interfered with the operation" of the public schools.[17] In a 1984 Alabama case, the court ruled that two tenured teachers who wanted to send their children to a virtually all-white Christian academy should be exempt from the school board policy prohibiting employees from sending their children to private schools.[18] The court distinguished this controversy from the 1975 *Cook* case on two grounds: First, in *Cook,* "the sole reason" why the teachers enrolled their children in private school was to avoid desegregation, while in this case segregation was not "the motivating factor" behind the teachers' decision; second, enrollment in the private academy is not "a serious threat to integration of the public schools."

Can a new school board refuse to reappoint a teacher because of his or her association with former board members?

No. In a small Texas school district, two political factions were vying for control of the school board. A teacher, Troy Burris, was friendly with members of the old board, whose policies he supported, and with the superintendent, who recommended him for reappointment. When a new board was elected that was hostile to the superintendent and the old board, it refused to approve the reappointment of Burris. The teacher claimed that the new board's action was based on his friendship with the old board and violated his First Amendment freedom of association. Although a school board may refuse to renew a teacher's contract for any legitimate reason, a federal appeals court ruled that it may not do so simply in retaliation for his support for and association with members of the former board.[19]

Can teachers be denied employment because the people they married are controversial or because of their divorce?

No. This would violate their constitutional right of free association. So ruled a federal court in the case of a middle school teacher who was denied a job because her husband was a controversial civil rights leader who helped organize a local school boycott.[20] The court concluded that the teacher could not be punished "because she elected to become the wife" of a civil rights activist. Similarly, a federal appeals court ruled that a school cannot refuse to rehire a teacher because of her divorce. According to this 1985 decision, "matters involving marriage and family relationships involve privacy rights that are constitutionally protected."[21]

Nevertheless, there are limits to a teacher's freedom of association in this area. These limits were confronted by a South Carolina teacher whose contract was not renewed because of his serious personal problems with his wife. On several occasions she had assaulted him with a bottle or a knife, and once burst into his classroom and threatened his life. A federal court noted that school officals in this case were faced with a "potentially explosive and dangerous" domestic conflict that had disrupted school activities. The court denied that a teacher's right to marry whom he wishes gives him the right "to engage in domestic altercations in the classroom of a public high school."[22]

Can a teacher be prohibited from marrying an administrator?

Yes. Or the board might transfer or dismiss an administrator for marrying a teacher. Either action might be legitimate to avoid conflicts of interest. Thus a Minnesota school board did not renew a high school principal's contract when he married a physical education teacher in violation of a board policy prohibiting administrator-teacher marriages. The principal claimed that this violated his constitutional rights. The court ruled, however, that the policy "does not deny people the right to marry; it only prohibits the employment of married couples in administrator-teacher situations."[23] The purpose of the rule is "a laudatory one—preventing conflicts of interest and favoritism." Situations where such conflicts might occur include teacher evaluation and recommendations, classroom and extracurricular assignments, disagreements among teachers, or school resource allocations. Therefore, because the interest of the state in avoiding such conflicts is strong and the impact of the policy on marriage itself is "so attenuated," the court upheld the board policy.

Similarly, a New York court ruled that a school district could transfer a teacher who married her assistant principal. Since district policy prohibited any employee supervising a "near relative" and since the assistant principal supervised his wife, the court held that the transfer was a reasonable action to avoid the "perception of favoritism on the part of other members of the teaching faculty."[24]

On the other hand, a Mississippi court ruled that an individual could not be prohibited from serving in the state legislature and voting on education laws simply because his wife was a public school teacher. According to the court, indirect, remote, insubstantial conflicts of interest should not be prohibited where the "interest is so small" that it "could not reasonably be expected to influence his judgment."[25]

Can teachers be prohibited from promoting political candidates in class?

Yes. An early California case provides an example of an educator who was punished for such behavior.[26] In 1922 a Sacramento teacher named Goldsmith suggested to his students that their parents support one of the candidates for school superintendent. According to Goldsmith, his candidate "would be more helpful to our department than a lady, and we need more men in our schools." As a result of these comments, the administration suspended him for "unprofessional conduct," and a state court supported this action. The judge observed that a teacher's "advocacy" of the election of a particular candidate before students in a public school and his attempts to influence students and their parents "introduced into the school questions wholly foreign to its purposes and objectives."

Can teachers wear political buttons, badges, or armbands to class?

Yes, as long as such symbols do not interfere with a teacher's classroom performance and are not an attempt to proselytize or indoctrinate students. A case in point occurred when a New York English teacher, Charles James, refused to stop wearing an armband to class to protest the Vietnam War. As a result he was dismissed for presenting only one point of view on a controversial public issue. A federal appeals court ruled in James's favor.[27] The court noted that teachers do not "shed their constitutional rights to freedom of speech or expression at the school-house gate" unless they cause substantial disruption.

On the other hand, since students may be a captive audience, there must be some restraint on the free expression of a teacher's view. Thus, if a teacher tries to persuade students that they should adopt his or her values, it is reasonable "to expect the state to protect impressionable children from such dogmatism." In James's case, however, the wearing of an armband did not interfere with his teaching, was not coercive, and was not an attempt to indoctrinate his students.

Can teachers be prohibited from encouraging or participating in demonstrations?

No. Such a broad prohibition would violate a teacher's constitutional rights. This was the ruling of a federal court in Alabama where the legislature barred raises to any teacher who "participates in, encourages or condones . . . any extracurricular demonstration."[28] The court acknowledged that a state may punish a teacher who disrupts schooling. Under the legislature's vague policy, however, teachers can be punished for encouraging a peaceful demonstration. According to the court, this policy is a "comprehensive interference with associational freedom which goes far beyond what might be justified in the protection of the state's legitimate interest."

Can administrators refuse to hire a teacher who participated in disruptions at another school?

Yes. Bruce Franklin, a Marxist English scholar, had his appointment rejected by the University of Colorado because of his participation in disruptions at Stanford University. Franklin argued that he never violated any criminal statutes. But a federal judge noted that schools need not tolerate political conduct "substantially disrupting school discipline even though that conduct was perhaps not unlawful."[29] The judge emphasized that he was not ruling against Franklin because of his political beliefs or his associations with radical political groups. Rather, it was because (1) there was "clear and convincing" evidence that Franklin's conduct at Stanford "materially and substantially interfered with university activities," and (2) this was a reasonable basis to conclude that he posed a "substantial threat of material disruption" at the University of Colorado.

TEACHERS AND PARTISAN POLITICS

Can a teacher elected to public office be required to resign?

Yes. Professor Mary Jane Galer was elected to the Georgia House of Delegates and requested an unpaid leave of absence. Because a state statute prohibited members of the legislature from being employed by a state agency, Galer's request was denied. She argued that the statute was unconstitutional because it restricted her right to hold office. The Georgia Supreme Court ruled that the law was a reasonable restriction on her rights because it furthered an important governmental interest.[30] Its purpose was to prevent "the obvious conflict of interests inherent in situations where an individual serves concurrently in two of the branches of state government." Thus the court ruled that Galer may be employed by her state college or by the legislature, but may not hold both positions. Although many schools grant leaves of absence to faculty members appointed or elected to political office, the *Galer* case indicates that they are under no constitutional obligation to do so.

Can a teacher be prohibited from running for political office?

Courts are split on this issue. Some hold that it is reasonable to require a teacher to resign before campaigning for public office; others feel that a general prohibition against running for any office is unconstitutional. In resolving this issue, one judge might focus on whether the prohibition is overly broad. Another judge might consider whether campaigning would interfere with the teacher's duties, whether the office is highly political or nonpartisan, or whether the position might involve a conflict of interests (e.g., a teacher running for the school board that employs her).

In Florida, for example, a law professor was dismissed after he filed to run for circuit judge because he violated a university rule prohibiting employees from engaging in "a political campaign for public office." The professor argued that the rule was unconstitutional, but a Florida court held that it was reasonable because

1. the demands on the time and energies of a candidate in a "warmly contested" political campaign would necessarily affect his efficiency as a teacher;
2. campaigning can bring political influences to bear on the students that might affect them detrimentally; and
3. the potential political involvement of a state university, which depends on public support from all political elements, is a major consideration supporting the reasonableness of the prohibition against teachers running for office.[31]

On the other hand, an Oregon court ruled that a state law prohibiting public employees from running for any political office was unconstitutional.[32] The court recognized that the state could bar some of its employees from campaigning for some offices to promote an efficient public service. This law, however, went much further than necessary and broadly restricted the First Amendment right of political expression. The court noted that "a revolution has occurred in the law relative to the state's power to limit federal First Amendment rights. Thirty years ago the statutes now under consideration would have been held to be constitutional." But in this case the court declared the law prohibiting public employees from running for state, federal, or nonpartisan office "unconstitutional because of overbreadth." It cannot be demonstrated, concluded the court, "that the good of the public service requires all of the prohibitions of the present statute."

Can a teacher be penalized because of his political opposition to a superintendent or board member?

No. Nathaniel Martin was a teacher and guidance counselor in Claiborne County for eleven years. After he supported a recall petition against three board members and opposed the election of the superintendent, Martin was told he would not be rehired "because of a reduction in force in the area of his employment." But the Mississippi Supreme Court concluded that the school's explanation was a pretext since there was no evidence of a funding shortage, no evidence that Martin was incompetent, or that the counseling needs would be less in the future than they had been in the past. According to the court, "where a teacher has engaged in constitutionally protected activity, and where the superintendent's reason for nonreemployment is shown to be false or a sham," the teacher is entitled to reinstatement.[33] In a similar Texas case, a federal judge went further and held several members of the school board personally liable for damages since their failure to rehire two teachers "because of their political associations was done in disregard of the teachers' clearly established constitutional rights."[34]

What if a teacher is not fired but only reassigned (with less salary) because of his support for an unsuccessful school board candidate? Is this still an infringement of his First Amendment rights? A federal appeals court ruled that it was. In this Oklahoma case, the court held that a teacher has a constitutional right to support any school board candidate and that retaliation in the form of "altered employment conditions instead of termination" is nevertheless an "unconstitutional infringement" of that right.[35]

Can teachers be prohibited from taking an active part in partisan politics?

Probably. Since the U.S. Supreme Court has upheld the Hatch Act, which prevents federal employees from being active in partisan politics, it is likely that school districts could impose similar restrictions on their teachers. The purpose of the Hatch Act is to reduce the hazards to fair and impartial government, prevent political parties from using public employees for political campaigns, and prohibit selection of government employees based on political performance. Yet the act does not bar all political activities. Employees are allowed to vote and contribute funds, to express their opinions on political subjects and candidates, to display political stickers and badges, and to take an active part in nonpartisan elections. Many school districts allow greater political freedom for their teachers. But a 1973 Supreme Court ruling concerning federal employees indicates that Hatch Act-type restrictions on teachers probably would not violate the U.S. Constitution although they may violate some state constitutions.[36]

Can teachers be prohibited from taking part in all political activity except voting?

No, ruled a federal court in a Texas case.[37] The court acknowledged that school boards can protect their educational system from undue political activity that may "materially and substantially interfere" with their schools. But a broad ban on *all* political activity went too far and violated the teacher's constitutional rights. This prohibition, wrote the judge, threatens popular government, not only "because it injures the individuals muzzled, but also because of its harmful effect on the community" in depriving it of the political participation of its teachers.

STUDENT ORGANIZATIONS

Is freedom of association a constitutional right?

Yes, it is. Although freedom of association is not directly mentioned in the Constitution, the Supreme Court has held the right to be "implicit" in the freedoms of speech, assembly, and petition. "Among the rights protected by the First Amendment," wrote Justice Lewis Powell, "is the right of individuals to associate to further their personal beliefs."[38] While courts have broadly protected this right among teachers and other adults, it has been more narrowly applied to students in the public schools.

Can secret societies be prohibited in public schools?

Yes. As early as 1909 the California legislature declared it unlawful for any public school student to become a member of any secret society or club. In defending this legislation, a state court wrote that such groups "tend to engender an undemocratic spirit of caste" and "to promote cliques" among students.[39] The judge noted that "regulations have recently been adopted by boards of education in many cities of the country" to curb the negative effects of secret organizations, and "courts have uniformly held valid reasonable rules adapted by school authorities to prevent the establishment" of such groups. This decision was written in 1912, and it is still the prevailing legal opinion on the subject.

Can schools prohibit students from belonging to fraternities, sororities, and other undemocratic organizations?

Yes. Although adults cannot be prohibited from joining undemocratic groups, courts have held that such prohibitions can apply to high school students "in their formative years." A California case concerned a former high school sorority that had given up its secret ritual, handshake, and Greek letter name and reorganized itself into the Manana Club. Despite these changes, the Sacramento School Board prohibited the Manana Club and other undemocratic organizations. As a result, one of the members of the Manana Club went to court to have the rule declared unconstitutional. She argued that the club was not secret and submitted in evidence its constitution, which described its objectives as being "literature, charity, and democracy." But a California appeals court found that the club had different purposes than its stated objectives and upheld the school regulations.[40]

The court said that schools had authority to restrict student social organizations that try to create a membership composed of the "socially elite" by "self-perpetuation, rushing, pledging," and admitting a select few from the student body. The Manana Club rules provided that only twenty girls from the Sacramento schools could be rushed each semester; each candidate had to be sponsored by three members, and new members were chosen by a secret process. Thus the court concluded that the purpose of these prohibited organizations is "not to foster democracy (as the Manana constitution preaches) but to frustrate democracy (as the Manana Club by its admitted activities practices)."

Do many states have legislation outlawing undemocratic high school organizations, and have such laws been upheld?

Yes. Although such legislation might seem inconsistent with the principles of the *Tinker* decision, judges have pointed out that statutes in about 25 states have outlawed high school fraternities, sororities, and organizations such as the Manana Club, and that numerous cases over the past 50 years have upheld such legislation against attack on the grounds of unconstitutionality. The 1966 case discussed above,[41] noted that the following states have legislation similar to California's, which makes it unlawful for any public school student to join "any fraternity, sorority or secret club": Arkansas, Colorado, Florida, Illinois, Indiana, Iowa, Kansas, Louisiana, Maine, Massachusetts (optional with local board), Michigan, Minnesota, Mississippi, Montana, Nebraska, New Jersey, Ohio, Oklahoma, Oregon, Pennsylvania, Rhode Island, Texas (limited), Vermont, Virginia, and Washington. A 1978 report added Maryland, Missouri, and New York (optional with local board) to the list of states that prohibit public schools from setting up secret organizations.[42]

Are schools required to recognize controversial student groups?

Probably. Public schools are not required to recognize any extracurricular student organizations. But if they recognize some political groups (e.g., Young Democrats or Republicans or a United Nations Club), then they cannot discriminate against other groups (e.g., socialists or conservatives) simply because of the unpopular or controversial quality of their ideas or goals.

In a Supreme Court case, Justice Powell ruled that college officials could not deny recognition to Students for a Democratic Society, a "leftist" organization whose philosophy was in conflict with that of the school.[43] Justice Powell wrote that "denial of recognition, without justification to college organizations," abridges their constitutional right of association. This is because nonrecognition usually restricts a group's ability to function by denying it use of school facilities such as meeting rooms, bulletin boards, and the school newspaper. The court ruled that basic disagreement with a group's philosophy was not justification for nonrecognition. Although this case did not involve high school students, the same principles are likely to apply to public high schools. Thus a federal court held that it was unconstitutional for a Michigan high school to deny recognition to the Young Socialist Alliance and other voluntary student groups, because they "advocate controversial ideas" and "stress one side of issues."[44]

Does recognition of an organization imply approval of its goals or programs?

No, courts generally hold that it does not.[45] The purpose of recognition is to enable school officials to be informed about the purposes and activities of an organization, to ensure that student groups understand and are willing to comply with reasonable school rules, and to establish procedures for governing the time, place, and manner in which groups may conduct their activities. If school officals used the term "registered" (rather than "recognized") student organizations, they might lessen the tendency of many parents and educators to erroneously believe that recognition implies approval.

Can schools regulate or restrict student organizations?

Yes. Administrators can require student groups to obey a variety of reasonable regulations governing the equitable and responsible use of school facilities. Groups that fail to comply with such regulations can be disciplined and barred from campus. Moreover, the Supreme Court ruled that school officials would be justified in refusing to recognize a proposed organization if there was evidence that the group was likely to be a disruptive influence and break "reasonable rules, interrupt classes, or substantially interfere" with other students' rights.[46]

Does the Equal Access Act protect student organizations?

Partly. Congress passed the Equal Access Act in 1984 to prohibit discrimination against student groups because of their political, religious, or philosophical ideas in public schools that allow extracurricular groups to meet on campus.[47] However, the Act does not limit the authority of administrators to prohibit all extracurricular organizations or to permit only curriculum-related groups which schools can then control. (See Chapter 8 on this topic.)

Must public schools recognize gay student groups?

The answer is uncertain, although courts have generally ruled in favor of gay college groups that have been denied recognition. Judges have reasoned that college students "of whatever sexual persuasion have the fundamental right to meet [and] discuss current problems" so long as they do not advocate unlawful activity.[48] It might also be argued that the Equal Access Act protects gay groups since it prohibits discrimination against any student meetings "on the basis of the . . . content of the speech."[49] However, there has not been an appellate court case on this topic in the public schools. Judges might give high school administrators wider latitude in restricting gay student groups among teenagers in their formative years on the grounds that the Equal Access Act does not apply to groups that "substantially interfere" with the school's responsibility "to protect the well-being of students."[50]

Are student religious groups entitled to recognition?

Yes, if not school sponsored. Federal law prohibits schools from denying equal access to student religious groups because of the "religious . . . content" of their speech.[51] On the other hand, federal appeals courts have held that public schools can deny recognition to student religious clubs because such recognition would "create an appearance of official support" in violation of the establishment clause of the First Amendment.[52] However, on June 5, 1990, the Supreme

Court upheld the Equal Access Act and ruled that student religious clubs can meet on the same basis as other extracurricular activities.[53] (For more on this topic, see Chapter 9.)

DEMONSTRATIONS AND PROTESTS

Do students have a right to demonstrate on campus?

Yes. School officials probably could not issue a total prohibition against all demonstrations anywhere on campus without violating students' First Amendment rights. Yet administrators clearly have the authority to protect safety, property, and normal school operations by placing reasonable, nondiscriminatory restrictions on the time, place, and manner of proposed demonstrations.

In Pennsylvania, a group of high school students were suspended for participating in a sit-in demonstration, although they attempted to conduct their protest in a peaceful and orderly fashion. The evidence indicated that some demonstrators were noisy and skipped classes, and that the demonstration made it necessary to relocate other students. Therefore, despite the students' peaceful intentions, the judge ruled against them because their protest substantially interfered with the educational process.[54] However, the court noted that the demonstration was not illegal merely because it was in school, because other students gathered to watch, or because school administrators were distracted from their regular duties. (Related questions appear in Chapter 8.)

Do peace groups have a right to recruit in public schools?

They probably do if the Armed Forces are allowed to recruit there. In Chicago, the Board of Education allowed military recruiters to disseminate literature, advertise in the school papers and on bulletin boards, and counsel students concerning careers in the armed services. However, the board denied a peace group the opportunity to distribute information and counsel students about "conscientious objection and legal alternatives to the draft," because they feared the group would use the schools "to propagandize their views on . . . the evils of war." But the group sued and won. According to the court, this is not a case of anyone's right to propagandize; it is an issue of "equal access" to discuss a subject the board already approved when it allowed military recruiters into the schools.[55] If military representatives are allowed to discuss military careers, then the peace group should be allowed an equal opportunity to discuss alternative careers. Otherwise the schools would be officially discriminating against a particular point of view.

Similarly, a federal court in Georgia ruled in 1988 that a local antiwar group should not be denied the same access as military recruiters—"to present peace-oriented educational and career opportunities to Atlanta public school students." In addition, the court held that school policy banning speakers who criticized other job opportunities or discouraged participation in a particular field were unconstitutional efforts to suppress the peace group's point of view.[56]

On the other hand, another federal court held that a Pennsylvania school was not required to make its facilities available to a student group for an antinuclear rally open to the public where such facilities have not been generally open.[57]

Can controversial speakers be prohibited from public schools?

Not simply because they are controversial or are likely to express unpopular views. Although public schools probably can prohibit *all* outside speakers, officials do not have the authority to discriminate against views with which they and most citizens or students disagree.

After a New Hampshire school official denied a socialist candidate the opportunity to speak, a federal court wrote that the First Amendment "encompasses the right to receive information and ideas," and its protection extends to listeners as well as speakers.[58] When a school chooses to provide a forum for outside speakers, it must do so in a way that is consistent with constitutional principles. According to the court, this means that (1) school officials may not influence a public forum by censoring the ideas, the speakers, or the audience; (2) the right of students to hear speakers cannot be left to the complete discretion of administrators; and (3) freedom of speech and assembly requires that "outside speakers be fairly selected and that equal time be given to opposing views."

In a 1985 Maine case, a school board, after several bomb threats, cancelled the observance of Tolerance Day and a homosexual speaker. The speaker and the program organizers alleged that the school violated their First Amendment rights. However, a state court upheld the board's action for two reasons: First, the board's motive was to prevent substantial disruption, not to restrict discussion of controversial ideas. And second, since Tolerance Day was to be part of the required school curriculum, the board had the discretion to change the program as long as it did not restrict discussion of homosexuality, prejudice, or other issues of concern.[59]

Can schools bar all outside political speakers?

No. A case confronting this issue arose in Oregon when a high school teacher invited a variety of political speakers, including a communist, to his class. Before the communist was to speak, the school board banned "all political speakers" from the high school. The ban was ruled unconstitutional by a federal court.[60]

The judge acknowledged that schools might exclude all speakers, unqualified speakers, or speakers who would cause disruption. But officials could not bar only "outside political speakers," nor could they contend that "political subjects are inappropriate in a high school curriculum." On the contrary, the court noted that political subjects are frequently discussed in schools and such discussions are often "required by law."

The judge acknowledged the problem faced by school officials in a community in which many people equate communism with "violence, deception and imperialism." He observed, however, that schools would eliminate much of their curriculum if they teach only about "pacifist, honest, and nonexpansionist societies." "I am firmly convinced," concluded the judge, "that a course designed to teach students that a free and democratic society is superior to those in which freedoms are sharply curtailed will fail entirely if it fails to teach one important lesson: that the power of the state is never so great that it can silence a man or woman simply because there are those who disagree."

Can schools prohibit suspended teachers from associating with students?

Under some circumstances, they can. In West Virginia, for example, a high school basketball coach was suspended for beating a student and, during the suspension, was prohibited "from any professional association with public school students." The coach claimed that this violated his constitutional right of association. But a federal court disagreed. It ruled that the administration had a compelling interest in seeing that the effectiveness of the coach's replacement was not undermined. According to the court, "the specter of a former authority figure competing with his replacement for the affection and respect of the students justified the restrictions imposed."[61]

SUMMARY

In past decades, the Supreme Court had been critical of teacher loyalty oaths since they tended to inhibit the exercise of First Amendment freedoms. Negative oaths (e.g., swearing that one does not belong to any subversive organization) were usually held unconstitutional. Similarly, oaths that were "overbroad," uncertain, and ambiguous were also struck down—especially when there were statutory procedures to "police" the oath and punish violators. Nevertheless, two kinds of oaths have been consistently upheld: (1) loyalty oaths drawn with precision and prohibiting clearly unlawful conduct, and (2) positive employment oaths affirming support for the state and federal constitutions or pledging to uphold professional standards.

Teachers cannot be dismissed simply because they are members of a revolutionary or subversive organization unless they have supported the organization's illegal activities. Similarly, teachers cannot be penalized because they associate with union organizers, political extremists, or unsuccessful school board candidates, or because their spouse engages in controversial activities unless competent evidence indicates that such behavior impairs the teacher's effectiveness. It is unclear whether teachers can be prohibited from sending their children to private, segregated schools. However, teachers can be prohibited from marrying an administrator.

In recent years, teachers' organizations have become powerful political machines, and individual teachers are no longer prohibited from engaging in all political activity. Today's teachers cannot be punished merely for wearing political symbols, for supporting particular candidates, or for participating in political demonstrations. On the other hand, they have no right to campaign for candidates in school, to indoctrinate students, or to urge disruptive political action. While in some districts teachers may run for and hold partisan political office, this is not a constitutional right; it usually depends on state legislation or local policy.

Although adults have the right to join secret and undemocratic organizations, courts have refused to grant these rights to public school students. Statutes in over 20 states have outlawed high school fraternities, sororities, and similar groups that choose their members in an undemocratic manner. Numerous cases during the past 60 years have upheld such laws against charges of unconstitutionality.

When school officials refuse to recognize a proposed student organization without justification, such action violates the students' constitutional rights of association. This means that if administrators deny recognition to a student group, they bear a "heavy burden" to demonstrate the appropriateness of their action. Furthermore, the Equal Access Act prohibits discrimination against student groups because of the religious, philosophic, or political content of their speech. On the other hand, schools may issue reasonable rules concerning the time, place, and manner in which student groups must conduct their activities; and they may deny recognition to groups that do not follow such rules.

When schools provide a forum for outside speakers, they must give equal time to opposing views and may not discriminate among proposed speakers or censor their ideas. Moreover, public schools may not ban all political speakers or all candidates for public office or prohibit views with which most students, teachers, or parents disagree. Student groups can be required to request approval of school officials before inviting an outside speaker. If a request is denied, there must be a fair and prompt hearing.

NOTES

1. As quoted in Robert R. Hamilton, LEGAL RIGHTS AND LIABILITIES OF TEACHERS 84 (Laramie, Wyo.: School Law Publications, 1956)
2. *Baggett v. Bullitt*, 377 U.S. 360 (1964).
3. *Id.*
4. *Whitehall v. Elkins*, 389 U.S. 54 (1967).
5. *Ohlson v. Phillips*, 304 F.Supp. 1152 (D. Col. 1969), *aff'd*, 397 U.S. 317 (1970).
6. *Id.*
7. *Id.*
8. *Cole v. Richardson*, 405 U.S. 676 (1972).
9. *Keyishian v. Board of Regents of New York*, 385 U.S. 589 (1967).
10. *Cooper v. Henslee*, 522 S.W.2d 391 (Ark. 1975).
11. *Cooper v. Ross*, 472 F.Supp. 802 (E.D. Ark. 1979). The focus of the state court

decision was the constitutionality of the Arkansas statute. The federal case concerned whether the university violated the professor's First Amendment rights by not reappointing him.

12. *Schmid* v. *Lovette*, 201 Cal. Rptr. 424 (Cal. App. 1 Dist. 1984).

13. *Missouri National Education Association* v. *New Madrid County R-1*, 810 F.2d 164 (8th Cir. 1987).

14. *South Carolina Education Association* v. *Campbell*, 697 F.Supp. 908 (D. S.C. 1988).

15. *Hattiesburg Municipal Separate School District* v. *Gates*, 461 So.2d. 730 (Miss. 1984).

16. *Cook* v. *Hudson*, 511 F.2d 744 (5th Cir. 1975).

17. *Brantley* v. *Surles*, 718 F.2d 1354 (5th Cir. 1983).

18. *Stough* v. *Crenshaw County Board of Education*, 744 F.2d 1479 (11th Cir. 1984).

19. *Burris* v. *Willis Independent School District*, 713 F.2d 1087 (5th Cir. 1983).

20. *Randle* v. *Indianola Municipal Separate School District*, 373 F.Supp. 766 (N.D. Miss. 1974).

21. *Littlejohn* v. *Rose*, 768 F.2d 765 (6th Cir. 1985).

22. *Mescia* v. *Berry*, 406 F.Supp. 1181 (D. S.C. 1974).

23. *Keckeisen* v. *Independent School District 612*, 509 F.2d 1062 (8th Cir. 1975), *cert. denied*, 423 U.S. 833 (1975).

24. *Solomon* v. *Quinones*, 531 N.Y.S.2d. 349 (1988).

25. *Smith* v. *Dorsey*, 530 So.2d. 513 (Miss. 1988); *Frazier* v. *State by and through Pittman*, 504 So.2d. 675 (Miss. 1987).

26. *Goldsmith* v. *Board of Education*, 225 P. 783 (Cal. 1924).

27. *Charles James* v. *Board of Education of Central District No. 1*, 461 F.2d 566 (2d Cir. 1972).

28. *Alabama Education Association* v. *Wallace*, 362 F.Supp. 682 (M.D. Ala. 1973).

29. *Franklin* v. *Atkins*, 409 F. Supp. 439 (D. Colo. 1976).

30. *Galer* v. *Board of Regents of the University System*, 236 S.E.2d 617 (Ga. 1977).

31. *Jones* v. *Board of Control*, 131 So.2d 713 (Fla. 1961).

32. *Minielly* v. *State*, 411 P.2d 69 (Ore. 1966).

33. *Claiborne County Board of Education* v. *Martin*, 500 So.2d 981 (Miss. 1986).

34. *Guerra* v. *Roma Independent School District*, 444 F.Supp. 812 (S.D. Tex. 1977).

35. *Childers* v. *Independent School District No. 1 of Bryan County, State of Oklahoma*, 676 F.2d 1338 (10th Cir. 1982).

36. *United States Civil Service Commission* v. *National Association of Letter Carriers, AFL-CIO*, 413 U.S. 548 (1973).

37. *Montgomery* v. *White*, 320 F.Supp. 303 (E.D. Tex. 1969).

38. *Healy* v. *James*, 408 U.S. 169 (1972).

39. *Bradford* v. *Board of Education*, 121 P. 929 (1912).

40. *Robinson* v. *Sacramento City Unified School District*, 53 Cal. Rptr. 781 (1966).

41. *Id*.

42. STATE LEGAL STANDARDS FOR THE PROVISION OF PUBLIC EDUCATION 32 (Washington, D.C.: National Institute of Education, 1978).

43. *Healy, supra*.

44. *Dixon* v. *Beresh*, 361 F.Supp. 253 (E.D. Mich. 1973).

45. *Gay Alliance of Students* v. *Matthews*, 544 F.2d 162 (4th Cir. 1976).

46. *Healy, supra*.

47. David Tatel and Elliot Minceberg, *The Equal Access Act Four Years Later: The Confusion Remains*, 51 ED. LAW REP. 11 (1989).

48. *Gay Alliance of Students, supra;* see also *Gay Student Services* v. *Texas A&M University,* 737 F.2d 1317 (5th Cir. 1984).
49. 20 U.S.C.A. § 4071(a) (1990).
50. *Id.* at § 4071 (c)(4) and (f).
51. *Id.* at § 4071(a).
52. *Brandon* v. *Board of Education of Guilderland Central School District,* 635 F.2d 971 (2d Cir. 1980).
53. *New York Times,* 6/5/90.
54. *Gebert* v. *Hoffman,* 336 F.Supp. 694 (E.D. Pa. 1972). For a more restrictive decision, see *Sword* v. *Fox,* 446 F.2d 1091 (4th Cir. 1971).
55. *Clergy and Laity Concerned* v. *Chicago Board of Education,* 586 F.Supp. 1408 (N.D. Ill. 1984).
56. *Searcey* v. *Crim,* 681 F.Supp. 821 (N.D. Ga. 1988).
57. *Student Coalition for Peace* v. *Lower Marion School District Board of School Directors,* 618 F.Supp. 53 (D.C. Pa. 1985). On appeal, the court ruled that the Equal Access Act of 1984 would apply to this case "only if a limited open forum existed after the Act became law." 776 F.2d 431 (3d Cir. 1985).
58. *Vail* v. *Board of Education of Portsmouth,* 354 F.Supp. 592 (D. N.H. 1973).
59. *Solmitz* v. *Maine School Administrative District No. 59,* 495 A.2d 812 (Me. 1985).
60. *Wilson* v. *Chancellor,* 418 F.Supp. 1358 (D. Ore. 1976).
61. *Cook* v. *Board of Education for Logan County,* 671 F.Supp. 1110 (S.D. W.Va. 1987).

CHAPTER 11

What Are My Rights under Due Process?

OVERVIEW

It is commonly accepted among lawyers that a right without adequate procedures to protect and enforce it is no right at all. This was recognized by the framers of the Constitution when they inserted the right to due process of law in both the Fifth and Fourteenth Amendments. This chapter focuses on the Fourteenth Amendment, for public schools are agencies of the state, and the amendment provides that no "State deprive any person of life, liberty, or property, without due process of law." Courts have held that actions of school officials and board members are state actions; therefore, the Fourteenth Amendment applies to them.

Due process may be thought of in ordinary language as "fair process," an attempt to secure justice in official actions. Most people gain their impressions of due process from television's presentation of criminal cases. This chapter centers around civil cases, where individuals find themselves in conflict with school officials concerning their jobs or some restrictions related to their work or schooling. In these matters, due process requires that governmental action not be arbitrary, unreasonable, or discriminatory and that fair procedures be followed by officials before any act by these officials would be carried out depriving anyone of "life, liberty, or property."

DUE PROCESS FOR TEACHERS

When is official action arbitrary or unreasonable?

Like many other concepts used to govern human affairs, terms such as "arbitrary," "discriminatory," or "unreasonable" are not easily and simply defined. Their legal meanings become clearer as we look at the ways courts have used and interpreted them. Various cases have held, for example, that it is arbitrary to dismiss teachers for membership in a controversial or even subversive organization. Since many members of such organizations are innocent of any wrongdoing and may not even be aware of the organization's purposes and activities, it is arbitrary to classify such members with those who knowingly participate in illegal activities.[1] Thus some classifications are arbitrary, while others are reasonable. It is reasonable to classify people according to age for purposes such as voting, driving a car, and running for the Senate; but it is unreasonable to use age classification for access to food or medical care. It has been held reasonable to classify males and females separately for military services, but arbitrary to classify them separately for purposes of voting or holding administrative positions in school.

Furthermore, as we have seen in earlier chapters, some courts consider it arbitrary to regulate teachers' or students' hair length, while others consider such policies reasonable. What is arbitrary or discriminatory is not always clear or simple. Courts tend to apply a three-step test to determine whether a law or policy is arbitrary: (1) They ask whether there is a legitimate social goal or objective to be attained by the law or policy, (2) they seek a rational connection between the objective and the means created to achieve it, and (3) they look for alternative and less restrictive ways of achieving the desired goal.

A further concern of courts when examining laws and policies under the due process clause is vagueness. If a law or policy is so vague that a reasonable person of ordinary intelligence cannot be guided by it, it is said to violate due process. Such policies often occur in schools that attempt to control the grooming of teachers and students and are not sufficiently specific in their stated policies or rules. For example, a requirement that "teachers must dress in good taste" would be void because it is too vague. To say that the principal will be the judge of what is in good taste does not cure the defect, for it gives arbitrary power to the principal and thus violates due process.

Many lawsuits filed under other provisions of the Constitution also allege a violation of the due process clause because policies or laws that involve racial, sexual, or other discrimination, or that abridge one's liberty, are also often unreasonable, arbitrary, or vague and therefore violate due process.* We now

---

* Courts and lawyers often distinguish *substantive* and *procedural* due process. Actions that are arbitrary, unreasonable, discriminatory, or based on vague rules are said to violate substantive due process; unfair procedures violate procedural due process. For most educators, such distinctions become needlessly technical.

turn to questions related to fair procedures, questions that most educators think about when the right to due process is mentioned.

Can local communities attach any condition they wish to the privilege of teaching?

No. Moreover, teaching can no longer be thought of as merely a privilege. Historically, the question of whether teaching was a right or a privilege was important because various conditions could be attached to the granting of a privilege, but rights could not be so restricted. Today it is clear that while no one has a right to public employment, unconstitutional conditions cannot be attached to a public job. For example, as a condition for teaching in its schools, a community cannot require that teachers be members of a certain religion or that they vote for candidates of a specific political party. As the Supreme Court has said: "We need not pause to consider whether an abstract right to public employment exists. It is sufficient to say that constitutional protection does extend to the public servant whose exclusion pursuant to a statute is patently arbitrary or discriminatory."[2]

Is there a distinction between tenured and probationary teachers in the right to due process?

Yes. This distinction was established and explained in Chapter 2 (see pages 22–26). Since the Fourteenth Amendment applies only if one is being deprived of "life, liberty, or property," the teacher who claims a denial of due process because job security is threatened must show a deprivation of one of these rights.

A tenured teacher has a reasonable expectancy that his or her position will be continuous. Such expectation of a "continuous contract" is the meaning of tenure, and courts have held that this is a sufficient "property" right to warrant the protection of the due process clause. Tenured teachers receive the full protection of due process. Probationary teachers have no continuous contract and therefore cannot make a claim to a property right on that basis. Other grounds may permit them to claim the protection of the due process clause, however.

The *Roth* Case

When David Roth, a nontenured assistant professor at a public institution, was informed that he would not be rehired for the upcoming academic year, he went to court.* He claimed that he was never given a notice or a hearing regarding any reasons for the nonrenewal of his contract. This, he alleged, violated his constitutional rights by depriving him of his "liberty" and "property" without due process of law.

---

* Although Roth was a college professor, the legal principles of this case apply equally to public elementary and secondary schools.

The Supreme Court disagreed with Roth.[3] The Court distinguished a probationary teacher from a tenured teacher and held that only the tenured teacher had a reasonable expectancy of continuous employment, which created a property interest meriting due process protection. The probationary teacher has a property interest only for the duration of the contract. Thus, if the probationary teacher is dismissed *during* the year of the contract, notice, a hearing, and reasons for dismissal are required. There is an important difference, however, between a dismissal during the term of the contract and a mere nonrenewal. Since the teacher does not have a right to a renewal of the contract, its nonrenewal violates no rights. That is the very meaning of the probationary period.

The Court then turned to the claim that the teacher's "liberty" interest was diminished. There are conceivable circumstances, reasoned the Court, where even a probationary teacher would have a right to a hearing. This would be the case if the employing school or its officials made statements against the teacher that were stigmatizing and thus seriously damaged possibilities for future employment. According to the Court, if in connection with the nonrenewal, the school damaged the teacher's "good name, reputation, honor or integrity . . . a notice and an opportunity to be heard are essential."

Unless local law requires it, schools are under no legal obligation to give reasons for not renewing the contract of a probationary teacher. If they give such reasons and allege incompetence, racism, sexism, mental or moral unfitness, fraud, or other damaging reasons, the teacher has a right to notice and a hearing where the validity of these charges are examined and refuted.[4]

In sum, the Supreme Court has ruled that important distinctions exist between tenured and probationary teachers related to the right to due process. In the ordinary case of the nonrenewal of a contract of a probationary teacher, there is no constitutional right to due process, for no property right is being violated. Under special circumstances, where the teacher's reputation is stigmatized by charges made by school officials, the teacher's liberty interest is implicated, and proper procedures must be followed to provide an opportunity for the teacher to refute those charges.

However, some states or local school districts do expand these due process rights to provide for minimal due process even for probationary teachers, though typically nothing more than a statement of the reasons for nonrenewal is required.

Can schools refuse to rehire probationary teachers for any reason whatever?

No. School officials do not have unlimited discretion not to renew the contract of probationary teachers. The Supreme Court in *Roth* said that only in the ordinary case of nonrenewal of a probationary teacher's contract is there no constitutional right to due process. Stigmatizing reasons for nonrenewal give rise to sufficient due process rights to enable teachers to clear their names.

Due process rights must also be granted if the probationary teacher's nonrenewal relates to some constitutionally protected activity (e.g., exercise of the right to free speech or union organizing). This principle was applied in the case of two teachers in the Miami–Dade County, Florida, Junior College. When the Board of Public Instruction of Dade County denied them tenure by refusing to hire them for a fourth year, the teachers claimed that the board's action was in retaliation for their union-organizing activities and also because one of them supported in her classroom some "new demands for campus freedom."

The district court upheld the board's right not to renew the probationary teachers' contract, but the circuit court of appeals reversed this ruling in a strongly worded opinion.[5] The court was not impressed by the argument that there is no right to public employment and that therefore the board may deny renewal of the contract at will. The chief judge wrote: "Equally unpersuasive is the argument that since there is no constitutional right to public employment, school officials only allowed these teachers contracts to expire. . . . The right sought to be vindicated is *not* a contractual one, nor could it be since no right to reemployment existed. What is at stake is the vindication of constitutional rights—the right not to be punished by the state or to suffer retaliation at its hand because a public employee persists in the exercise of First Amendment rights."

The judge quoted from leading Supreme Court cases to support his position: "To state that a person does not have a constitutional right to government employment is only to say that he must comply with reasonable, lawful, and nondiscriminatory terms laid down by the proper authorities."[6] Furthermore, "constitutional protection does extend to the public servant whose exclusion pursuant to a statute is patently arbitrary or discriminatory."[7] Recent cases have reaffirmed these principles. For example, in 1978 three Missouri teachers found their jobs in jeopardy because they had been active in the Missouri branch of the National Education Association and had spoken out against the school board at public meetings concerned with salary increases. The courts ordered their reinstatement because it found that their terminations were motivated by their exercise of First Amendment rights.[8] In West Virginia, the court reinstated three teachers and awarded them back pay when it found that their transfers or dismissals were in retaliation for political activities on behalf of a school board candidate.[9] The West Virginia court said that "the law, applicable to the merits of this case is clear: A non-policy-making, non-confidential government employee may not be discharged from a job that he or she is satisfactorily performing upon the sole ground of his political beliefs or activities."

Thus, even probationary teachers may exercise their constitutional rights. If a probationer presents evidence to indicate that nonrenewal is in retaliation for the exercise of such rights, due process must be available to determine whether or not the nonrenewal is so motivated. If the facts indicate that the sole motivation for nonrenewal was a constitutionally protected activity, the termination will not stand. If there are mixed reasons for nonrenewal, the outcome may be different.

The *Mt. Healthy* Case

Doyle, a public school teacher in Ohio, went to court to challenge the action of the school board not to reappoint him. Doyle was very active in the Teacher's Association; in fact, he had served as its president. During his presidency, but not directly connected with his role in the association, he had gotten into an argument and even an altercation with another teacher, which led to a one-day suspension for both teachers. He had also gotten into arguments with cafeteria employees over the amount of spaghetti served him, had referred to students as "sons of bitches," and had made obscene gestures at two girls in the cafeteria who disobeyed him. In his capacity as president of the Teachers' Association, he had called the local radio station and conveyed critical remarks to them about his principal's memorandum concerning a dress code for teachers and how such a code might influence public support of a bond issue.

Doyle contended that he had a constitutional right to communicate with the radio station and that his exercise of such a right played a "substantial" part in the board's decision not to renew his contract. The district court agreed with Doyle and ordered his reinstatement with back pay. After the court of appeals affirmed this decision, the case went to the Supreme Court.

The Supreme Court, upholding the constitutional rights of probationary teachers, said that "Doyle's claims under the First and Fourth Amendments are not defeated by the fact that he did not have tenure."[10] He might establish a claim to reinstatement if the decision not to rehire him was based on his exercise of a constitutional right. Nevertheless, the Court asked whether other legitimate grounds, independent of any First Amendment rights, were involved in not extending tenure to Doyle. If there were other professional grounds not to renew the contract, the fact that the school board included some impermissible grounds in its decision would not save the teacher's job.

The Court tried to balance the rights of the individual probationary teacher with the important social interest in conducting effective and efficient public schools. If the individual can show that the protected activity was a "substantial factor" or a "motivating factor" in the board's decision not to renew the contract, the board may still show by a preponderance of evidence that the teacher would not have been reemployed even in the absence of the protected conduct. Thus the Supreme Court sent the case back to the lower courts to determine in the light of these principles.

Various lower courts have applied the *Mt. Healthy* test to their cases. For example, a Louisiana teacher challenged the nonrenewal of his contract and claimed that his freedom of expression was violated by the action of the school board. Although the teacher could show that "his constitutionally protected conduct was a motivating factor in the board's decision," the court ruled that the principal's negative evaluations were sufficient for the board to reach the same conclusion.[11] By contrast, a Texas court ruled on behalf of teachers who showed that the only credible explanation for the nonrenewal of their contracts was their political activities on behalf of opponents of three recently elected board members. [12] (A related question appears on page 194.)

What is procedural due process?

In the final analysis, the legal concept of procedural due process refers to fair procedures. There is no single, technical definition for this concept; its basic elements are flexible and must be applied and interpreted in light of the unique facts and circumstances of each case. As a general rule, fairness would require that before a teacher is deprived of any substantial liberty or property interest, there ought to be adequate notice and a hearing before an impartial tribunal where the teacher's side of the conflict is presented. A sense of fairness also includes the right to be represented by a lawyer or a friend, to present evidence and to cross-examine witnesses, to receive a written copy of the findings and conclusions, and to have an opportunity to appeal.

In addition to the constitutional right to due process, most states also have statutes that establish procedures for the termination of teachers. When such laws exist, they are strictly enforced by courts, and boards of education must follow them meticulously.

School board policies must also be followed, but they don't have the same force as state laws. For example, a probationary teacher in Wyoming was terminated without being evaluated four times during the year, which was the school's policy. The teacher claimed that her right to due process was violated because the school board did not follow its own policies. However, the state court ruled that she had no property interest in the position and thus was not entitled to a statement of reasons for the nonrenewal. She was only entitled to a notice of nonrenewal by March 15 as prescribed by state law.[13]

Is a school board a fair tribunal for the hearing?

Yes, according to various court decisions. Although it would seem that the board represents the administration and the community in conflict with the individual teacher who is being dismissed or whose contract is not being renewed, the Supreme Court ruled that this fact alone does not disqualify the board as a decision maker if the hearing is otherwise fair.[14] At a typical school board hearing, strict legal procedures need not be used, for these are administrative hearings and not court proceedings. Technical rules of evidence do not apply, but the proceedings must be orderly.[15]

Must state laws be strictly followed?

Yes, they must be, in states that have enacted statutes to govern nonrenewals or dismissals. For example, a probationary teacher in Ohio claimed that her notice of nonrenewal was late and that therefore she was entitled to reemployment for the ensuing year. The facts showed that she was aware the board had not renewed her contract and that she was not available to receive the notice when attempts were made to deliver it at her home. Nevertheless, the Ohio Supreme Court ruled in her favor because she did not purposely avoid receiving the notice, and the school board had not exerted the necessary efforts to comply with the requirements of the statute.[16]

Questions also arise concerning the adequacy of the substance of the notice. For example, Alabama law requires adequate notice that specifies the grounds for the administrative action. When one principal wrote a letter to a teacher stating: "You have not done well enough for me to recommend that you come back next year," the state's supreme court ruled that the state statute was not satisfied by this letter.[17] Some states require two notices, one that specifies the deficiencies at a specified time prior to the later notice of dismissal charges. The purpose of the earlier notice is to give the teacher time to overcome the specified deficiencies. When a dismissed tenured teacher in Missouri challenged the adequacy of both notices, the court ruled for the school board.[18] The court recognized the dilemma of the board as follows: "If the board sets forth the charges . . . at length and in detail including a recital of incidents to support the charges, it is contended that new and different charges have been made. If it states them in a cryptic way, it is contended that they are not set forth with particularity."

Following State Law May Not Be Enough: The *Loudermill* Case

In a 1985 case that arose in Cleveland, Ohio, the Supreme Court clarified some aspects of the due process protections to be accorded to tenured state employees under the Fourteenth Amendment. While the plaintiff, Loudermill, was a security guard, under the wording of the state law he could be fired only "for cause," thus his situation is analogous to that of tenured teachers.

According to the Court, following procedures specified by the state law may not be sufficient to satisfy the constitutional requirements of due process. The latter requires "notice and an opportunity to respond. The opportunity to present reasons, either in person or in writing, why proposed action should not be taken is a fundamental due process requirement. The tenured public employee is entitled to oral or written notice of the charges against him, an explanation of the employer's evidence, and an opportunity to present his side of the story."[19] In this case, when Loudermill received a hearing only after he was dismissed, he went to court. In the final appeal, the Supreme Court ruled in his favor. It held that since a tenured employee has a property right to continued employment, he has a right to a hearing *prior* to being terminated.

DUE PROCESS FOR STUDENTS

Many of the oppressive features of schooling have been challenged and to some extent changed with the increasing application of constitutional rights to life in school. One area of dramatic change, mandated by important decisions of the Supreme Court and further implemented by various decisions of lower courts, is the right of students to due process of law in school-related controversies. This section also explores other aspects of discipline including controversies related to corporal punishment and "search and seizure" in schools.

What is the current status of the doctrine of *in loco parentis?*

In loco parentis is not as strong as it once was, but it is still often invoked by the courts. It means "in place of the parents," and has been used historically to justify the power and authority of school officials over students at school or while traveling to and from school. Although the doctrine gave substantial authority to school officials in years past, many courts and legislatures have limited its applicability. It is odd, for example, when parents notify schools not to use corporal punishment on their children, to justify such punishment with an appeal to *in loco parentis.* As more and more courts have recognized that constitutional rights apply to students and schools, the *in loco parentis* doctrine has been weakened, though it has not been completely eradicated.

Must schools follow due process in cases of short suspension?

Yes. However, the legal requirements are not onerous or unduly demanding if the disciplinary violation is a minor one. The Supreme Court addressed this issue in *Goss* v. *Lopez.*[20] Dwight Lopez and several other students were suspended from school in Columbus, Ohio, during the 1970–1971 academic year without receiving a hearing. Some of the students were suspended for documented acts of violence, but others, Lopez among them, were suspended even though they claimed to be innocent bystanders of demonstrations or disturbances. Moreover, they were never informed of what they were accused of doing. The students, who were suspended for up to ten days without a hearing, went to court and claimed that their right to due process was violated. When the federal district court agreed with them, the administrators appealed to the U.S. Supreme Court. In a 5–4 opinion, the Court ruled in favor of the students and discussed several issues of importance to students, teachers, and administrators.

The Court reiterated the key principle of the *Tinker* case, that "young people do not 'shed their constitutional rights' at the schoolhouse door." Justice White, writing for the majority, indicated that the Constitution does not require states to establish schools, but once they do, students have a property right in them, which may not be withdrawn without "fundamentally fair procedures." Clearly, said the Court, the Constitution protects students in cases of expulsion from the public schools. Furthermore, some degree of due process is required even in cases of short-term suspension.

A suspension for up to ten days is not so minor a punishment that it may be imposed "in complete disregard of the Due Process Clause," wrote Justice White. Such exclusion from school is a serious event in the life of the child, and it becomes even more serious if the misconduct is recorded in the student's file. Such a record is likely to damage the student's standing with teachers and "interfere with later opportunities for higher education and employment." Thus it is clear that the law requires schools to respect students' constitutional right to due process in both serious and minor disciplinary matters that might lead to either expulsion or suspension from school.

What process is due in minor disciplinary cases?

The seriousness of the possible penalty influences the extent and thoroughness of the due process requirement. Since due process is a flexible concept and not a fixed or rigid set of requirements, some minimal but fair procedures will satisfy the courts in cases that might lead to short-term suspension. As a minimum, students facing suspension "must be given some kind of notice and afforded some kind of hearing."

Notice of the charges may be oral or written, and a student who denies the charges must be given "an explanation of the evidence the authorities have and an opportunity to present his side of the story." The central concern of the Court is that there be at least "rudimentary precautions against unfair or mistaken findings of misconduct and arbitrary expulsion from school." Thus, the Court does not turn schools into courtrooms and does not place unreasonable burdens on educators faced with disciplinary problems. Most schools had followed such fair procedures long before the *Goss* case arose.

What process is due in serious cases?

Serious disciplinary cases, by contrast, may require extensive and thorough procedures. By "serious cases" is meant those that might lead to long-term suspension or expulsion. Since such actions are likely to have important consequences on students' educational and even occupational life, their property interests are in serious jeopardy, and meticulous procedures are required.

Cases involving serious disciplinary violations call for a written notice specifying the charges, the time and place of the hearing, and a description of procedures to be followed at the hearing. Students should know what evidence will be used against them, the names of witnesses who will testify, and the substance of witnesses' testimony. Students should have the right to cross-examine witnesses, as well as to present witnesses and evidence on their own behalf. A written or taped record of the proceeding should be available to students, together with the findings and recommendation of the group conducting the hearing (usually the school board). The right of appeal should also be clearly stated.[21] Although the *Dixon* case, from which these requirements were taken, involved college students, courts, including the Supreme Court, have referred to *Dixon* with approval in various cases involving high school students.

Do courts always allow the cross-examination of witnesses?

There are conflicting cases on the right to confront and cross-examine accusing witnesses. Even the Supreme Court said that a "full-dress judicial hearing, with the right to cross-examine witnesses" may not always be required. A Connecticut case ruled that confrontation and cross-examination may be dispensed with if extenuating circumstances or persuasive evidence reveals that the accusing witnesses will be inhibited to a significant degree or fearful for their personal safety due to probable revenge or retaliation.[22] A Kansas court ruled similarly.[23]

Several cases have held that hearsay evidence may be used in school disciplinary hearings, unlike in courts of law. Thus, in a recent Wisconsin case, a student whose ring was stolen, did not testify at the expulsion hearing of the accused student. The court reviewed *Goss* as well as other relevant cases and rejected technical legal rules of evidence, proclaiming: "[A] student's right to due process is satisfied even though some of the testimony presented was hearsay given by members of the school staff."[24] But in another expulsion case, a New Jersey court required that the accusing witnesses be available for cross-examination.[25] The witnesses' fear of physical reprisal was no justification for depriving the accused of the right to confront and examine witnesses. It is a community obligation, ruled the court, to protect such witnesses against retaliation.

Do students have a right to have lawyers represent them?

There is no generally applicable answer to this question. Clearly there is no right to representation in connection with short-term suspensions. According to the Court in *Goss,* "further formalizing the suspension process and escalating its formality and adversary nature may not only make it too costly as a regular disciplinary tool but also destroy its effectiveness as part of the teaching process." On the other hand, courts have held that lawyers might attend serious disciplinary hearings to observe the procedures and give assistance to the student. This happened, for example, when a senior in a New York high school was accused of cheating on a state Regents Examination. Since this is an important exam in New York, and since a charge of cheating could lead to very serious consequences, the state court upheld the student's right to be assisted by counsel.[26] A case involving a college student came to the same conclusion.[27]

Do "Miranda rights" apply to school situations?

No, they do not. In 1966 the Supreme Court held in *Miranda* v. *Arizona* that the Fifth Amendment privilege against self-incrimination applies to those under questioning while in official custody related to a criminal investigation.[28] This means that the person "deprived of his freedom of action in any significant way" must be informed of his right to remain silent, that anything he says may be used against him, and that he has a right to the assistance of a lawyer. Such rules, however, do not apply when school officials detain students for questioning[29]—they have no right even to have their parents present. Since the *Miranda* rule derives from the Fifth Amendment provision that a person shall not be "compelled in a criminal case to be a witness against himself," and since public school disciplinary proceedings and inquiries are not criminal proceedings, *Miranda* does not apply.

Are there disciplinary situations where due process is not a prerequisite?

Yes. In two situations teachers or school administrators may proceed without first observing any formalities of due process. The first involves the myriad of trivial disciplinary matters routinely experienced in schools. In situations involving minor infractions of rules or nonperformance of required tasks, students are given a variety of "punishments" ranging from brief detentions to extra work, verbal chastisement, being sent to the principal's office, and so forth. The legal maxim *de minimis non curat lex* (the law does not deal with trifles) is applicable to these situations, and schools ought to rely on their knowledge of pedagogical principles to deal with such matters. For example, a federal court in Maine held that a student placed on "school probation" after returning from disciplinary expulsion was not denied any liberty or property interest, making due process inapplicable.[30]

The second exception involves emergencies in which educators must act quickly to perserve the safety of persons or property. The Supreme Court recognized in *Goss* that emergencies occur in school that would make notice and hearing prior to action impracticable because the situation presents danger to persons or property. In such situations, the only legal requirement is that fair procedures be followed "as soon as practicable after removal of the danger or disruption."

At least one appeals court also held that participation in interscholastic athletics is not a property interest protected by the due process clause.[31] The case involved a 17-year-old student who claimed that the interscholastic league rule that made him ineligible to participate in high school football, when he moved from one town to another, denied him his constitutional rights. The court was concerned that to escalate to "constitutional magnitude" a youth's desire to play high school football would trivialize the Constitution.

Could the punishment itself violate due process?

Yes, it could. Due process requires fair procedures on the one hand and fairness in punishment on the other. That is, the punishment itself must not be so excessive as to be arbitrary and grossly unfair. For example, when two students who vandalized a school were suspended pending an investigation, and their suspension actually turned into an expulsion for the balance of the school year, the court ruled that the school officials violated both *procedural* and *substantive* due process.[32] Fair procedures were violated because there was neither an expulsion hearing nor a notice of the charges against the students. Substantive due process rights were violated because school officials never determined when the suspension would end, which was unfair to the students. This case suggests that care must be exercised in the use of indefinite suspension when investigating a case, lest it turn into a de facto expulsion and thus violate substantive due process.

Is there a due process requirement for guidance conferences?

No. Under ordinary circumstances, a guidance conference is not considered to be a disciplinary proceeding. For example, guidance conferences related to the appropriate placement of a student or concerning progress in scheduled courses are not disciplinary matters. Absent special circumstances, the student is not being deprived of liberty or property; therefore there is no constitutional right to due process. In special circumstances, such right is granted by statute (e.g., in the case of exceptional students or bilingual students). By state statute or local policy it is always possible to expand the due process rights of students beyond those granted by the Constitution. Our discussion has focused on the interpretation of the constitutional provisions that apply to all public schools. Nevertheless, as in all other controversies, the importance of state law and local policy must not be underestimated.

Can schools create general rules to govern student behavior?

Yes, they can, as long as such rules are sufficiently clear to guide student behavior. For example, a rule requiring students to be in their assigned homerooms and in their seats at the time the school bell rings at 8:30 a.m. is a legally valid general rule. It is clear and unambiguous. By contrast, consider a rule that required students "to dress in good taste" and avoid "extremes in style." Under this rule a student in Arcata, California, was suspended because he had long hair. The student and his parents went to court seeking reinstatement and claimed that the rule was so vague that it violated his right to due process. The California Supreme Court agreed with the student and found that the rule was void because it was too vague.[33] The court said that "a law violates due process if it is so vague and standardless that it leaves the public uncertain as to the conduct it prohibits or leaves judges or jurors free to decide, without any legally fixed standards, what is prohibited and what is not in each case."

Similarly, a school rule that is too broad will not stand up in court. The written regulations of a school in Texas gave the principal power to make rules "in the best interest of the school." When the principal acted under this regulation and expelled two students for publishing an underground newspaper, the students went to court, claiming the rule to be vague and overly broad. The court agreed with the students and said that "school rules probably need not be as narrow as criminal statutes, but if school officials contemplate severe punishment they must do so on the basis of a rule which is drawn so as to reasonably inform the student what specific conduct is proscribed."[34]

When a principal has the power to do anything "in the best interest of the school," there are no clear or objective standards by which students can guide their behavior. The rule may even cover constitutionally protected activities such as free speech and press. Therefore the rule is unconstitutional.

Have due process requirements turned classrooms and schools into courtrooms?

No. When the Supreme Court ruled in *Goss* that even short-term suspensions require some modicum of due process, a hue and cry arose across the land. School administrators, parents, and teachers were upset and feared that the decision would force school officials to consult lawyers before they could take any disciplinary measures in schools. These fears were ill based. Careful reading of *Goss* and other cases indicates that the legal requirements are not at all excessive and that there is no need for lawyers to be at the side of administrators or teachers. Conscientious educators used fair procedures long before these cases ever went to court, and their procedures amply satisfy the law.

On the other hand, oppressive, authoritarian procedures that do not respect students' rights to know why they are being disciplined and do not provide opportunities for students to present their defense in a fair way are crumbling as a result of the application of the Constitution to the schools. In sum, one may think of the right to due process as applying to student disciplinary matters on a continuum represented in the following diagram:

May act without due process:	*Some modicum of due process is necessary:*	*Extensive, careful due process is required:*
Trivial or very minor matters, or emergencies. The latter must be followed by due process as soon as possible.	Disciplinary matters that may lead to short-term suspensions or entry on the students' record.	Disciplinary matters that may result in long-term suspension or expulsion, or in a significant penalty such as a short suspension during final exams.

CORPORAL PUNISHMENT

Is reasonable corporal punishment unconstitutional?

No. The Constitution is silent on this matter, as it is silent on education in general. Thus courts have held that education is a function of state governments (under the reserved powers of Article X of the Constitution) and that states may further delegate power over schooling to local governments. At this date, twenty states and the District of Columbia prohibit the use of corporal punishment: Hawaii, Maine, Massachusetts, New Hampshire, New Jersey, New York, Rhode Island, California, Nebraska, Wisconsin, Virginia, Alabama, Connecticut, Iowa, Michigan, Minnesota, North Dakota, Oregon, South Dakota, and Vermont. Some of these states prohibit corporal punishment by law, while others, such as New York, by school board policy. Efforts are also being made in other states to outlaw the use of such punishment. Furthermore, some local communities outlaw the practice in states where the state law does not forbid it. Some school districts that allow corporal punishment restrict its administration in various ways, in which case the restrictions must be followed. The most common restriction is that an administrator is the only person authorized to spank students and then only in the presence of an adult witness. In any event, it is clear that ordinary corporal punishment does not violate the Constitution.

Is excessive corporal punishment unconstitutional?

It might be, depending on the severity of the punishment. In Dade County, Florida, James Ingraham and Roosevelt Andrews, junior high school students, were severely paddled during the 1970-1971 school year. In fact, Ingraham was so harshly beaten that the resulting hematoma required medical attention, and he missed 11 days of school. The paddling Andrews received included being struck on his arms, depriving him the use of an arm for a week.

At the time of the paddling, Dade County schools used corporal punishment as one means of maintaining discipline. Simultaneously, a Florida law forbade punishment that was "degrading or unduly severe" or that took place prior to consultation with the principal or the teacher in charge of the school. The students filed suit against several school administrators and claimed that the severe beating they received constituted cruel and unusual punishment. The district court, the court of appeals, and finally the Supreme Court all ruled that the beating, although excessive and unreasonable, did not violate the Eighth Amendment, which prohibits cruel and unusual punishment.[35]

Does that mean that the Court recommends physical punishment of students or condones excessive punishment? Not at all. Whether school-children and youth ought to be physically punished is not a legal matter. It is a policy question for educators to decide with appropriate consideration of psychological, developmental, and other factors. Even when such punishment is allowed, it must remain within reasonable limits. To be "reasonable," punishment must relate to an educational purpose and not be merely an expression of teacher anger, frustration, or malice. The severity of the punishment should relate to the gravity of the offense and should consider the ability of the student to bear it. Therefore the size, age, sex, and physical and emotional condition of the child must be considered. Excessive punishment is unreasonable, and the law has always provided ways for legal redress against it. Students may sue the perpetrators for money damages for the suffering endured as well as seek an indictment for assault and battery. The Supreme Court has ruled that these traditional remedies are sufficient to deter educators and minimize abuse. The Court examined the history of the Eighth Amendment and concluded that it was never intended to apply to schools but was created to control the punishment of criminals, who are incarcerated in closed institutions. The very "openness of the public school and its supervision by the community afford significant safeguards against the kind of abuse from which the Eighth Amendment protects the prisoner."

Must due process be used before administering corporal punishment?

The Court ruled that existing remedies would suffice and the addition of procedural safeguards while protecting student rights "would entail a significant intrusion into an area of primary educational responsibility." Thus the question of whether to have corporal punishment is for legislatures and local school boards to decide. Courts will intrude only when the punishment is excessive and unreasonable.

A different issue was raised and decided in 1980 by the Court of Appeals for the Fourth Circuit. It ruled that excessive corporal punishment in a public school might be a violation of "constitutional rights given protection under the rubric of substantive due process."[36] The court spoke of "the right to be free of state intrusions into realms of personal privacy and bodily security through means so brutal, demeaning, and harmful as literally to shock the conscience of a court. The existence of this right to ultimate bodily security—the most fundamental aspect of personal privacy—is unmistakably established in our constitutional decisions as an attribute of the ordered liberty that is the concern of substantive due process."

In this case it was alleged that a young girl was so severely paddled in school that she was badly bruised and required 10 days' hospitalization and treatment "of traumatic injury to the soft tissue of the left hip and thigh, and trauma to the soft tissue of ecchymosis of the left buttock," with possible injuries to her lower back and spine. The court held that the student's substantive due process rights were violated if the evidence showed that "the force applied caused injury so severe, was so disproportionate to the need presented and was so inspired by malice or sadism rather than a merely careless or unwise excess of zeal that it amounted to a brutal and inhumane abuse of official power literally shocking to the conscience."

An important New Mexico case came to the same conclusion in 1987.[37] There, nine year old Teresa Garcia was excessively beaten on two separate occasions with a split wooden paddle. On the first occasion a teacher held her upside down by the ankles while Theresa Miera, the principal, beat her repeatedly "on the front of her leg between the knee and the waist." Teresa bled, had welts on her leg and a two-inch cut that left a permanent scar. The second beating, about a month later, caused severe bruises on her buttocks, shocking a physician who treated her and causing a nurse to say that if Teresa had received this type of injury at home the nurse "would have called [the police department's] Protective Services," reporting child abuse.

The Court of Appeals for the 10th Circuit ruled that this type of excessive beating is so brutal and offensive to human dignity as to shock the conscience. Therefore, ruled the court, the excessive punishment violated Teresa's constitutional right to substantive due process. The court identified three levels of corporal punishment: "Punishments that do not exceed the traditional common law standard of reasonableness are not actionable; punishments that exceed the common law standard without adequate state remedies violate procedural due process rights; and finally, punishments that are so grossly excessive as to be shocking to the conscience violate substantive due process rights, without regard to the adequacy of state remedies." The Supreme Court refused to review the case, thus at least tacitly approving it.

There is a developing trend among Federal appeals courts to hold grossly excessive corporal punishment violative of substantive due process. The Fifth Circuit ruled otherwise in *Ingraham* but since *Ingraham*, both Fourth and Tenth Circuits ruled in favor of protecting students' rights and the Supreme Court declined to overrule them.

Thus, while corporal punishment does not necessarily require prior procedural due process, and while it does not violate the Eighth Amendment prohibition against cruel and unusual punishment, excessive punishment might violate the substantive due process rights embodied in the Fourteenth Amendment.

Can parents forbid the use of corporal punishment?

In general, no. If a state allows corporal punishment, parental objection to the practice will not necessarily prevail. The Supreme Court so ruled in a North Carolina case in which a sixth-grade boy was spanked for violating a school rule against throwing balls at certain specified times.[38] Virginia Baker had requested that her son not be spanked or paddled, for she opposed such practices in principle. While the law of North Carolina allowed the use of force reasonably necessary "to restrain or correct pupils and to maintain order," Baker claimed the law was unconstitutional because it allowed such punishment over parental objections. Though recognizing the parents' basic right to supervise the upbringing of children, the Court also considered the "legitimate and substantial interest" of the state "in maintaining order and discipline in the public schools." In the final analysis, since both professional and popular opinion are split on the question of the use of corporal punishment, the Court refused to allow "the wishes of a parent to restrict school officials' discretion in deciding the methods to be used in . . . maintaining discipline."

Some states have passed laws that provide for prior written parental approval before a student may be spanked. At times, local school districts create their own policies regulating this matter. In the absence of state legislation or local regulation, it is clear that schools do not have to get parental approval to use corporal punishment, and, in fact, may use it over the objections of parents. As a general rule, school discipline is a local matter, and school boards may adopt reasonable rules and regulations to conduct their schools efficiently. The authority of school personnel, in the conduct of the ordinary affairs of the school, derives in part from the doctrine of *in loco parentis* introduced earlier in this chapter.

Can students be disciplined for conduct outside school?

Yes, if the rule they violate is reasonably connected to the operation of the school. A Texas court so ruled, upholding the suspension of a student for drinking vodka on school grounds, violating a known school rule.[39] If the alleged wrong took place away from the school and the school grounds, school officials should allow the civil authorities to handle the matter.[40] However, when a student's conduct gets him or her in trouble with the civil authorities, that does not preclude the schools from applying appropriate disciplinary measures if the behavior is connected to the school. Punishment by both school and outside authorities does not constitute double jeopardy, which is a technical legal concept that applies to criminal proceedings. School disciplinary matters are not criminal proceedings.

Can schools lower grades or withhold diplomas as disciplinary measures?

Courts are divided on this issue. In the past, schools often withheld diplomas as punishment and teachers often lowered students' grades for misbehaving in class. The trend among educators is to assign separate grades for academic work and for behavior, or "citizenship." As a general rule, the law does not intrude into disputes over grading policies or practices. These are matters for educators to decide. Nevertheless, if a student can show that a grade was lowered for disciplinary reasons or that the teacher acted out of prejudice or malice, the courts will listen and help. The burden of proof is on the student to establish that the reasons for the low grade were illegitimate and not related to the quality of the work. This is a difficult burden of proof, and there are no cases reported wherein a student below the college level has succeeded in such a suit.

Diplomas should not be withheld as punishment for an alleged violation of a school rule. The reason for this principle is that the diploma is a symbol and recognition of academic accomplishment and not a reward for good behavior. Misbehavior should be faced directly through disciplinary procedures, not indirectly through the withholding of a symbol of academic accomplishment.

Although there are few cases in point, there are some that have upheld school officials' right to reduce a student's grade in addition to a penalty such as suspension from school. In a case involving two high school seniors in Texas who were suspended for three days and given zeros for the three days' graded school work for consuming alcohol on school grounds, the court upheld both school punishments.[41] The court ruled that the punishments did not injure either the property or liberty rights of the students and thus did not violate their due process rights.

In the absence of state statutes controlling the imposition of what some consider to be a double penalty, courts are likely to respect the discretion of school officials and will not substitute their judgment for those of educators. However, if the penalty is a severe one, the courts will scrutinize official action to ensure that both procedural and substantive due process rights were respected.

By contrast, a Pennsylvania court struck down a policy that provided for a reduction in grades in all classes by two percentage points for each day of suspension. When an eleventh-grade student on a field trip to New York drank a glass of wine while with friends in a restaurant, she was suspended for five days and expelled from the cheerleading squad and the National Honor Society. When the student and her parents challenged the grade reduction policy, the court struck it down. According to the court, the reduction of the grade would misrepresent academic achievement and such misrepresentation would be both improper and illegal.[42]

Is it unconstitutional for schools to require passing grades as a precondition for participating in extracurricular activities?

No, it is not, ruled the Texas Supreme Court. The so-called "no pass, no play" rule required that students wishing to participate in extracurricular activities, including sports, must earn grades no lower than 70 on a scale of 100 in an academic class. When the rule was challenged by students as a violation of the equal protection and due process clauses of the Fourteenth Amendment, the district court ruled in their favor. The state supreme court, however, reversed that ruling.

The highest court of Texas held that participation in extracurricular activities is not a fundamental right akin to student speech or religion. Furthermore, the rule does not burden an inherently suspect class of students, such as a racial, ethnic, or religious group. Therefore, applying the rational basis test, the court found the rule to be reasonably related to a legitimate state objective by providing an incentive for students to keep up their performance in academic subjects.[43]

SCHOOL SEARCHES

Can school officials search student lockers?

Yes, they may, if they have reasonable grounds to suspect that something illegal or dangerous is hidden in the locker. In recent years, students have objected to locker searches on the grounds that since they were unauthorized, a search without a warrant violates the Fourth Amendment right against illegal search and seizure.

The *Overton* Case

In a high school in New York, police showed the vice principal a search warrant and with his help searched the lockers of two students. They found four marijuana cigarettes in Carlos Overton's locker. When the search warrant turned out to be defective, the student claimed that the entire search was illegal and therefore the evidence obtained could not be used in court. The police and the school claimed that the vice principal gave consent for the search; therefore, since no unauthorized search took place, the evidence found could be used. The court ruled against the student and upheld the validity of the search and the use of the evidence.[44] The court held that students had exclusive use of the lockers vis-à-vis other students but not in relation to school authorities. School officials have the locker combinations, and if they have reason to suspect that something illegal or dangerous is hidden in a locker, they have a right to inspect it. In fact, the New York court went further and said that "not only have the school authorities the right to inspect but the right becomes a duty when suspicion arises that something of an illegal nature may be secreted there."

In typical situations away from school, law enforcement officials need "probable cause" to secure a search warrant to search a person's home, a rented locker, or even an occupied telephone booth. Schools, however, are special environments where school officials have the duty and responsibility for the safety, health, and learning of children. Therefore, less demanding standards are applied by courts to searches conducted by school personnel than by law enforcement officials.

New *Jersey* v. *T.L.O.*

Because of conflicting decisions handed down by lower courts, the Supreme Court rendered an opinion in January 1985 related to the authority of school officials to search students for contraband.

The facts accepted by the Court were that a teacher, upon entering the girls' restroom, found T.L.O. and another student holding lighted cigarettes. Since school rules forbade smoking there, the girls were escorted to the assistant vice principal's office. When questioned, T.L.O. denied smoking at all. At the request of the official she opened her purse, where, in addition to cigarettes, there was drug paraphernalia and evidence that she had sold drugs. After examining the purse, the assistant vice principal summoned T.L.O.'s mother and the police.[45]

A divided Supreme Court said school searches are justified "when there are reasonable grounds for suspecting that the search will turn up evidence that the student has violated or is violating either the law or the rules of the school." The Court rejected the Fourth Amendment requirement of probable cause as inapplicable to school situations. Instead, expressing confidence that educators will behave "according to the dictates of reason and common sense," Justice White, writing for the majority, said that the proper standard for searches by educators is "reasonableness, under all the circumstances." Reasonableness "involves a twofold inquiry: first, one must consider 'whether the . . . action was justified at its inception'; . . . second, one must determine whether the search as actually conducted was 'reasonably related in scope to the circumstances which justified the interference in the first place.' "

Justice White concluded that the initial search for the cigarettes was reasonable, since finding cigarettes in the purse "would both corroborate the report that she had been smoking and undermine the credibility of her defense to the charge of smoking." When drug paraphernalia was plainly visible in the purse, the second search for marijuana was also considered reasonable by the Court. The Court also explicitly rejected the applicability of the *in loco parentis* doctrine, which would hold that since the school's authority is the same as that of the parents, therefore it is not subject to the Fourth Amendment. Since school authorities are state agents for purposes of constitutional law, they are exercising public rather than parental authority when conducting searches of students.

While the Court was divided in its analysis, educators can be guided by the standard applied by the Court. However, several issues related to school searches remain unresolved. As Justice White indicated, the Supreme Court has not yet ruled on

1. the search of lockers, desks, and other storage areas provided by schools, and what standards should be used for searching such areas;
2. searches by educators at the request of law enforcement officials;
3. whether or not "individualized suspicion" is an essential part of the standard of reasonableness; and
4. whether or not the "exclusionary rule applies to the fruits of unlawful searches conducted by school authorities."

The Court as a whole has not yet resolved issues related to the use of search dogs, or the standards to be used for searching student automobiles. It is quite probable that these and other issues will be addressed as more cases percolate up through our appellate courts.

Courts below the U.S. Supreme Court level have applied the *T.L.O.* principles to a variety of cases. For example, the Court of Appeals of Alaska ruled on a case involving the search of a student's car by school officials.[46] In this case a teacher in a library noticed a student with glassy eyes, face flushed, behaving in a way that led the teacher to suspect the student was under the influence of alcohol. When the "safety/security home school coordinator" was called, he escorted the student into the storeroom for a talk. The student bumped into large objects and swayed as he walked, his speech was slurred, and there was an odor of alcohol on him. In the assistant principal's office school officials suspected a combination of alcohol and drug use during the lunch hour, and after discussion the student gave them his car keys and signed a form consenting to the search of his car.

When cocaine was found in the ashtray of the car, the student wanted the judge to exclude the evidence, claiming the search to be illegal. The court, following *T.L.O.*, ruled that the search was proper in its inception and its scope. However, the court held that the consent form was void for it was not freely given by the intoxicated student, but that under the circumstances the school officials had reasonable grounds to suspect drug use and, particularly because the student's car was improperly parked in the parking lot, it was reasonable to search the car as well.

By contrast, a Pennsylvania court declared invalid a locker search by school officials that produced some marijuana cigarettes in a jacket pocket.[47] In this case the student was observed getting a pack of cigarettes out of his locker and giving one of the cigarettes to another student. The assistant principal took the cigarette and the pack away and then searched the locker. The court, applying the *T.L.O.* standard, found (a) that students do have a reasonable expectancy of privacy in their jacket that they take to school, which expectation they do not lose by placing the jacket in the school locker, and (b) that once the school officials seized the cigarette and the pack, they had no reasonable basis to suspect that there would be more in the locker. Catching the juvenile with cigarettes "formed a pretext for a search for drugs" in violation of the Fourteenth Amendment.

An interesting case arose in Michigan, where a school security guard apprehended a female student ducking behind a parked car in the school parking lot, during class time.[48] When she emptied her purse after being ordered to do so, it was found to contain several "readmittance slips" that the student should not have had. A further search of the student for drugs was ordered by the vice principal. In a suit by the student, the court held that her constitutional rights were violated. The court reasoned that *T.L.O.* does not justify the search just because *some* school rule or law was violated by the student. The administrator must show that the "student's conduct creates a reasonable suspicion that a specific rule or law has been violated and that a search could reasonably be expected to produce evidence of that violation." Courts have also held consistently that the *T.L.O.* test of reasonable suspicion applies to locker searches.[49]

Variations on school-related searches are legion. For example, after receiving reports of stolen items, the vice principal interviewed several students and focused her attention on four who were alone in the locker room at the time of the theft. Although she did invite the police liaison officer to be present in the building to accompany her, she conducted the investigation independently. After the vice principal found some of the stolen items, the police officer participated in the search by "patting down" a girl. The court upheld the search by the vice principal as justified by reasonable suspicion based on the information she received. The court distinguished between a search conducted "with" the police present and "at the request (behest)" of law enforcement personnel. The *T.L.O.*

standard applies in the former and a warrant requirement in the latter.[50]

In a different type of case, the principal searched a student's hotel room for alcohol during a school-sponsored field trip. The district court applied the *T.L.O.* analysis, but limited itself to *T.L.O.* as it applies to in-school searches. The appeals court found the *T.L.O.* standard relevant, but went further and applied the *in loco parentis* doctrine as well and held the search to be reasonable.[51]

Thus, school officials must be careful in following the guiding principles laid down by the Supreme Court in *T.L.O.* v. *New Jersey* and the *in loco parentis* doctrine, which may further complicate search and seizure cases, particularly on field trips. Some courts no longer apply the *in loco parentis* doctrine, while others do, particularly in school-sponsored after-school activities. In such situations courts are likely to give school authorities more leeway to search under suspicious circumstances.

Can school officials search students' clothing?

Yes. However, there are important differences between searching lockers, which are school property, and searching students' clothes, which are not. Because clothing or body searches entail a great danger of invasion of privacy, courts have imposed high standards of protection against such searches. For example, a 17-year-old student was subjected to a body search when he was observed entering a bathroom with a fellow student twice within the same hour, and leaving within a few seconds. For months he had been suspected of dealing in drugs. The search revealed illegal drugs, yet the Court of Appeals of New York excluded the evidence and ruled the search unconstitutional.[52] Though the court recognized the widespread use of drugs and the need to protect the school environment, it held that even these considerations did "not permit random, causeless searches" that might result in "psychological damage to sensitive children" and expose them to serious consequences, such as possible criminal convictions.

An extreme example is that of a school that conducted a strip-search of an entire fifth-grade class over a report of $3 missing from a student's coat pocket. The search, which was conducted by separating boys and girls, was fruitless. The court considered the school's action to be excessive and thus illegal.[53]

As when other student rights are violated, courts may award money damages for illegal and unauthorized searches. For example, $7500 in damages was awarded to a student in connection with a strip-search a federal court found to be illegal.[54] The Second Circuit Court of Appeals indicated that "reasonable suspicion" might suffice to search students' lockers, but for highly invasive searches, such as body or strip-searches, a higher standard is required (i.e., "probable cause"). The distinction between these two standards is not entirely clear, but in law they are significantly different. "Probable cause" is also the standard used by law enforcement officials when they request a search warrant from a court.

Can the police search school lockers or students without search warrants?

No. In general, the same legal principles apply to police behavior in and out of schools. Nevertheless, school officials often cooperate with the police in warrantless searches. The question becomes whether evidence so gathered may be used in criminal proceedings against students.

The Supreme Court developed the "exclusionary rule" whereby illegally obtained evidence may not be used in court. Cases have raised the question whether evidence obtained in locker searches through the cooperation of police and school officials falls within the "exclusionary rule." So far, courts are divided on this question with some courts excluding such evidence and others allowing it if school officials had at least reasonable suspicion concerning the particular student's locker.

An unusual case arose when police and school officials, with the aid of specially trained dogs, planned and conducted a search in the junior and senior high schools of Highland, Indiana. On a predetermined day, students were kept in their first-period classes for two and a half hours while a team of handlers led the dogs on a room-to-room inspection tour. Particular students singled out by the dogs were asked to empty their pockets and purses, and some of them were strip-searched in the nurse's office. With this dragnet, seventeen students were caught with illegal drugs. Of these, twelve withdrew from school voluntarily, two were suspended, and three were expelled. Five sets of parents whose children were strip-searched went to court, though four of them withdrew before trial.

In the final analysis, the U.S. District Court ruled that the strip-searches were illegal in that they violated the Fourth Amendment right against unreasonable search and seizure.[55] The Court did not consider a dog alert to be a reasonable suspicion sufficient to warrant a strip-search. On the other hand, it saw nothing wrong with the use of dogs and with asking suspected students to empty their pockets or purses. The court ruled on the *in loco parentis* doctrine to uphold the action of the administrators and the school board to use the canine units to search students in every classroom if the school officials felt they had reasonable suspicion of drug violations. On appeal, the Seventh Circuit Court of Appeals upheld the right of school officials to use dogs in an exploratory sniffing of students.[56] There were strong dissenting opinions in this case, followed by widespread criticism when the court ruled that the sniffing of students was not a "search." One important aspect of this case was a prior agreement between school officials and the police that illegal materials discovered during the search would not be used in any criminal investigations or proceedings.

Doberman pinschers and German shepherds were also used in a drug-detection program involving the Goosecreek School District in Texas. The dogs, with the aid of trainers, sniffed students, lockers, and cars for the presence of drugs they were trained to recognize.[57] The search yielded only a bottle of perfume, but some students searched filed suit claiming their right to be free from unreasonable searches had been violated.

In the final analysis, the appellate court held that the use of trained dogs to sniff *objects* is not a search. When objects and their odors occupy public space, a "public smell" is analogous to seeing something in "plain view," and therefore sniffing cars or lockers does not constitute a search at all. When a dog alerts its handler to a locker or car it might be grounds for reasonable suspicion and thus enable school officials to check for contraband. The court, however, reached a different conclusion regarding the search of persons. Since a personal search is a more intrusive invasion of privacy, the court held that using dogs to sniff students was a search and that, before a body search could be conducted, school officials would have to have reasonable cause to believe that a *particular* student possessed drugs or other forbidden substances.

In the *Goosecreek* case, the Fifth Circuit Court rejected the reasoning of the Seventh Circuit Court which saw nothing objectionable in the use of dogs to sniff students and did not consider it to be a search. Although the full Supreme Court has not yet decided a case involving the use of dogs to search students, Justice Brennan expressed a clear and strong personal view when he said, "I cannot agree that the . . . school officials' use of the trained police dogs did not constitute a search."[58]

Can a school system require that all teachers submit to urine tests for drugs?

No it cannot, for that would violate the Fourth Amendment. Various courts have so ruled, and it is clear that there must be resonable suspicion about a particular teacher before a urine test may be required.[59]

Can a school system require school bus drivers to submit to a routine urine test for drugs?

Yes, it can, if it is reasonable under the circumstances, ruled a U.S. Appeals Court in the District of Columbia.[60] In this case, the school system instituted a routine, mandatory drug-testing policy for employees in the Transportation Branch. The program was instituted because of evidence of widespread drug use by employees whose main duty was the daily transportation of handicapped children to and from school. The court examined the program when it was challenged by an employee who was discharged when she tested positive for drug use. Applying the *T.L.O.* test, the court balanced the individual's expectancy of privacy against the reasonableness of the governmental action attempting to protect a public interest. On balance, the court upheld the requirement since the system had a serious safety concern in the transportation of the students; the intrusion on employees' privacy was minimal because the drug testing was conducted as part of a routine, reasonable, annual medical examination; and the school system agreed to test its employees only in a manner that would validly detect the type of drug abuse with which it was legitimately concerned. Therefore, the required drug-testing program was not unreasonable.

May students be given a urine test to detect or prevent drug abuse?

As a general rule the answer is no, but special circumstances may justify urine tests. Since schools seldom use such tests, there are very few reported cases. One state court struck down a required yearly urine test as a violation of students' reasonable expectations of privacy.[61] On the other hand, a federal appeals court upheld a random urine testing program applicable only to high school interscholastic athletes and cheerleaders.[62] The program was carefully designed to check for controlled substances and performance-enhancing drugs, it contained provisions to limit the invasion of privacy, results were double-checked and could be challenged, and the information obtained was kept confidential.

The court upheld the program even though it was not based on individual suspicion but was applied to all athletes and cheerleaders. "Interscholastic athletes have diminished expectations of privacy, and have voluntarily chosen to participate in an activity which subjects them to pervasive regulation of off-campus behavior; the school's interest in preserving a drug-free athletic program is substantial, and cannot adequately be furthered by less intrusive measures; the [school district] program adequately limits the discretion of the officials performing the search; and the information sought is intended to be used solely for noncriminal educational and rehabilitative purposes."

SUMMARY

This chapter presented the major dimensions of due process rights of teachers and students. It is clear that laws or policies that are arbitrary, capricious, unreasonable, or overly vague violate the due process clause of the Fourteenth Amendment. Lawyers and courts refer to these as "violations of substantive due process." There are also "procedural due process" rights based on the same amendment, where it prohibits states from depriving anyone of "life, liberty or property" without fair procedures.

Tenured teachers have a "property" interest in their continuing contract, and any attempts to suspend or dismiss them must be carried out with full observance of fair procedures. Statutes usually specify the steps that are part of such procedures, and these must be meticulously followed. Although all teachers have a right to due process if they are dismissed *during* the term of their contract, probationary teachers do not have a "property" right in continuous employment; therefore, if their employment is not renewed, they may not claim the constitutional right to due process. Nevertheless, if the announced grounds for the nonrenewal are stigmatizing, if their reputation is damaged and thus their opportunities for further employment are diminished, due process must be observed so that the stigmatizing charges can be challenged. Probationary teachers also have a right to due process if the grounds for nonrenewal were constitutionally protected activities (e.g., controversial speech or unionizing activity).

If a teacher has a constitutional right to due process, the administrative hearing before the board must be orderly and fair but it need not be formal and technical. Elements of a fair procedure include a written notice of the charges; a hearing before an impartial tribunal; an opportunity to present evidence and cross-examine witnesses; a right to representation; a written statement of the findings, conclusions, and recommendations; and the right to appeal. In addition to the constitutional right to due process, many states provide some due process by state law. Such laws must be followed scrupulously by school boards, and courts will enforce them strictly.

Historically, schools all too often have used arbitrary and authoritarian disciplinary methods to control student behavior. These practices have been altered in some places by more enlightened education theories and in others by legal challenges that claimed the due process clause of the Constitution applies to the schools. Students and their parents have challenged administrative authority to suspend and expel students without open and fair procedures, the use of corporal punishment in schools, and the practice of searching students and their lockers.

The U.S. Supreme Court has ruled that the right to due process applies to the schools, for a suspension or expulsion affects the property or liberty interests of students, protected by the Fourteenth Amendment. Such interests may not be diminished without due process of law. The Court has ruled that even a short suspension requires some modicum of due process. But the courts do not want to turn schools into courtrooms and recognize the need for administrative authority and discretion. Therefore, a brief, informal process usually satisfies the law in cases where the punishment might be a short suspension. More serious infractions, ones that are likely to lead to long-term suspensions, entries in school records, or expulsions, require more meticulous due process. While no fixed formula for such process exists, it should include a written notice specifying the charges; a hearing at which the student should have an opportunity to respond to the charges, present evidence, cross-examine witnesses, and be represented by his parents or by counsel; a fair tribunal; a written statement of the findings and conclusions; and the right to appeal. A student who constitutes a danger to people or property may be removed from school immediately as long as due process procedures follow such removal as soon as practicable.

As a general rule, school discipline is a matter within the discretion of school authorities and local school boards. The practice of corporal punishment in public schools has been challenged. Only nineteen states clearly prohibit corporal punishment, though some require parental consent. In addition, some school districts prohibit it through local policy. Where challenged, courts have upheld the legality of *reasonable* use of corporal punishment. Excessive brutal punishment is nowhere sanctioned by the law; if used, educators may be sued for money damages as well as prosecuted for assault and battery. But even excessive punishment does not constitute "cruel and unusual punishment" under the Constitution, for the Supreme Court has ruled that the Eighth Amendment was intended to apply to "closed" institutions, like prisons, and not to schools. Two appeals courts ruled, however, that excessive corporal punishment may be a violation of substantive due process protected by the Fourteenth Amendment.

School lockers may be searched by appropriate school officials if they have reasonable suspicion that unlawful or dangerous materials are hidden there. Similarly, the Supreme Court held that students' purses may be searched. The search of students' clothing, or "strip searches," are more invasive, and therefore merit greater protection. While the Supreme Court has not ruled on such cases, lower courts indicate that a standard akin to "probable cause" must be used by educators, which means that they must have evidence from highly reliable sources that a particular student is hiding illegal or dangerous materials. Mass searches or arbitrary ones (e.g., search every seventh locker on alternate Tuesdays) are frowned upon by courts and violate the Constitution. As a general rule, the police need a search warrant before they conduct locker searches in schools. Evidence gathered in warrantless searches, or without the student's consent, is excluded by some courts but allowed in by others on the theory that school administrators may consent on behalf of the students. Many courts are concerned that such collaboration between administrators and the police undermines the relationship between administrators and students.

Trained dogs may be used to search lockers or cars, but students may be sniffed by search dogs only when there are reasonable grounds to suspect particular students. If a dog's reliability has been established, lockers and cars may be searched when the dog alerts a handler to them. However, a dog's alert is not sufficient to warrant a strip search of a student.

To date no court has upheld a random urine analysis requirement for either teachers or students. However, at least one federal appeals court has upheld mandatory urine testing for drugs for employees involved in pupil transportation, when there was strong evidence of widespread drug use among such workers.

NOTES

1. *Wieman* v. *Updegraff*, 344 U.S. 183 (1952).
2. *Id.*
3. *Board of Regents* v. *Roth*, 408 U.S. 564 (1972).
4. *Lombard* v. *Board of Education of City of New York*, 502 F.2d 631 (2d Cir. 1974); *Huntley* v. *North Carolina State Board of Education*, 493 F.2d 1016 (4th Cir. 1974); *McGhee* v. *Draper*, 564 F.2d 903 (10th Cir. 1977); *Perry* v. *Sindermann*, 408 U.S. 593 (1972).
5. *Pred* v. *Board of Public Instruction*, 415 F.2d 851 (5th Cir. 1969).
6. *Slochower* v. *Board of Higher Education*, 350 U.S. 551 (1965).

7. *Wieman* v. *Updegraff*, 344 U.S. 183 (1952).

8. *Greminger* v. *Seaborne*, 584 F.2d 275 (8th Cir. 1978).

9. *Miller* v. *Board of Education of the County of Lincoln*, 450 F.Supp. 106 (S.D. W.Va. 1978).

10. *Mt. Healthy City School District Board of Education* v. *Doyle*, 429 U.S. 274 (1977).

11. *Foreman* v. *Vermillion Parish School Board*, 353 So.2d 471 (La. App. 1978).

12. *Guerra* v. *Roma Independent School District*, 444 F.Supp. 812 (S.D. Tex. 1977).

13. *Roberts* v. *Lincoln County School District No. 1*, 676 P.2d 577 (Wyo. 1984).

14. *Hortonville District* v. *Hortonville Education Association*, 426 U.S. 482 (1976).

15. *Adams* v. *Professional Practices Commission*, 524 P.2d 932 (Okla. 1974).

16. *State ex rel. Curry* v. *Grand Valley Local Schools Board of Education*, 375 N.E.2d 48 (Ohio 1978).

17. *Johnson* v. *Selma Board of Education*, 356 So.2d 649 (Ala. 1978).

18. *Rafael* v. *Meramac Valley R-111 Board of Education*, 591 S.W.2d 309 (Mo. App. 1978).

19. *Cleveland Board of Education* v. *Loudermill—Parma Board of Education*, 105 S.Ct. 1487 (1985).

20. *Goss* v. *Lopez*, 419 U.S. 565 (1975).

21. *Dixon* v. *Alabama State Board of Education*, 294 F.2d 150 (5th Cir. 1961).

22. *DeJesus* v. *Penberthy*, 344 F.Supp. 70 (D. Conn. 1971).

23. *Smith* v. *Miller*, 514 P.2d 377 (Kan. 1973).

24. *Racine Unified School District* v. *Thompson*, 321 N.W.2d 334 (H. App. Wisc. 1982).

25. *Tibbs* v. *Board of Education of Township of Franklin*, 584 A.2d 179 (N.J. 1971).

26. *Goldwyn* v. *Allen*, 281 N.Y.S.2d 899 (Sup. Ct. N.Y. 1967).

27. *Gabrilowitz* v. *Newman*, 582 F.2d 100 (lst Cir. 1978).

28. *Miranda* v. *Arizona*, 377 U.S. 201 (1966).

29. *Pollnow* v. *Glennon*, 594 F.Supp. 220 (S.D. N.Y. 1984).

30. *Boynton* v. *Casey*, 543 F.Supp. 995 (D. Me. 1982).

31. *Hardy* v. *University Interscholastic League*, 759 F.2d 1233 (5th Cir. 1985).

32. *Darby* v. *School Superintendent*, 544 F.Supp. 428 (W.D. Mich. 1982).

33. *Meyers* v. *Arcata Union High School District*, 75 Cal. Rptr. 68 (Cal. 1969).

34. *Sullivan* v. *Houston Independent School District*, 333 F.Supp. 1149 (S.D. Tex. 1971).

35. *Ingraham* v. *Wright*, 420 U.S. 651 (1977).

36. *Faye Elizabeth Hall et al.* v. *G. Garrison Tawney et al.*, 621 F.2d 607 (4th Cir. 1980).

37. *Garcia* v. *Miera*, 817 F.2d 650 (10th Cir. 1987) *cert. denied*, 108 S.Ct. 1220 (1988).

38. *Baker* v. *Owens*, 395 F.Supp. 294 (M.D. N.C. 1975), *aff'd*, 423 U.S. 907 (1975).

39. *Wingfield* v. *Fort Bend Independent School District*, (D.C. S.D. Texas No. 72-H-232, 1973).

40. *Howard* v. *Clark*, 299 N.Y.S.2d 65 (1969).

41. *New Braunfels Independent School District* v. *Armke*, 658 S.W.2d 330 (Tex. App. 1983).

42. *Katzman* v. *Cumberland Valley School District*, 479 A.2d 671 (Pa. Commw. Ct. 1984).

43. *Spring Branch I.S.D.* v. *Stamas*, No. C-4184, slip. op. (Tex. 1985).

44. *People* v. *Overton*, 249 N.E.2d 366 (N.Y. 1969).
45. *New Jersey* v. *T.L.O.*, 105 S.Ct. 733 (1985).
46. *Shamberg* v. *State of Alaska*, 762 P.2nd 488 (Alaska App. 1988).
47. *In the Interest of Guy Dumas, a Minor*, 515 A.2d 984 (Pa. Super. 1986).
48. *Cales* v. *Howell Public Schools*, 635 F.Supp. 454 (E.D. Mich. 1985).
49. *State* v. *Brooks*, 718 p.2d 837 (Wash. 1986); *R.D.L.* v. *State*, 499 90.2d 31 (Fla. App.1986).
50. *Cason* v. *Cook*, 810 F.2d 188 (8th Cir. 1987).
51. *Webb* v. *McCullough*, 828 F.2d 1151 (6th Cir. 1987).
52. *New York* v. *Scott*, 358 N.Y.S.2d 403 (1974).
53. *Bellnier* v. *Lund*, 438 F. Supp. 47 (N.D. N.Y. 1977).
54. *M.M.* v. *Anker*, 607 F.2d 588 (2d Cir. 1979).
55. *Doe* v. *Renfrow, Superintendent of Highland Town District*, 475 F.Supp. 1012 (N.D. Ind. 1979).
56. *Doe* v. *Renfrow*, 631 F.2d 91 (7th Cir. 1980), *cert. denied*, 451 U.S. 1022 (1981).
57. *Horton* v. *Goosecreek Independent School District*, 690 F.2d 470 (5th Cir. 1982), *cert. denied*, 51 U.S.L.W. 3919 (1983).
58. *Doe* v. *Renfrow*, 631 F.2d 91 (7th Cir. 1980), *cert. denied*, 451 U.S. 1022, at 1025 (1981).
59. *Patchogue-Medford Congress of Teachers* v. *Board of Educ.*, 510 N.E.2d 325 (N.Y. 1987).
60. *Jones* v. *McKenzie*, 833 F.2d 335 (D.C. Cir. 1987).
61. *Odenheim* v. *Carlestadt-East Rutherford Regional School Dist.*, 510 A.2d 709 (N.J. Super. Ct. Ch. Div. 1985).
62. *Schaill* v. *Tippecanoe School Corp.*, 864 F.2d 1309 (7th Cir. 1988).

CHAPTER 12

How Free Is My Personal Life?

OVERVIEW

In the past, teachers who violated their community's moral standards either resigned or were quickly dismissed. Few educators doubted that teachers could be fired for adultery, drunkenness, homosexual conduct, illegal drug use, committing a felony, or becoming pregnant while single, but community consensus about what constitutes immoral conduct has broken down in recent years. The concept of morality seems to vary according to time and place. As the California Supreme Court observed: "Today's morals may be tomorrow's ancient and absurd customs." Moreover, many educators believe that their personal behavior away from school is their own business. Yet many administrators argue that educators teach by example, and thus should be adult models for their students and should conform to the moral standards of the community. This chapter examines how courts have resolved this conflict between teacher freedom and community control. It focuses on three questions: What constitutes immoral conduct for teachers? When can teachers be punished for such behavior? And can schools concern themselves with other aspects of a teacher's personal life, such as age, weight, residency, or citizenship?

IMMORAL CONDUCT

The *Morrison* Case[1]

In 1969 the California Supreme Court rejected the notion that teachers can automatically be dismissed for immoral behavior. The case involved Marc

235

Morrison, who engaged in a brief homosexual relationship with another teacher. About a year later, the other teacher reported the incident to Morrison's superintendent. This led the board of education to revoke Morrison's teaching credentials on the grounds of immoral and unprofessional conduct. The board defended its action by saying that teachers take the place of parents during school hours and should be models of good conduct, that state law requires teachers to impress on their pupils "principles of morality," that homosexual behavior is contrary to the moral standards of the people of California, and that the board of education is required to revoke a teacher's credentials for immoral conduct.

Despite these arguments, the California court ruled in favor of Morrison. The court explained that it was dangerous to allow the terms "immoral" and "unprofessional" to be interpreted broadly. To many people, "immoral conduct" includes laziness, gluttony, selfishness, and cowardice. To others, "unprofessional conduct" for teachers includes signing petitions, opposing majority opinions, and drinking alcoholic beverages. Therefore, unless these terms are defined carefully and narrowly, they could be applied to most teachers in the state. Furthermore, the court ruled that the board should not be able to dismiss an educator because it disapproved of his personal, private conduct unless the conduct is clearly related to his professional work. According to the court, when a teacher's job is not affected, his private behavior is his own business and should not be a basis for discipline.

But how can a board determine whether a teacher's behavior affects his job in such a way that he is unfit to teach? In making this decision, the court suggested that the board consider all the circumstances. Here there was no evidence that Morrison's conduct affected his teaching. There was no evidence that he "even considered any improper relationship with any student," that he "failed to teach the principles of morality," or that the single homosexual incident "affected his relationship with his co-workers." Therefore, the court ruled against the board because it failed to present evidence that Morrison's retention in the profession would be harmful. In the words of the court: "An individual can be removed from the teaching profession only upon a showing that his retention in the profession poses a significant danger of harm to either students, school employees, or others who might be affected by his actions as a teacher."

Morrison marked a change in the way many courts considered questions of teachers' immoral conduct. In the past, the fact that a teacher engaged in behavior a community considered immoral would have been enough to support his dismissal. After *Morrison,* other courts began to rule that teachers could not be dismissed simply because of such conduct unless there was evidence that it was clearly related to teacher effectiveness. Thus a federal court in Oregon ruled in favor of a teacher who was dismissed because she acknowledged that she was a "practicing homosexual."[2] Judge Solomon held that the statute allowing teachers to be dismissed for immorality simply because they are homosexual was unconstitutionally vague because it permits "erratic and prejudicial exercises of authority" and does not require a connection between the alleged conduct and teaching.

When can a teacher be dismissed for homosexual behavior?

This depends on a variety of circumstances, such as whether the conduct is considered private or public. In California, for example, the board of education revoked the teaching credentials of Thomas Sarac after he was arrested and convicted for making a "homosexual advance" to a plainclothes policeman at a public beach; and the court ruled in favor of the board.[3] The California Supreme Court distinguished the *Sarac* ruling from the *Morrison* decision on the grounds that the circumstances were different. Unlike Morrison, Sarac admitted a recent history of homosexual activity and pleaded guilty to a criminal charge arising from a public homosexual advance.[4]

In Nebraska, a high school teacher was dismissed for making a homosexual advance to a typewriter salesman in the teachers' lounge. Although there was no direct evidence that the incident impaired the teacher's efficiency, a 1988 decision upheld the dismissal, reasoning that such sexual advances in school are "a clear departure from moral behavior and professional standards" and indicate "unfitness to teach."[5]

In Oregon a court upheld the dismissal of a teacher for homosexual conduct that was observed by undercover police in the rear of an adult bookstore.[6] According to the judge, engaging in sexual activity in a public place violates contemporary moral standards; and once the behavior became known among the parents of his pupils, "his ability to function as a teacher was severely impaired." In short, the court found that the teacher's public immoral behavior, combined with community knowledge and parental complaints, justified his dismissal.

On the other hand, the Supreme Court of Washington sustained the dismissal of James Gaylord even though his sexual behavior was not public. Gaylord, an excellent high school teacher, was fired after he admitted to his vice principal that he was a homosexual.[7] The Washington court pointed out that a teacher's efficiency is determined by his relations with students and their parents, fellow teachers, and school administrators. The judge noted that "at least one student plus several administrators, teachers, and parents publicly objected to Gaylord remaining on the teaching staff" and they testified that his continued presence "would create problems." According to the court, this evidence supported the school's concern that the continued presence of Gaylord after he voluntarily became known as a homosexual would result in confusion, fear, and parental concern, which would impair his efficiency as a teacher.

A related decision involved an Ohio guidance counselor who told a school secretary, the assistant principal, and several colleagues that she was bisexual and had a female lover.[8] When she was not rehired because of these and other comments, she sued, arguing that her speech should have been protected by the First Amendment. But a divided appeals court ruled that her statements about her sexual preferences were not protected since the First Amendment only protects a teacher when she speaks about matters of "public concern" and not about her "personal interests."

Can teachers be fired for advocating legalization of homosexual activity?

Probably not. In Oklahoma, a law was passed permitting teachers to be dismissed for public homosexual "conduct" or "activity." In 1984 a federal appeals court upheld part of the law, punishing homosexual "activity" that is "indiscreet and not practiced in private."[9] But the prohibition against homosexual "conduct" was unconstitutional since it defined such conduct to include "advocating" or "promoting" homosexual activity in a way that could come to the attention of school children or employees. Thus a teacher could violate the law by appearing on television or before the legislature to urge repeal of an antisodomy statute. However, firing teachers for advocating legal or social change violates the First Amendment. Therefore, such restrictions on teachers' rights are only permitted if the state proves they are "necessary" to prevent disruption or insure effective teaching, and the state proved neither. The Supreme Court reviewed this case and was evenly divided. As a result, the appeals court decision stands.

Can teachers be dismissed for being unwed mothers?

Decisions vary. One view is reflected in a federal decision upholding the action of Omaha officials who fired a junior high school teacher "because of her being pregnant and unwed."[10] The court noted that a teacher who develops a good relationship with her students "is likely to be a model to those students in wide-ranging respects, including personal values." This teacher had developed such a relationship with her students, who knew that she was unmarried and pregnant. Therefore, the court said that it was reasonable for the school board to believe that permitting the teacher to remain in the classroom would be viewed by the students as condoning pregnancy out of wedlock. The court concluded that "there is a rational connection between the plaintiff's pregnancy out of wedlock and the school board's interest in conserving marital values, when acts probably destructive of those values are revealed, verbally or non-verbally, in the classroom."*

On the other hand, the trend of decision is illustrated by a federal appeals court case involving a Mississippi rule that automatically disqualified school employees who were parents of illegitimate children.[11] The policy led administrators to investigate and reject several present and prospective employees. Officials offered these reasons for the rule: unwed parenthood is proof of immoral conduct, unwed parents are improper role models for students, and such teachers contribute to the problem of student pregnancy.

In rejecting these reasons, the judge explained that "present immorality"

---

* This decision was later reversed on procedural grounds by a divided appeals court.

does not necessarily follow from unwed parenthood. Under the school rule, a teacher "could live an impeccable life yet be barred as unfit for employment for an event . . . occurring at any time in the past." This policy, wrote the court, "equates the single fact of the illegitimate birth with irredeemable moral disease. Such a presumption is not only patently absurd, it is mischievous and prejudicial, requiring those who administer the policy to investigate the parental status of school employees and prospective applicants. Where no stigma may have existed before, such inquisitions by over-zealous officialdom can rapidly create it."

The court also did not agree that unwed parents would be improper models. The judge doubted that students would seek information on the private family life of teachers and then try to emulate them. Moreover, the school district offered no evidence, beyond speculation, that the presence of unwed parents in school contributed to student pregnancy. Finally, the court noted that "unwed mothers only, not unwed fathers" were penalized by the policy. For these reasons, the court ruled that the policy violated the constitutional right to equal protection. In a related 1986 decision involving an Illinois teacher who was fired for being unmarried and pregnant and for deciding to raise her child as a single parent, a judge wrote: "Under the overwhelming weight of authority, it is beyond question that [the teacher] had a substantive due process right to conceive and raise her child out of wedlock without unwarranted . . . School Board intrusion."[12]

Can teachers be dismissed for immoral or unprofessional conduct with students?

Yes. Although most courts will not allow teachers to be dismissed for immorality with other adults unless there is evidence that such conduct will negatively affect their teaching, judges rule differently concerning immoral behavior with students. In these cases courts are generally quite strict, especially in the area of sexual relations with students.

Joseph Stubblefield was a teacher in a California junior college. After teaching one night, he drove one of his female students to a deserted side street and parked. Later a deputy sheriff stopped to investigate and discovered Stubblefield and the student involved in a sexual relationship. After recognizing the deputy, Stubblefield knocked him down and drove away at speeds of 80 to 100 miles per hour before he finally pulled over. Because of these events, the teacher was dismissed for immoral conduct.

Stubblefield argued that the evidence against him concerned only his out-of-school conduct, not his teaching. But a California appeals court supported his dismissal.[13] The court noted that "there are certain professions which impose upon persons attracted to them, responsibilities and limitations on freedom of action which do not exist in regard to other callings. Public officials such as . . . school teachers fall into such a category." Therefore, "as a minimum, responsible conduct on the part of a teacher, even at the college level, excludes meretricious relationships with his students." According to the court, Stubblefield's assault on the police officer, his misconduct with his student, and the notoriety of his behavior were evidence of his unfitness to teach. In conclusion the court wrote: "The integrity of the educational system under which teachers wield considerable power in the grading of students and the granting or with-holding of certificates and diplomas is clearly threatened when teachers become involved in relationships with students such as is indicated by the conduct here."

Similarly, an Illinois court upheld the dismissal of a Peoria teacher because he was discovered partially undressed playing strip poker in his automobile with a female high school student.[14] In a Washington case, teacher Gary Denton was discharged after a high school student he had dated became pregnant. Denton admitted being the prospective father. But he claimed his discharge was improper since his girl friend was not a student at his school, and there was no evidence that their relationship had a negative impact on his teaching. The court ruled that no direct evidence is needed when the sexual misconduct involves "a teacher and a minor student."[15] The court held that in such a situation a school board may properly conclude that "the conduct is inherently harmful to the teacher-student relation, and thus to the school district."

In Michigan, an appeals court upheld the firing of a tenured teacher because of an "unprofessional relationship" with one of her 17-year-old high school students.[16] She had been warned to avoid "the appearance of impropriety" with male students, but the teacher visited the student's apartment several times (one time over night), and allowed him to drive her car without a license. Although there was no proof that the teacher's conduct had an adverse effect on other students or teachers, the court ruled that her dismissal was supported by "competent, material, and substantial evidence."

In a recent New York case, a state court upheld the dismissal of a tenured teacher, Bernard Weaver, for insubordination for refusing to obey an order to stop living with a 16-year-old former male student who was still attending school in the district.[17] Weaver encouraged and assisted the student to leave home (he "waited outside the student's house with a loaded gun") despite the mother's strong objections.

Can a teacher be dismissed for sexual conduct with a student that occurred years before?

Yes. In a Minnesota case, a principal was discharged for sexual abuse of a student that occurred twelve to sixteen years before, when the student was in the first to fifth grades.[18] The superintendent learned of the incident from the former student when he became a father and was concerned for his own children. The teacher argued that the remoteness of the alleged behavior denied him due process. A state court ruled, however, that the seriousness of the sexual contact with the student "required dismissal" even though it occurred years before.

Can a teacher be dismissed for sexual advances toward students?

Yes. Cases indicate that courts tend to be quite strict in this area. For example, a Pennsylvania court upheld the dismissal of a teacher because of two incidents involving his proposal to "spank" two of his female high school students, which each perceived as a sexual advance.[19] Although the teacher admitted he had sexual fantasies about spanking the girls, he denied that his *conduct* was immoral. The court acknowledged that a teacher "cannot be found guilty of immorality based solely on his admitted fantasies." But when teachers discuss sex with students, this is often a serious problem "because of the significant influence teachers exert." According to the court, when such a discussion is not related to the curriculum, a school board can conclude that the conduct is improper.

In a related Alabama case, Montgomery teacher Howard Kilpatrick was discharged for immoral conduct because he made "sexual advances towards female students." The teacher claimed that the term "immoral conduct" was unconstitutionally vague and could include innocuous activity. Although the judge acknowledged that the "ultimate reach" of the term immorality was not clear, he did not feel there was any problem about vagueness in this case. According to the judge, any teacher can be expected to know that sexual advances toward students "cannot be condoned in the classroom setting."[20] Similarly, a state court upheld the firing of a Colorado high school teacher because of his "horseplay" with several female students on a field trip.[21] This consisted of tickling them all over their bodies and carrying on a vulgar and sexually suggestive dialogue. The teacher viewed his behavior as an attempt to act his "natural self to gain rapport" with his students. But the court, viewing his conduct as "sordid," ruled that it had "no legitimate professional purpose," and upheld his dismissal. Similarly, in a New York case, the court approved the discharge of a teacher for "intolerable behavior" that included kissing the girls in his sixth-grade class, patting them "on the behind," and permitting obscene jokes and profanity in his classroom.[22]

On the other hand, an Illinois court ruled in favor of a guidance counselor who was dismissed for hugging and stroking a fifth-grade girl and letting her sit on his knee. Experts disagreed about the wisdom of the counselor's professional conduct. A state court ruled, however, that in this case it was not immoral for the counselor "to hug or stroke a crying, distraught ten-year-old child" or to permit her to sit on his knee "while they discussed her school work and her family situation."[23]

Can teachers be punished for talking to their students about sex?

Sometimes. Talking about sex may subject a teacher to disciplinary action, especially when such talk is not related to the curriculum. A high school band instructor in Florida was dismissed for making remarks in a coed class relating to virginity and premarital sex relations. A state court sustained his discharge for immorality because of his "unbecoming and unnecessary risque remarks."[24] The judge concluded that "instructors in our schools should not be permitted to so risquely discuss sex problems in our teenage mixed classes as to cause embarrassment to the children or to involve in them other feelings not incident to the course of study being pursued."

In a similar Wisconsin case, a state court upheld the dismissal of a Milwaukee teacher because of a series of discussions about sex in his twelfth-grade speech classes.[25] Specifically, he explained the operation of houses of prostitution and indicated which students were old enough to be admitted; he told stories about intercourse with a cow and about the size of a penis; and he discussed premarital sex in an approving way. The teacher argued that the speech curriculum was broad enough to include sex education, which was never specifically prohibited. But the court concluded that the teacher's discussions transcended the bounds "of propriety of the contemporary community" and constituted immoral conduct. And in a New York case, a tenured photography instructor was fired for showing his eleventh- and twelfth-grade students a "pornographic film that included scenes involving oral sex."[26]

On the other hand, a Mississippi teacher who merely answered a student's question about sex on one occasion was held not guilty of immoral behavior.[27] After several boys in an eighth-grade spelling class asked "What is a queer?" she briefly discussed homosexuality. Although some parents objected, a federal court ruled that this single incident was not enough to disqualify the teacher. While the judge questioned the judgment of a woman teacher discussing such a subject with young boys, he concluded that such a discussion was "certainly not an act 'repulsive to the minimum standards of decency' required of public school teachers." In other cases where teachers have been dismissed for using objectionable language in the classroom, courts have sometimes ruled that their actions are protected by their right to freedom of speech under the First and Fourteenth Amendments. (For a detailed discussion of this issue, see Chapter 8.)

Can a teacher be fired for using profanity or abusive language toward students?

Yes. In Colorado, a music teacher took a troublesome student outside the high school and told him he was a "disgrace to the band," an "SOB," and a "fucking asshole." As a result, the director was dismissed since he previously had been ordered "not to use profanity in dealing with the students."[28] Similarly, a Pennsylvania foreign-language teacher was fired for calling a 14-year-old student a "slut" and implying that she was a prostitute. In upholding the dismissal, the court explained that school officials must be able to protect students from abusive language by teachers, which, in this case, was "totally inappropriate."[29]

In Omaha, a teacher was fired for calling black students "dumb niggers" in a racially mixed class. According to the Nebraska Supreme Court, it is as immoral for teachers to use such language (which is "humiliating, painful, and harmful") as it is to teach students to cheat.[30] "There may have been a time," wrote the court, when it was thought appropriate to "refer to each other as 'kikes' or 'wops' or 'shanty Irish' or 'nigger.'" But, "thankfully, we have overcome that disgrace. And those who insist on making such words a part of their vocabulary must be labeled by the public as immoral."

In a controversial Indiana case, a divided appeals court even upheld the dismissal of a teacher for immorality because she may have said, "Fuck you" during class. In a skeptical comment on the conflicting evidence, the court wrote: "The School Board chose to believe that a mature grade-school teacher with 12 years of experience and an unblemished record would stand in the middle of her 5th-grade art class and mindlessly utter a barracksroom obscenity in response to a student's question."[31] Although other judges might have ruled differently, this court held that the board had adequate evidence to believe the students who testified against the teacher and that the harsh penalty was not an abuse of the board's discretion. However, in a dissenting opinion, Judge Canover wrote that the record revealed the absence of a fair hearing and "a mockery of justice." (This case illustrates the extreme reluctance of some judges to overturn the findings and judgment of a school board.)

Can teachers be dismissed because of rumors of immoral conduct?

No. If teachers are terminated for immoral conduct, such action should be based on fact, not rumor. This was the ruling in the case of Annabel Stoddard, a divorced mother who taught in a small, religiously oriented Wyoming community.[32] Stoddard was a competent teacher, but her contract was not renewed. Despite the official written reasons given for her nonrenewal, the evidence indicated that the real reasons were because of "rumors that she was having an affair" and because she was unattractive and did not attend church regularly. As a result of this evidence, a federal court ruled that the school officials were "motivated by constitutionally impermissible reasons" in not renewing her contract, and she was awarded $33,000 in "compensatory damages."

Moreover, an Iowa court ruled that even an admission of adultery does not make a person automatically unfit to teach.[33] The case involved an excellent teacher whose certification was revoked after he was discovered committing adultery. The court ruled that this "isolated incident" was not grounds for revocation when there was no evidence to indicate it would adversely affect his teaching.

Are there other reasons why teachers have been dismissed on grounds of immoral or unprofessional conduct?

Yes. A tenured California elementary teacher was dismissed after she was arrested by an undercover policeman for openly engaging in sexual activity with three different men at a swingers' club party in Los Angeles. A state court upheld her dismissal because her conduct at the semipublic party reflected "a total lack of concern for privacy, decorum or preservation of her dignity and reputation" and indicated "a serious defect of moral character, normal prudence, and good common sense."[34]

In Ohio, a counselor who was also a wrestling coach was dismissed for telling a student to lie about his weight during a wrestling tournament. As a result, he resigned as coach, but argued that this conduct should not affect his position as guidance counselor. The court disagreed. It ruled that telling a student to lie and cheat was immorality that related directly to his performance as a teacher.[35]

In Missouri the state supreme court upheld the dismissal of a building trades teacher for immoral conduct because he permitted male students to "engage in sexual harassment" of the only female student by repeatedly using obscene and sexually explicit language toward her, by displaying a "suggestive centerfold," and by using a plastic phallus to embarrass her.[36]

A New Jersey court upheld the dismissal of a male tenured music teacher, Paul Monroe Grossman, after he underwent "sex-reassignment" surgery.[37] The operation changed his external anatomy to that of a female, Paula Miriam Grossman, who began to live and dress as a woman. While there was conflicting testimony about Grossman's probable future effectiveness, the court supported her termination because of "potential psychological harm to students" if she were retained.

On the other hand, a Pennsylvania court recently ruled in favor of two teachers who were punished for engaging in a water fight with their students on the last day of school. Since administrators had clearly prohibited such conduct, the teachers were found guilty of immoral conduct and suspended for 15 days. The judge, however, noted that immorality usually involves "sexual improprieties, stealing," or "illegal gambling." Therefore, the court concluded that, although the teachers' conduct in this case was "most inappropriate and an error in judgment," it was "not immoral."[38]

Does a school have to warn teachers before dismissing them for immoral or unprofessional conduct?

Not if the misconduct is serious or a clear violation of professional ethics. Thus, a Minnesota guidance counselor was discharged for a series of unprofessional incidents including breaching the confidence of students (e.g., he disclosed an incest victim's confidences in a social setting to teachers who had no need for the information). The teacher argued that he should have been warned about his deficiencies and given an opportunity to remedy them. But the state court rejected his argument.[39] "It should not be necessary," wrote the judge, "to tell a counselor that his conduct is inappropriate when the conduct clearly violates [his] code of ethics."

Can a teacher be dismissed for excessive drinking?

Yes. California teacher Joseph Watson was denied a secondary teaching credential on grounds of immorality because of six convictions involving the use of alcohol. Although there was no proof that his convictions affected his teaching, the court ruled that the evidence amply demonstrated his unfitness to teach.[40] First, Watson's use of alcohol had gotten out of control and indicated that he did not have the proper attitude necessary for successfully counseling students away from the harmful effects of alcohol, as state law requires. Second, being arrested as a "public drunk" and for driving under the influence of alcohol was a poor example for high school students. Through his behavior, Watson had repeatedly violated important community values and jeopardized the welfare of his students and the public. Finally, the judge wrote: "I don't know what better evidence there could be of immorality than a series of criminal convictions."

In a related Wyoming case, a state court upheld the dismissal of a teacher who was found drunk in school in front of his students and had to be removed from class by other teachers.[41] Similarly, an Arizona court ruled that a teacher could be dismissed after pleading guilty to fighting and "disturbing the peace by being under the influence of intoxicants."[42] On the other hand, the Supreme Court of Montana ruled that convictions for driving while intoxicated were not enough to discharge a teacher for immorality.[43] In this 1976 case, a teacher was arrested and pleaded guilty to "driving under the influence" for the third time. Based on this "conviction," he was dismissed. In overruling the school authorities, the Montana court held that "violations for driving under the influence of intoxicating liquor" are not in themselves "tantamount to immorality." To sustain the dismissal of such a teacher, the court indicated that school officials would have to present evidence indicating that the convictions would affect the teacher's professional performance.

Can a teacher be dismissed for allowing students to drink at the teacher's home?

Yes, especially if the drinking is excessive. On December 27, 1979, two 16-year-old students asked teacher Archie Vivian if they could play pool at his house. There, they gave Vivian a bottle of whiskey "as a Christmas gift." Although the teacher had only one drink, the girls helped themselves and finished the bottle. Vivian saw them do this and did not attempt to stop them. As a result, one of the girls became intoxicated and passed out, the incident became public, and the teacher was dismissed.

Witnesses testified that Vivian (who had not been disciplined in 23 years of teaching) could soon overcome the adverse effects of this incident. In response, the judge wrote: "No doubt, Vivian can at some time in the future regain his ability to teach"; but schools are not established to rehabilitate teachers.[44] In upholding Vivian's dismissal, the court concluded that the district "was entitled to a teacher who would be an effective role model and teacher on the date of his discharge, not the following day, or the following month."

Can a teacher be dismissed for allowing students to use drugs in the teacher's home?

Yes. In Kentucky, two tenured teachers, Greg and Donnie Wood, were fired for allowing two 15-year-old students to participate in a marijuana smoking party in their home. The Wood brothers argued that they should not have been fired for "acts committed during off-duty hours, during the summer . . . and in the privacy of their own apartment." However, the state supreme court disagreed. The court acknowledged that teachers should not be dismissed for every "private shortcoming that might come to the attention of the Board of Education." However, in this case, the court held that smoking marijuana with two students was "serious misconduct of an immoral and criminal nature" and that there was a direct connection between the off-campus misconduct and the teachers' in-school role "as a moral example for the students."[45]

Can a teacher be dismissed for lying?

It depends on the facts of the case. In Kentucky, a teacher called in sick in order to drive a coal truck to Ohio and later falsely swore that he was ill in order to collect sick leave for that day. As a result, a state court upheld his dismissal for conduct unbecoming a teacher.[46]

In California, however, a court reached a different result in the case of a teacher who was fired for calling in sick so she could attend a landing of the space shuttle. The judge acknowledged that the teacher's behavior constituted unprofessional conduct for which she might have been suspended. But, in view of the teacher's "previously unblemished record," the court agreed with a state Commission on Professional Competence that dismissal was excessive punishment for her behavior.[47]

In another California case concerning a teacher who was dismissed for dishonesty for misusing her sick leave, a court noted that "dishonest conduct may range from the smallest fib to the most flagrant lie." Therefore, it ruled that "not every falsehood will constitute 'dishonesty' as a ground for dismissal."[48] Instead, the court said that judges should weigh the seriousness of the dishonesty in each case and consider a number of factors including the likelihood of its recurrence, extenuating or aggravating circumstances, motivation, the extent of publicity, its likely effect on students, and the proximity or remoteness of the conduct.

Will courts reverse penalties against teachers that seem harsh?

Not usually. Although courts are willing to overturn a school board's decision for constitutional or procedural reasons, most judges are reluctant to reverse a penalty imposed by a board because it seems harsh. In Colorado, for example, Patricia Blaine, a high school teacher and cheerleading coach, was dismissed for not stopping her cheerleaders from drinking beer in their motel room during a basketball tournament. Blaine admitted poor judgment, but said she didn't "make a scene and throw the beer away" because she wanted to keep the cheerleaders "safe, supervised, and in their room." Since Blaine failed to stop the drinking, a majority of the Colorado Supreme Court refused to hold that the dismissal "was such an unwarranted form of discipline as to constitute an abuse of school board discretion."[49] However, in a dissenting opinion, three justices emphasized that Blaine was "a concerned and well-intentioned, but inexperienced chaperone" who tried "a non-confrontive approach" to control the cheerleaders during a night of widespread partying. Although the dissenters agreed that Blaine "erred in judgment," they concluded that her conduct "simply did not warrant the devastating sanction of dismissal."[50]

In some cases, however, the penalty of the board, which seems relatively light in view of the seriousness of the offense, is still challenged by the teacher. In New York, for example, a driver education and industrial arts teacher was convicted and jailed for negligent homicide in a widely publicized hit and run auto accident that killed a teenage biker. As a result, the teacher was suspended for two years. Even though he taught driving, the teacher argued that there was no connection between the accident and his ability to teach. But the court disagreed and concluded that "the adverse effect of this particular notorious conviction and sentence on a teacher's legitimate function" is "self-evident."[51]

CRIMINAL CONDUCT

Is conviction for a felony grounds for dismissal?

Usually, a teacher who is convicted of a serious crime, such as a felony, can be dismissed. This was the ruling of a Delaware court in the case of Leon Skripchuk, an outstanding industrial arts teacher.[52] After Skripchuk pleaded guilty to charges of theft and aggravated assault with a gun, he was dismissed for immorality. This was the only blemish in his long teaching career, and experts testified that it was "most unlikely" that he would ever again be involved in similar criminal conduct. But school officials testified that his conviction, which received widespread publicity, would make parents fearful and would impair his teaching effectiveness. In view of the seriousness of this crime, the court ruled that the teacher's actions were "unquestionably immoral," and his termination was reasonable. In a similar Florida case, a state court upheld the dismissal of a teacher who pleaded guilty to manslaughter after killing her husband with a shotgun.[53] The court held that under the circumstances, her guilty plea was sufficient evidence of immorality.

On the other hand, a California court pointed out that not all felonies involve immoral behavior or crimes of such seriousness that by themselves they would be sufficient to justify dismissing a teacher.[54] This view was endorsed by the Washington Supreme Court in a case involving a teacher who was fired after being convicted of grand larceny for purchasing a stolen motorcycle.[55] The court ruled that a teacher should not be dismissed unless the school district shows that his criminal conduct "materially and substantially" affects his teaching. According to the court, "simply labeling an instructor as a convicted felon will not justify a discharge." This is especially true in this case, where the teacher might not have known the motorcycle was stolen when he bought it, where he received support from students, parents, and other teachers, and where the conviction had no adverse effect on his teaching.

Does conviction for a misdemeanor justify dismissal?

Not usually. But it may if the misdemeanor constitutes a crime of moral turpitude or unprofessional conduct. For example, in Alaska, a tenured teacher was dismissed after being convicted of illegally diverting electricity from the power company to his home. The board characterized the teacher's crime as a "form of larceny or theft . . . involving moral turpitude." The Alaska Supreme Court agreed.[56] The court wrote: "The legislature, in enacting certain criminal statutes, has established minimum acceptable moral standards for the state as a whole. If a teacher cannot abide by these standards, his or her fitness as a teacher is necessarily called into question."

Similarly, in Minnesota, social studies teacher Donald Shelton was discharged for unprofessional conduct after being convicted for theft from a company he ran with two other teachers. Shelton made restitution and argued that he should not be fired since the conviction for this misdemeanor did not impair his teaching. However, the school board claimed that Shelton's fitness "was directly affected" since he teaches business ethics and "lost his credibility to teach such values." A state court agreed. The judge added that, because of Shelton's theft from fellow teachers and the resulting animosity, his "continued presence in this small district will result in . . . an unsatisfactory learning environment."[57]

Is shoplifting sufficient grounds for teacher dismissal?

Judges differ on this issue. Some believe conviction for shoplifting is a sufficient basis for dismissal; others hold that schools must prove that the crime impairs teacher effectiveness. A case illustrating this conflict involved Arlene Golden, a West Virginia guidance counselor, who was fined $100 for shoplifting at a local mall. Although there were mitigating circumstances indicating that the counselor was "totally distraught" at the time, the board dismissed her, believing that her conviction constituted immoral conduct. But the West Virginia Supreme Court ruled in Golden's favor because there was no evidence that the counselor's conviction had any relationship to her professional effectiveness.[58] Since the only competent evidence was favorable to Golden, the court ruled that the board could not conclude she was unfit as a counselor.

In a strong dissenting opinion that reflects the views of other courts, Judge Neely wrote: "What type of example does a confessed shoplifter set for impressionable teenagers? . . . I can hear the dialogue now in the guidance office of this particular counselor: 'Say, Miss Golden, do you know a good fence for some clean, hot jewelry?' . . . The result in this case is absurd."[59]

In a Pennsylvania shoplifting case, a state court upheld the right of a school board to dismiss a teacher for shoplifting on grounds of immorality. According to the court, immorality includes conduct that offends community morals and is "a bad example to the youth whose ideals a teacher is supposed to foster." Clearly, wrote the court, "shoplifting falls squarely within this definition."[60]

Should conviction for a serious crime preclude future employment as a teacher?

Not necessarily. According to some courts, commission of a crime is not always sufficient to permanently bar a person from teaching. In considering this issue, the liberal California Supreme Court wrote that dismissal for illegal conduct is reasonable only under two conditions: (1) the teacher's conduct must be "sufficiently notorious" that students know or are likely to learn of it, and (2) "the teacher must continue to model his past conduct." According to the court: "The teacher who committed an indiscretion, paid the penalty, and now seeks to discourage his students from committing similar acts may well be a more effective supporter of legal and moral standards than the one who has never been found to violate those standards. Since these conditions will vary from case to case, proof that one has at some past time committed a crime should not in itself suffice to demonstrate that he is not now and never will be a suitable behavior model for his students."[61]

A related New Mexico case involved Geronimo Garcia, a teacher who had been found guilty of sexual misconduct with his 13-year-old stepdaughter.[62] After completing his three-year probation, Garcia applied for renewal of his teaching certification. Medical testimony indicated that the teacher had been rehabilitated. But others testified that parents would feel uncomfortable with any teacher convicted of sexual misconduct with a minor. The court acknowledged that a person convicted of a crime such as this, which is related to the teaching of children, has the burden of showing he has been rehabilitated. They ruled, however, that Garcia met that burden. Those who testified against the teacher had no personal knowledge of Garcia's present condition or his professional performance; therefore such testimony "is not relevant to a determination of rehabilitation."[63] Since the only competent evidence indicated that Garcia had been rehabilitated, the court ruled in his favor.

Can teachers be suspended on the basis of a criminal indictment?

Yes, if the alleged misconduct relates to their job as teacher (e.g., stealing school funds or molesting students). In Massachusetts, the state courts have broadly interpreted the concept of "misconduct in employment." In one case, a court sustained the suspension of a junior high school teacher after his indictment for "possession, with intent to distribute, cocaine."[64] There was no evidence that the teacher engaged in misconduct with school personnel or students. However, the judge reasoned that because of the teacher's position as role model, because of the increased use of drugs among students, and because his conduct was in "direct conflict with the message his teaching should impart," school officials should have discretion to consider the cocaine indictment to be "an indictment for misconduct in office." In a subsequent case, another court used the role model argument to sustain the suspension of two teachers who were indicted for welfare fraud of $32,000.[65]

Can teachers be dismissed because of criminal charges against them?

Not simply because of the charges or the publicity surrounding them. In Florida, after a teacher was arrested for possession of illegal marijuana and alcohol, the charges were dropped when it was found that both illegal substances belonged to his brother. Nevertheless, the teacher was dismissed because the school board believed his "effectiveness as a teacher has been impaired." But a state appeals court rejected this argument.[66] "Otherwise," wrote the judge, "whenever a teacher is accused of a crime and is subsequently exonerated with no evidence being presented to tie the teacher to the crime, the school board could, nevertheless, dismiss the teacher because the attendant publicity has impaired the teacher's effectiveness." Such a rule, concluded the court, "would be improper."

On the other hand, acquittal of a criminal charge, such as selling drugs to students, does not prevent a school from dismissing a teacher on those grounds. To convict someone of a crime, the state must prove he is guilty "beyond a reasonable doubt." But to dismiss a teacher, a school board need only show "by a preponderance of the evidence" that he engaged in immoral or criminal conduct that impaired his teaching.

Can a teacher be fired for taking school property of relatively little value?

Yes, even when the property is later returned. In 1984 a Missouri court upheld the dismissal of a tenured teacher-librarian who, during an eight-year period, took the following property from the school: a teapot, $20 from baseball gate receipts, and a set of books. The court explained: "The taking of property belonging to another without consent, notwithstanding its return when confronted with such wrongdoing, breaches even the most relaxed standards of acceptable human behavior, particularly so with regard to those who occupy positions which bring them in close, daily contact with young persons of an impressionable age."[67]

Can a teacher be punished for considering a crime?

No. David Bogart, a Kansas teacher, was charged with possession of marijuana because of drugs his son kept in his room. Although Bogart was cleared of the charge, he was dismissed by the school committee for "conduct unbecoming an instructor." Before the committee, Bogart admitted that he considered trying to protect his son and taking the blame himself, though he did not. But a federal court held that this was not a lawful basis for dismissal.[68] "It is fortunate," wrote the court, "the state is not allowed to penalize its citizens for their thoughts, for it would be the rare and either mindless, supine, or super-saintly citizen who has not at some time contemplated and then rejected the illegal."

Can a teacher be dismissed for the use or possession of illegal drugs?

It depends on the circumstances. Courts, for example, might not support the firing of a teacher solely because he once was indicted for possessing a small amount of marijuana. But they would probably support a dismissal based on evidence of a widely publicized conviction combined with testimony indicating how the teacher's criminal behavior would undermine his effectiveness as a teacher. The California courts have decided these four relevant cases on this question.

Arthur Comings's teacher certification was revoked for immoral and unprofessional conduct based on evidence that he had been convicted for possession of marijuana. But at Comings's hearing no evidence was presented indicating whether his conduct adversely affected students or fellow teachers, the likelihood of its recurrence, the teacher's motives, or other evidence concerning his unfitness to teach. Under these circumstances, the court held that there was not sufficient evidence to revoke Comings's certification.[69] The court said it was not ruling that marijuana offenders must be permitted to teach, only that they cannot be dismissed without adequate evidence of their unfitness.

In a later case, a California appeals court ruled that teacher Theodor Judge could not be discharged after being convicted for cultivating one marijuana plant.[70] The judge wrote that in this case, "a felony conviction, standing by itself is not a ground for discipline in the absence of moral turpitude," and "marijuana related offenses need not necessarily always be crimes of moral turpitude . . . measured by the morals of our day."

Barnet Brennan was the teaching principal of a California school when she wrote an affidavit in support of a friend who had been convicted of possessing marijuana. In the sworn statement, she said: "Marijuana is not harmful to my knowledge, because I have been using it since 1949 almost daily, with only beneficial results." Because Brennan's statement attracted wide publicity and her students learned of its content, she was dismissed and went to court. Brennan argued that she should not be penalized when there was no evidence that her statement had a negative effect on students. The court responded that the school acted so promptly after learning of the affidavit that there was little time for such evidence to develop. Here, said the court, there was "competent evidence" on the "likely" effect of Brennan's conduct on students. As one witness testified: "I would be inclined to believe that the pupil would be thinking, 'If my teacher can gain her ends by breaking the law, then I, too, can gain my ends by breaking the law!' "[71]

In a related case, art teacher Selwyn Jones was fined for possessing marijuana while on a trip to Hawaii. His conduct was reported in the *San Francisco Chronicle* and reached the attention of Daly City school officials, who dismissed him. At a hearing the vice principal testified that Jones's return to the school would adversely affect its art department, faculty, student body, and parents because many of these persons had expressed "disapproval" or "concern" at reinstating a teacher convicted of using marijuana. According to the vice principal, Jones's return "would be an example in opposition to the instructions we are giving to the students" concerning drug use; in fact, his return would "work against the total goals of our school." Based on this "substantial evidence" concerning Jones's fitness to teach, the court upheld his dismissal.[72]

LIFE STYLE

Does the right to privacy protect teachers' personal lives?

It might. In 1985 a federal appeals court ruled that a school could not refuse to renew a teacher's contract because of her pending divorce.[73] The nonrenewal decision was based on some parents' worry that too many divorcees were teaching in the school and the superintendent's concern for the school's image in the community. While the court acknowledged that the school could deny reemployment for any legitimate reason, it could not take such action in violation of the teacher's "constitutional right to privacy." Although the outer limits of this right may not be clear, the court ruled that "matters relating to marriage and family relationships involve privacy rights that are constitutionally protected against unwarranted government interference." Thus, a school cannot refuse to hire a teacher simply because of her "constitutionally protected decision to seek a divorce."

When Virginia teacher Pamela Ponton was forced to take a leave because she was pregnant and unmarried, she argued that this violated her right to privacy. A federal judge agreed and ruled that the constitutional "right to privacy encompasses decisions regarding whether to have a child" and "protects the right to have a child out of wedlock."[74] The school board had argued that unmarried pregnant teachers set a bad example for their students. In rejecting this role model theory, the judge doubted "that students would have even been aware" that Ponton was unmarried; and, even if they had, "the mere knowledge that the teacher had gotten pregnant out of wedlock would seem to have a fairly minimal impact on them." The court concluded that the school's interest "in support of the coerced leave of absence is, at best, very weak" and does not outweigh Ponton's constitutional right to privacy.

Can a teacher be prohibited from breastfeeding her child in school?

Not necessarily. In Orange County, Florida, Janice Dike, an elementary schoolteacher, challenged her principal's refusal to allow her to breastfeed her child in school. To avoid interference with her duties, Dike arranged to have her child brought to school during her duty-free lunch period, and she nursed the baby in a private room. However, the principal ordered her to stop because of a rule prohibiting teachers from bringing their children to work. A trial judge dismissed Dike's suit as "frivolous," but an appeals court disagreed.[75]

The court ruled that the Constitution "protects from undue state interference citizens' freedom of personal choice" in some areas of family life which the court described as "rights of personal privacy" or "fundamental personal liberties." According to the court, this right or liberty interest includes breastfeeding—"the most elemental form of parental care." The court's ruling does not mean that schools cannot restrict this protected liberty to prevent disruption or insure that teachers perform their duties. However, a school can only interfere with this right when it is clearly necessary to do so.

Can an unmarried teacher be dismissed for living with someone of the opposite sex?

It depends on the circumstances. Kathleen Sullivan, an elementary teacher, began living with a male friend in a small, rural South Dakota town. When 140 residents petitioned for her dismissal because of her unwed cohabitation, Sullivan's principal asked her to change her living arrangement. Sullivan replied that whom she lived with was her business, not a school matter. As a result, Sullivan was fired because she violated local mores, was a "bad example" for her students, and would not get parental cooperation due to her improper conduct. Sullivan claimed that her dismissal violated her right to privacy.

Although the court acknowledged that this case posed "very difficult constitutional issues," it ruled in favor of the school board.[76] First, it wrote that the scope and limits of the "newly evolving constitutional right to privacy" are not clear. Second, even if courts rule that the Constitution does protect a teacher's personal life style, this would not necessarily resolve a case such as this. A court would still have to balance the privacy interest of the teacher against the legitimate interest of the board in promoting the education of its students.

On the other hand, a Florida appeals court ruled that a single teacher could not be fired simply because she lived with a man.[77] The case involved a high school Spanish teacher who was dismissed because she lived with a boyfriend for a month and later spent the night with him on occasion. The school board alleged that such cohabitation showed that the teacher lacked good judgment and that she failed "to conform to the moral standards established by the vast majority of teachers" in the county, and that such conduct "reduces her effectiveness." Despite these allegations, there was no evidence that the cohabitation did in fact reduce her effectiveness, and there was substantial testimony that she was an excellent teacher. Moreover, there was no evidence that her relationships were common knowledge until the matter was publicized by the board. Under these circumstances, the court ruled that the private sexual relationships of a teacher are not "good cause" for termination "unless it is shown that such conduct adversely affects the ability to teach."

Can a teacher be fired for using vulgar or "obscene" language off campus?

Probably not, although it may depend on where and with whom the language is used.

In Ohio, a court protected a high school teacher in a case involving two offensive letters.[78] The letters were sent to a former student who had just graduated; they were found by the student's mother, who was shocked by their language and gave them to the police. As a result, local newspapers wrote several stories about the letters. The prosecuting attorney said that they contained hard-core obscenity and that "a person who would write letters of this kind is not fit to be a school teacher." Subsequently the school board terminated the teacher's contract on grounds of immorality, but a state court ruled in his favor.

The letters, wrote the court, contain language that many adults would find "gross, vulgar, and offensive" and that some 18-year-old males would find "unsurprising and fairly routine." Moreover, there was no evidence that these letters adversely affected the schools—except after public disclosure. And this, wrote the judge, "was the result not of any misconduct on [the teacher's] part, but of misconduct on the part of others." The court concluded that a teacher's private conduct is a proper concern of his employer only when it affects him as a teacher; "his private acts are his own business and may not be the basis of discipline" as long as his professional achievement is not affected.

AGE, CITIZENSHIP, AND PHYSICAL FITNESS

Can teachers be fired because of age?

Yes and no. On January 1, 1979, the Age Discrimination in Employment Act Amendment of 1978 became effective. This statute abolished mandatory retirement at age 65 for teachers; however, it still permits forced retirement at 70 years of age.* The cases that follow reflect the arguments and law on both sides of this issue.

The *Palmer* Case[80]

When New York kindergarten teacher Lois Palmer was told that she had to retire because she had reached the age of 70, she sued. She was willing and able to continue teaching and claimed that compulsory retirement at age 70 violated the equal protection clause of the Constitution by unfairly creating "an irrebuttable presumption of incompetency based on age." But a federal appeals court disagreed.

According to the appeals court, states might require mandatory retirement for teachers to open up employment for younger teachers, to make more places available for minorities, to bring new people with fresh ideas in contact with students, or to assure predictability in administering pension plans. "A compul-

---

* The act broadly prohibits age discrimination in employment and the 1978 amendments apply "to individuals who are at least 40 years of age but less than 70."[79]

sory retirement system," wrote the court, "is rationally related to the fulfillment of any or all of these legitimate state objectives."

The court acknowledged the "debilitating effects" that compulsory retirement has on many able people. But these considerations "must be weighed against the social goals that compulsory retirement furthers." The court concluded that the resolution of these competing social goals is best left to the legislative process. Thus courts generally have found a "rational basis" for supporting compulsory retirement at 70.

The *Kuhar* Case[81]

When Raymond Kuhar argued that he should not be required to retire at 65, his Pennsylvania school district defended mandatory retirement with the same arguments used by the court to justify its decision in *Palmer*. But another federal court ruled in Kuhar's favor. Why? Because Kuhar's case was tried after the president signed the Age Discrimination in Employment Act Amendments, which raised the age of mandatory retirement from 65 to 70. The court noted that congressional policy underlying the act indicated that:

1. Mandatory retirement based solely on age is arbitrary, and age alone is a poor indicator of ability.
2. There is evidence that mandatory retirement decreases life expectancy and that the right to work as long as one can is basic to the right to survive.
3. Mandatory retirement will have little effect on recruiting younger people or providing job opportunities for minorities and women, and it is a poor method for eliminating incompetent or unproductive people.
4. Research indicates that older workers are as good or better than younger co-workers "with regard to dependability, judgment, work quality, work volume, human relations, [and] absenteeism."

The school district presented evidence to indicate that Kuhar's job involved considerable pressure, that a younger person should be favored, and that its mandatory retirement policy was therefore reasonable. But the court labeled such arguments "speculative and conjectural." It concluded that the new national policy "to the effect that 70 years is the earliest time for mandatory retirement" of state employees should apply to Kuhar. In short, under current federal law, mandatory retirement for teachers is illegal at 65 but permissible at 70.

Can an educator be demoted because of approaching retirement?

No. In Illinois, two administrators were reclassified as teachers at lower salaries after they notified their superintendent of their plans to retire in two years. The district said the reclassification was based on its "concern about continuity." The educators, however, argued that this violated their rights under the Age

Discrimination and Employment Act (ADEA), and a federal court agreed.[82] To establish a violation of ADEA, a plaintiff must prove "an adverse employment decision was made because of his age." He need not prove that age was the only factor motivating his employer, only that age was a "determining factor." Since the judge found that the district would not have reclassified the educators but for their intent to retire, and that such an action was "inexorably linked with age," the court concluded that the demotion violated the ADEA.

Is a teacher entitled to a hearing before being retired at 70?

No. Connecticut has a Teacher Retirement Act which provides for mandatory retirement at age 70 and allows school boards discretion to employ teachers beyond that age. But when Armand Zimmerman asked the Bradford School Board for a third renewal of his contract beyond the retirement age, the board refused. It provided no hearing or explanation other than his age. Zimmerman claimed that to terminate his contract without a hearing because of his age was a violation of his right to equal protection of the laws, since older teachers are treated differently than younger teachers. In rejecting this claim, the judge wrote that the U.S. Supreme Court has "clearly established that mandatory retirement laws that do not provide for a hearing do not violate an individual's rights to due process or equal protection."[83]

Can teachers be fired because of obesity?

Probably not. Although weight may be a relevant factor in considering whether teachers can perform their jobs effectively, cases indicate that teachers cannot be fired solely because of obesity. Elizabeth Blodgett, a 42-year-old physical education teacher from California, was not rehired because her overweight condition allegedly rendered her "unfit for service." Blodgett was 5 feet 7 inches tall and weighed about 225 pounds. Although she was following a medical diet, her principal recommended she not be rehired because she was unable "to serve as a model of health and vigor" and was "restricted in her ability to perform or teach aspects of the physical education program [such as] modern dance, trampoline, gymnastics, track and field."

Blodgett argued that obesity may justify discharging a teacher only when her weight "has impaired her ability to function effectively." Since the evidence in this case indicated she had been a successful teacher and coach, Blodgett felt that the school acted arbitrarily in refusing to rehire her. The court agreed.[84] As to her inability to serve as a "model of health," the court wrote: "Any requirement that the teachers embody all the qualities which they hope to instill in their students will be utterly impossible of fulfillment." As for the contention that the teacher set a bad example, which her students might imitate, the court observed that "obesity, by its very nature, does not inspire emulation." Furthermore, there was extensive testimony that physical education teachers "need not excel at demonstration in order to perform their instructional duties competently and well." Since there was no evidence that Blodgett's weight had a negative effect on her teaching, the court concluded that her termination was arbitrary and ruled in her favor.

In a related New York case, Nancy Parolisi was denied a teaching license solely because she was overweight. Although she had established an excellent record during three terms of teaching, a Board of Examiner's physical fitness policy excluded candidates who were "extremely overweight or underweight." While Parolisi was admittedly overweight, the court ruled that "obesity, standing alone, is not reasonably related to the ability to teach or to maintain discipline."[85] In a related New York case, the Commissioner of Education ruled that school officials lacked authority to order a teacher to visit a doctor to develop "an appropriate weight loss program" and to visit a dentist "to improve the condition and appearance of his teeth."[86]

Can teachers be denied certification because they are not citizens?

Yes. Although several federal laws prohibit discrimination based on "national origin," the U.S. Supreme Court ruled that a state could prohibit individuals from becoming certified as public school teachers if they were not citizens or applying for citizenship.[87]

The case involved two qualified New York teachers who applied for elementary certification but were turned down because they were not American citizens. In a 5–4 decision, Justice Powell noted that the distinction between alien and citizen is ordinarily irrelevant to private activity. But it is fundamental to certain state functions, especially teaching, which "goes to the heart of representative government." The court emphasized that teachers "play a crucial part in developing students' attitude toward government and understanding of the role of citizens in our society." Moreover, a teacher "serves as a role model for his students, exerting a subtle but important influence over their perceptions and values." According to Justice Powell, all public school teachers, not just those who teach government or civics, may influence student attitudes toward the political process and a citizen's responsibilities. And schools "may regard all teachers as having an obligation to promote civic virtues" in the classes. Therefore, the court ruled that the state's citizenship requirement for teachers was rationally related "to a legitimate state interest."

Can teachers be required to reside in their school districts?

Most courts say yes. In 1972 the Cincinnati School Board established a policy that required any employee hired after that year to either reside in the district or agree to establish residency there within 90 days. Terry Wardwell, who was hired to teach, challenged the policy as discriminating against new teachers since those already hired may live outside the district. But a federal appeals court held that there was a "rational basis" for the residency requirement.[88] Its reasonable purposes included employing teachers who are "deeply committed to an urban educational system," are less likely to engage in illegal strikes and more likely to help obtain passage of school taxes, and are more likely to be involved in school and community activities and to gain an understanding of the racial, social, and economic problems of the children they teach. The judge acknowledged that the rule's "limited applicability" to new teachers was "its most questionable feature." However, since the rule is designed to achieve a reasonable purpose, the court concluded that it is not unconstitutional "because it did not apply to all teachers."

A few courts have ruled against residency requirements. In a Kansas case, for example, a federal court held that a local residency requirement was "too crude" and arbitrary to meet its "avowed purpose." The judge observed that the district offered "no proof that residents . . . are more effective teachers than non-residents."[89] However, as the Arkansas Supreme Court noted in a recent decision upholding residency requirements: "School boards are increasingly requiring employees to maintain residence within the school district and challenges have been rejected by a majority of federal and state courts."[90]

Can teachers be denied jobs because they are handicapped?

No, not merely because of their handicap. In 1973 Congress passed Section 504 of the Rehabilitation Act which stated that "no otherwise qualified individual . . . shall, solely by reason of his handicap, be excluded from participation . . . or be subjected to discrimination under any program" receiving federal funds.[91]

In many school situations, the question arises concerning what the statute means by an "otherwise qualified individual." In one case, a federal court explained that the term does not mean that a handicapped individual must be hired despite his handicap. Rather it prohibits the nonhiring of a handicapped individual when the disability does not prevent that individual from performing the job.[92] (For related material on handicapped students, see Chapter 15.)

Can an educator be barred from teaching because of AIDS?

Probably not. After Vincent Chalk was diagnosed as having AIDS, the Orange County School Department transferred him to a nonteaching job. On the basis of extensive medical evidence, Chalk claimed that, as a teacher, he posed no health risk to students or other school staff. In a 1988 decision, a federal appeals court agreed and ruled that Chalk's transfer violated his rights under Section 504 of the Rehabilitation Act that prohibits discrimination against otherwise qualified handicapped people.[93]

The court acknowledged that "a person who poses a significant risk of communicating an infectious disease to others in the workplace will not be otherwise qualified." However, the judge emphasized that "there is *no* evidence" of "any appreciable risk of transmitting the AIDS virus under the circumstances likely to occur in the ordinary school setting." The court recognized that, despite this medical opinion, there is widespread confusion about AIDS, and some people want to exclude anyone with the virus from the schools. However, the judge pointed out that the purpose of Section 504 was "to insure that handicapped individuals are not denied jobs or other benefits because of the prejudiced attitudes or ignorance of others." Therefore, since all medical evidence indicated that Chalk's illness was not communicable in the normal classroom, it ruled that he could not be barred from teaching because he had AIDS.

SUMMARY

An increasing number of courts now hold that teachers cannot be dismissed for personal conduct simply because it is contrary to the mores of a community. Thus the fact that a teacher has done something most people regard as immoral (e.g., smoking marijuana, committing adultery, engaging in homosexual activity, or using vulgar language) is not by itself sufficient grounds for dismissal. To dismiss such a teacher there must be substantial evidence that the immorality is likely to have a negative effect on his or her teaching. As long as a teacher's competence is unaffected, most courts hold that private behavior is a teacher's own business. In addition, some judges are applying the new constitutional "right to privacy" to protect teachers' personal behavior.

On the other hand, courts usually uphold the dismissal of teachers whose immoral conduct becomes known through their own fault and, as a result, has a negative impact on their teaching effectiveness. They may be *suspended* because of a criminal indictment if the alleged crime relates to their job; but they may not be *dismissed* simply because of a serious criminal charge if they are not guilty. In cases of notoriously illegal or immoral behavior, some courts allow teachers to be fired even without evidence that the conduct impaired their teaching. For example, in cases involving repeated convictions for drunk driving, armed assault, shoplifting, or illegal drug use, some judges say that the negative impact of such behavior is obvious. Whether being known as a homosexual, being an unwed mother, or committing a crime could result in dismissal probably would depend on the circumstances. Courts might consider the size, the sophistication, and the values of the community; the notoriety of the activity; the reaction of the students and parents; when the conduct took place; whether it occurred in the community where the teacher is employed; and its impact on other teachers.

In cases of immoral conduct with students, courts tend to be strict. Evidence of a single sexual relationship between a teacher and a student would probably be enough to sustain a teacher's dismissal even if the relationship occurred years before and even if no other students, teachers, or parents knew about it. Similarly, a teacher who made sexual advances toward students, told them to cheat, showed them pornographic films, smoked marijuana, drank excessively, or used obscene language with them would probably receive no protection from the courts. Teachers also could be disciplined for allowing students to drink or sexually harass others.

In addition to immoral behavior, schools also consider other aspects of teachers' personal lives, such as age, weight, residency, and citizenship, when deciding whether to employ or rehire them. Under current federal law, it is illegal to discriminate against a teacher solely because of a handicap or to compel a teacher to retire before the age of 70. In addition, cases indicate that a teacher cannot be fired merely because of obesity. On the other hand, a state may refuse to hire teachers if they are not U.S. citizens or applying for citizenship or refuse to live in the school district.

As the cases in this chapter have indicated, the law concerning the removal of teachers for immoral or illegal conduct is not always precise. There are no recent Supreme Court opinions on the topic, and decisions in different states sometimes appear inconsistent. Much depends on the circumstances of the case. Nevertheless, most courts recognize that teachers should not be penalized for their private behavior unless it has a clear impact on their effectiveness as educators.

NOTES

1. *Morrison* v. *State Board of Education*, 461 P.2d 375 (Cal. 1969).
2. *Burton* v. *Cascade School District Union High School No. 5*, 353 F.Supp. 254 (D. Ore. 1973).
3. *Sarac* v. *State Board of Education*, 57 Cal. Rptr. 69 (1967).
4. *Id.*
5. *Stephens* v. *Board of Education, School District No. 5*, 429 N.W.2d 722 (Neb. 1988).
6. *Ross* v. *Springfield School District No. 19*, 691 P.2d 509 (Ore. App. 1984).
7. *Gaylord* v. *Tacoma School District No. 10*, 559 P.2d 1340 (Wash. 1977).
8. *Rowland* v. *Mad River Local School District, Montgomery County, Ohio*, 730 F.2d 444 (6th Cir. 1984).
9. *National Gay Task Force* v. *Board of Education of Oklahoma City*, 729 F.2d 1270 (10th Cir. 1984).
10. *Brown* v. *Bathke*, 416 F.Supp. 1194 (D. Neb. 1976), *rev'd*, 566 F.2d 588 (8th Cir. 1977).
11. *Andrews* v. *Drew Municipal Separate School District*, 507 F.2d 611 (5th Cir. 1975).
12. *Eckmann* v. *Board of Education of Hawthorn School District*, 636 F.Supp. 1214 (N.D.Ill. 1986).
13. *Board of Trustees of Compton Junior College District* v. *Stubblefield*, 94 Cal. Rptr. 318 (1971).
14. *Yang* v. *Special Charter School District No. 150, Peoria County*, 296 N.E.2d 74 (Ill. 1973).
15. *Denton* v. *South Kitsap School District No. 402*, 516 P.2d 1080 (Wash. 1973).
16. *Clark* v. *Ann Arbor School District*, 344 N.W.2d 48 (Mich. App. 1983).
17. *Weaver* v. *Board of Education of Pine Plains Central School District*, 514 N.Y.S.2d 473 (1987).
18. *Fisher* v. *Independent School District No. 622*, 357 N.W.2d 152 (Minn. App. 1984).
19. *Penn-Delco School District* v. *Urso*, 382 A.2d 162 (Pa. 1978).
20. *Kilpatrick* v. *Wright*, 437 F.Supp. 397 (M.D. Ala. 1977).
21. *Weissman* v. *Board of Education of Jefferson County School District No. R-1*, 547 P.2d 1267 (Colo. 1976).

22. *Katz* v. *Ambach*, 472 N.Y.S.2d 492 (App. Div. 1984).

23. *Board of Education of Tonica Community High School District No. 360* v. *Sickley*, 479 N.E.2d 1142 (Ill. App. 1985).

24. *Pyle* v. *Washington County School Board*, 238 So.2d 121 (Fla. 1970).

25. *State* v. *Board of School Directors of Milwaukee*, 111 N.W.2d 198 (Wis. 1961).

26. *Shurgin* v. *Ambach*, 442 N.Y.S.2d 212 (App. Div. 1981).

27. *United States* v. *Coffeeville Consolidated School District*, 365 F.Supp. 990 (N.D. Miss. 1973).

28. *Ware* v. *Morgan County School District*, 748 P.2d 1295 (Colo. 1988).

29. *Bovino* v. *Board of School Directors of the Indiana Area School District*, 377 A.2d 1284 (Penn. 1977).

30. *Clarke* v. *Board of Education of the School District of Omaha*, 338 N.W.2d 272 (Neb. 1983).

31. *Fiscus* v. *Central School District of Greene County*, 509 N.E.2d 1137 (Ind. App. 1987).

32. *Stoddard* v. *School District No. 1, Lincoln County, Wyoming*, 590 F.2d 829 (10th Cir. 1979).

33. *Erb* v. *Iowa State Board of Instruction*, 216 N.W.2d 339 (Iowa 1974).

34. *Pettit* v. *State Board of Education*, 513 P.2d 889 (Cal. 1973).

35. *Florian* v. *Highland Local School District Board of Education*, 570 F.Supp. 1358 (N.D. Ohio 1983).

36. *Ross* v. *Robb*, 662 S.W.2d 257 (Mo. 1983).

37. *In re Grossman*, 316 A.2d 39 (N.J. 1974).

38. *Everett Area School District* v. *Ault* 548 A.2d 1341 (Pa. Cmwlth. 1988).

39. *Downie* v. *Independent School District No. 141*, 367 N.W.2d 913 (Minn. App. 1985).

40. *Watson* v. *State Board of Education*, 99 Cal. Rptr. 468 (Cal. App. 1971).

41. *Tracy* v. *School District No. 22, Sheridan County, Wyoming*, 243 P.2d 932 (Wyo. 1952).

42. *Williams* v. *School District No. 40 of Gila County*, 417 P.2d 376 (Ariz. 1966).

43. *Lindgren* v. *Board of Trustees, High School District No. 1*, 558 P.2d 468 (Mont. 1976).

44. *Coupeville School District No. 204* v. *Vivian*, 677 P.2d 192 (Wash. App. 1984).

45. *Board of Education of Hopkins County* v. *Wood*, 717 S.W.2d 837 (Ky. 1986).

46. *Board of Education of Laurel County* v. *McCollum*, 721 S.W.2d 703 (Ky. 1986).

47. *Fontana Unified School District* v. *Burman*, 246 Cal. Rptr. 865 (Cal. App. 1988).

48. *Bassett Unified School District* v. *Commission on Professional Responsibility*, 247 Cal. Rptr. 865 (Cal. App. 1988).

49. *Blaine* v. *Moffat County School District*, 748 P.2d 1280 (Colo. 1988).

50. *Id.* at 1294.

51. *Ellis* v. *Ambach*, 508 N.Y.S.2d 624 (1986).

52. *Skripchuk* v. *Austin*, 379 A.2d 1142 (Del. 1977).

53. *Kiner* v. *State Board of Education*, 344 So.2d 657 (Fla. 1977).

54. *Board of Trustees of Santa Maria Joint Union High School District* v. *Judge*, 123 Cal. Rptr. 830 (1975).

55. *Hoagland* v. *Mount Vernon School District No. 320*, 623 P.2d 1156 (Wash. 1981).

56. *Kenai Peninsula Borough Board of Education* v. *Brown*, 691 P.2d 1034 (Alaska 1984).

57. *Matter of Shelton*, 408 N.W.2d 594 (Minn. App. 1987).

58. *Golden* v. *Board of Education of the County of Harrison*, 285 S.E.2d 665 (W.Va. 1982).
59. *Id.* at 670.
60. *Lesley* v. *Oxford Area School District*, 420 A.2d 764 (Pa. 1980).
61. *Board of Education of Long Beach Unified School District* v. *Jack M.*, 139 Cal. Rptr. 700 (1977).
62. *Garcia* v. *State Board of Education*, 694 P.2d 1371 (N.M. App. 1984).
63. The court also noted that the state legislature intended "to encourage the rehabilitation of criminal offenders by removing barriers to their employment." *Id.*
64. *Dupree* v. *School Committee of Boston*, 446 N.E.2d 1099 (Mass. App. 1983).
65. *Perryman* v. *School Committee of Boston*, 458 N.E.2d 748 (Mass. App. 1983).
66. *Baker* v. *School Board of Marion County*, 450 So.2d 1194 (Fla. App. 5 Dist. 1984).
67. *Kimble* v. *Worth County R-111 Board of Education*, 669 S.W.2d 949 (Mo. App. 1984).
68. *Bogart* v. *Unified School District No. 298 of Lincoln County, Kansas*, 432 F.Supp. 895 (D. Kan. 1977).
69. *Comings* v. *State Board of Education*, 100 Cal. Rptr. 73 (1972).
70. *Board of Trustees of Santa Maria Joint Union High School District* v. *Judge*, 123 Cal. Rptr. 830 (1975).
71. *Governing Board* v. *Brennan*, 95 Cal. Rptr. 712 (Cal. App. 1971).
72. *Jefferson Union High School District* v. *Jones*, 100 Cal. Rptr. 73 (1972). Jones was decided together with *Comings, supra.*
73. *Littlejohn* v. *Rose*, 768 F.2d 765 (6th Cir. 1985).
74. *Ponton* v. *Newport News School Board*, 632 F.Supp. 1056 (E.D. Va. 1986).
75. *Dike* v. *School Board of Orange County, Florida*, 650 F.2d 783 (5th Cir. 1981).
76. *Sullivan* v. *Meade Independent School District, No. 101*, 530 F.2d 799 (8th Cir. 1976).
77. *Sherburne* v. *School Board of Suwannee County*, 455 So.2d 1057 (Fla. App. 1984).
78. *Jarvella* v. *Willoughby-East Lake City School District*, 233 N.E.2d 143 (Ohio 1967).
79. 29 U.S.C.A. §631(a); §621 (1985). The law also provides that mandatory retirement below the age of 70 shall not be unlawful "where age is a bona fide occupational qualification reasonably necessary to the normal occupation." 29 U.S.C.A §623(f)(1)(1985).
80. *Palmer* v. *Ticcione*, 576 F.2d 459 (2d. Cir. 1978).
81. *Kuhar* v. *Greensburg-Salem School District*, 466 F.Supp. 806 (W.D. Pa. 1979).
82. *Equal Employment Opportunity Commission* v. *Community Unified School District No. 9*, 642 F.Supp. 902 (S.D. Ill. 1986).
83. *Zimmerman* v. *Board of Education of Town of Bradford*, 597 F.Supp. 72 (D. Conn. 1984).
84. *Blodgett* v. *Board of Trustees, Tamalpais Union High School District*, 97 Cal. Rptr. 406 (1971).
85. *Parolisi* v. *Board of Examiners of City of New York*, 285 N.Y.S.2d 936 (1967).
86. *Mermer* v. *Constantine*, 520 N.Y.S.2d 264 (1987).
87. *Ambach* v. *Norwick*, 441 U.S. 68 (1979).
88. *Wardwell* v. *Board of Education of City School District of Cincinnati*, 529 F.2d 625 (6th Cir. 1976).
89. *Hanson* v. *Unified School District No. 500, Wyandotte County*, 364 F.Supp. 330 (D. Kan.· 1973).

90. *McClelland* v. *Paris Public Schools*, 742 S.W.2d 907 (Ark. 1988). As the court noted, those challenging these requirements usually have the difficult burden of proving that they are "not rationally related to any legitimate objective." For more on this issue and a critique of the criteria used by courts in judging these cases, see Bruce Beezer, *School Employees and Continuous Residency Policies: Is Competence Related to Immobility*, 41 ED. LAW REP. 21 (1987).
91. 29 U.S.C.A §794 (1989).
92. *Carmi* v. *Metropolitan St. Louis Sewer District*, 471 F.Supp. 119 (E.D. Mo. 1979).
93. *Chalk* v. *United States District Court*, 840 F.2d 701 (9th Cir. 1988).

CHAPTER 13

Am I Protected against Racial Discrimination?

OVERVIEW

Many scholarly studies have established that American culture, throughout its history, has been fraught with racism. There have been regional differences in the openness and intensity of racial discrimination, but rare indeed is the community that can claim to have been completely free from it. Even at the beginning of the twentieth century, blacks were "considered by many whites, North and South, to be depraved, comic, childlike, or debased persons."[1]

Schools, like other institutions in American culture, have reflected this widespread prejudice against blacks, Native Americans, Orientals, and Latins. Many social forces have interacted to influence the schools, including the courts and the law. While no claim is made here that law is the most important force influencing attitudes toward different racial groups, it is recognized as one important influence on people in general and public schools in particular.

This chapter examines the impact of the courts and the law on racial discrimination against students and school personnel in the light of the Supreme Court ruling that segregation in schools is unconstitutional.

SCHOOL DESEGREGATION

Why is racial segregation in schools unconstitutional?

The equal protection clause of the Fourteenth Amendment has been the major legal vehicle used to challenge various aspects of racial discrimination in public life. Section I specifies that "no State shall . . . deny to any person within its jurisdiction the equal protection of the laws." Early in the history of the amendment, it was determined that since public schools are state institutions, actions by public school officials and employees are *state* actions. However, the famous case of *Plessy* v. *Ferguson*[2] established the principle that separate but equal facilities satisfy the equal protection clause of the amendment. Though *Plessy* involved public transportation facilities, the Supreme Court used it as precedent in a public school conflict in 1927.[3] A successful challenge to the "separate but equal" doctrine did not arise until 1954, in the landmark case of *Brown* v. *Board of Education*. This is not to say that segregated education went unchallenged until the *Brown* case. Between *Plessy* in 1896 and *Brown* in 1954, many lawsuits challenged the separate but equal doctrine, particularly in graduate and professional schools. Several such suits succeeded because it was not possible for the southern states engaged in segregated schooling to provide law schools or medical schools of equal quality in separate facilities for blacks and whites. These suits ultimately prepared the way for Linda Brown's successful legal action.

The *Brown* Case[4]

Linda Brown, an elementary school student in Topeka, Kansas, filed suit challenging a Kansas law that sanctioned the racially separate schools she was attending. The district court found "that segregation in public education has a detrimental effect upon Negro children" but upheld the arrangement since schools for white children and black children "were substantially equal with respect to buildings, transportation, curricula, and educational qualifications of teachers." When Brown appealed to the Supreme Court, school officials argued that the Fourteenth Amendment was never meant to apply to the schools and that in any event, the *Plessy* principle of "separate but equal" should be followed and the Kansas law upheld.

Was the Fourteenth Amendment meant to apply to public schools? Chief Justice Earl Warren, writing for a unanimous Court, answered in the affirmative. He wrote that the amendment must be considered in the light of current facts and conditions and not those of 1868 when the amendment was adopted. Only by considering the importance of public schools in the middle of the twentieth century could it be determined whether segregated schooling deprives students of equal protection of the law. Other judges and scholars have voiced the same conviction by asserting that the Constitution and its amendments stay alive by constant application to new conditions, lest they become mere "parchment under glass."

Courts do not follow precedents blindly, however. Changing conditions, as well as new knowledge generated by the sciences, may lead to the overruling of a precedent. This is precisely what happened in the *Brown* case.

The Court recognized that education has become "perhaps the most important function of state and local governments. . . . It is the very foundation of good citizenship. Today it is a principal instrument in awakening the child to cultural values, in preparing him for later professional training, and in helping him to adjust normally to his environment. In these days, it is doubtful that any child may reasonably be expected to succeed in life if he is denied the opportunity of an education. Such an opportunity, where the state has undertaken to provide it, is a right which must be available to all on equal terms."

The Court then considered evidence offered by social scientists concerning the impact of segregation on school children and concluded that "segregation . . . has a detrimental effect upon the colored children. The impact is greater when it has the sanction of the law; for the policy of separating the races is usually interpreted as denoting the inferiority of the Negro group. A sense of inferiority affects the motivation of the child to learn. Segregation with the sanction of law, therefore, has a tendency to retard the educational and mental development of Negro children and to deprive them of some of the benefits they would receive in a racially integrated school system." Thus, in rejecting *Plessy* v. *Ferguson* the Court concluded that "in the field of public education the doctrine of 'separate but equal' has no place. Separate educational facilities are inherently unequal."

How soon must schools desegregate?

Each community has its unique history of segregation, its unique traffic and residential pattern, and its own educational system, so the Court considered it unwise to pronounce one formula or timetable for desegregation applicable throughout the country. Instead, after hearing arguments on behalf of various possible remedies, the Court ordered that schools must desegregate "with all deliberate speed." Local school districts were to create desegregation plans, under the supervision of federal district courts, which are the courts closest to each locality. Thus, school authorities were given the primary responsibility to solve local educational problems, but local courts were to decide whether the school officials acted in "good faith implementation of the governing constitutional principles."[5] This decision is commonly known as *Brown II*.

Are parents free to choose which schools their children will attend?

No, they are not, if their choices will perpetuate segregated schooling. This question arose after *Brown,* when various arrangements were created to delay and even avoid the mandate of the Court. Some localities even closed their public schools and then used public funds to support segregated private schools. Such subterfuge was ruled unconstitutional.[6]

The "freedom-of-choice" plan appealed to many parents and politicians. The plan gave individual families the choice of where to send their children to school, and it was quickly adopted in many communities and legislatures. One such plan was challenged in New Kent County, Virginia, where segregated schools existed under a law enacted in 1902. In the three years of operation of the "freedom-of-choice" plan, not a single white child chose to attend what had historically been the black school, and 85 percent of the black children continued to attend the all-black school. The dual system of schooling had not been eliminated 11 years after *Brown I* and 10 years after *Brown II*.

The Supreme Court struck down the "freedom-of-choice" plan in this community as ineffective. In the words of the Court: "'Freedom-of-Choice' is not a Sacred Talisman; it is only a means to a constitutionally required end—the abolition of the system of segregation and its effects. If the means prove effective, it is acceptable, but if it fails to undo segregation, other means must be used to achieve this end. The school officials have the continuing duty to take whatever action may be necessary to create a 'unitary, nonracial system.'" A lower court gave a simple, pragmatic test for similar cases: "The only school desegregation plan that meets constitutional standards is one that works."[7]

Must all one-race schools be eliminated?

Not necessarily. Geographic factors, population concentrations, location of schools, traffic patterns, and good-faith attempts to create a unitary school system must all be taken into consideration. The Supreme Court addressed this question in the *Swann* case.[8] The North Carolina schools in this 1965 case had adopted a desegregation plan that was being challenged during the 1968–1969 school year as inadequate. Chief Justice Burger, in writing for a unanimous Court, recognized that in large cities minority groups are often concentrated in one part of the city. In some situations, certain schools remain all or largely of one race until new schools can be built or the neighborhood changes. Thus the mere existence of such schools is not in itself proof of unconstitutional segregation. Nevertheless, the courts will carefully scrutinize such arrangements, and the presumption is against such schools. District officials have the burden of showing that single-race schools are genuinely nondiscriminatory.

Can racial quotas be used in attempts to desegregate schools?

It depends on how such quotas are used. The Supreme Court ruled in *Swann* that "the constitutional command to desegregate schools does not mean that every school in every community must always reflect the racial composition of the school system as a whole." Thus, if a mathematical quota were used that required a particular percentage of racial mixing, the Court would disapprove. On the other hand, it is legitimate to use mathematical ratios as starting points or as general goals in efforts to achieve racial balance in a previously segregated school system.

Are there limits to using buses for desegregation?

Yes, in a general sense. Courts have recognized that "bus transportation has been an integral part of the public school system for years, and was perhaps the single most important factor in the transition from the one-room schoolhouse to the consolidated school." During the year that the *Swann* case went to court, 18 million public school children, or about 39 percent of the nation's enrollment, were bused to school. The Supreme Court has accepted bus transportation as an important tool of desegregation. Its use may be limited "when the time or distance of travel is so great as to either risk the health of the children or significantly impinge on the educational process." Furthermore, "it hardly needs stating that the limits on time of travel will vary with many factors, but probably with none more than the age of the students."

Can an ethnic group be exempt from desegregation?

No. This was illustrated in San Francisco when Chinese parents brought suit to exclude their children from a citywide desegregation plan. The children attended neighborhood elementary schools that enrolled mostly Chinese-American students. Parents valued this enrollment pattern, for it helped them maintain and perpetuate their subculture and the Chinese language. They expressed fear that a dispersal of Chinese-American students, as part of an overall plan to achieve racial balance, would destroy their subculture and make it more difficult to teach their children the Chinese language. They also argued that San Francisco never had a dual school system so it need not create a unitary one. Moreover, claimed the parents, San Francisco had no rules or regulations segregating the races; district officials merely drew attendance lines to determine who goes to which school.

The district court ruled that if school officials draw attendance lines knowing that the lines maintain or heighten racial imbalance, their actions constitute officially imposed segregation and are therefore unconstitutional. The fact that San Francisco never had an official dual system is irrelevant. It developed such a system partly by the location of different racial groups and partly by the actions of school officials in arranging and rearranging attendance lines.

While sympathetic to the concern of the parents, the court ruled that the Chinese-American students must participate in the overall desegregation of the schools. Nevertheless, the court also supported efforts to develop bilingual classes for Chinese-speaking children, as well as courses that taught the "cultural background and heritages of various racial and ethnic groups."[9]

Is unintentional segregation against the law?

No. Since the Fourteenth Amendment forbids the state from denying anyone the equal protection of the law, some state action or actions by state officials must be identified as discriminatory action. In the early years of school desegregation, attention focused on southern states because they typically had laws that explicitly mandated or permitted segregated schooling. Such laws led courts to distinguish de jure and de facto segregation. *De jure* meant "by law"; *de facto* meant "as a matter of fact." The former was a violation of the Constitution; the latter was not.

As more and more cases were brought to court, in northern as well as southern communities, it became clear that segregation often occurs without explicit laws yet with the help of state, municipal, and school officials. Are such actions de jure? Yes, said the courts, for any action by governmental officials in the course of their duties is action "under color of the law." Examples of such official actions are the drawing of school district lines and attendance zones, zoning ordinances, creating housing and other residential restrictions, governmental support or insurance of home loans, and governmental enforcement of restrictive covenants in deeds to private property. All these practices have been used to create residential segregation and hence segregated schools. When the Supreme Court established these legal principles, it became clear that de jure segregation has occurred in virtually every city in the nation. School boards often contributed to such segregation without malice or bad faith but simply by being unaware of the consequences of their actions. Nonetheless, *their actions were intentional* in establishing district lines, attendance zones, location of new schools, hiring policies, and so forth.

This was illustrated in 1984 in San Jose, California, when a circuit court held that considering the cumulative impact of all the evidence, there was segregative intent behind the policies and actions of the school board. Among other actions, the board built new schools, rebuilt schools, used portable buildings, and closed schools in a manner that intensified racial imbalance. While the board's public pronouncements repeatedly declared its intentions to create a better racial balance, its actions, including its refusal to use busing to achieve integration while it bused one-third of its students for other purposes, maintained and even intensified segregation.[10]

In 1979 the Supreme Court ruled once again, in cases involving Columbus and Dayton, Ohio, that intentional acts by school or other governmental officials were required for de jure segregation to be established.[11] If such acts occurred, the school district had the affirmative duty to eliminate all vestiges of segregation, even if the acts occurred years ago. In Dayton, for example, the segregative acts occurred 20 years previously, but the city never completely overcame the effects of past segregation; therefore, said the Court, the duty to do so was never completely satisfied.

A different type of case arose in 1985 in Yonkers, New York, where concentrated subsidized housing together with a neighborhood school policy intensified segregated schooling. The court held this development to be unconstitutional. Although city officials and school board members were "separate actors" under state law, the way the mayor appointed members of the board made this legal separation "an artificial and constitutionally insignificant one." The city and the board "created a consistency between housing and school policy" that clearly preserved existing patterns of racial segregation and thus engaged in unconstitutional actions."[12]

If part of a school district is segregated, must the entire district undergo desegregation?

That depends on what portion of the school district is unconstitutionally segregated. The Court ruled in a case involving Denver, Colorado, that if a substantial portion of the district is unlawfully segregated, the entire district must be involved in the remedy. How much is a "substantial portion"? That depends on the circumstances; the district court closest to the facts is in the best position to determine whether the segregation is substantial enough to have an impact on the student composition in the entire district.[13]

What if a desegregated district becomes resegregated?

A community may desegregate its schools, yet, as a result of population shifts and without any official action, resegregation may occur. Is there a duty to desegregate all over again? No, ruled the Supreme Court in a case from Pasadena, California.[14] Once the school district creates a "racially neutral system of student assignment" it does not have to readjust attendance zones when population shifts occur because no official action caused the new imbalance. The new segregation is de facto and thus not unconstitutional.

After achieving unitary status, may a school board modify its busing plan?

Yes it may, ruled a federal appeals court in 1986 in a case involving the school system of Norfolk, Virginia.[15] Norfolk, pursuant to a court-approved desegregation plan that involved busing, achieved a unitary status and in 1975 received a court order recognizing this status. Thereafter the school system stopped its busing, changed to a neighborhood plan, and shifted its sixth graders to middle schools where busing continued. When plaintiffs challenged the end of elementary school busing, the courts ruled that in a unitary system busing is a policy decision within the discretion of the school board as long as the board's intent in creating the policy was not racial discrimination.

In a similar case, however, involving the schools of Oklahoma City, a same level court ruled otherwise.[16] It held that a past finding of unitariness, by itself, does not prevent a renewal of litigation. Furthermore, said the court, in such cases the plaintiff need not prove the changes were motivated by a discriminatory intent. Perhaps the conflicting holdings of these cases will be addressed by the Supreme Court in the future.

To further illustrate the complexity of school desegregation, we point to Topeka, Kansas, once again. There, on October 6, 1986, hearings opened in a case that is now called *Brown III*.[17] Plaintiffs claimed that Topeka never fully complied with the order to establish a unitary, integrated school system. The defendant school district responded that it has complied with all court orders and legal requirements to desegregate and that the plaintiffs must prove that intentional state action caused the current segregation. It is likely that *Brown III* will also reach the Supreme Court to decide the extent to which a school district must continue its efforts to develop and maintain unitary schools or whether once it achieves unitary status it can return to a neighborhood school policy that may well lead to resegregation.

Can desegregation plans cross district lines to include suburbs with the city in the same plan?

Yes and no. This question has arisen in metropolitan areas where the core city, made up predominantly of racial minorities, is surrounded by suburbs that are predominantly white. In Detroit, for example, the city population (64 percent black, 36 percent white) made it impossible to achieve substantial desegregation within the city. Yet people living in Detroit's suburbs (81 percent white, 19 percent black) objected to a metropolitan area desegregation plan that would have included busing students across district lines.

Proponents of the "metropolitan plan" (also known as "cross-district plan") argued that since education is a state function and the state only delegates its responsibility to local districts, Michigan had the obligation to desegregate Detroit's schools. Since many other governmental functions are performed on a regional basis rather than a citywide basis, there is no compelling reason why school desegregation should not be regionalized. District and appeals courts agreed, but the Supreme Court rejected this line of argument. In a close decision (5–4), the Court ruled that desegregation must take place within the city of Detroit because that is where the constitutional violation occurred: "the scope of the remedy is determined by the nature and extent of the constitutional violation."[18]

Chief Justice Burger noted, however, that "an interdistrict remedy might be in order where the racially discriminatory acts of one or more districts caused racial segregation in an adjacent district, or where district lines have been deliberately drawn on the basis of race." A case in Wilmington, Delaware, involved just such facts. When the evidence showed cross-district collaboration through official policies that created segregated schooling, and when it was clear that an interdistrict remedy was feasible, the court ordered such a remedy. The Supreme Court affirmed this decision.[19]

Three school districts were involved in a legal action that sought interdistrict remedy in the Little Rock, Arkansas, area in 1984. The district court found that the three school districts engaged in racially discriminatory acts resulting in substantial interdistrict segregation. When a comprehensive examination of the entire situation indicated that these violations could be corrected only by a substantial interdistrict remedy, the court ordered a consolidated plan encompassing the three districts. The plan included a racial composition standard for each school (± 25% of the racial makeup of the student population), a uniform grade structure (K-6, 7-9, 10-12) "so as to enhance the ability of students to move about the district more freely," a careful, court-supervised plan for busing, and a plan for magnet schools.

The court, realizing the need for public support to achieve desegregation, required the school to hold "no less than three public meetings within their district for the purpose of explaining the . . . consolidation plan to their patrons and allowing constructive criticism." In sum, since the three districts collaborated to bring about unconstitutional segregation, they have an "affirmative obligation to eliminate segregation 'root and branch.'"[20]

In Benton Harbor, Michigan, not only did the court order an interdistrict remedy for unconstitutional segregative acts engaged in by the four school districts involved, but it also held the State of Michigan responsible for purposely violating both the U.S. and Michigan constitutions. As part of the remedy, the state was ordered to pay a substantial portion of the transportation costs entailed in the interdistrict remedy.[21]

By contrast, in a Cincinnati, Ohio, area school desegregation case, the court dismissed claims for an interdistrict remedy because there was not substantial evidence presented, only "unsubstantiated speculation" of interdistrict racial segregation.[22]

Do state constitutions and laws relate to desegregation?

Yes. Since the Constitution is the basic law of the land, no federal law, state constitution, or state law may contradict it. State constitutions, laws, and policies may go further than the federal Constitution, as long as they are not inconsistent with it. For example, several states have erased the de jure–de facto distinction by state law or policies of state boards of education, and made them both illegal. Examples of such states are Connecticut, Illinois, New Jersey, and New York. Similarly, California eliminated the distinction by its state constitution.[23]

Once a state chooses to do more to desegregate its schools than the Fourteenth Amendment requires, may it recede on its commitment?

Yes, it may, ruled the Supreme Court in 1982 in a case involving the Los Angeles Unified School District. In a previous ruling, the California Supreme Court held that the state constitution forbade both de facto and de jure segregation. Thereafter, in 1979, the voters of California ratified an amendment (Proposition I) to their constitution which in effect repealed state antidiscrimination laws. The U.S. Supreme Court held that a simple repeal does not constitute an invalid racial discrimination and that the people of a state may experiment with different laws in addressing problems of a heterogenous population. Thus, it was proper for Californians to decide that the Fourteenth Amendment standards were more appropriate than standards repealed by Proposition I. In effect, the state went back to the requirement that intent to segregate must be proven to uphold a claim of unconstitutional action.[24]

Very different results were reached in the State of Washington involving the so-called Seattle Plan for desegregation. This statewide initiative allowed students to go to schools outside their neighborhoods for various purposes, such as special education, to avoid overcrowding, because of the lack of certain physical facilities, but *not* for purposes of achieving racial integration. In other words, there was to be extensive use of mandatory busing, but busing was permitted only for nonracial reasons and forbidden for racial desegregation. The U.S.

Supreme Court struck down this initiative; it is clearly quite different from the simple repeal of a law involved in the Los Angeles case discussed previously.[25]

Can private schools exclude black students?

No. Many private schools genuinely welcome students from all racial, ethnic, and religious groups, but some schools accept applications only from Caucasians or certain religious denominations. The First Amendment of the Constitution protects freedom of religion and thus the creation and maintenance of separate, private religious schools. No such protection is extended to racial prejudice, however. When black parents brought suit against a private school that denied admission to their children, the Supreme Court ruled in favor of the parents.[26]

Since no state action is involved when a private school denies admission, why did the Court rule for the parents? A federal law protects the equal right to enter into contracts.[27] The Court ruled that this law prohibits private, commercially operated schools from denying admission to an applicant simply on the basis of race. Even private schools must submit to reasonable government regulation. The only exception is for a religious school where the religion itself forbids racially integrated schooling. However, as we explain below, such schools run the risk of losing their tax exemption.

In a highly controversial case the Court reexamined this post–Civil War statute and significantly restricted its coverage. The Court ruled in 1989 that this federal law does prohibit "racial discrimination in the making and enforcement of private contracts," but it does not address racial discrimination or harassment on the job. The latter actions must be litigated under Title VII of the Civil Rights Act of 1964.[28] Prior to the 1989 decision it was generally understood that the earlier post–Civil War statute encompassed racial discrimination in the making and enforcement of contracts as well as discrimination or harassment on the job or during the life of the contract. Since the earlier law provided broader coverage, a longer statute of limitations, and money damages, as well as other advantages, the recent decision of the Court is generally viewed by civil rights advocates as restrictive and conservative.

Sectarian private schools may also lose their tax exempt status if they engage in racial discrimination. The Supreme Court upheld the authority of the Internal Revenue Service (IRS) to deny tax-exempt status to Bob Jones University. The facts showed that, while Bob Jones University allowed blacks to enroll as students, it denied admission to those who engaged in and/or advocated interracial dating or marriage.

The university argued that when the IRS denied its tax exemption, it violated the university's rights to free exercise of religion. The IRS, on the other hand, maintained that the tax code that grants exemptions applies only to institutions that are "charitable," are consistent with public interest, and are not at odds with the common conscience of the community. Since racial discrimination in education is contrary to public policy, institutions which practice it cannot be "charitable" within the intent of Congress as embodied in the relevant sections of the Internal Revenue Code.[29] The Supreme Court upheld the argument of the IRS and held that discrimination on the basis of racial association is a form of racial discrimination.[30] In all likelihood, the same principles would apply to subcollegiate schools that engage in race discrimination.

RACIAL DISCRIMINATION AGAINST TEACHERS AND STAFF

Does the *Brown* case apply to teachers and staff?

Yes. While *Brown I* dealt with the general constitutional principles related to desegregation, the Court addressed the question of judicial remedy a year later in *Brown II*. Considering the appropriate remedies, the Court was mindful that the wide variety of local conditions would make a single monolithic order inappropriate. Therefore it generated several guiding principles. First, it required that school districts "make a prompt and reasonable start toward full compliance" with the ruling in *Brown I* and proceed "with all deliberate speed." Second, it gave supervisory responsibility to the district courts to oversee school officials as they proceeded with good-faith implementation to desegregate the schools. The courts were to be "guided by equitable principles," which has traditionally meant "a practical flexibility in shaping remedies and by a facility for adjusting and reconciling public and private needs." Third, courts may consider "the physical condition of the school plant, the school transportation system, personnel," and other factors in supervising good-faith compliance.[31] Courts have relied heavily on *Brown II* in the breadth of their discretionary powers and in considering the role of teachers, administrators, and staff in efforts to desegregate schools.

Can schools still delay desegregation?

No. Massive resistance met the Supreme Court's ruling in the *Brown* case. The resistance took many forms, some blatant and some subtle, but schools were not desegregating. Therefore, 15 years later, the Court declared that the doctrine of desegregating "with all deliberate speed" had run its course. It was time to direct schools that they may no longer operate a dual school system based on race or color but must "begin immediately to operate as unitary systems within which no person is to be effectively excluded from any school because of race or color"[32]

How quickly must faculty and staff be desegregated?

That depends on the local situation, including the racial composition of the teaching force and the staff, as well as the overall plan to desegregate in good faith. For example, in Montgomery County, Alabama, the district court required the immediate desegregation of "the substitute teachers, the student teachers, [and] the night faculties," since this could be accomplished without any administrative problems. The desegregation of the regular faculties was ordered on a slower, more gradual basis. The Supreme Court approved the actions of the district court, saying that it has repeatedly recognized faculty and staff desegregation "to be an important aspect of the basic task of achieving a public school system wholly free from racial discrimination."[33]

Can minorities be dismissed when reductions occur as a result of desegregation?

Yes, but only if objective criteria are used to make the reduction decisions. This question arose in many school districts that maintained a dual system, one for black students and the other for whites. There were many underenrolled classes and small schools with administrators in charge of each school. When unitary school districts were being formed as a result of court-ordered desegregation it became clear that many communities had been supporting a surplus of teachers and administrators as a price of segregation. As a result, when the schools were consolidated, many black educators lost their jobs. When some black educators in Mississippi challenged such practices, the courts generated some guiding principles.

In Jackson, Mississippi, the U.S. Court of Appeals, in connection with a suit to desegregate the schools, ordered that principals, teachers, teacher aides, and staff who work with children be so assigned within the district that "in no case will the racial composition of a staff indicate that a school is intended for Negro students or white students." Subsequent hiring should be conducted so that the racial composition of teachers and staff within each school will reflect the racial composition in the entire school system.[34] Moreover, if there is to be any reduction in the number of administrators, faculty, or staff, or if there are any demotions, members to be demoted or dismissed "must be selected on the basis of objective and reasonable and nondiscriminatory standards from among all the staff of the school district." If demotions or dismissals occur, no replacements may be made by hiring or promoting a person of a different race or national origin from that of the dismissed or demoted individual until each displaced staff member who is qualified has had an opportunity to fill the vacancy. This is the *Singleton* principle.

Where do we get the objective criteria for use in dismissals or demotions?

Criteria must be developed by the school district for use in connection with demotions or dismissals. Such nonracial objective criteria must be available for public inspection.

Do faculty and staff members have access to the evaluations?

Yes. This was a requirement in the *Singleton* case and many subsequent courts, including the Supreme Court, have referred to the *Singleton* principles with approval.

What is a demotion?

Singleton held that a demotion is any reassignment that (1) leads to less pay or less responsibility, (2) requires less skill than the previous assignment, or (3) requires a teacher to teach a subject or grade other than one for which he or she is certified or for which he or she has had substantial experience within the past five years.

Must objective criteria always be used before a black teacher can be dismissed?

No, not always, only when faculty reduction accompanies school desegregation. This question arose concerning Watts, a black teacher who taught for 25 years in the Tuscaloosa County school system in Alabama, 24 of those years in all-black schools. When the schools were desegregated pursuant to a court order in 1970, she was transferred to a predominantly white school. According to the testimony presented at the trial, Watts had severe discipline problems, which she could not master. The school board suspended her a year later and held hearings with respect to her competence. She called no witnesses on her own behalf, nor did she cross-examine those who testified about her lack of competence.

When the hearings resulted in her dismissal for incompetence, she appealed to a state administrative commission, and when that agency upheld the decision of the school board, she went to court. The court held that the *Singleton* principles that require the application of objective criteria before a teacher can be dismissed govern only reductions resulting from court-ordered conversion to a unitary system. In Watts's case, there was no faculty or staff reduction immediately before or following desegregation. Courts will be reluctant "to intrude upon the internal affairs of local school authorities in such matters as teacher competency." Thus, if there is substantial evidence to support the board's finding of incompetence, courts will not substitute their judgment for that of the board. The appeals court upheld the dismissal of Watts.[35]

Can school boards hire by race to fill vacancies?

Yes and no. In a school district undergoing court-ordered desegregation to overcome the results of past unconstitutional actions, the district court may order school officials to take race into account when filing vacancies. This happened in Boston where the district court, as part of an overall plan of desegregation, ordered (1) the hiring of black and white teachers on a one-to-one basis until the percentage of black faculty reaches 20 percent, (2) the creation of an affirmative action program to recruit black faculty until their proportion reaches 25 percent of the faculty, (3) a coordinator of minority recruitment and a recruiting budget for 1975–1976 of no less than $120,000, and (4) periodic reports to the court on recruiting and hiring.[36]

The same question arose in Alabama when a school board practice of filling "white vacancies" and "black vacancies" was challenged. The court ruled that if a school district is not involved in a desegregation process, and if there are no reductions, dismissals, or hirings in connection with such desegregation, then boards must seek the most qualified applicants, regardless of race.[37]

Can schools override seniority and tenure in favor of integration when layoffs are necessary?

This depends on the situation. This question arose in Boston in 1982, in one of the series of lawsuits involving the desegregation of the city schools. Pursuant to the initial district court order in 1974 to desegregate the schools of Boston, a systematic effort was made to hire black faculty and administrators until they made up 20 percent of the workforce. When massive layoffs threatened as a result of a budget crisis in 1981, questions arose concerning the validity of court orders to maintain the 20 percent proportion of minority educators when such action would override seniority and tenure rights of whites. The district court ordered maintenance of such ratios and the circuit court of appeals affirmed this order.

The appeals court relied on principles laid down by the Supreme Court in 1977 in *Milliken* v. *Bradley* where the Court said "the nature of the desegregation remedy is to be determined by the nature and scope of the constitutional violation."[38] Furthermore, "the decree must indeed be *remedial* in nature, that is, it must be designed as nearly as possible to restore the victims of discriminatory conduct to the position they would have occupied in the absence of such conduct." The court further relied on *Milliken,* asserting that local authorities should be given the discretion to manage their own affairs consistent with the Constitution. "If, however, school authorities fail in their affirmative obligations . . . judicial authority may be invoked."[39] Thus the appeals court upheld the order overriding seniority in favor of integration.

In a similar case involving the schools of Buffalo, New York, a court order specified a racial quota that superseded contractual and statutory rights. Evidence showed that the school system consistently hired a disproportionately small percentage of minority staff and assigned them to schools with large proportions of minority students. The court ordered the school system to hire black and white teachers on a one-to-one basis until the staff consisted of 21 percent black teachers in each tenure area; to maintain such ratio of black and white staff in each area in case of future layoffs; and to apply the same one-to-one hiring rule to any recall of laid-off, probationary, and permanent teachers.

The appeals court upheld these requirements imposed by the district court in the face of proven past practices of discrimination. It did indicate, however, that on the recall provision, the district court order was harsh in its treatment of laid-off, probationary, and permanent teachers, unless it was a "demonstrable necessity" that their rights be so impaired.[40]

By contrast, the Sixth Circuit Court of Appeals struck down a quota system based on racial percentages that overrode contractual and statutory tenure rights in a 1983 case involving Kalamazoo, Michigan. In Kalamazoo, pursuant to court orders, the schools desegregated and made a good faith effort over a 10-

year period to remedy the effects of past discrimination. In the face of threatened layoffs, the district court imposed a quota to maintain the percentage of blacks hired. The appeals court held that a more flexible affirmative action plan with goals rather than quotas should be used. According to the court, seniority and tenure rights of teachers should be overridden only when it is *necessary* and not merely *reasonable* to "vindicate the rights of students." In this case, there was no evidence to prove such necessity.[41]

Recently, in the *Wygant* case, the Supreme Court ruled on a voluntary plan calling for quotas in hiring, layoffs, and recalls that was included in a collective bargaining contract, binding on teachers. *Wygant* involved a Michigan school district collective bargaining contract in which the board and the teachers agreed to a layoff plan designed to maintain the racial composition of the faculty, a plan in which seniority provisions might in some instances be superseded. The appeals court held the plan to be a reasonable means of remedying the chronic underrepresentation of minority teachers on the teaching force and therefore not a violation of the Constitution.[42]

Although previously the Supreme Court has not ruled on a public sector voluntary quota plan, it did rule on a related matter in the *Weber* case in 1979. That case was brought under Title VII and the Court ruled that Title VII does not forbid "private employers and unions from voluntarily agreeing upon bona fide affirmative action plans that accord racial preferences" designed to overcome racial problems in the work force.[43]

The *Weber* case, however, addressed neither the question of voluntary affirmative action in the public sector through a collective bargaining contract nor the constitutional issue of equal protection since the case was based on Title VII, a federal law.

On appeal the Supreme Court struck down the *Wygant* voluntary quota plan and concluded that the layoff provision violated the equal protection clause of the Fourteenth Amendment. The Court distinguished affirmative action from layoff plans, supporting the former but striking down the latter if racial classification is used in the layoff plan unless there was convincing evidence of prior racial discrimination in the particular school district. Since there was no such evidence presented in the *Wygant* case the voluntarily bargained layoff plan that used racial classification to override seniority was declared unconstitutional.[44]

Educators often use the role model theory to support affirmative action as well as racial preference in layoffs. In the *Wygant* case the Court thought the argument based on this theory too weak to support a racially based layoff plan. It distinguished hiring goals from layoff plans, noting that the former "impose a diffuse burden" while the latter "impose the entire burden of achieving racial equality on particular individuals, often resulting in serious disruption of their lives. That burden is too intrusive." Or, as the Court succinctly phrased it, "Denial of a future employment opportunity is not as intrusive as loss of an existing job."

In two related cases involving firefighters in Cleveland, Ohio, and sheet metal workers in New York City, the Court reiterated the constitutionality of affirmative action plans as a way of remedying past discrimination against minority groups when other approaches have not succeeded.[45]

Can voluntary affirmative action plans be agreed upon between school districts and unions?

Yes, they can be, for such efforts are consistent with policies approved by Congress and the Office of the President as well as various decisions of the Supreme Court. However, even voluntary plans will be carefully scrutinized by the Court, for any official policy or action that takes race or ethnicity into account is suspect and must be justified by a compelling governmental interest. Thus, as we saw in *Wygant*, as well as in other cases,[46] voluntary race-conscious affirmative action plans will be upheld for hiring and/or promotion, to overcome historic patterns of discrimination. Layoff plans or plans that contradict seniority, however, have been struck down as too intrusive and hurtful of identifiable employees.

Must principals be selected on a nondiscriminatory basis?

Yes, the selection of principals must be based on professional qualifications. If a school district is either reducing or increasing the number of its administrators and these changes are not in connection with desegregation, it is not required that objective criteria be used to select new administrators. If a black teacher claims nonpromotion to a principalship because of race, the burden of proof is on the teacher to support such a claim. Cases have held that this could be established by showing a large reduction in the number of black administrators in a district that had no reduction in the percentage of white administrators. The burden of proof then falls on the school board to show that there were nondiscriminatory reasons for its actions.[47]

Can a minority counselor be demoted?

Yes, if there are adequate nonracial reasons for the demotion. In El Paso, Texas, Eduardo Molina, a Mexican-American high school teacher, was appointed school counselor. After serving in that capacity for three years at two different schools, he was demoted to classroom teaching. Molina claimed that his demotion reflected his ethnic status and his involvement in Mexican-American affairs. The school district claimed that the demotion was based on his unsatisfactory performance as a counselor and his inability to get along with students, faculty, and other counselors.

The court was satisfied with the evidence establishing Molina's unsatisfactory performance as a counselor. Even though there was also evidence of discrimination in the school system at large, in the opinion of the court there were sufficient nondiscriminatory reasons for demoting this particular individual.[48]

Can teachers be transferred to promote desegregation?

Courts tend to uphold such transfers as a way of promoting faculty desegregation. For example, when a white teacher in San Bernardino, California, went to court challenging a transfer based on her race, the court upheld the board's action. According to the court, there was no violation of the Fourteenth Amendment because she continued teaching with the same position, salary, and benefits. Furthermore, she had no due process right to a hearing in connection with the transfer.[49]

By contrast, a federal district court struck down a policy adopted by the Philadelphia schools that specified percentage quotas for the employment of blacks and the transfer of teachers on the basis of race. The court held the policy to violate Title VII of the Civil Rights Act of 1964.[50] In this school district, desegregation had been achieved to the satisfaction of federal law and there was no evidence that resegregation would occur. According to the court, "the involuntary transfer of a teacher from a particular school solely on the basis of race and the imposed restriction on the selection of a new school solely on the basis of race constitutes racial discrimination with respect to the terms and conditions of employment."[51]

Thus, it seems that school districts may consider race in the transfer of teachers to achieve desegregation. It is quite likely, however, that once desegregation is achieved, race should not be a key consideration in the transfer of teachers or in their choices among schools.

A different kind of case arose involving a white counselor in Flint, Michigan. There, a federal court held that there was no violation of the equal protection clause when a white counselor was demoted to classroom teacher. This action was part of the board of education's affirmative action program in light of a history of discrimination against blacks in the school system.[52]

Can objective tests be used to screen applicants for jobs even if more blacks than whites fail the test?

Yes, if the tests are reasonable and relevant to the job for which people are being screened. The Supreme Court, in a case involving the recruiting of police officers, said that it has "not embraced the proposition that a law or other official act, without regard to whether it reflects a racially discriminatory purpose, is unconstitutional solely because it has a racially disproportionate impact."[53] This became a very important case because, earlier, some courts had ruled that a law or official act was unconstitutional if it had a discriminatory intent, purpose, or impact. Thus, to declare such tests unconstitutional today, the Court would require that the intent to discriminate be shown.

Must an employee prove intentional discrimination by the employer?

Yes, ruled the Supreme Court. The requirement of the showing of intent to discriminate was highlighted by the Court once again in the 1989 *City of*

Richmond case, involving a 30 percent "set aside" plan for minority subcontractors.[54] The Court ruled such a plan unconstitutional as violative of the Equal Protection Clause, unless plaintiffs have proven that the City of Richmond has practiced racial discrimination against such subcontractors in the past. Furthermore, the Court also ruled in 1989 that the employee always bears the burden of proof in claims of discrimination and it is not enough merely to show statistical disparities in the racial composition of the work force.[55]

Can objective tests be used for certification or pay if they disproportionately fail more blacks than whites?

Yes, if the tests are valid and reliable and are not used with the purpose and intent of discriminating against any race. In South Carolina, they used the National Teacher Examination (NTE) to screen people for certification. Candidates had to achieve a minimum score to be certified to teach in the state, and their pay levels were also determined by their scores. The use of the test was challenged because more blacks than whites failed to acquire the minimum score, and this allegedly created a racial classification in violation of the Fourteenth Amendment as well as Title VII of the Civil Rights Act of 1964.

The Supreme Court, after examining the NTE used to screen candidates for certification, concluded that the test was a well-developed instrument reasonably calculated to assess the presence or absence of knowledge. It also found that the test was not created or used with the intent to discriminate; therefore its use was proper and legal.[56]

In the same case, the court held that using the NTE to determine the level of teachers' pay was reasonable and rationally connected to a legitimate state interest. A unitary pay system had been introduced in South Carolina together with the new basis for certification. The court found that the reason for the new arrangement was the state's desire to use its limited resources to improve the quality of the teaching force "and to put whatever monetary incentives were available in the salary schedule to that task." Thus, finding no discriminatory intent in the use of the NTE for salary purposes, the court upheld the state policy.

How do courts determine employment discrimination—by the racial composition of the schools or of the larger area?

The latter, according to the Supreme Court. In a case in St. Louis County, Missouri, the school district suggested that the comparison be made between the teacher work force and the student population. The Court rejected this position and held that "a proper comparison was between the racial composition of [the] teaching staff and the racial composition of the qualified public school teacher population in the relevant labor market."[57]

SUMMARY

Schools are at the center of the storm as various interest groups attempt to put their ideas into practice and use the schools to attain their social goals. The meaning of the equal protection clause is generally agreed upon in bold outlines by the courts, even though many details and "legal wrinkles" still have to be ironed out. The major remaining tasks are those of implementation, to carry out the Supreme Court's clear pronouncement in the landmark *Brown* case that "in the field of public education the doctrine of 'separate but equal' has no place."

Brown I declared that segregated public schools are unconstitutional; *Brown II* ordered schools to desegregate "with all deliberate speed." Most communities resisted the Court's mandate. As legal challenges were mounted against the different forms of resistance to desegregation, courts tended to respect various plans to overcome historic patterns of racial separation as long as the plans were advanced in good faith and were likely to work.

Busing is a legitimate means by which schools may desegregate. Factors such as time and distance to be traveled must be considered in any plan for busing children, and the age of the children is a vital factor. Quotas may not be used as fixed requirements in attempts to achieve racially balanced schools, but they may be used as general goals in a previously segregated school system. In a school district undergoing desegregation all racial groups must participate; no group may be exempt.

The Fourteenth Amendment prohibition against segregated schooling applies to the entire country and to all situations where official acts were involved in the creation or perpetuation of segregated schooling. Any intentional act that has a segregative impact is unconstitutional, however indirect or hidden the act may be. Not only the laws of the state and the formal policies of a school district must be examined to determine whether de jure segregation exists, but other official actions as well. These include the drawing of school attendance zones, zoning ordinances, residential restrictions, government support for housing and insurance, and all other actions used to create residential and therefore school segregation.

The Supreme Court has ruled that if a substantial portion of a city has been unlawfully segregated, the entire school district must be involved in the remedy. On the other hand, once a school district has undergone legitimate desegregation and through ordinary events, without any official action, some resegregation occurs, the U.S. Constitution does not require a new effort to desegregate. Such a situation would be a *de facto* segregation and thus not unconstitutional.

Efforts to create metropolitan area desegregation plans have met with mixed results in the courts. If there is evidence to prove that officials of a city and its surrounding suburbs collaborated in the creation of a city heavily populated by racial minorities with suburbs largely populated by whites, a plan for interdistrict desegregation will be ordered. In the absence of such cooperation (or collusion), the district lines will be respected by the courts and the remedy will have to be restricted to the area wherein the constitutional violation occurred.

In any effort to achieve desegregation, both federal and state laws must be consulted. All public schools must meet the minimum requirements of the national Constitution and the federal laws; state laws and constitutions may provide some remedies that go beyond the federal law. Private schools may not exclude students on the grounds of race. The Supreme Court ruled that federal law protects the equal right to enter into contracts, thus a private nonsectarian school may not deny admission to an otherwise qualified applicant simply on the basis of race.

The general principles pronounced by the Court in *Brown* apply to all aspects of schooling including teachers and staff. Racial segregation is unconstitutional, and racial discrimination in all forms is illegal. This does not mean that race cannot be taken into account when teachers and staff are assigned. *Swann* makes a strong argument for the assignment of teachers and staff to enhance faculty desegregation and specifically rejects the notion that teachers must always be assigned on a "color blind" basis. The implementation of desegregation is a complex and demanding task. As the Supreme Court said,

> There is no universal answer to complex problems of desegregation; there is obviously no one plan that will do the job in every case. The matter must be assessed in light of the circumstances present and the options available in each instance. It is incumbent upon the school board to establish that its proposed plan promises meaningful and immediate progress toward disestablishing state imposed segregation. It is incumbent upon the district court to weigh that claim in light of the facts at hand and in light of any alternatives which may be shown as feasible and more promising in their effectiveness.[58]

Desegregation with "all deliberate speed" has run its course, and schools must begin to desegregate immediately. Nevertheless, courts still allow individual school districts reasonable time to achieve desegregation as long as they are proceeding in good faith. If in the process of desegregation a surplus of teachers, administrators, or staff appears, individuals to be dismissed or demoted must be selected on the basis of objective, reasonable, and nondiscriminatory criteria. In ordinary cases of reduction in force, or in dismissals based on incompetence, in the absence of desegregation, courts will allow school districts to follow their usual procedures.

If racial quotas are imposed by a court order as a remedy for past discrimination, such quotas may also be applied to layoffs in case of a budget crisis as well as to a program of recalls in order to maintain racial balance even where seniority and tenure are superseded. In the absence of a court-ordered desegregation plan, when a collective bargaining agreement specifies quotas for layoffs and recalls that override seniority and tenure provisions, the plan will be upheld only if there is substantial evidence of prior racial discrimination in the particular school district. A voluntary layoff plan that includes racial classification may not override seniority or tenure in the absence of a history of discrimination in the particular governmental unit. On the other hand, affirmative action plans stating goals and hiring procedures that are aimed at achieving racial balance in the teaching force or school staff have been upheld by the Supreme Court. In the eyes of the law, the distinction between goals and quotas is important; the latter will be upheld only if temporary and either ordered by a court or adopted by a governmental unit with a history of substantial discrimination.

Objective tests may be used by public schools and state agencies in the process of certification, as well as in deciding where to place teachers on a salary scale, if the objective tests are reasonable, relevant to the occupational tasks, and were not created with the intent to discriminate. The fact that the tests have a disproportionate negative impact on a racial or ethnic minority does not invalidate an otherwise acceptable test.

In sum, the courts continue their efforts to apply the equal protection clause of the Fourteenth Amendment to the functioning of all school personnel. The problems change with changing times and conditions, but the principles of the *Brown* case are still alive and powerful in situations related to the racial integration of schools and school personnel.

NOTES

1. J.W. Peltason, 58 LONELY MEN: SOUTHERN FEDERAL JUDGES AND SCHOOL DESEGREGATION (Urbana: University of Illinois Press, 1971).
2. 163 U.S. 537 (1896).
3. *Gong Lum* v. *Rice*, 275 U.S. 78 (1927).
4. 347 U.S. 483 (1954).
5. This decision is known as *Brown II, Brown* v. *Board of Education*, 349 U.S. 294 (1955).
6. *Griffin* v. *Prince Edward County*, 377 U.S. 218 (1964).
7. *U.S.* v. *Jefferson*, 372 F.2d 836 (5th Cir. 1966).
8. *Swann* v. *Charlotte-Mecklenburg Board of Education*, 402 U.S. 1 (1971).
9. *Lee* v. *Johnson*, 404 U.S. 1215 (1971).
10. *Diaz* v. *San Jose Unified School District*, 733 F.2d 660 (9th Cir. 1984).
11. *Columbus Board of Education* v. *Penick; Dayton Board of Education* v. *Brinkman*, 443 U.S. 449 and 526 (1979).
12. *U.S.* v. *Yonkers Board of Education*, No. 80 CIV 6761 (LBS), 54 U.S.L.W. 2296 (December 10, 1985).
13. *Keyes* v. *School District No. 1*, Denver, Colo., 413 U.S. 189 (1974).
14. *Pasadena City Board of Education* v. *Spangler*, 427 U.S. 424 (1976).
15. *Riddick* v. *School Board of Norfolk*, 784 F.2d 521 (4th Cir. 1986), *cert. denied*, 107 S.Ct. 420 (1986).
16. *Dowell* v. *Board of Education of the Oklahoma City Pub. Schools*, 795 F.2s 1516 (10th Cir. 1986).
17. In the U.S. District Court for the District of Kansas, Case No. T-316.

18. *Bradley* v. *Milliken*, 418 U.S. 717 (1974).

19. *Evans* v. *Buchanan*, 393 F.Supp. 428 (D. Del. 1975).

20. *Little Rock School District* v. *Pulaski County Special School District No. 1, et al*, 597 F.Supp. 1220 (D.C. Ark. 1984).

21. *Berry* v. *School District of the City of Benton Harbor*, 564 F.Supp. 617 (W.D. Mich. 1983).

22. *Bronson* v. *Board of Education for the Cincinnati Public Schools*, 578 F.Supp. 1091 (S.D. Ohio 1984).

23. *Crawford* v. *Board of Education in City of Los Angeles*, 551 P.2d 28 (Cal. 1976).

24. *Crawford* v. *Board of Education*, 102 S.Ct. 3211 (1982).

25. *Washington* v. *School District No. 1*, 102 S.Ct. 3187 (1982).

26. *Runyon* v. *McCrary*, 427 U.S. 160 (1976).

27. 42. U.S.C. § 1981.

28. *Patterson* v. *McLean Credit Union*, 57 L.W. 4705 (6-13-89).

29. I.R.C. of 1954, 501(c)(3).

30. *Bob Jones University* v. *United States*, 103 S.Ct. 2017 (1983).

31. *Brown* v. *Board of Education, supra*.

32. *Alexander* v. *Holmes County Board of Education*, 396 U.S. 19 (1969).

33. *U.S.* v. *Montgomery Board of Education*, 395 U.S. 225 (1969).

34. *Singleton* v. *Jackson Municipal Separate School District*, 419 F.2d 1211 (5th Cir. 1970).

35. *Lee* v. *Tuscaloosa County Board of Education*, 591 F.2d 324 (5th Cir. 1978).

36. *Morgan* v. *Kerrigan*, 509 F.2d 580 (2d Cir. 1974).

37. *Lee* v. *Conecuh County Board of Education*, 464 F.Supp. 333 (S.D. Ala. 1979).

38. 433 U.S. 267 (1977).

39. *Morgan* v. *O'Bryant*, 671 F.2d 23 (lst Cir. 1982).

40. *Arthur* v. *Nyquist*, 712 F.2d 816 (2d Cir. 1983).

41. *Oliver* v. *Kalamazoo Board of Education*, 706 F.2d 757 (6th Cir. 1983).

42. *Wygant* v. *Jackson Board of Education*, 746 F.2d 1152 (6th Cir. 1984).

43. *United Steel Workers of America* v. *Weber*, 443 U.S. 193 (1979).

44. *Wygant* v. *Jackson Board of Education*, 54 L.W. 4479 (May 19, 1986).

45. *Firefighters* v. *Cleveland*, 54 L.W. 5005 (June 24, 1986).

46. *International Association of Firefighters* v. *City of Cleveland*, 54 L.W. 5005 (1986).

47. *Lee* v. *Conecuh County Board of Education*, 464 F.Supp. 333 (S.D. Ala. 1979).

48. *Molina* v. *El Paso Independent School District*, 583 F.2d 213 (5th Cir. 1978).

49. *Bolin* v. *San Bernardino City Unified School District*, 202 Cal. Rptr. 416 (Cal. App. 1984).

50. 42 U.S.C. 2000e2(a).

51. *Kromnick* v. *School District of Philadelphia*, 555 F.Supp. 249 (E.D.Pa. 1983).

52. *Marsh* v. *Board of Education of City of Flint*, 581 F.Supp. 614 (E.D. Mich. 1984).

53. *Washington* v. *Davis*, 426 U.S. 229 (1976).

54. *City of Richmond* v. *J. A. Croson*, 57 L.W. 4132 (1-24-1989).

55. Wards Cove Packing Co. v. *Antonio*, 57 L.W. 4583 (6-5-1989).

56. *United States of America* v. *State of South Carolina*, 434 U.S. 1026 (1978).

57. *Hazelwood* v. *United States*, 433 U.S. 299 (1977).

58. *Green* v. *County School Board*, 391 U.S. 430 (1968).

CHAPTER 14

Am I Protected against Sex Discrimination?

OVERVIEW

The history of sex discrimination among teachers is well documented. In recent years we have seen a variety of challenges to such discrimination, and many school policies have been revised in the light of court cases, legislation, and a new public concern for equal treatment of men and women. This chapter examines questions concerning equal pay, promotions, marriage, pregnancy, maternity leaves, sexual harassment, and other forms of discrimination as they affect teachers.

In the past, both the culture at large and our schools functioned as if there were significant differences between males and females that should be reflected in schooling. Though some of these practices persist, many have been challenged. This chapter summarizes these challenges by examining questions regarding students and equal access to school sports, curricular exclusions, discriminatory admissions policies, and separate schools, and by examining questions related to married or pregnant students.

SEX DISCRIMINATION AGAINST TEACHERS

Can schools pay men more than women?

No. Under both the Equal Pay Act of 1963[1] and Title VII of the Civil Rights Act of 1964,[2] sex cannot be used as the basis of a pay disparity between individuals who perform substantially the same work. A pay difference is permissible, however, if based on factors other than sex, such as experience or qualifications. Thus, in a recent New York case,[3] the court dismissed a claim that Title VII was violated where elementary school principals were paid less than high school principals. The court rejected the plaintiff's argument that, while a majority of both elementary and high school principals were male, the elementary principals were paid less because they traditionally supervise women teachers. The court explained that the mere fact that a lower paid job was "traditionally female" is not enough to establish Title VII violation; the critical question, rather, is whether any present violation exists. In examining the current situation, the court found that the salary difference was justified by factors other than sex: the high school principal's job entailed greater responsibility and effort due to the size of the staff and student body, the larger budget, and other nonsex factors.

When can schools pay some teachers more than others?

Schools' salaries may be based on formal preparation and experience, and thus teachers may be placed on different steps of a schedule based on those factors. Given objectively equal preparation and experience, some teachers may be paid more than others if such additional pay is based on merit or additional duties. These standards, however, must apply equally to men and women. (Biology is not merit!)

Can coaches receive extra pay?

Yes. Schools can create policies to pay for extra duties, whether these duties involve coaching, drama, outing club, or others.

Can male coaches receive more pay than female coaches?

The principle of equal pay for equivalent work has been difficult to apply in the area of coaching. Historically, significant disparities existed in favor of male coaches. While Title IX of the Education Amendments of 1972[4] has equalized some aspects of the funding of athletics, it has not been applied to coaching because Congress intended this particular law to apply to students and not to coaches.

The federal Equal Pay Act of 1963 and similar state laws have been used to challenge unequal pay. In one such case,[5] for example, female junior high school coaches brought suit when they were paid less than the male coaches in the same sports. The court explained that, under the Equal Pay Act, the female coaches could prevail only if they could show that their coaching jobs were substantially similar to the male coaches' jobs. Examining their respective duties, the court found that there were no significant differences between the male and female teams in terms of number of students, length of season, or number of practice sessions, and concluded that the work of the male and female coaches was substantially similar and required the same skill, effort, and responsibility, except that the female track coach worked longer hours than the male coach. The court therefore awarded back pay to the female coaches.

In a similar case,[6] however, the court found that a salary difference (ranging from $50 to $580) was not a violation where different hours of work were required for female volleyball coaches and male football coaches.

Can the scale of compensation be different for coaching boys and for coaching girls?

Yes, it can, ruled the Appellate Court of Illinois in a suit filed by four women in Proviso Township High School.[7] Plaintiffs alleged violations of both the federal Equal Pay Act and the Illinois Constitution of 1970, article I, section 18. The women claimed they received lower pay because they were women. Such a claim, if supported by evidence, would violate both the federal Equal Pay Act and the Illinois Constitution, which contains the equivalent of an equal rights amendment.

The facts showed that the collective bargaining agreement between the school board and the local teachers' union specified coaching compensation in detail. The contract referred to "men coaches" and "women coaches." However, the evidence showed, and parties to the suit conceded, that "men" and "women" did not refer to the gender of the coaches, but the sex of the students participating in athletics. In fact, there were instances of males coaching girls in some sports and, in one instance, a female coached a boys' team. Some women coaches who worked with boys' teams received a higher salary than men who coached girls' teams. In light of these facts, the court ruled there was no discrimination based on sex proven by the plaintiffs and there was nothing illegal about the differential pay.

Does coupling a teaching position with coaching constitute sex discrimination?

It may depending on the circumstances. An interesting case arose in Arizona where the Amphitheater Unified School District required applicants for a teaching position in biology to have the ability to coach varsity football. A female applicant who did not even make it into the list of finalists for the position went to court, claiming sex discrimination under Title VII.[8]

Title VII prohibits discrimination in employment on the basis of race, color, religion, sex, and national origin. The term "discrimination" has been interpreted by the U.S. Supreme Court to include two different concepts:

> "Disparate treatment" . . . is the most easily understood type of discrimination. The employer simply treats some people less favorably than others because of their race, religion, sex or national origin. Proof of discriminatory motive is critical, although it can in some situations be inferred from the mere fact of differences in treatment. . . . Claims of disparate treatment may be distinguished from claims that stress "disparate impact." The latter involve employment practices that are facially neutral in their treatment of different

groups but that in fact fall more harshly on one group than another and cannot be justified by business necessity. Proof of discriminatory motive . . . is not required under a disparate impact theory. . . .[9]

A plaintiff bringing a charge of disparate treatment has the burden of proving each of the following:

1. that he or she belongs to the protected class;
2. that he or she applied and was qualified for the position;
3. that despite such qualifications, plaintiff was rejected; and
4. that after plaintiff's rejection, the position remained open and the employer continued to seek similarly qualified applicants.[10]

Once the plaintiff has met this burden of proving a *prima facie* case, then the employer must establish a legitimate, nondiscriminatory reason for the actions taken. If the employer can do so, the plaintiff must then show the reason given by the employer was merely a pretext.

In the Arizona case mentioned above, however, the teacher was not claiming "disparate treatment," but was using the theory of "disparate impact" to establish discrimination. In such a case, the plaintiff must show a causal connection between the employment practice and the differing treatment of a protected group. Most commonly, statistics are used to show that an employment practice disproportionately disadvantages women or men. Until recently, once the plaintiff had shown disparate impact, the employer then had the burden of proving "business necessity," that the challenged employment practice was necessary for the safe and efficient operation of the business. There must be a compelling reason for the practice without acceptable alternatives to accomplish the same business goals.

When applying this standard, the Arizona court held that the school district presented no evidence that less discriminatory hiring practices had been attempted and had failed "and there was in fact substantial evidence that hiring alternatives were available and were not used." The Arizona court recognized that it might be possible for a school district "to show business necessity in the practice of coupling addendums (extra coaching assignments) and academic contracts." However, the burden of proving that was on the school district and, in this case, it did not prove such necessity.

If this case were decided today, however, the result might well be different. In 1989, the U.S. Supreme Court decided a case[11] in which it redefined business necessity in deference to employer goals and also transferred the burden of proof on this issue to the plaintiff. In this case, called *Ward's Cove*, the Court said that a practice can be a business necessity without being "essential" or "indispensable," and thus made business necessity a less strict standard. Even more significantly, the Court transferred the burden of proof to the plaintiff. Thus, the teacher who claims that an employment practice has a discriminatory disparate impact will now have to show not only the disproportionate disadvantage to women but also the absence of business necessity on the employer's part. Although we will have to await future decisions to see how *Ward's Cove* is applied in the educational setting, it is clear that the Court has significantly undermined the disparate impact theory as a method of challenging employment practices as discriminatory.

Can schools prefer males over females in administrative positions?

No. In matters of promotion and in the selection of administrators, sex is not a relevant factor. It would be a violation of the equal protection clause of the Fourteenth Amendment to give preference to either sex over the other in the selection of school administrators. Such preference would be arbitrary because there is no rational connection between sex and administrative competence in public schools. An exception to this general principle might be the selection of a dean of girls or dean of boys in schools where the job descriptions specify some duties that are particularly sensitive and where being a male or female would be a job-related qualification.

Similarly, such a preference would be a violation of Title VII. In a recent Alabama case,[12] for example, the court found that a woman assistant principal who had applied for, but had been denied, 13 administrative positions over a four-year period had been discriminated against when a man was chosen in every case and among the reasons given was that "a woman could not handle the responsibilities such as sports and cleaning, that went along with a high school principalship."

Can gender be a relevant factor in selecting a school counselor?

Yes it can, ruled the Montana Supreme Court in 1984. The school in this case already had a male counselor, and in its search for a second counselor, males were excluded from consideration. Stone challenged his exclusion. The court ruled that gender in this situation was a bona fide occupational qualification for the position might call for special sensitivities in relationships with female students. Thus, in this instance, discrimination based on sex was reasonable.[13]

Sex discrimination may appear in the selection or promotion process in other ways as well. For example, an unsuccessful applicant for promotion showed evidence of her outstanding credentials and excellent work record and the successful applicant's poor work record, unprofessional and dishonest behavior, and intimate sexual relationship with the supervisor. The appeals court held that this was sufficient to prove sex discrimination even though there was no "direct evidence of an explicit sexual relationship." The requirement of proof of sexual intercourse "would establish a patently absurd legal principle." Evidence of sexual encounters short of intercourse is sufficient. While this case involved nurses and a chief medical officer, the legal principles would be equally applicable to educators.[14]

Are there other forms of discrimination based on sex?

Yes, there are. Courts will examine each situation and apply the relevant legal principles. An example is the case of a female kindergarten teacher who refused to undergo physical examination by the school district's male physician, after an extended sick leave. She was willing to submit a certificate from her own physician or, at her own expense, from any *female* physician selected by the superintendent or recommended by the local medical society. She claimed it was against her religion to be examined by a male physician. When suspended, she went to court. The circuit court held the board's action to be arbitrary and therefore a violation of her right to substantive due process. One of the judges also ruled in her favor on the grounds that her constitutional right to privacy was violated.[15]

MARRIAGE AND PREGNANCY

Can teachers be dismissed for getting married?

Not public school teachers. Whatever rules of celibacy private schools may wish to impose on their teachers, public schools can no longer fire teachers for entering wedlock. This is not to say that teachers always had such a freedom. Historically many communities had contractual provisions forbidding marriage or did so by rule of the school board. Economic and/or moral justifications were offered for such rules. Today, courts would strike down such rules as being arbitrary, against public policy, and a violation of the "liberty" provision of the Fourteenth Amendment.

Must pregnant teachers take specified maternity leaves?

Until recently, most school systems required that teachers who became pregnant take a leave of absence without pay at the fourth or fifth month of their pregnancy. Furthermore, they usually specified that the teacher could not return to work for a certain period of time after having the baby. Many schools required the new mother to stay home for at least six months; some schools specified even longer leaves. In recent years, women have gone to court to challenge such school policies; they claimed that such policies were arbitrary as they violated due process. School boards maintained that such policies were legitimate, for they were reasonably related to the maintenance of an orderly efficient school system. These and related issues have been argued in court and were faced recently by the U.S. Supreme Court.

The *LaFleur* and *Cohen* Cases[16]

The Cleveland Board of Education adopted a rule in 1952 that required pregnant schoolteachers to take a leave of absence without pay beginning five months before the expected birth of their child. A teacher on a maternity leave was not allowed to return to work until the beginning of the next semester that followed the date when her child attained the age of three months. A doctor's health certificate was required as a prerequisite for return. Moreover, the teacher on maternity leave was not guaranteed reemployment but was merely given priority for a position for which she qualified. Failure to comply with the mandatory leave provision was grounds for dismissal.

The Ohio rule was in effect in 1971 when Jo Carol LaFleur, a junior high school teacher, became pregnant. She did not wish to take an unpaid leave but wanted to teach until the end of the school year. Her child was expected late in July. By the school district requirement, she had to commence her leave in March 1971. LaFleur filed suit in a U.S. district court challenging the constitutionality of the maternity leave rule. She lost, but on appeal the Court of Appeals for the Sixth Circuit ruled in her favor.

At the same time, a similar case was working its way through the courts in Virginia. Susan Cohen challenged a school board maternity leave regulation requiring pregnant teachers to take unpaid leaves of absence at least four months before delivery. In this case the district court ruled in her favor, but the Court of Appeals of the Fourth Circuit upheld the constitutionality of the regulation.

Since two courts of appeal reached contradictory conclusions on essentially the same facts, the U.S. Supreme Court agreed to decide the constitutionality of the school boards' rules. The Court has often recognized that freedom of personal choice in matters of marriage and family life is one of the liberties protected under the due process clause of the Fourteenth Amendment. Among other things, this means that there can be no unreasonable or arbitrary governmental regulation of one's freedom "to bear or beget a child."

The school boards argued that their regulations were not unreasonable but in fact were necessary for the efficient operation of the schools. They gave two reasons for the rules: (1) Such rules maintain continuity of classroom instruction, since advance knowledge of when a pregnant teacher will begin her leave makes it possible to arrange for a qualified substitute; and (2) some pregnant teachers became physically incapable of performing their duties, and thus the leave policy protects the health of the teacher and her unborn child at the same time that it ensures the presence in the classroom of a physically capable teacher.

The Court recognized continuity of instruction as a significant and legitimate concern of school boards. Advance notice of pregnancy leaves undoubtedly facilitates administrative planning for continuity. Nevertheless, the absolute requirement of taking a leave at the fourth or fifth month of pregnancy is arbitrary and does not necessarily help continuity in instruction. Teachers become pregnant at different times, and thus their leaves must begin at different times. Therefore the Court held that "the arbitrary cutoff dates embodied in the mandatory leave rules before us have no rational relationship to the valid state interest of preserving continuity of instruction."

On the second argument of the school boards, the physical incapacities of pregnant teachers, the court also thought it desirable to keep physically unfit teachers out of the classroom. Furthermore, it accepted the fact that *some* teachers are unable to perform their duties during the late months of pregnancy. However, *all* pregnant teachers should not be mandated to take a leave, ruled the Court, for such a regulation sweeps too broadly. It presumes that all pregnant teachers become physically incapacitated after a certain time, and there is no individual determination of abilities. A rule that contains a conclusive presumption that is neither necessarily nor universally true is overly broad and thus violates the due process clause of the Fourteenth Amendment.

What about rules that limit the teacher's eligibility to return to work after giving birth? The Cleveland rule made the teacher ineligible to return until the beginning of the semester following the child's age of three months. The Virginia rule allowed the return at any time upon submission of a satisfactory medical certificate. Once again, the school boards offered continuity of instruction and physical competence as reasons for the rules.

The Court ruled that the three-month age provision of the Cleveland rule was wholly arbitrary and irrational: "The age limitation serves no legitimate state interest, and unnecessarily penalizes the female teacher for asserting her right to bear children." Since each child will reach the age of three months at a different time, the purpose of continuity is not served by the rule. Thus the Cleveland rule was struck down as a violation of the due process clause of the Fourteenth Amendment, while the Virginia rule was upheld.

In sum, a school policy that requires all pregnant teachers to begin leaves at the fourth or fifth month of pregnancy may be administratively convenient, but it conclusively presumes such women to be unfit to teach past those dates. Such presumption is overly broad and unduly penalizes female teachers who bear children; therefore the policy is unconstitutional. A "return policy" that specifies any number of months or years after childbirth before the teacher may return to work is invalid because it is arbitrary.

What are reasonable requirements in a maternity-leave policy?

School officials may require a written notice of intention to begin a pregnancy leave as well as a notice of intention of the date of return. They may also require a medical certificate attesting to the medical competence of the teacher to continue or resume her work. This would amount to a complete individualization of maternity-leave practices.

On the other hand, if the school district wanted to provide continuity of instruction, it could create a policy requiring teachers to commence their maternity leaves at the beginning of the semester during which they expect to deliver. The policy could also require that they not return until the beginning of the semester following delivery.

Can teachers be dismissed because of pregnancy?

Absurd as it may seem today, some cases have held, as recently as 1945, that pregnancy can constitute "neglect of duty" or "incompetency" and be grounds for dismissal since it renders a teacher unable to carry out her job. More recently, the law has recognized the right "to bear and beget a child" as one of the liberties protected by the due process clause of the Fourteenth Amendment. Married pregnant teachers would undoubtedly be protected in their right to bear children. In a recent case,[17] for example, a Virginia court held that a school district that forced a pregnant and unmarried female teacher to take a leave of absence from teaching violated her right to privacy as well as her statutory rights under Title VII. (Questions concerning the pregnancy of unmarried teachers are discussed in Chapter 12.)

Do teachers on maternity leave receive disability and other employment benefits?

Yes, they do. Laws today generally require employers to treat pregnancy disability the same way as any other disability. A Pennsylvania court held, for example, that discrimination based on pregnancy constitutes sex discrimination.[18] While this case was decided specifically under Pennsylvania law, it reflects general principles applicable in other jurisdictions as well. The federal Pregnancy Discrimination Act, an amendment to Title VII of the Civil Rights Act of 1964, prohibits discrimination against pregnant women. It even requires employers to provide medical benefits for pregnancy-related conditions of employee's spouses the same as is generally provided to spouses for other medical conditions.[19] The U.S. Supreme Court has ruled, however, that the Pregnancy Discrimination Act, while mandating equal treatment regardless of pregnancy, does not prohibit a state from requiring employers to give women unpaid pregnancy leave and then to reinstate them to their jobs when other disabled employees are not given such "special treatment."[20] The Court found that such a state law does not compel employers to treat pregnant employees *better* than other disabled employees; it merely establishes benefits that employers must, at a minimum, provide to pregnant workers.

A school district's maternity and sick leave policy, as well as leave without pay policy, will be carefully considered by the courts as illustrated by a recent case in Colorado. In this case, the district policy stated: "Maternity leave will be granted with full pay for the total number of accrued days of sick leave and at full pay less the substitute's regular pay within the same contract year." In accordance with this policy, Pamela Pastor requested her sick leave days first, at full pay, to be continued at full pay less the cost of the substitute for the remainder of the school year.

At first, the superintendent claimed that this request would "directly affect the efficiency of the school operation." Later he noted that the school would not suffer and recommended a leave without pay. The school board granted the first

50 days at full pay pursuant to its maternity leave policy, but the rest of the leave would be without pay and not under the maternity leave policy. The court, however, held the district to its policy and granted the teacher's request since it was clearly covered under the explicit language of the policy.[21]

When pregnant teachers are contemplating taking a leave they must carefully consider district policies related to sick leaves, maternity leaves, personal leaves, leaves without pay, and any other leave provisions. Once they make their decision it might be extremely difficult or even impossible for them to select a more favorable alternative. Courts have held that the burden of proof is on the teacher who later claims to be a victim of unlawful discrimination.[22]

Recently, an interesting case arose that brought into conflict the rights of a private, religious school on the one hand and a teacher's right to be free from sex discrimination on the other. In Dayton, Ohio, a teacher informed the principal of a private, religious school that she was pregnant. The principal notified her that her contract would not be renewed "because of our desire to have a mother home with pre-school age children." When the teacher consulted an attorney who threatened to sue the school, she was fired for not following the biblical chain-of-command for resolving disputes among church members.

When the teacher filed sex discrimination charges with the Ohio Civil Rights Commission the school went to the federal court to prohibit enforcement of the state statute against it, claiming that such enforcement would violate the First Amendment. In reaching its decision, the court weighed the state's interest in prohibiting discrimination against the genuinely held religious beliefs of the members of the church-school. On balance, the court ruled in favor of the religious school on the grounds that (1) its actions were based on bona fide religious beliefs, (2) the controls exercised by the civil rights commission would place undue burdens on the school's right to free exercise of religion, and (3) the commission's jurisdiction would require continuous, comprehensive surveillance of the school and this would constitute excessive entanglement of church and state.[23]

Are teachers protected against sexual harassment?

Yes, they are. In fact, they always have been, but under different legal principles. However, before we look at the principles that protect teachers, we should clarify the meaning of sexual harassment. Since Title VII of the Civil Rights Act of 1964 and Title IX of the 1972 Education Amendments are the legal bases for sexual harassment actions, the regulations that interpret these laws give us a guide to the meaning of such harassment.

The guidelines of the U.S. Equal Employment Opportunity Commission (EEOC), which administers Title VII, indicate that sexual harassment refers to unwelcome sexual advances, requests for sexual favors, and other verbal or physical conduct of a sexual nature when (1) submission to such conduct is made either explicitly or implicitly a term or condition of one's employment, (2) submission to or rejection of such conduct is used as a basis for employment decisions, or (3) such conduct has the purpose or effect of substantially interfering with one's work performance or creating an intimidating, hostile, or offensive work environment.[24] In its first decision in a sexual harassment case, *Meritor Savings Bank* v. *Vinson*,[25] the U.S. Supreme Court approved these guidelines and held that a claim of "hostile environment" sexual harassment is a form of sex discrimination actionable under Title VII.

The primary purpose of laws and regulations related to sexual harassment is to protect women in the workplace, since historically they were victims of widespread abuse, intimidation, and exploitation. Most often, such abuse came from supervisors and bosses who were in positions of power over rewards and promotions. In education, this meant that principals, supervisors, and other administrators occupied these positions and often used their power to extract sexual favors.

Historically, this kind of behavior was treated as immoral and unprofessional conduct, and many administrators lost their jobs or were otherwise disciplined. Even today, it is most likely that actions against administrators guilty of immoral and unprofessional conduct will proceed on that basis (see Chapter 12). However, it is clear that all educators are bound by the same principles, not only administrators. Teachers who harass teachers, secretaries, or even administrators, may be guilty of immoral and unprofessional conduct, or sexual harassment. It is also clear that sexual advances or relations with students constitute such conduct (see Chapter 12). An important distinction between students and adults is that minor students are legally incapable of consenting to such activities, whereas for behavior to constitute sexual harassment of adults, it must be *unwanted* sexual advances or other conduct. In short, genuinely consensual sexual behavior is not grounds for sexual harassment.[26] Whether or not the advances or verbal behavior were unwanted is a question of fact and must be determined by taking all relevant evidence into consideration.

A significant legal development in connection with sexual harassment is the principle that holds employers liable for the actions of supervising personnel when the employer knows or *should know* of the supervisor's behavior. The Court in *Meritor Savings Bank* v. *Vinson* did not specifically define when this principle applies to hold an employer liable for sexual harassment at work. In general, however, schools are less likely to be liable if they have antidiscrimination policy that includes specific sexual harassment language and an accessible complaint procedure. For example, in a recent Washington case,[27] the court found that a school district was not liable for the alleged sexual or racial harassment of a woman custodian by her immediate male supervisor where the district responded to her complaint by conducting a prompt investigation but then reasonably concluded that the problem was due to personality differences between the two workers.

SCHOOL SPORTS

Must girls and boys have equal access to school sports?

This area of schooling has turned out to be both complex and controversial. Because no simple answer is appropriate to this question, a variety of questions must be explored.

Can girls try out for the boys' team in noncontact sports?

This question was raised in 1972 when Peggy Brenden was the top-ranked 18-year-old woman tennis player in her area of Minnesota. Because there was little interest in tennis among the girls at St. Cloud Technical High School, where Brenden was a senior, she wanted to play on the boys' team. The boys' team had a coach and a full schedule of interscholastic matches, neither of which was available for girls. Peggy was told that she could not try out for the boys' team because the Minnesota State High School League rules forbade girls' participation on boys' teams, and vice versa.

Brenden went to court, claiming that her right to equal protection and due process were violated. She requested an injunction against the enforcement of the rules that prevented her from interscholastic athletic participation.[28] The school contended that the rule was reasonable and that its aim was to achieve fair competition among all student athletes. They claimed that the basis for separating boys and girls in sport activities was because significant physiological differences exist between boys and girls and because the growth patterns of the two sexes are so different.

Was the separation of girls and boys in athletic activities arbitrary and therefore a violation of the girls' constitutional rights? The federal district court was guided by legal principles set forth by the U.S. Supreme Court: "A classification must be reasonable and not arbitrary, and must rest upon some ground of difference having a fair and substantial relation to the object of the legislation, so that all persons similarly circumstanced shall be treated alike."[29]

The Court recognized substantial physiological differences between boys and girls in muscle mass, size of the heart, and construction of the pelvic area, which "may, on the average, prevent the great majority of women from competing on an equal level with the great majority of males." Thus, these differences may form the basis for classifying by sex in athletic competition and thus separating boys and girls. Nevertheless, the statistical picture, though accurate for large populations, does not accurately portray all individuals. Peggy Brenden did not fit the statistical abstraction and had reached a high level of performance in her chosen sport. There was no evidence that she would in any way be damaged by competing in the boys' league, nor did any evidence suggest that boys would be harmed by her participation. (The school officials had also argued that separate sports programs were desirable to encourage more participation by all boys and girls.)

In sum, the court ruled that Brenden was prevented from playing interscholastic tennis "on the basis of the fact of sex and sex alone." The school offered no competitive athletic programs for girls. Therefore the court held that the rules as applied to Brenden were unreasonable, discriminatory, and thus unconstitutional and that she must be allowed to try out for the boys' team.

Other courts have also ruled that in noncontact sports such as golf, swimming, or cross-country skiing, where no teams exist for girls, they may compete for positions on boys' teams. Where competitive teams are available for both boys and girls, most courts were satisfied with the provision of separate teams, even though the quality of competition tends to be higher for the boys.[30]

How has Title IX affected school sports?

Congress made a significant impact on sex discrimination in schools by enacting Title IX of the Education Amendments of 1972.[31] This law provides that "no person in the United States shall on the basis of sex be excluded from participation, be denied the benefits of, or be subjected to discrimination under any education program or act or activity receiving Federal financial assistance." Title IX is relied upon in many situations to strike down discrimination against students based on sex because it is specifically aimed at such discrimination, whereas the clauses of the Fourteenth Amendment are much more general and abstract.

The regulations interpreting Title IX specifically allow separate teams for boys and girls in contact sports, such as football, basketball, and wrestling. They also require separate teams "in situations where the provision of only one team would not 'accommodate the interests and abilities of members of both sexes.'" But what about situations where one or two girls want to play a contact sport where only a boys' team exists?

Such a case arose in Yellow Springs, Ohio, where two girls tried out successfully for the boys' basketball team at the middle school level. However, the rules of the Ohio High School Athletic Association (OHSAA) prohibited coed teams in interscholastic contact sports, and basketball is defined as a contact sport. Since the OHSAA rules apply to middle schools and since virtually all secondary schools in Ohio belong to OHSAA and are governed by its rules, Yellow Springs filed suit to test whether the rules of the association violated federal law, specifically Title IX.[32]

The Sixth Circuit Court held that the rules of OHSAA were more restrictive than Title IX, so the schools need not follow these rules. Title IX *requires* schools to allow girls to try out for a boys' team if there is no girls' team in the same noncontact sport at that school. Even if there is a girls' team, explained the court, but it is not as strong as the boys', the girl is allowed to try out for the boys' team. And in contact sports Title IX does not specifically prohibit girls from trying out for the boys' team; it leaves that to the discretion of the school. Thus, the school may allow girls to try out for the boys' basketball team and OHSAA can neither prevent this, nor exclude the teams from the league for having a coed team. In short, Title IX takes precedence over league rules.

In a similar suit, action was brought by a 13-year-old female against the school district because of her exclusion from the junior high school football team. The school offered football for boys only and volleyball for girls only. While the evidence indicated that, in general, 13-year-old females have a higher potential for injury in mixed-sex football than 13-year-old males, there was no evidence offered to show that the plaintiff, Nicole Force, could not safely play junior high school football.

The court applied the intermediate test for equal protection and held that a school that would use a gender-based classification must have an "exceedingly persuasive justification" for its action. The rules of an interscholastic athletic association do not validate an otherwise unconstitutional act. While the goal of the school was to provide safe programs, the exclusion does not bear a substantial relationship to this goal. Schools do not exclude boys who are likely to be injured and thus the rule reflects historic "paternalistic" attitudes toward females. The court would uphold school policies or practices based on actual differences between the sexes, but not broad generalizations "which—while perhaps empirically supported as *generalizations*—do not hold true for all members of a sex."[33]

Some students chose to sue under the Constitution despite the availability of Title IX. Such was the case in Colorado, where the state athletic association forbade coeducational interscholastic contact sports. Hoover, a high school student, went to court when she was prevented from playing on the boys' soccer team.[34] The athletic association argued that the aim of the rule was physical safety: to prevent girls from being harmed. The court rejected this position as "patronizing protection to females" and said that "the failure to establish any physical criteria to protect small or weak males destroys the credibility of the reasoning urged in support of the sex classification." The court held that the rule was in violation of the equal protection clause in that it arbitrarily separated girls and boys by sex without regard to the wide range of individual variations within each group. Similarly, a Nebraska state association rule that broadly forbade girls from competing in wrestling fell in a Fourteenth Amendment challenge.[35]

Cases have even held that portions of Title IX are unconstitutional. For example, a district court ruled in an Ohio case that the Title IX regulations that allow for the separation of boys and girls in contact sports are unconstitutional. According to the court, governmental policies based on a presumption that girls are uniformly physically weaker or inferior to boys are arbitrary and thus violate due process.[36] This case seems to go further than others, for it strikes down distinctions between contact and noncontact sports.[37]

Can boys try out for the girls' team in noncontact sports?

In general they have no right to do so, although the law does not prohibit it. A reverse discrimination suit was brought by a group of boys in Arizona who wanted to try out for the girls' volleyball team. Their school sponsored only girls' volleyball teams and the Arizona Interscholastic Association (AIA) policy precluded boys from playing on girls' teams even though the converse was not the case. The issue before the court was whether or not the AIA policy violated the equal protection clause of the Fourteenth Amendment.

The equal protection clause is implicated when a classification treats persons similarly situated in different ways. When a gender-based classification occurs, the courts will ask whether such classification serves an important governmental objective and whether it is substantially related to the achievement of those objectives. The governmental objectives in this situation were the provisions of equal opportunities for males and females to participate in sports and to overcome the historic discrimination women suffered in this respect in the past. The court ruled the exclusion of boys was substantially related to these interests in light of the physiological differences between males and females as they relate to the skills involved in the sport of volleyball. It is generally recognized that males would have an undue advantage competing against females for positions on a volleyball team and thus, their participation would reduce rather than enhance equal opportunities for females. In the words of the court: "While equality in specific sports is a worthwhile ideal, it should not be purchased at the expense of ultimate equality of opportunity to participate in sports."[38]

What effect do state Equal Rights amendments have?

Although many states have added Equal Rights amendments (ERAs) to their constitutions, the legal meaning of such amendments is not yet clearly established. There is no uniformity among the states on just what the amendments mean for coeducational athletic competition, and it is probable that variations will persist from state to state because such state constitutional provisions are interpreted by the courts of the respective states and not by the U.S. Supreme Court.

Under a state ERA, a Washington case[39] ruled that girls are allowed to try out for the football team on an equal basis with boys. A Pennsylvania case[40] similarly ruled that under its state's ERA, boys and girls may try out for all school teams, including those in contact sports. Massachusetts also has an ERA and, consequently, when the Massachusetts legislature was considering enacting a law prohibiting girls from participating with boys in contact sports, the advice of the state supreme court was sought.[41] The Justices advised that such a law would be inconsistent with the state's ERA. However, they specifically declined to render an opinion whether such a law would be valid "if equal facilities were available for men and women in a particular sport which was available separately for each sex."

What options are available to victims of sex discrimination?

Students who believe that they are victims of sex discrimination may sue under the U.S. Constitution, Title IX, state ERAs, and other state laws. As a general rule, schools are under no obligation to provide interscholastic athletics. If they have such a program, however, it should be available on an equal basis for boys and girls. Some courts are satisfied with separate teams as long as similar coaching, support, and a competitive schedule are available for each sex. Others have ruled that all sports, even contact sports, must be equally available for boys and girls. Because state laws vary and state ERAs have been variously interpreted, when controversies arise, it is very important to check the applicable state law as well as the prior opinion of federal courts for the area.

Must schools provide equal funds for girls' and boys' sports?

Schools must fund sports for both sexes equitably, though exact mathematical equality is not necessary. Title IX forbids discrimination in financial support for sports in equipment and coaching. Fairness and equity are the guiding principles, for each sport activity has its unique needs and costs. If the sports are comparable, such as tennis teams for girls and boys, or swimming or golf teams for each sex, substantial equality is easier to determine. In dealing with high-cost and high-revenue sports, such as football or basketball, questions of equity and comparability become much more complex. Title IX regulations provide that, in determining whether there is equal opportunity in athletics, a number of factors are to be examined, including the physical facilities and assignment of coaches, and that unequal monetary expenditures alone do not constitute discrimination.[42]

Can some courses in the curriculum be restricted to boys only or to girls only?

In general, no. Girls and boys must have access to the full curriculum on an equal basis without the imposition of stereotypic views of what girls and boys ought to be. The historic exclusion of girls from shop courses and boys from cooking or home economics is no longer legal and laws such as the Carl D. Perkins Vocational Education Act[43] provide that schools should develop programs to eliminate sex bias and stereotyping in vocational education. Title IX, state laws, and local political pressures have erased any legal bases of such exclusions, though in some schools they are perpetuated through custom and informal pressures. Guidance counselors, teachers, parents, and others who advise students have important roles to play in this area, together with peer pressures that tend to be so important in secondary schools. While the law is clear in forbidding such restrictions, ingrained attitudes often perpetuate practices that force students into believing that some courses are for boys only and some for girls only. Nothing in the law prevents schools from separating boys and girls for instruction in highly sensitive areas, such as sex education.

Does Title IX prohibit sex discrimination in all aspects of a school's education program?

Title IX prohibits discrimination based on sex in connection with all education programs or activities at public or private schools which receive federal financial assistance. In *Grove City College* v. *Bell*,[44] the U.S. Supreme Court narrowed the application of the law when it held that Title IX only prohibited discrimination in the particular program being funded, and not discrimination in the entire institution. Congress reacted by voting to overturn the Court's decision by enacting the Civil Rights Restoration Act of 1987.[45] This act amended Title IX, as well as other civil rights acts, to provide that a "program or activity" means all of the operations of an educational institution. In other words, a school that receives federal support for its programs in departments A, B, and C may no longer discriminate on the basis of sex in departments D, E, and F.

SEPARATE SCHOOLS AND SEPARATE STANDARDS

Can public schools provide separate schools for boys and girls?

The answer depends on the facts of the particular situation. In Philadelphia, for example, the school system maintained separate high schools for academically talented boys and girls. When evidence showed that the separate schools were genuinely equal in terms of size, prestige, and academic quality, a federal court upheld the arrangement. School officials argued that there were educational merits of such separation during the years of early adolescence, and the court was reluctant to substitute its judgment of what is educationally sound for the judgment of educators. Applying the "rational basis" test, the court concluded that such an arrangement was reasonable.[46]

Could schools compel students to attend sex-segregated schools?

Probably not. The foregoing cases involved voluntary attendance at boys' and girls' schools and only by those who qualified on the basis of academic examination. In Hinds County, Mississippi, an entire school district was sex-segregated as part of a racial desegregation plan. A circuit court struck down this arrangement as a violation of the Equal Educational Opportunities Act of 1974.[47] Thus it seems that a limited, *voluntary* plan of sex-segregated schooling is acceptable whereas a *compulsory* one is not, particularly if it might be construed to be a vestige of historic patterns of racial segregation.

Can schools set different admission standards for boys and girls?

No. Such practices violate the equal protection clause of the Fourteenth Amendment. A case arose in Boston where girls had to score 133 or above on a standardized test to gain entrance into Girls Latin School, compared with a score of 120 or above for boys who wanted to enter Boys Latin School. Although the different scores were based on the different capacities of the two school buildings, the court struck down the arrangement as discriminatory.[48]

Admission policies or procedures based on sexual discrimination will be struck down if it is established that their intent is discriminatory. The First Circuit Court of Appeals so ruled in 1985 in a case that originated over ten years earlier when a young woman was denied admission to the Massachusetts Maritime Academy. According to testimony, when she applied for admission, the director of admissions told her that she would be admitted to the academy only if she went to Sweden to undergo a sex change operation. These comments, together with other evidence, clearly established that discriminatory intent underlay admission policies. The academy claimed exemption from Title IX because it has traditionally and continually from its establishment had a policy of admitting students of only one sex. Title IX grants exemption in such a case.

The court held that this exemption applied only to legal action brought under Title IX, but not to action brought pursuant to the Constitution as denial of equal protection or under other federal laws which prohibit gender discrimination.[49] Therefore the discriminatory admission policies of the academy were held to be unconstitutional.

Can schools set different standards for boys and girls when awarding scholarships?

No. In a 1989 case,[50] a federal court issued an injunction to prevent the state of New York from awarding merit scholarships solely on the basis of scores on the Scholastic Aptitude Test (SAT). A group of female high school seniors challenged this practice as discriminatory under Title IX based on the fact that females scored lower on the SAT than did males. In 1988, for example, they showed that males scored approximately 435 and 498 on the verbal and math sections respectively, while females scored 422 and 455. The court ruled, in a case of first impression, that the female students could prove discrimination under Title IX by showing disparate impact. Applying the traditional Title VII analysis of disparate impact, the court found that the plaintiffs had established a prima facie case of discrimination, and therefore shifted the burden to the state to establish a business necessity for its practice of relying solely on SAT scores. Determining that business necessity in the educational setting meant a "manifest relationship between the use of the SAT and the award of academic achievement in high school," the court held that the state had not met this burden. The court explained that the SAT was not designed to measure achievement and was never validated for that purpose. The court then ordered the state to discontinue use of the SAT and, instead, to use a combination of grades and SAT scores in selecting 1989 scholarship winners. Since the court did not rule that the SAT itself was biased, the case does not have immediate widespread impact. However, if this case leads to other challenges to validated uses of standardized tests, such as the SAT and LSAT, its impact would be very significant. For example, colleges and universities that use these tests in admissions would be likely targets for lawsuits alleging both sex and race discrimination.

Can school districts provide alternative separate schools for pregnant students?

Yes, they may, as long as the alternative is a genuine option that students may choose. Several cities have provided such alternatives where the curriculum also reflects the special needs of the pregnant students.

Can married students be required to attend adult school instead of regular day school?

No. Many school districts used to force married and/or pregnant students out of school by requiring them to choose between no schooling or adult or correspondence courses. The school districts stated reasons such as (1) the presence of pregnant students encourages immoral behavior among students, (2) their presence encourages early marriages, (3) their presence encourages "sex talk" in schools, and (4) pregnant students suffer psychological harm in school. In spite of these reasons, the courts protected the right of these students to continue attending regular schools.

Courts have not been impressed with the reasons stated above because no reliable evidence has been found to support them. In fact, psychological evidence shows that pregnant students suffer more by exclusion than from attendance in regular day school. Moreover, the courts have pointed out that where state laws make public education available up to a certain age, students have a right to attend even if they are married and/or pregnant.[51]

Can married students be excluded from extracurricular activities?

While earlier cases upheld such exclusions, the current trend of legal decisions is against them. Why did earlier cases uphold such restrictions against married students? The *Kissick* case gives the typical reasons used by schools and courts to reach such conclusions.

The *Kissick* Case[52]

The Garland Public School in Texas had a policy that barred "married students or previously married students . . . from participating in athletic or other exhibitions" and from holding "class offices or other positions of honor." When 16-year-old Jerry Kissick, Jr., a letterman in football, married a 15-year-old-girl, he received notice from the school barring him from further athletic participation, based on the school policy. Kissick, who planned to earn a college scholarship with his football prowess, filed suit claiming that the school policy was unreasonable and discriminatory and that it violated his Fourteenth Amendment rights to due process and equal protection. School officials argued that the policy was adopted in order to discourage "teen-age" marriages, which often lead to dropping out of school. They also indicated that Kissick's right to continue his academic work was untouched and that only his participation in football, an extracurricular activity, was denied.

The evidence showed overwhelming parental support for the school policy. There was a high rate of juvenile marriage at Garland School; many of the married students dropped out of school, and of those who remained, a high proportion experienced a drop in grades. A psychologist also testified in favor of the policy.

The court upheld the school policy and recognized the earlier dominant view that "Boards of Education, rather than Courts, are charged with the important and difficult duty of operating the public schools. . . . The Court's duty, regardless of its personal views, is to uphold the Board's regulation unless it is generally viewed as being arbitrary and unreasonable." In effect, the court accepted the distinction between academic and extracurricular activities and upheld the right of school officials to control access to the latter.

The trend of recent decisions is more accurately reflected in the *Davis* case in Ohio.[53] This case involved a similar policy: excluding married students from school-sponsored athletic and other extracurricular activities. When Davis challenged the policy in court, the policy was struck down. The court acknowledged the importance of extracurricular activities and considered exclusion from them to be a significant deprivation. The *Tinker* case was used by the judge to examine whether the school rule was necessary to maintain appropriate discipline or whether it was part of an "enclave of totalitarianism." Since Davis's marriage did not lead to any "material or substantial" interference with school discipline, the court ruled in his favor.

In sum, the current legal trend is to protect students' rights to participate in both curricular and extracurricular activities, whether the students remain single, get married, or become pregnant. Health and safety considerations may be used by school officials in making individual decisions, and officials may also act to prevent significant disruption of the schooling processes.

SUMMARY

Recent changes in public attitudes, together with important court rulings and new legislation, have led to significant reductions in sex discrimination in public schools. It is no longer legal to pay men more than women for the same work, though differences in pay are still acceptable if based on material differences in work load. Merit pay is proper if based on meritorious work but not if it is based on sexual differences.

Males may no longer be given preference over females in administrative positions or in other job assignments. Sex may still be considered a relevant factor in assignments where some duties call for particular sensitivities concerning boys or girls.

Courts have rejected the time-honored policies of schools that mandated maternity leave at the fifth month of pregnancy and did not allow the teacher to return to work for three months after delivery. Such policies were arbitrary and therefore violated the Fourteenth Amendment. Current school policies must allow the teacher and her physician to decide when to take the leave and when to return, or the policies must be based on the schools' needs for continuity of instruction. Arbitrary cutoff dates are illegal. Teachers may not be dismissed for getting married or for becoming pregnant; and for purposes of sick-leave pay, pregnancy leaves must be treated the same as disability leaves.

Sex discrimination and stereotyping in the school life of students have also been challenged in recent years. It is no longer legally acceptable to exclude girls or boys from parts of the curriculum, though in practice cultural pressures remain influential. Preferential treatment of boys in school athletics has spawned many lawsuits as well as new legislation. As a result, girls and boys must have equal access to noncontact sports, on separate teams if the schools provide them, and on integrated teams if only one team is available in the particular sport. Schedules, coaching, equipment, and other support must be comparable for girls' and boys' teams. Title IX and its regulations are the most important laws to achieve equal treatment of the sexes in public schools.

Several states have enacted Equal Rights amendments, which also must be considered in sex-related controversies in those particular states. There is no uniform interpretation of such amendments in the area of school sports. Some courts, for example, interpret state ERAs as mandating equal access even in contact sports, while courts in other states allow the separation of the sexes in such athletic activities.

Different admission standards for girls and boys to selective public schools are unconstitutional, but separate facilities are currently acceptable if they are genuinely equal. Married and/or pregnant students may not be excluded from school nor compelled to attend separate classes, separate schools, or evening classes. Similarly, courts now tend to protect the rights of such students to participate in extracurricular activities, though health and safety considerations may always be used to exclude an individual from a particular activity.

In general, though some vestiges of inequality and stereotyping remain as a function of tradition and habit, significant strides have been made in recent years toward the eradication of sex discrimination in the public schools.

NOTES

1. 29 U.S.C. § 1206.
2. 42 U.S.C. § 2000(e) et seq.
3. *Siegel v. Board of Education of City School Dist. of City of New York*, 713 F.Supp. 54 (E.D.N.Y. 1989).
4. 20 U.S.C. § 1681.
5. *EEOC v. Madison Community School Dist. No. 12*, 818 F.2d 577 (7th Cir., 1987).
6. *McCullar Human Rights Commission*, 158 Ill.App.3d 1011, 511 N.E.2d 1375 (1987).
7. *Erickson, et al. v. Board of Education, Proviso Township High School, District No. 209, Cook County, Illinois*, 458 N.E.2d 84 (Ill. App. 1983).

8. *Civil Rights Division* v. *Amphitheater Unified School Dist. No. 10*, 680 P.2d 517 (Ariz. App. 1983).
9. *International Brotherhood of Teamsters* v. *U.S.*, 431 U.S. 324, 335, n. 15 (1977).
10. *McDonnell Douglas Corporation* v. *Green*, 411 U.S. 792 (1973).
11. *Ward's Cove Packing Company, Inc.* v. *Antonio*, 109 S.Ct. 2115 (1989).
12. *Tye* v. *Houston County Board of Education*, 681 F.Supp. 740 (M.D. Ala. 1987).
13. *Stone* v. *Belgrade School District No. 44*, 703 P.2d 136 (Mont. 1984).
14. *King* v. *Palmer*, No. 184-5750, CA-DC (December 3, 1985).
15. *Gargiul* v. *Tompkins*, 704 F.2d 661 (2d Cir. 1983), *aff'g dismissal of claim for suspension pay*, 790 F.2d 265 (2d Cir. 1986).
16. *Cleveland Board of Education* v. *LaFleur; Cohen* v. *Chesterfield County School Board*, 414 U.S. 632 (1974).
17. *Ponton* v. *Newport News School Board*, 632 F.Supp. 1056 (E.D. Va. 1986).
18. *Dallastown Area School District* v. *Com. Pennsylvania Human Relations Commission*, 460 A.2d 878 (Pa. Cmwlth. 1983).
19. 42 U.S.C. § 2000e(k); *United Teachers—Los Angeles* v. *Board of Education of City of Los Angeles*, 712 F.2d 1349 (9th Cir. 1983).
20. *California Federal Savings and Loan Association* v. *Guerra*, 479 U.S. 272 (1987).
21. *Pastor* v. *San Juan School District No. 1*, 699 P.2d 418 (Colo. App. 1985).
22. *Jericho Union Free School District* v. *New York Human Rights Appeal Board*, 468 N.Y.S.2d 393 (A.D. 2 Dept. 1983).
23. *Dayton Christian Schools, Inc.* v. *Ohio Civil Rights Commission*, 766 F.2d 932 (6th Cir. 1985).
24. 29 C.F.R. § 1604.11.
25. 477 U.S. 57 (1986).
26. See *Keppler* v. *Hinsdale Township High School Dist. 86*, 715 F.Supp. 862 (N.D. Ill. 1989).
27. *Fisher* v. *Tacoma School Dist. No. 10*, 53 Wash.App. 591, 769 P.2d 318 (1989).
28. *Brenden* v. *Independent School District 742*, 342 F.Supp. 1224 (D. Minn. 1972), *aff'd*, 477 F.2d 1292 (8th Cir. 1973).
29. *Reed* v. *Reed*, 404 U.S. 71 (1971).
30. See, for example, *Bucha* v. *Illinois High School Association*, 351 F.Supp. 69 (N.D. Ill. 1972); *O'Connor* v. *Board of Education*, 645 F.2d 578 (7th Cir. 1981), *cert. denied*, 454 U.S. 1084 (1981), *on remand*, 545 F.Supp. 376 (1981).
31. 20 U.S.C. § 1681.
32. *Yellow Springs, etc.* v. *Ohio High School Athletic Association*, 647 F.2d 651 (6th Cir. 1981).
33. *Force* v. *Pierce City R-VI School District*, 570 F.Supp. 1020 (W.D. Mo. 1983).
34. *Hoover* v. *Meiklejohn*, 430 F.Supp. 164 (D. Colo. 1977).
35. *Stephani* v. *Nebraska School Activities Association*, 684 F.Supp. 626 (D. Neb. 1988).
36. *Yellow Springs Exempted Village School District Board of Education* v. *Ohio High School Athletic Association*, 443 F.Supp. 753 (S.D. Ohio 1978).
37. *Id.*
38. *Clark, etc.* v. *Arizona Interscholastic Association*, 695 F.2d 1126 (9th Cir. 1982).
39. *Darrin* v. *Gould*, 85 Wash.2d 859, 54 P.2d 882 (1975).
40. *Commonwealth of Pennsylvania, Packel* v. *Pennsylvania Interscholastic Athletic Association*, 334 A.2d 839 (Commw. Ct. 1975).

41. *Opinion of the Justices Re House Bill No. 6723*, Mass. Adv. Sh. 2728, Massachusetts Supreme Judicial Court (December 22, 1977).

42. 34 C.F.R. § 106.41.

43. 20 U.S.C. § 2301.

44. 465 U.S. 555 (1984).

45. 20 U.S.C. § 1681.

46. *Vorchheimer* v. *School District*, 532 F.2d 880 (3d Cir. 1976), *aff'd*, 430 U.S. 703 (1977).

47. *U.S.* v. *Hinds County*, 560 F.2d 619 (5th Cir. 1977).

48. *Bray* v. *Lee*, 377 F.Supp. 934 (D. Mass. 1972).

49. *U.S.* v. *Massachusetts Maritime Academy*, 762 F.2d 142 (1st Cir. 1985); *see also, Mississippi University for Women* v. *Hogan*, 458 U.S. 718 (1982).

50. *Sharif* v. *New York State Education Department*, 709 F.Supp. 345 (S.D.N.Y. 1989).

51. *Alvin Independent School District* v. *Cooper*, 404 S.W.2d 76 (Tex. 1966).

52. *Kissick* v. *Garland Independent School District*, 330 S.W.2d 708 (Tex. 1959).

53. *Davis* v. *Meek*, 344 F.Supp. 298 (N.D. Ohio 1972).

CHAPTER 15

Are There Special Rights
for Handicapped and
Non-English-Speaking Students?

OVERVIEW

In recent years, much public attention has focused on exceptional children and on children with limited English-speaking ability. Perceived inequalities in their education have been challenged in courts and debated by legislative bodies. As a result of court cases, legislation, and political activism, significant gains toward the achievement of equal educational opportunities have been registered by these groups. This chapter examines the major developments in each of these areas, first as they relate to students with special needs and then the emerging law related to bilingual-bicultural education.

Until recently, the compulsory education laws of most states made exceptions for children who were retarded, emotionally disturbed, deaf, blind, or otherwise handicapped. For various reasons, most of them based on ignorance, prejudice, or finance, many parents kept these children out of school with the consent of local school officials and the sanction of state laws. When handicapped children attended school, it was all too often in an aura of charity for which they and their parents were to be grateful.

Recent developments have brought substantial changes in attitudes toward the handicapped and in laws related to their schooling. These changes are based in part on scientific evidence that has reliably established that all humans can learn and benefit from appropriate education and training. The changes are also due to the civil rights movements of the 1950s and 1960s, which reverberated throughout the American culture and stimulated the handicapped to make their claims on the basis of right and not of charity.

Historically, the language in all public schools has been English. Children who spoke little or no English had no choice in the language of instruction and, typically, no special help to acquire the language. It was generally assumed that such children would pick up English through their daily interaction in and out of school, as well as through the efforts of kind-hearted teachers. Americanization, as expressed in the "melting pot" ideal, relied on English as the common language necessary for survival and success in school and in the worlds of commerce and industry.

Indeed, for millions of children, sons and daughters of immigrants and first-generation Americans, schools became important places for language acquisition and an important step up the mythical ladder of success in the new world. For countless others, however, schools were unfriendly places conducted in a strange tongue where too many teachers had little sympathy for non-English-speaking students. These students left school early and, by and large, became industrial workers and unskilled laborers in various segments of our economy. As immigration continued and "the melting pot refused to melt," serious questions began to surface about the rights of minorities whose mother tongue was other than English. They too had their consciousness raised by the civil rights movements in the latter half of the century, and they began to organize and assert their rights and those of their school-age children.

EDUCATING THE HANDICAPPED

Are the rights of handicapped children based on the Constitution, federal legislation, or both?

On both. Earlier challenges to excluding and misclassifying handicapped children were based on the Constitution. These challenges (discussed below) helped raise public consciousness about the issue to the point where state and federal laws were enacted to ensure the schooling rights of *all* children. It is interesting to realize that a landmark case in school desegregation, the *Brown* case, was heavily relied upon to establish the right to education of all children and bring the federal government into an important role in public education. A key paragraph of *Brown*, often used by advocates of the rights of handicapped children, recognizes the pervasive influence and importance of education in contemporary American life.

> Today, education is perhaps the most important function of state and local governments. Compulsory school attendance laws and the great expenditures for education both demonstrate our recognition of the importance of education to our democratic society. It is required in the performance of our most basic public responsibilities, even service in the armed forces. It is the very foundation of good citizenship. Today it is a principal instrument in awakening the child to cultural values, in preparing him for later professional training, and in

helping him to adjust normally to his environment. In these days, it is doubt-ful that any child may reasonably be expected to succeed in life if he is denied the opportunity of an education. Such an opportunity, where the state has undertaken to provide it, is a right which must be made available to all on equal terms.[1]

What key constitutional provisions are related to the rights of handicapped children?

Historically, two kinds of practices worked to the educational disadvantage of handicapped children: exclusion from school and misclassification. *Exclusion* occurs when a school-age child is denied access to schooling or is provided grossly inappropriate education. The phrase "functional exclusion" is also used to describe grossly inappropriate placement, as exemplified by the placement of retarded children in regular classes with no special assistance for the children or the teacher, or the placement of non-English-speaking children in an English-speaking school program without special assistance. *Misclassification* occurs when a child is erroneously assessed, placed, or tracked in a school program. Both exclusion and misclassification have been attacked on constitutional grounds.

The *PARC* Case[2]

In 1971 the laws of Pennsylvania, like those of many other states, kept children out of public schools if they were certified by psychologists as "uneducable and untrainable." In that year a lawsuit was filed on behalf of 17 children by their parents and by the Pennsylvania Association for Retarded Children (PARC), requesting that the state law and practices based on it be declared violations of the equal protection and due process clauses of the Constitution. They claimed that the laws (1) violated due process by not giving parents a notice and a hearing, (2) denied equal protection by assuming certain children to be uneduca-ble without a rational basis in fact, and (3) guaranteed education for all chil-dren, but arbitrarily and capriciously excluded retarded children.

When the federal district court ruled that retarded children may not be excluded from public schools, the contending parties worked out an agreement. The Consent Agreement, approved by the court, acquired the force of law, binding on both parties. The decision became a landmark (together with the *Mills* case, which follows), for it gave retarded children in the state access to public schools as well as tuition and maintenance costs at qualified institutions (or home instruction where that was appropriate). In addition, careful and elabo-rate due process is provided before any child may be placed in special classes or before any change in such placement may be made.

PARC incorporated into the law the conviction of knowledgeable profes-sionals regarding the educability of retarded children. Expert testimony indicated that all mentally retarded persons are capable of benefiting from a program of education and training; that the greatest number of retarded persons, given such education and training, are capable of achieving self-sufficiency, and the remaining few, with education and training, are capable of achieving some degree of self-care; and that the earlier education and training begins, the more thoroughly and the more efficiently a mentally retarded person can benefit.

The court recognized the danger of misclassification and mislabeling; labeling a child "retarded" and placing him in a class for the retarded creates a handicap and a stigma. The parties to the suit agreed that mild cases of retardation can be integrated with normal children, or "mainstreamed," but that most retarded students need special classes taught by qualified teachers. It was also agreed that homebound instruction was the least desirable alternative; when it was used as a last resort, qualified teachers must be involved. Such arrangements must be reevaluated every three months, with proper notice to the parent or guardian, who may request a hearing on the case.

The *Mills* Case[3]

Mills was filed in Washington, D.C., and challenged exclusion and misclassification practices related not only to retarded children but to all handicapped children. This case also challenged the practice of suspending and expelling from school children the schools did not want to serve.

The court found that of the approximately 22,000 handicapped children in the D.C. school district, close to 18,000 were "not being furnished with programs of specialized education." They were either excluded completely, or inappropriately placed. In the words of the court:

> The defendants' conduct here, denying plaintiffs and their class not just an equal publicly supported education but all publicly supported education while providing such education to other children, is a violation of the Due Process Clause.
>
> Not only are plaintiffs and their class denied the publicly supported education, to which they are entitled, many are suspended or expelled from regular schooling or specialized instruction or reassigned without any prior hearing and are given no periodic review thereafter. Due process of law requires a hearing prior to exclusion.

School officials argued that not enough funds were available for the appropriate schooling of all children and that handicapped children were particularly expensive to educate. The court did not accept their argument. If funds are inadequate, ruled the court, they must nevertheless be used equally for all children and in particular, no child should be completely excluded. As the court said: "The inadequacies of the District of Columbia Public School System, whether occasioned by insufficient funding or administrative inefficiency, certainly cannot be permitted to bear more heavily on the 'exceptional' or handicapped child than on the normal child."

The *PARC* and *Mills* cases established the constitutional basis to attack the exclusion from schooling and misclassification of handicapped children. They paved the way for the conviction that the equal protection and due process clauses protect the right of such children to access to public schools and free and appropriate education. They also opened the way for major federal legislation, setting nationwide standards for the education of handicapped children and served as the "blue print" for Public Law 94-142, discussed below.

What major federal laws establish the rights of handicapped children?

The most important federal laws related to the rights of handicapped students are Public Law 94-142, the Education of All Handicapped Children Act, enacted in 1975;[4] and section 504, the Rehabilitation Act of 1973.[5] These two federal laws overshadow all other federal legislation related to educating the handicapped. P.L. 94-142 makes certain federal funds available to schools that comply with its requirements. Section 504 would cut off *any and all* federal funds from schools that discriminate against the handicapped. Thus, the two laws have the same objectives, but section 504 applies a broader sanction, namely the cutting off of funds, whereas P.L. 94-142 would only withhold funds under its allocation formula.

Public Law 94-142

When Congress enacted the Education of All Handicapped Children Act in 1975, it found that there were more than 8 million handicapped children in the country and that over half of them were not receiving an appropriate education. Furthermore, approximately 1 million were completely excluded from the public schools. In the preamble, in addition to recognizing these disturbing facts, Congress stated that the main purpose of the act was to assure that states provide all handicapped children with "a free appropriate public education and related services designed to meet their unique needs." While Congress recognized that education remains a state responsibility, it also acknowledged that federal assistance was necessary "to assure equal protection of the law."

The law specified that all handicapped children between the ages of 3 and 18 must have "free appropriate public education" by September 1, 1978; all such children between the ages of 3 and 21 must be accommodated by September 1, 1980. Since schooling is basically a state responsibility, however, P.L. 94-142 applies only to the ages covered by state laws. For example, if state law exempts children from ages 3 to 5 or from 18 to 21, the federal law cannot extend to those age groups. A 1986 amendment to the act, Public Law 99-457, extended the mandate downward, to include infants and toddlers. This new directive emphasizes minimizing (1) developmental delays seen in very young children, (2) the cost of education when they reach school age, and (3) the likelihood of institutionalization.

Who are the handicapped?

Federal regulations define "handicapped children" to include those who are mentally retarded, hard of hearing, deaf, speech impaired, visually handicapped, seriously emotionally disturbed, orthopedically impaired, other health impaired, deaf-blind, multihandicapped, or with specific learning disabilities and who, because of these impairments, need special education and related services. Regulations published in 1977 further define each of these terms.

Can schools require parents to pay for the cost of educating handicapped children?

No. The law specifies that such education must be free. Since special education in public or private schools is often expensive, school officials have tried various ways to shift all or part of the cost on to the parents. Courts, however, have consistently held that public schools have the obligation to provide appropriate education, including testing, guidance, and other special and support services, at no cost to the parents. This principle holds whether the schooling is provided in public or private facilities. The only exception occurs when appropriate free public facilities are available for a particular child, but the parents choose a private facility instead. In that case, they must bear the cost of the private education. There are also disagreements among public agencies about who should bear what costs with certain kinds of handicapped children.

What is the legal meaning of "appropriate" education?

P.L. 94-142 and its regulations conceive of an "appropriate" education as one designed specifically to meet the unique needs of the particular handicapped child. Thus an individual educational program or plan (IEP) must be drawn up for each child under the law, and such plan is to be carried out in an appropriate educational setting.

It is not enough to provide "equal" access, in the sense of identical schooling for handicapped and nonhandicapped children. Without special provisions and support services, handicapped students might not gain anything from instruction, even though they are physically exposed to the same experiences as the other children. Such treatment is referred to as "functional exclusion" by courts and lawyers. One important case considered functional exclusion as similar to the placement of non-English-speaking students in ordinary classrooms without support services. They "are certain to find their classroom experiences wholly incomprehensible and in no way meaningful."[6] In *Fialkowski,* children with the mental abilities of preschoolers were placed in a program that emphasized reading and writing skills way beyond their abilities. This was held to be inappropriate placement and does not satisfy the law.

The requirements of appropriateness and the IEP are best considered as complementary notions. The IEP is a tailor-made plan that follows careful assessment and evaluation of a particular student's abilities and disabilities. Curricular plans and instructional approaches are based on such evaluation, and periodic assessments follow to ascertain progress and the continuing appropriateness of the plan. The education provided must be comparable to that offered the nonhandicapped, the procedural safeguards are provided in order to keep parents informed and to solicit their participation in the appropriate placement of their children. Moreover, when state laws set higher standards for the education of exceptional children than those required by the Education of the Handicapped Act (EHA),* the higher standards must be followed. Various courts have so ruled, including cases in New Jersey[7] and Massachusetts.[8]

The *Rowley* Case

In 1982 the Supreme Court interpreted the phrase "free appropriate public education" guaranteed under the EHA. *Rowley* involved a hearing-impaired first-grade student "mainstreamed" in a regular first-grade classroom. She was assisted by a hearing aid and her IEP included a speech therapist for three hours each week and a special tutor one hour a day. Her parents argued that under the law Amy Rowley was entitled to the services of a qualified sign-language interpreter in order to gain the maximum from her school experiences. School authorities pointed to Amy's successful progress, citing that she was performing "better than the average child in her classes," and, after repeated consultation, denied the request.

When Amy's parents sued, the lower courts ruled in their favor, interpreting the law to require services to maximize each child's potential. However, on the final appeal, the Supreme Court disagreed. The Court noted that Amy was progressing satisfactorily and was receiving "personalized instruction and related services." Since all procedural requirements of the law were followed, and since Amy's education was "adequate," the Court held that the EHA was not violated.[9]

It is perfectly acceptable for states or local communities to provide for more services than those specified by federal law, as long as they do not provide less. It appears to be the case, at this time, that the federal law requires only that the IEP enable the particular student to *benefit* from schooling, and that the procedural requirements of EHA be carefully observed.

What are the "related services" required by the EHA?

The *Rowley* case relied to a large extent on the EHA requirement that schools provide "related services" needed for the appropriate education of handicapped children. The definition of related services in the act is "transportation, and

---

* The law was originally called the Education for All Handicapped Children Act (EAHCA).

such developmental, corrective, and other support services (including speech pathology and audiology, psychological services, physical and occupational therapy, recreation, and medical and counseling services, except that such medical services shall be for diagnostic and evaluative purposes only) as may be required to assist the handicapped child to benefit from special education, and includes the early identification and assessment of handicapping conditions in children."[10]

Because of the ambiguity of phrases such as "medical services" and because of the high cost of some services required to educate certain types of handicapped students, there has been an inordinate number of cases litigated under the EHA and under section 504 of the Rehabilitation Act of 1973. To cite an extreme example, a federal appeals court in 1984 granted a seriously emotionally disturbed student an educational placement under the EHA that costs $88,000 per year, in preference to the school board's choice of placement that costs $55,000 per year.[11] To put this in perspective, the national average expenditure per student was approximately $3000 during the same year. The question of what "related services" schools must provide was central in the case of Amber Tatro, an eight-year-old girl.

The *Tatro* Case

Amber Tatro, born with spina bifida, suffered from orthopedic and speech impairments and a bladder condition which prevented her from emptying her bladder voluntarily. She had to be catheterized every three to four hours to avoid injury to her kidneys. Is such periodic catheterization during school hours a "related service" or an excluded medical service? The school district drew up an IEP that was quite comprehensive except that it made no provision for school personnel to administer the "clean intermittent catheterization" (CIC) in accordance with accepted medical practice. CIC is a simple procedure that can be learned in about an hour and requires about five minutes to administer.

While the district court initially held that CIC was not a related service arising from the need to educate, the appeals court and then the Supreme Court ruled otherwise.[12] They held that CIC is a related service because it makes it possible for the handicapped child to remain in school during the day without which she cannot be educated. It is not significantly different from dispensing necessary medicine or administering emergency injections pursuant to medical authorization, which are also related services. It is highly probable that litigation will continue to arise concerning the meaning of "related services" and especially concerning the distinction between medical services that are excluded and school health services that are to be provided.

A federal court in New Jersey, for example, held in 1983 that psychotherapy might be a related service within the context of the EHA. This ruling was upheld on appeal where the court noted that, since Congress under the EHA specifically authorized psychological and counseling services, it must have intended to provide psychotherapy as well, particularly if they are the kinds of services that could be performed by qualified social workers, psychologists, or counselors.[13] There is doubt about the inclusion of psychotherapy that could be provided only by a psychiatrist, whose services might be categorized as medical services.

Extensive in-school nursing services are not likely to be considered a related service under the EHA. A Pennsylvania court so held in the case of a seven-year-old child named Bevin, whose severe, multiple handicaps required constant care by a specially trained nurse.[14] Bevin had fetal face syndrome, was profoundly mentally handicapped, suffered from spastic quadriplegia and a seizure disorder, and was legally blind. She was fed and given medicine through a gastrostomy tube and breathed through a tracheostomy tube. Without a doubt, the services of a trained nurse were necessary to enable her to be in school, in a classroom with six handicapped students, one teacher, and two aides. Nursing services cost $1,850 a month in 1984–85, excluding close to $1,000 additional monthly expenses for Bevin outside school. The court concluded that neither the EHA, its regulations, nor case law would include such extensive and expensive nursing care under related services.

A recent case further raised questions about the state's responsibility under the EHA to educate children so severely and profoundly handicapped as to raise doubts about their educability even at minimal levels.

The *Timothy W.* Case

In the case of *Timothy W.*, the Federal district court for the District of New Hampshire held that the school district was not required by law to provide special education for Timothy because the child "was not capable of benefiting from special education." The Court of Appeals, however, reversed this decision.[15]

Timothy, born two months prematurely, suffered from a variety of serious problems from the time of his birth. As a result, he is multiply handicapped and severely mentally retarded, to the point that some pediatricians testified that he "had no educational potential" and that parts of his brain were destroyed. The district court, ruling against special education for Timothy, held that "under New Hampshire law, an initial decision must be made concerning the ability of a handicapped child to benefit from special education before an entitlement to the education can exist." The appeals court, however, rejected the criterion of "ability to benefit," and ruled that the wording of the EHA is clear concerning zero reject, that is, *all* handicapped children are entitled to a free appropriate education. Furthermore, noted the court, Congress made its intent clear "that the most severely handicapped be given priority" under the act.

The case of *Timothy W.* was so extreme that it elicited comments, pro and con, from a variety of sources. There are those who claim that public school funds, particularly in times of limited resources, ought not to be used for children like Timothy, particularly since public schools lack the professional expertise to provide for such needs. Even those quite sympathetic to the needs of Timothy and his parents urge closer cooperation among relevant social

service agencies and the schools, so that schools will not be exclusively responsible for services beyond their competence and their resources. It is likely that
further litigation will clarify schools' responsibilities in this complex area of
"related services" and there are also political moves afoot to address the implicit policy questions through legislation.

What are the due process rights of parents and children under P.L. 94-142?

It was clear to Congress that in the past, parents were all too often left out of
educational decisions that were crucial in the lives of their handicapped children. The current law has changed that and requires at least the following:

1. Prior written notice must be given a reasonable time before any proposed change in the child's educational program, together with a written
   explanation of the procedures to be followed in effecting the change.
2. All notices must be written in "language understandable to the general
   public" and in the primary language of the parents. If the parents
   cannot read, the notices must be interpreted to them orally or by other
   means.
3. The testing of children must be nondiscriminatory in language, race, or
   culture.
4. There is a right to independent testing and evaluation, free or at low
   cost.
5. Parents must have access to the records relevant to the case and the
   right to have the records explained, to make copies, and to amend
   records parents consider to be inaccurate, misleading, or an invasion of
   privacy; and the right to a hearing on the issue if the school refuses to
   amend the records.
6. Opportunity for a fair and impartial hearing must be conducted by the
   State Educational Agency (SEA) or local school district, *not* by the
   employee "involved in the education or care of the child." At any
   hearing, parents have the right to be represented by a lawyer or an
   individual trained in the problems of handicapped children; the right to
   present evidence and to subpoena, confront, and cross-examine witnesses; and the right to obtain a transcript of the hearing and a written
   decision by the hearing officer. Parents may appeal the decision to the
   SEA and, if they are still not satisfied, may appeal the SEA ruling in
   court.
7. The student has a right to remain in current placement until the due
   process proceedings are completed. A child who is just beginning school
   may be enrolled until the proceedings determining proper placement are
   completed.
8. A "surrogate parent" will be appointed for children who are wards of
   the state or whose parents or guardians are unknown or unavailable.

9. The child's records are confidential. Parents and the student may restrict access to the records; they have a right to be informed before any information in the file is destroyed and a right to be told to whom information has been disclosed.

While further details are given in regulations interpreting the law, the foregoing list presents the main procedural safeguards.

A case involving a high school student in Danbury, Connecticut, illustrates the powerful due process protection afforded special-needs students by P.L. 94-142. School records indicated that Kathy Stuart had a variety of academic deficiencies as a consequence of a combination of learning disabilities and limited intelligence. When, as punishment for disruptive behavior, the school wanted to expel her, she went to court. The federal district court believed that she was exactly the type of student intended to be protected by the federal law. While it interpreted the law and its regulations to allow short-term suspensions or new placements of disruptive handicapped students after following due process, it prohibited their expulsion. As the court stated: "The expulsion of handicapped children not only jeopardizes their right to an education in the least restrictive environment, but is inconsistent with the procedures established by the Handicapped Act for changing the placement of disruptive children."[16]

Can handicapped students be suspended or expelled from school?

Yes, they can be, but under the law some alternative educational placement must be found for the handicapped student expelled from school. Such students may be subject to discipline like any other students *if* their misbehavior is not a result of their handicapping condition and if mandated procedures are followed.[17] Long-term suspension or expulsion, however, is considered to be a change in educational placement and is allowed only after following procedures specified by law.[18] As a last resort, the student would have a right to continue his education by being taught at home, or in some appropriate but more restrictive institution.

Can handicapped students whose behavior is dangerous be given long-term suspensions?

No, they cannot, ruled the Supreme Court in the 1988 case of *Honig* v. *Doe*.[19] Doe, a 17-year-old special education student whose IEP explicitly recognized a propensity for aggressive acts, acted in an explosive manner when taunted by a fellow student. He "choked the student with sufficient force to leave abrasions" on the neck, and "kicked out a school window" while being escorted to the principal's office afterward. When the school system proceeded with a summary long-term suspension, suit was filed on behalf of Doe. The issue before the court was whether or not the EHA implicitly contained a "dangerousness exception" to the "stay-put" provision. In the final analysis the Court ruled that there is no such exception explicit or implicit in the EHA. In fact, the "stay-put" provision was intended to remove the unilateral authority school officials traditionally exercised to exclude disabled students, "particularly emotionally disabled students from school." School officials, however, are not left hamstrung. If a student is dangerous to self or others, he may be temporarily suspended for up to 10 school days. During this "cooling down" period officials can initiate review of the IEP and work with the parents to agree on an interim placement. If the parents "of a truly dangerous child adamantly refuse to permit any change in placement, the 10-day respite gives school officials an opportunity to involve the aid of the courts," to approve a new placement.

Thus, the Court ruled that there is no "dangerousness exception" to the "stay-put" rule, but there are ways, consistent with the EHA's due process provisions, to deal with disruptive or even dangerous students, to protect their rights while also protecting an orderly learning environment in our schools.

What is the least restrictive educational alternative?

Historically, handicapped children tended to be segregated from the nonhandicapped. Various reasons were advanced for such isolation, but, in recent years, these reasons have been challenged and in most instances rejected. Current law requires that handicapped students be educated in "the least restrictive alternative" program. In brief, this means that the handicapped child should be educated in a setting that deviates least from the regular nonhandicapped program yet is appropriate for the particular child.

Courts have recognized that various educational arrangements, or "treatments," have been "restrictive" in the legal sense. For example, segregation of the handicapped that further handicaps or stigmatizes them is restrictive in the eyes of the law. So is the use of medication for many children. If a child's ability to learn is aided through medication, that use might be justifiable; if the chemical treatment merely restrains a child for the convenience of the staff, that use is "restrictive."

Mattie T. v. *Holliday* capsulizes the provisions of the federal law regarding "the least restrictive alternative" educational placement of a child: "The Bureau of Education for the Handicapped Guidelines establish, inter alia, two important steps to be taken by school districts . . . : (1) 'a variety of program alternatives (e.g., continuum of education services) must be available in every L.E.A. [local educational agency] to meet the varying needs of handicapped children' and (2) an individual determination of the appropriate program alternatives must be made for each child in conformance with the procedures for nondiscriminatory evaluations."[20]

The principle of least restrictive alternative educational placement is what is popularly referred to as "mainstreaming." The law does not require that each child be mainstreamed, that is, fully integrated with nonhandicapped students. Such placement is appropriate for some children; others might benefit more by spending part of the day mainstreamed and part of the day in special classes with specially prepared teachers. Students who cannot handle either arrangement may have to be in special classes all day, which is preferable to separate special schools. Finally, such schools are preferable to home schooling, although home schooling is better than no schooling at all. This principle was confirmed in a 1988 case involving two hearing-impaired students, where the acquisition of oral language skills outweighed benefits to be acquired from mainstreaming.[21]

Is private schooling an alternative available under the law?

Yes, it is, if no appropriate public facilities are available that can effectively meet the needs of the particular student. Public funds must be used to pay for the child's education including room and board and transportation, where necessary, and there should be no extra costs to the parents. Parents must be careful, however, not to make a unilateral decision to place their children in a private school and hope to recover the costs from the local school district. They should follow the procedures specified in the EHA. If they acted unilaterally, they will not recover their costs, except in two types of situations: (1) if the court finds that had they selected otherwise, the child's physical health would have been endangered, and (2) when educational officials "acted in bad faith" by denying them the procedures guaranteed by the EHA.[22]

The law gives courts discretion in this matter, and the Supreme Court ruled in 1985 that parents may be reimbursed even if they chose to place their children unilaterally in disagreement with public officials, if such placement is deemed to be the proper one through appeal procedures specified by the law. Without this possibility, reasoned the Court, the child of poor parents might have to spend years in an inappropriate educational placement awaiting the outcome of the case. However, the parent takes a risk of not being reimbursed when the child is unilaterally moved to a private school.[23]

What if the parents and the school disagree concerning the placement of the child?

The law is clear that such disagreements must be resolved through a fair procedure: "Disagreements between a parent and a public agency regarding the availability of a program appropriate for the child, and the question of financial responsibility, are subject to the due process procedure."[24] Under federal law, local schools also have the obligation to locate all children who might fit the criteria, specified by law, to receive services provided the handicapped. Though some schools have urged that this obligation is properly placed on parents, courts have rejected this view. Courts have held that parents are not always in the best position to recognize that their children are not functioning well academically or that special support services are available to help with a particular handicap. Parents may or may not be aware of due process provisions provided by law, nor have the expert advice available to schools. Therefore, particularly with respect to children already in school, the duty rests with the provider of services to identify children in need of special services. Efforts are under way in several states to extend to regular students similar rights to "appropriate educational programs" currently available to the handicapped. For example, the Wisconsin legislature enacted laws in 1980 which give students and their parents a wide range of choices if they are dissatisfied with their assignment in public schools. (Reported in *NOLPE Notes*, October 1980, pp. 3–4.)

Educators' discretion is respected by courts as was illustrated in a case where school officials changed a handicapped student's placement because they considered his psychosexual disorder and overt sexual behavior disruptive of the educational process and dangerous to the physical and emotional health of other students. On behalf of the student it was argued that his placement could not be changed until after he exhausted all administrative and judicial appeals. The federal courts ruled, however, that school officials have the discretion to change the placement when there is clear evidence that the student endangers himself or others or threatens to disrupt a safe school environment.[25]

Can handicapped children ever be excluded from a school activity?

Yes, they can, if the school has substantial justification for the exclusion. Cases have arisen when students who were wholly or partially blind in one eye were not allowed to participate in contact sports. The schools excluded them from participation because of the risk of injury to their sighted eye. Courts would not overturn the educators' decision because school officials had a reasonable basis to act as they did. To win such a case, students would either have to show that school officials had no reasonable grounds for their action or that the students would suffer irreparable harm by not having an opportunity to participate in the contact sport.[26]

Similarly, the U.S. Supreme Court upheld the exclusion of a severely hearing-impaired student from a nursing program to which she applied. The student sued under section 504, which prohibits discrimination against "otherwise qualified handicapped" individuals. The Court found that the student was not "otherwise qualified" for "otherwise qualified [means] otherwise able to function sufficiently in the position sought in spite of the handicap, if proper training and facilities are suitable and available." However, the Court said that section 504 does not "compel the college to undertake affirmative action that would dispense with the need for effective oral communication in the college's nursing program."[27]

Thus it is clear that the handicapped can be excluded from some school activities or programs, but only if sound educational grounds exist for such exclusion. Such grounds might relate to health and safety considerations or to requirements inherent in the program that the handicapped person cannot meet without support services.

What does the law require for program "accessibility"?

For some years now, concerns have been expressed about the difficulties that certain handicapped persons have experienced in gaining physical access to buildings. The Architectural Barriers Act, which became law in 1968, addressed some of these issues and incorporated certain standards to be applied in buildings "designed, constructed, or altered" after the effective date of the law. A 1976 amendment to this act extended its application, but the most fundamental regulation of program accessibility is derived from section 504, which provides that no qualified handicapped person, "because facilities are inaccessible to or unusable by handicapped persons," shall be denied benefits, be excluded from participation, or otherwise be subjected to discrimination.

Under this law, schools and all other programs receiving federal assistance must make facilities and programs accessible through the use of ramps, sufficiently wide doors, elevators, accessible lavatory facilities, interpreters, support services, and other modifications of existing facilities and programs that might be necessary. This does not mean that every *building* on a campus must be modified, but that each *program* must be accessible. In their efforts to make programs accessible to the handicapped, schools must take care that they do not segregate or isolate them from nonhandicapped students. Much of this can be achieved through careful scheduling, relocating offices, making services available at alternate accessible sites, new construction, and the remodeling of existing facilities.

In addition to the federal law, many states have enacted laws against architectural barriers and on behalf of accessibility by the handicapped. State laws cover public places that do not necessarily receive federal support and are thus beyond the reach of section 504, such as local parks, public toilets, elevators, stairs, doors, ramps, and sidewalks.

Must schools provide year-round schooling for handicapped children?

There is no clear legal answer to this question. For certain handicapped children the summer break is too long and they regress educationally. This is particularly the case for the severely retarded. When suits were brought on their behalf to extend the school year beyond the traditional 180 days, lower federal courts ruled in favor of the extension as a way of providing individualized appropriate schooling.[28] The Supreme Court, however, overturned one of these cases without comment, thus casting some doubt on the current status of the law.[29] We must wait for further legal developments to get a clear answer to our question.

Do children with AIDS qualify for special education?

Having AIDS or testing positive for HIV virus are not grounds to automatically exclude a child from school. In fact, courts have ruled that children have a right and duty to attend school, and barring special complications, AIDS does not diminish this right. A federal district court so held, for example, in 1987, when a parent group claimed that an emotionally disturbed child who tested positive for HIV virus should be excluded from school under the state's contagious disease law.[30] The court held that the child had a right to attend school under the EHA, and barring special factors, positive testing for HIV virus alone is insufficient grounds for denying that right.

A child may become eligible for special education if he or she becomes handicapped due to the disease.[31] However, in the early stages of having the disease, the child may not be qualified for special education.

Section 504 must also be considered in these cases since it has a broader definition of "handicapped," to include those who are "regarded as having an impairment."[32] In two recent cases involving young children infected with the AIDS virus as a result of blood transfusions, the courts considered the relevance of both the EHA and Section 504. The first case involved a 5-year-old boy who was excluded from school after a biting incident. The court concluded that the child was "handicapped" under section 504 and was "otherwise qualified" to attend school. After considering the best available medical evidence, the court concluded that any risk of transmitting the AIDS virus in connection with attending kindergarten is remote and cannot be used as a basis for excluding the child.[33]

The second case, decided in 1988, involved a 7-year-old trainable, mentally handicapped (TMH) child with AIDS, who was not toilet trained, had a disease that can cause blood to appear in the saliva, and sucked her thumb. The federal court of appeals ruled that she had a right to special education and that the "remote theoretical possibility" of transmitting the virus was insufficient risk to exclude her from the TMH class. The appeals court sent the case back to the trial court to determine whether or not the child was "otherwise qualified" or could be made so through some reasonable accommodations as required by Section 504.[34]

Since the incidence of children with AIDS is increasing, particularly among minority children, we may expect further legal developments related to their right to education and their inclusion under the EHA and Section 504.

BILINGUAL-BICULTURAL EDUCATION

Are there federal laws that apply to the schooling of non-English-speaking children?

Yes, there are, the most important among them being Title VI of the Civil Rights Act of 1964[35] and the Bilingual Education Act of 1974 amended in 1988.[36] The most significant case in this area is *Lau* v. *Nichols*.

The *Lau* Case[37]

Among the thousands of Chinese-American students attending public schools in San Francisco, approximately 3,000 spoke little or no English, and of these, close to 1,800 received no special services designed to meet their linguistic needs. In 1970 these students and their parents filed suit in a federal district court and claimed that their right to equal protection under the Fourteenth Amendment of the Constitution, as well as their rights under Title VI of the

Civil Rights Act of 1964, were being denied by the public schools. The main issue was whether non-English-speaking students are denied an equal educational opportunity when taught in a language they cannot understand. Title VI provides that "no person in the United States shall, on the ground of race, color or national origin, be excluded from participation in, be denied the benefit of, or be subjected to discrimination under any program or activity receiving Federal financial assistance."

The district court considered Title VI and the Fourteenth Amendment together and concluded that the non-English-speaking children did not have any of their rights violated when "the same education [was] made available on the same terms and conditions to the other tens of thousands of students in the San Francisco Unified School District" as to these students. When the Ninth Circuit affirmed this ruling, the case was appealed to the U.S. Supreme Court. The Court ruled in favor of the students and their parents, basing its decision on Title VI and deliberately not ruling on constitutional grounds. (The Court will, as a general policy, avoid ruling on a constitutional issue if it can dispose of the case on statutory grounds.)

While the lower courts were satisfied that the provision of identical educational services to all students would satisfy the law, the Supreme Court disagreed. It held that students who understand little or no English are denied equal opportunities when English is the sole medium of instruction and when there are no systematic efforts to teach that language to non-English-speaking students. "Under these state-imposed standards there is no equal treatment merely by providing students with the same facilities, textbooks, teachers, and curriculum; for students who do not understand English are effectively foreclosed from any meaningful education."

The Court did not specify what schools should do for these students, for remedies are usually left to educators under the supervision of district court judges who are more aware of local conditions. Various educational arrangements might satisfy the courts, including ESL (English as a second language), bilingual education, or a combination of both. In fact, disagreements over appropriate remedies have spawned further lawsuits as well as governmental regulations to guide school districts. The most important feature of any plan is its effectiveness.

Since *Lau,* several other cases based on Title VI have resulted in court orders requiring bilingual programs in schools.[38] These cases, however, require such instruction only if children have limited English-speaking abilities. For example, when a group of Chicano school children claimed that their school programs were inappropriate because they were "oriented for middle-class, Anglo children . . . staffed with non-Chicano personnel who do not understand and cannot relate with Chicano students who are linguistically and culturally different," the courts rejected their claims.[39] The court found that the plaintiffs did not prove the necessary facts to show violation of either Title VI or the Fourteenth Amendment.

Similarly, children of Mexican-American and Yaqui Indian origin went to court to compel the schools to provide bilingual-bicultural education. They wanted not only bilingual education for students deficient in English but continuous instruction in English and in the child's native language, Spanish or Yaqui, from kindergarten through high school. The district court ruled against them, and the court of appeals agreed.[40] The court held that education, though important, is not a fundamental right under the Constitution. "Differences in the treatment of students in the educational process, which in themselves do not violate specific constitutional provisions, do not violate the . . . Equal Protection Clause if such differences are rationally related to legitimate state interests."

It is clear, however, that the result reached in *Lau* is still good law today. As the 5th Circuit Court recently said: "[T]he essential holding of Lau, i.e., that schools are not free to ignore the need of limited English speaking children for language assistance to enable them to participate in the instructional program of the district, has now been legislated by Congress, acting pursuant to its power to enforce the [equal protection clause of the] fourteenth amendment."[41]

What are the rights of parents in these issues?

The first bilingual education act became law in 1968; following *Lau*, Congress passed a second act in 1974, which is commonly referred to as the Bilingual Education Act. Among its various provisions the law specifies that programs "of bilingual education shall be developed in consultation with parents of children of limited English-speaking ability, teachers, and, where applicable, secondary school students." It is clear that the law intends to integrate these students, whenever practicable, with English-speaking students and separate them for special instruction only when necessary. For example, they should attend regular classes in art, music, physical education, and other courses where language skills are not of central importance to instruction. The 1988 act reaffirms these principles, appropriates funds through 1993, and details the federal regulation relevant to bilingual education.

Are there state laws that provide special instruction for non-English-speaking students?

Yes, in some states. Massachusetts, Texas, California, Illinois, and Connecticut have laws related to bilingual education that predate the *Lau* decision and federal legislation. The federal law, of course, applies to all public schools, but state laws may go further than the federal law and provide more extensive education for non-English-speaking students.

It must be recognized that the federal law provides only transitional bilingual education and only for students of no or limited English ability. Thus, schools are not required to provide any special instruction for students who benefit from instruction in English. Most state laws similarly provide only for transitional bilingual education, but states or local schools may, at their discretion, provide further instruction in the students' native language.

Do federal laws apply to students who speak "black English"?

Yes, ruled a district court in Michigan. Suit was filed by black students living in a low-income housing project located in an affluent section of Ann Arbor, near the University of Michigan. They claimed that their language, black English, was a distinct language that was different from standard English. They further claimed that they were denied equal educational opportunities because their language constituted a barrier to their learning and using the written materials of the school, which were in standard English. The students alleged that section 1703(f) of Title 20 of the U.S. Code was violated by the school. This statute provides: "No state shall deny equal educational opportunity to an individual on account of his or her race, color, sex, or national origin, by (f) the failure by an educational agency to take appropriate action to overcome language barriers that impede equal participation by its students in its instructional program."

Evidence showed that the school provided various services to students including speech and language specialists, school psychologists, individualized instruction, and tutoring. Nevertheless, the court found that the teachers' lack of awareness and knowledge of black English, the home language of the children, was in part the reason for their not learning. Thus the school board was ordered to develop a plan whereby teachers would become aware of the language used in students' homes and in the community so that they might identify children who used the dialect and in turn use that knowledge to instruct them more effectively in standard English. The court did not require the creation of a bilingual program, nor did it require the teaching of black English. It did find that the teachers' lack of knowledge in this area denied students equal educational opportunities.[42]

SUMMARY

Until very recently, handicapped children were by and large excluded from schooling and misclassified and improperly placed in educational programs. Case law as well as legislative enactments have changed this dramatically. While significant developments have occurred in some states through state legislation, the most powerful developments are embodied in Public Law 94-142, the Education for All Handicapped Children Act of 1975, and in section 504 of the Rehabilitation Act of 1973. Taken together, these laws mandate that free and appropriate education, with all necessary support services, be available to all handicapped children and youth in America. In fact, while P.L. 94-142 originally applied to children between the ages of 3 and 21, a 1986 amendment applied it to infants and toddlers as well; section 504 has no age limit and forbids discrimination against the handicapped in any program or activity receiving federal support. To qualify for federal funds under P.L. 94-142, states must comply with standards set forth by law, which include individual education plans, nondiscriminatory assessment, appropriate placement of children in the least restrictive educational alternative, periodic reevaluation, and full due process rights for parents as well as students.

When no appropriate public school placement is available for a particular child, he or she may be placed in a private school at no extra cost to the parents. Thus it is clear that major strides have been made toward extending equal protection of the law and due process to all school-aged handicapped children. This is not to say that all their educational and social problems have been resolved. Important obstacles still prevent their full functioning in our society. Some of these obstacles relate to social prejudices and others to the lack of professional knowledge and even trained personnel. Nevertheless, the legal standards and tools are substantially in place to help the handicapped achieve their full human potential.

Significant strides have also been made to provide equal educational opportunities for children of limited English-speaking ability. These developments contrast dramatically with our historic attitude of "sink or swim" toward such students. Attempts to use the Fourteenth Amendment's equal protection clause on behalf of such students have not been successful. Title VI of the Civil Rights Act of 1964 was relied on by the Supreme Court in the landmark case of *Lau* v. *Nichols* to require transitional bilingual education for children who cannot benefit from instruction in English. *Lau* was followed by the Bilingual Education Act of 1974, and of 1988, which similarly mandate bilingual education for children of limited English-speaking ability. The law provides for parental participation in program planning, personnel preparation, and other support services. Several states have laws that further provide for bilingual education, some of which go beyond transitional, bilingual education and provide for maintenance instruction to help perpetuate the students' second language.

Thus it is clear that in recent years both the Constitution and legislation have been used to gain a significant degree of equality in education for handicapped and limited-English-ability students.

NOTES

1. *Brown* v. *Board of Education*, 347 U.S. 483 (1954).
2. *Pennsylvania Association for Retarded Children* v. *Commonwealth of Pennsylvania*, 343 F.Supp. 279 (E.D. Pa. 1972).
3. *Mills* v. *Board of Education of the District of Columbia*, 348 F.Supp. 866 (D. D.C. 1972).
4. 20 U.S.C. § 1401, 1402, 1411-20.
5. 29 U.S.C. § 794. Final regulations published at 42 Fed. Reg. 22676 (May 4, 1977) (codified as 45CFR84). Section 504 is brief and to the point: "No otherwise qualified handicapped individual in the United States, as defined in section 7(6), shall, solely by reason of his handicap, be excluded from the participation in, be denied

the benefits of, or be subjected to discrimination under any program or activity receiving Federal financial assistance."

6. *Fialkowski* v. *Shapp*, 405 F.Supp. 946 (E.D. Pa. 1975).
7. *Geis* v. *Board of Education of Parsippany-Troy Hills*, 599 F.Supp. 269 (D. N.J. 1984).
8. *David* v. *Dartmouth School Committee*, 615 F.Supp. 639 (D. Mass. 1984).
9. *Board of Education* v. *Rowley*, 458 U.S. 176 (1982).
10. 20 U.S.C. § 1401 (17) 1982.
11. *Clevenger* v. *Oak Ridge School Board*, 744 F.2d 514 (6th Cir. 1984).
12. *Irving Independent School District* v. *Tatro*, 104 S.Ct. 3371 (1984).
13. *T.G. and P.G.* v. *Board of Education*, 576 F.Supp. 420 (D. N.J. 1983), *aff'd. mem.*, 738 F.2d 425 (3d Cir. 1984), *cert. denied*, 105 S. Ct. 592 (1984). *(Piscataway Township Board of Education* v. *T.G.).*
14. *Bevin* v. *Wright*, 666 F.Supp. 71 (W.D.Pa. 1987).
15. *Timothy W.* v. *Rochester, New Hampshire, School District*, 875 F.2d 954 (1989).
16. *Stuart* v. *Nappi*, 443 F.Supp. 1235 (D. Conn. 1978).
17. *S-1* v. *Turlington*, 635 F.2d 342 (5th Cir. 1981), *cert. denied*, 445 U.S. 1020 (1981).
18. *See Sherry* v. *New York State Education Department*, 479 F.Supp. 1328 (W.D. N.Y. 1979); *Keelin* v. *Grubbs*, 682 F.2d 595 (6th Cir. 1982).
19. *Honig* v. *Doe*, 108 S.Ct. 592 (1988).
20. *Mattie T.* v. *Holliday*, C.A. 75-31-5 (N.D. Miss. July 28, 1977).
21. *Visco* v. *The School District of Pittsburgh*, 684 F. Supp. 1310 (1988).
22. *Anderson* v. *Thompson*, 658 F.2d 1205 (7th Cir. 1981).
23. *Burlington School Committee* v. *Department of Education, Commonwealth of Massachusetts*, 105 S.Ct. 1996 (1985).
24. 45 CFR 121 a. 403(b).
25. *Jackson* v. *Franklin County School Board*, 765 F.2d 535 (5th Cir. 1985).
26. *Kampmeier* v. *Nyquist*, 553 F.2d 296 (2d Cir. 1977).
27. *Southeastern Community College* v. *Davis*, 442 U.S. 397 (1979).
28. *Battle* v. *Pennsylvania*, 629 F.2d 269 (3d. Cir. 1980).
29. *Georgia Association of Retarded Citizens* v. *McDaniel*, 511 F.Supp. 1263 (N.D. Ga. 1981), *aff'd*, 716 F.2d 1565 (11th Cir. 1983), *vacated*, 52 L.W. 3932 (1984).
30. *Parents and Child, Code No. 870901W* v. *Group I/II/III/IV Defendants*, 676 F.Supp. 1072 (1987).
31. *District 27 Community School Board* v *Board of Education of The City of New York*, 502 N.Y.S. 2d 235 (1986).
32. Section 504 of the Rehabilitation Act of 1973 and the EHA both protect the rights of the handicapped, but are enforced by different agencies. Section 504 is broader in its coverage, since it also includes individuals addicted to alcohol or drugs. Furthermore, Section 504 extends civil rights protection beyond the school years and into the workplace as well.
33. *Thomas* v. *Atascadero Unified School District*, 662 F. Supp. 376 (C.D. Cal. 1987).
34. *Martinez* v. *School Board*, 861 F.2d 1502 (11th Cir. 1988).
35. 42 U.S.C. § 2000d (1970).
36. 20 U.S.C. § 800b; 20 U.S.C. 3281-3341 (1988).
37. *Lau* v. *Nichols*, 414 U.S. 563 (1974).
38. *Serna* v. *Portales Municipal Schools*, 499 F.Supp. 1147 (10th Cir. 1974); *Aspira* v.

Board of Education of City of New York, 423 F.Supp. 647 (S.D. N.Y. 1976); and *Rios* v. *Read,* 480 F.Supp. 14 (E.D. N.Y. 1978).

39. *Otero* v. *Mesa County Valley School District No. 51,* 408 F.Supp. 162 (D. Colo. 1975).
40. *Guadalupe Organization, Inc.* v. *Temple Elementary School District No. 3,* 557 F.2d 1022 (9th Cir. 1978).
41. *Castenada* v. *Pickard,* 648 F.2d 989 (5th Cir. 1981).
42. *Martin Luther King, Jr., Elementary School Children* v. *Michigan Board of Education,* 473 F.Supp. 1371 (E.D. Mich. 1979).

CHAPTER 16

Who Controls Student Records?

OVERVIEW

In 1974 Congress passed the Family Educational Rights and Privacy Act (also known as FERPA or the Buckley Amendment) to define who may and may not see student records. The law guarantees that parents have access to their children's school records; it also prohibits release of the records without parental permission, except to those who have a legitimate "right to know." Many administrators, teachers, and guidance counselors felt the act would cause more harm than good. Some teachers decided to put nothing critical in student records, fearing that any negative information could become the basis for a possible libel suit. Counselors were concerned that able students would be handicapped by a law that required nonconfidential recommendations, since all such recommendations would tend to sound the same and simply consist of positive platitudes. And many administrators saw this as another legislative intervention in the field of education, creating additional unnecessary procedures and paperwork and threatening to cut off federal funds for noncompliance. In view of these concerns, this chapter examines the reasons for the act, what the act does and does not require, and some of its consequences and controversies.

THE BUCKLEY AMENDMENT

Why did Congress pass the Buckley Amendment?

Congress acted because of abuses in the use of student records, especially the tendency of schools to provide access to the records to outsiders but to deny access to students and their parents. The establishment of health, guidance, and psychological records on students was originally a progressive development. It enabled teachers, counselors, and administrators to have access to information about the "whole child," not just about grades and subjects studied. In subsequent years, many schools developed extensive records on each student. In New York City, for example, student records typically included a guidance record of the counselor's evaluations of aptitude; behavior and personality characteristics; disciplinary referral cards; recommendations for tracking; a teacher's anecdotal file on student behavior; and cards containing standardized test results, grades, and health information. These records were open to government inspectors, employers, and other nonschool personnel. But they were not open to parents.[1]

As the quantity of information grew, so did the abuses. One mother was told she had no right to see records that resulted in her son's being transferred to a class for the mentally retarded. A father, attending a routine parent-teacher conference, discovered in teachers' comments in his son's record that he was "strangely introspective" in the third grade, "unnaturally interested in girls" in the fifth grade, and had developed "peculiar political ideas" by the time he was twelve.[2] Edward Van Allen, who was told by teachers that his son needed psychological treatment, had to get a judicial order to see all of the school's records on the boy.[3] During the 1960s, researchers found that the CIA and the FBI had complete access to student files in more than 60 percent of the school districts, while parents had access in only about 15 percent.[4]

A few years before the Buckley Amendment was passed, a group of prominent educators and lawyers reported these problems in school recordkeeping:

1. Pupils and their parents typically have little knowledge of what information about them is contained in school records or of how it is used.
2. Policies for regulating access to records by nonschool personnel do not exist in most school systems.
3. The secrecy with which school records are usually maintained makes it difficult for parents to assess their accuracy, and formal procedures for challenging erroneous information generally do not exist.[5]

The report concluded that these deficiencies "constitute a serious threat to individual privacy in the United States." Although many state and local regulations to control misuse of student records were developed during the 1960s, they were neither uniform nor comprehensive. Because of all these problems, Congress passed the Family Educational Rights and Privacy Act (FERPA), which also will be referred to as the Buckley Amendment.

What are the main features of the act?

The Buckley Amendment contains five important features:

1. It requires school districts to establish a written policy concerning student records and to inform parents of their rights under the act each year.

2. It guarantees parents the right to inspect and review the educational records of their children.
3. It establishes procedures through which parents can challenge the accuracy of student records.
4. It protects the confidentiality of student records by preventing disclosure of personally identifiable information to outsiders without prior parental consent.
5. It entitles parents to file complaints with the FERPA Office concerning alleged failures to comply with the act.

The act applies to all schools receiving federal education funds, either directly or indirectly. Parents may assert their children's rights of access and consent until they become 18 years old or begin attending a postsecondary institution; after this, these rights will "only be accorded to . . . the student."[6]

RIGHT OF ACCESS

What education records are accessible under the act?

Education records include any information compiled by a school that is directly related to a current student regardless of whether the record is in handwriting, print, tape, film, microfilm, or microfiche.

How does the act guarantee access to parents and students?

The Buckley Amendment states that no federal funds will be made available to any school that prevents parents from exercising "the right to inspect and review the education records of their children." This includes the right (1) to be informed about the kinds and location of education records maintained by the school and the officials responsible for them and (2) to receive an explanation or interpretation of the records if requested. Officials must comply with a parental request to inspect records "within a reasonable time, but in no case more than 45 days after the request." Either parent (including a noncustodial parent) has the right to inspect them, unless prohibited by court order. Although a school may not deny parental access to student records, it may for a legitimate reason deny a request for a copy of such records.

In a court case on this point, former students sued their college for not sending out certified copies of their transcripts because they failed to repay their student loans. The students claimed that the Buckley Amendment required the college to send out their records when they requested them. A federal court disagreed.[7] It ruled that the amendment was "for the inspection of records by students and their parents, not for the release of records to outside parties."[8]

Do parents have the right to see teachers' personal notes about their students?

No. The Buckley Amendment does not give parents the right to review the personal notes of teachers and administrators if these records are in their "sole possession" and are not revealed to any other individual except a substitute teacher.

What other records are not accessible?

Eligible students do not have the right to see records of a physician, psychologist, or other recognized professional used *only* in connection with their treatment. Parents have no right to see records of a law enforcement unit of the school maintained *solely* for police purposes; or job-related records of students who are employees of the school.

Can students waive their right of access?

Yes. Individuals who are applicants for admission to postsecondary institutions may waive their right to inspect confidential letters of recommendation. Although institutions may not require such waivers "as a condition of admission," they may "request" them. These waivers must be signed by the individual students, regardless of age, rather than by their parents. Just as a college is not required to permit students to see these confidential recommendations, so it may also prohibit students from inspecting the financial statements of their parents.

How does the Buckley Amendment restrict access to outsiders?

The act requires that a school obtain "the written consent of the parent . . . before disclosing personally identifiable information from the education records of a student." The consent must be signed and dated and include the specific records to be disclosed and the purpose and the individual or group to whom the disclosure may be made. Schools must keep a file of all requests for access to a student's record; the file must indicate who made the request and the legitimate interests in seeking the information.

Can a parent who has custody of a child prohibit the other parent from gaining access to the educational records of their child?

No. In a New York case, Michike Page, who had legal custody of her son Eric, asked the school not to permit Eric's father to see their son's educational records. In ruling that neither parent could be denied access to their son's records under FERPA, the judge wrote that despite "some inconvenience," schools should make educational information "available to both parents of every child fortunate enough to have two parents interested in his welfare."[9]

Are there exceptions to the consent requirement?

Yes, there are several. For example, prior consent is not required when education records are shared (1) with teachers or administrators of the same school who have "legitimate educational interests," (2) with officials of another school in which the student seeks to enroll (provided the parents are notified), (3) with persons for whom the information is necessary "to protect the health or safety of the student or other individuals," and (4) in connection with financial aid for which a student has applied.

Does FERPA prohibit a school from releasing a teacher's college transcript without the teacher's consent?

No. In Texas, a parent concerned about the quality of public education, requested access to the academic records of a teacher under the state's Open Records Act. The teacher, Rebecca Holt, and the superintendent claimed that the disclosure of Holt's college transcript would violate her privacy rights under FERPA. But a federal appeals court disagreed. It ruled that FERPA was only intended to protect student records, not the records of a person employed by the school. Because Holt was a teacher and not a student, the judge ruled that her college transcript was not an educational record protected from disclosure by FERPA.[10] However, a teacher's personnel file may be protected from public disclosure under the laws of some states.

Does the Buckley Amendment require schools to restrict distribution of personal student information in school newspapers?

It depends upon the source of the information. In defending their seizure of a school newspaper that contained personal information about a student's suspension, school officials argued that the Buckley Amendment prevented schools from disclosing such information about their students. However, the court ruled that the act could not justify the seizure. Although some of the information in the newspaper would fall within the act's protection "if the source of that information had been school records," the court wrote that "the Amendment cannot be deemed to extend to information which is derived from a source independent of school records."[11]

In a related case, the University of North Carolina Law School argued that its official faculty meetings could not be open to the public because the meetings might concern the personally identifiable educational records of students, and this would be inconsistent with the Buckley Amendment. The court ruled that the amendment does not prohibit open faculty meetings that might discuss student records, although it might penalize schools that have a regular practice of releasing such information.[12]

Can courts require schools to disclose personal information about students without their parents' permission?

Yes, under certain conditions. A case occurred in New York when a group of parents claimed that the schools failed to provide their children with adequate bilingual education. As part of their suit, the parents asked a federal court to order the schools to provide the names, test results, class schedules, and other information about bilingual students who had English deficiencies. The school refused, claiming that the Buckley Amendment prohibited them from disclosing this information without parental consent. The court ruled that the school may disclose such "personally identifiable information" if it does so in compliance with a judicial order and if those seeking the order "demonstrate a genuine need for the information that outweighs the privacy interest of the student." Since this information was essential to determine whether the suit was justified, the court ruled that a genuine need was shown.[13]

The school also expressed concern about violating the act's requirement that they notify all parents of students concerned before disclosure. Since several hundred students were potentially involved, the judge said that the school could meet this requirement by making "a reasonable effort" to notify the parents by publishing a notice in Spanish and in English in the local newspapers. The court explained that the act did not establish a school-student privilege analogous to an attorney-client privilege, but merely sought to deter schools from releasing personal student information unless there were appropriate educational, medical, or legal reasons. The act, concluded the court, was certainly not intended "as a cloak" for allegedly discriminatory practices.

What information about students can be shared without consent?

A school can disclose "directory information" from the education records of a student without requiring prior parental consent. Directory information includes such facts as a student's name, address, phone number, date and place of birth, field of study, sports activities, dates of attendance, awards received, and similar information. Before freely releasing such information, a school must try to notify parents of current students about what facts it regards as directory information and of the parents' right to refuse to permit the release of such information. It is the parents' obligation to notify the school in writing if they refuse. A school may release directory information about former students without first trying to notify them, however.

A school also has the discretion not to designate directory information. In a New York case, Francis Krauss asked Nassau Community College to give him the names and addresses of all students to be enrolled in the fall of 1983.[14] The school refused and Krauss sued, arguing that this was directory information that should be provided under the Buckley Amendment. The court noted that under FERPA, a school *may* disclose such information. However, in this case, the college chose not to include student names and addresses as directory information, and therefore its refusal to disclose such information did not violate the act. On the other hand, another New York court ruled that the FERPA does not *prohibit* a school from giving parents of an injured student the names and addresses of all pupils taking gym at the time of the accident since this was designated directory information and therefore was not privileged under the act.[15]

In some situations a school may even be required to provide information about students to outsiders. This occurred in a 1987 Missouri case in which a state appeals court ruled that a local district must disclose its students' names, addresses, and telephone listings which were requested by a local teachers' association.[16] The court concluded that disclosure of the requested information under the state's Sunshine Law was not barred by FERPA since it had been designated "directory information" by the school district.

Does FERPA prevent administrators from sharing critical information about students with teachers?

No. A recent article on Youth Records, Privacy Rights and Public Safety in *Education Weekly* described three criminal incidents by students in schools and suggested that the crimes might have been prevented if information in the students' records could have been shared.[17] The article implied that the Buckley Amendment prevented the sharing of such information and that school administrators believed it even barred the release of students' names and addresses to police investigating the crimes. While some administrators may honestly believe these errors, the Buckley Amendment is not to blame. As we have noted above (and as the article failed to point out), the Amendment does *not* prohibit administrators from sharing information with teachers who have "legitimate educational interests" in the information or with anyone for whom the information is necessary to protect the health and safety of students or teachers.

OTHER RIGHTS

Can schools destroy student records?

Yes. If state law does not determine how long student records must be kept, schools may destroy some or all of a student's educational records at any time, except where there is an outstanding request to inspect them.

Must parents be informed of their rights under the Buckley Amendment?

Yes. Every school must give parents of all current students "annual notice" of their rights under the act, where they can obtain copies of the school's policy for implementing and protecting these rights, and their "right to file complaints" for the school's failure to comply with the act. In addition, the act requires that elementary and secondary schools find a way to "effectively notify parents" of students whose primary language is not English.

Do parents have a right to challenge their children's records?

Yes. If the parents of a student believe that a school record is "inaccurate or misleading or violates the privacy or other rights of the student," they may request that the school amend it. If the school refuses, it must so inform the parents and advise them of their rights to a hearing. The hearing may be conducted by anyone "who does not have a direct interest" in its outcome.

Parents must be given "a full and fair opportunity" to present their evidence and may be represented by counsel, at their own expense, if they wish. The school must make its decision in writing "based solely on the evidence presented at the hearing," which must include the reasons and evidence to support its decision.

If, as a result of the hearing, the school decides the record was inaccurate or misleading, it must amend the record accordingly. But if the school decides that the information was correct, it must inform the parents of "the right to place in the education records of the student a statement commenting upon the information . . . and/or setting forth any reasons for disagreeing with the decision" of the school. Such explanation must be maintained by the school as part of the student's record; if the contested portion of the record is disclosed to anyone, the explanation must also be disclosed.

LEGAL ENFORCEMENT

Are there any procedures to enforce the Buckley Amendment?

Yes. There are detailed federal regulations concerning enforcement. The Family Educational Rights and Privacy Act Office of the Department of Education has been established to "investigate, process, and review violations and complaints." After receiving written complaints regarding alleged violations, the office will notify the school involved and provide an opportunity to respond. After its investigation, the office will send its findings to the complainant and the school. If there has been a violation, the office will indicate the specific steps the school must take to be in compliance. If the school does not comply, a review board hearing will be held. If the review board determines "that compliance cannot be secured by voluntary means," federal education funds will be terminated. FERPA, however, does not provide individual citizens with a legal right to enforce the act through the courts. According to a federal appeals decision, "enforcement is solely in the hands" of the Department of Education.[18]

Thousands of complaints have been received by the Privacy Act Office, and about 80 percent of them have been resolved informally through phone calls to the school districts involved. As of November 1989, there have been about 325 formal investigations.[19] No cases have yet been referred to the review board; thus federal funds have never been terminated for noncompliance.

In addition to enforcing the act, the Family Educational Rights and Privacy Act Office tries to help educators understand it. Its staff will consult with teachers and administrators by letter or phone and will answer questions concerning the act, its regulations, and their interpretation and application in specific school districts.[20]

Can parents sue schools for violating their FERPA rights?

Perhaps. FERPA itself does not provide for an individual to sue a school district for violations; instead, it requires the Secretary of Education to enforce the act. However, a federal appeals court has ruled that a parent can bring suit under Section 1983 of the federal civil rights laws which allows individuals to sue government officials who violate their rights.* In this New York case, a divorced father who had joint custody, unsuccessfully tried for 11 months to get information from school officials about his children's educational progress. Since FERPA does not prohibit a private suit under Section 1983, the court ruled that judges may award compensation to parents where their FERPA rights are violated and where damages can be proved.[21]

What have been the results of FERPA?

Initially schools were slow to comply with the statute. Federal regulations for implementation were not published until a year and a half after the act became law in 1974. But as hundreds of complaints have been filed with the Washington enforcement office each year, information about the act has increased, and compliance has become more widespread.

According to some observers, two notable results of the Buckley Amendment have been the destruction of old records and the improvement of new ones. After the law was passed, many schools across the country conducted "massive housecleanings" of records. Emptying school files of "undesirable material," wrote Lucy Knight, "remains the single most effective way for a school to attempt compliance with the Buckley Amendment."[22] Second, the quality of student records and the caliber of recommendations "has improved substantially," according to Chester Nolte. This, wrote Professor Nolte, reflects the fact that under the act teachers, principals, and counselors "must adhere to absolute truth, rather than opinion, when writing reports on individual students."[23]

Fears that teachers would be sued for libel if they wrote anything negative in student records have been greatly exaggerated. There is little chance of students winning libel suits against teachers whose comments are based on firsthand observation, are accurate, and are educationally relevant (For more on libel, see Chapter 6.)

Three other areas of misunderstanding have regularly occurred concerning the act. First, many educators are still unaware that access applies to all student records, not just to the cumulative file. Second, many parents believe the act gives them the right to challenge the fairness of a student grade. Although the act does allow parents to question whether a teacher's grade was recorded accurately, it does not allow them to challenge the reasonableness of the grade that was assigned.[24] Third, many administrators are not aware that the parental

---

* For more on individual liability under Section 1983, see Chapter 4, pages 56–64.

right to inspect and review the educational records of their children applies equally to noncustodial parents who do not live with their children (unless their access has been prohibited by a court order).

SUMMARY

Abuses in the use of student records led Congress to pass the Family Educational Rights and Privacy Act (the Buckley Amendment) in 1974. The act has several important features. First, it guarantees parents the right to inspect and review their children's educational records (excluding teachers' personal notes about students). Second, it limits access to student records by providing that such records cannot be released to outsiders without a parent's written consent. However, such consent is not required when the records are shared with teachers in the school who have a "legitimate educational interest" in the student, or when they are released pursuant to a court order. Third, the act gives parents the right to challenge recorded information that is "inaccurate, misleading, or otherwise in violation of privacy or other rights of students." It also gives parents the right to place an explanation in the record of any information with which they disagree. Students who apply to college may waive their right to inspect confidential letters of recommendation. And when students become 18 or begin attending a postsecondary institution, they assume their parents' rights under the act. Although the act imposed additional administrative responsibilities on the schools, it has generally led to an improvement in the quality and accuracy of student records.

NOTES

1. Diane Divoky, *Cumulative Records: Assault on Privacy*, LEARNING MAGAZINE, 9 (September 1973).
2. *Id.*
3. *Van Allen v. McCleary*, 211 N.Y.S.2d 501 (1961).
4. Michael Stone, *Off the Record: The Emerging Right to Control One's School Files*, 5 N.Y.U. *Rev. L. & Soc. Change*, 39, 42 (1975).
5. Divoky, *supra*, at 10.
6. The text of the act is contained in the *United States Code Annotated* Title 20 § 1232g (1989). Regulations for implementing the act can be found in the CODE OF FEDERAL REGULATIONS, Title 34, Part 99 (1989). Quotations about the act in this chapter are from the *Code of Regulations*, unless otherwise indicated.
7. *Girardier v. Webster College*, 421 F.Supp. 45 (E.D. Mo. 1976), 563 F.2d 1267 (8th Cir. 1977).
8. On the other hand, where a student's debt for college loans has been legally discharged by a bankruptcy court, "schools could not withhold a transcript as a means of forcing collection of [such] a debt." *Johnson v. Edinboro State College*, 728 F.2d 163 (3d Cir. 1984).

9. *Page* v. *Rotterdam-Mohanasen Central School District*, 441 N.Y.S.2d 323 (1981).
10. *Klein Independent School District* v. *Mattox*, 830 F.2d 576 (5th Cir. 1987).
11. *Frasca* v. *Andrews*, 463 F.Supp. 1043 (E.D.N.Y. 1979).
12. *Student Bar Association Board of Governors* v. *Byrd*, 239 S.E.2d 415 (N.C. 1977).
13. *Rios* v. *Read*, 73 F.R.D. 589 (E.D.N.Y. 1977).
14. *Krauss* v. *Nassau Community College*, 469 N.Y.S.2d 553 (Supp. 1983).
15. *Staub* v. *East Greenbush School District No. 1*, 491 N.Y.S.2d 87 (Supp. 1985).
16. *Oregon County R-IV School District* v. *LeMon*, 739 S.W.2d 553 (Mo.App. 1987).
17. *Privacy Rights and Public Safety Concerns: Debate Stirs Over Access to Youth Records*, EDUCATION WEEKLY, June 21, 1989, p. 1.
18. *Girardier* v. *Webster College*, 563 F.2d 1267 (8th Cir. 1977).
19. Telephone interview with LeRoy Rooker, Director, Family Policy and Regulations Office (November 13, 1989).
20. For copies of the regulations or a Model Policy Document for elementary and secondary schools, teachers can contact the Family Educational Rights and Privacy Act Office, U.S. Department of Education, 400 Maryland Avenue, S.W., Washington, DC 20202, or phone (202) 732-2057.
21. *Fay* v. *South Colonie Central School District*, 802 F.2d 21 (2nd Cir. 1986).
22. Lucy Knight, *Facts About Mr. Buckley's Amendment*, AMERICAN EDUCATION, June 1977, at 6.
23. M. Chester Nolte, *American School Board Journal*, 38 (April 1977).
24. Telephone interview with LeRoy Rooker (November 13, 1989).

CHAPTER 17

Must All Children
Go to School?

OVERVIEW

Universal, publicly supported education is a uniquely American idea, one that has been borrowed from us by many other nations. Based on the conviction that an enlightened citizenry can best serve the needs of society, the states provide free schools for children and youth, and require them to attend. Thus, since every state provides schools at public expense, schooling is a *right* provided not by the U.S. Constitution but by each state.

Furthermore, it becomes clear to see that, where attendance is compulsory, children and youth have a *duty* to attend school. (All of the states in our country have compulsory attendance laws, but the age of mandatory school attendance varies, beginning at ages 6, 7, or 8 and extending through ages 15 to 18, depending on the wording of the specific state statute.)

With the rise of compulsory schooling came disagreements concerning the constitutionality of such compulsion and proposals for alternatives to the public schools. Laws requiring that children attend school have been uniformly sustained, and it is clear today that there is no constitutional provision violated by such a mandate.[1]

Nevertheless, specific questions continue to arise regarding such matters as conflicts between parents' rights and compulsory schooling, educational choice, home schooling, and parental objection to teaching materials or to the curriculum. This chapter examines how the issues of compulsory education and curriculum objections have been dealt with in court.

COMPULSORY SCHOOLING
AND PARENTS' RIGHTS

Must all children attend public schools?

In 1922 Oregon passed a law, effective September 1, 1926, requiring every parent or guardian of a child between the ages of 8 and 16 to send such child "to a public school for the period of time a public school shall be held during the current year." Failure to comply with the law was a misdemeanor. The Society of Sisters, a religious organization that maintained various schools in Oregon, challenged the state law claiming it to be unconstitutional in that it took away property rights arbitrarily, in violation of the due process clause of the Fourteenth Amendment.

No questions were raised about the right of the state to require school attendance or regulate all schools; what was questioned was the requirement that all children attend *public* schools. To this challenge, the Supreme Court, recognizing the basic right of parents and guardians "to direct the upbringing and education of children under their control," said: "The fundamental theory of liberty upon which all governments in this Union repose excludes any general power of the state to standardize its children by forcing them to accept instruction from public teachers only. The child is not the mere creature of the state; those who nurture him and direct his destiny have the right, coupled with the high duty, to recognize and prepare him for additional obligations."[2]

Since this *Pierce* case, courts have uniformly held that a state's requirement that children attend school can be met either through public or private schools; furthermore, if the school is private, it may be either religious or secular.

If parents have religious objections to schooling, can they avoid sending their children to school?

No, not in states that have compulsory education laws. Nevertheless, a variation on this question led to a partial exemption from schooling for children of the Amish religion. Several Amish parents in Wisconsin decided not to send their 14- and 15-year-old children to school beyond the eighth grade, in violation of the state's compulsory attendance law. The parents claimed that high school attendance would be destructive of the children's religious beliefs and, ultimately, of the Amish way of life. The Amish way rejects material success, competition, intellectual and scientific accomplishment, self-distinction, and other values central to the curriculum and the social climate in high schools. The parents further claimed that competition in classwork, sports, and peer pressure would alienate Amish children from their families and from their close-knit, cooperative, agrarian, religion-based lives.

The Amish did not object to elementary schooling, for they believed in the necessity of the three Rs to read the Bible, to be good farmers and citizens, and to be able to interact occasionally with non-Amish people. The Supreme Court, after considering the conflicting interests of the State of Wisconsin and the Amish, exempted the students from schooling beyond the eighth grade. The Court based its decision on the religious freedom clause of the First Amendment and in effect considered the Amish way of life as an acceptable alternative to formal secondary education. Protecting the Amish, the Court wrote that "there can be no assumption that today's majority is 'right' and the Amish and others like them are 'wrong.' A way of life that is odd or even erratic but interferes with no rights or interest of others is not to be condemned because it is different."[3]

A related question appears in Chapter 9.

Can other parents, individually or in groups, avoid the requirements of compulsory schooling?

No. The Amish case cannot be used as legal precedent for those who simply disagree with today's schools or who even form "religious" groups to gain exemption from schooling. As Justice Burger wrote: "A way of life, however virtuous and admirable, may not be interposed as a barrier to reasonable state regulation of education if it is based on purely secular considerations. . . . It cannot be overemphasized that we are not dealing with a way of life and mode of education by a group claiming to have recently discovered some 'progressive' or more enlighted [sic] process for rearing children for modern life."

Thus, parental rights to guide the upbringing of their children are respected by allowing parents to choose among existing schools or even set up new schools. At the same time, the compulsory laws of the states are upheld, mandating that all children go to some school.

HOME SCHOOLING

Can parents educate their children at home?

State laws that mandate school attendance for children usually provide for alternative ways of satisfying that requirement. The most common equivalent is private schooling that meets certain minimum state requirements related to health and safety, curriculum, and teacher qualification. Some states allow for alternatives to public schools as long as such alternatives are "equivalent" in scope and quality. Still others provide that alternatives to public schooling must meet the approval of the local superintendent of schools and/or the school board. In considering whether parents have the choice of educating their school-age children at home, in general the answer is yes, but only if the requirements of their particular state statute are satisfied. State laws vary in their wording, and courts have interpreted these laws differently, so one must look carefully at the law of the particular state where the question of home teaching arises.

A typical state law requires that the alternative to public schooling include teaching "the branches of education taught to children of corresponding age and grade in public schools," that the education be "equivalent," and that some systematic reporting be made to the local school superintendent to enable the state to supervise the alternative schooling. Disagreements often arise concerning the meaning of "equivalent" education as well as the qualification of the parents to teach their children. Roughly speaking, courts can be characterized as bringing a liberal or a strict interpretation to such state statutes.

All courts are more concerned with the requirement that the child be educated than with the specific form or place of that education. Some courts place the burden on the parent to prove that the home teaching is adequate and equivalent to the public schools, while others place the burden of proof on the state or school officials to show that the particular home schooling is not adequate. Where the burden of proof is placed is very important in a lawsuit, for the party that has the burden of proof must present the initial evidence to establish the claim it is making. If the initial evidence is insufficient, the case is dismissed; if it is sufficient, the other side must refute it in order to prevail. Which side has the burden of proof is usually indicated by the relevant state statute under which the suit is brought.

The liberal interpretation can be exemplified by an Illinois case where parents were accused of violating the state compulsory education law by teaching their seven-year-old daughter at home. At the trial, evidence proved that her mother, "who had two years of college and some training in pedagogy and educational psychology," taught her at home for five hours each day and that the child could perform comparably with average third-grade students. Nevertheless, the laws of Illinois made no specific provision for home teaching, only for "private or parochial school where children were taught the branches of education, taught to children of corresponding age and grade in public schools." The parents claimed that their daughter was attending a "private school" within the meaning of the state law, since she was receiving instruction comparable to that of the public school.

The Supreme Court of Illinois agreed with the parents, noting that the purpose of the law "is that all children shall be educated, not that they shall be educated in a particular manner or place."[4] The court was satisfied that the intent of the law in specifying "private school" as an alternative included the "place and nature of instruction" provided in this case. While wanting to protect children against educational deprivation, the law did not intend to punish conscientious parents. In the words of the Illinois court: "The law is not made to punish those who provide their children with instruction equal or superior to that obtainable in the public schools. It is made for the parent who fails or refuses to properly educate his child."

State courts using a strict interpretation of the law tend to emphasize that the requirement of equivalent instruction includes qualified and even certified teachers. Some states specify that certification is the evidence necessary to prove qualification for home teaching. California is one of these states, and the court of appeals there ruled that children enrolled in a correspondence course were not receiving equivalent instruction.[5]

In a case that arose in Maine in 1983 the court held that the state has the power to impose reasonable regulations for the duration and control of basic education. When parents refused to submit their plans for home schooling to school authorities for approval, they were fined on the grounds that their children were habitually truant.[6] Similarly a Kansas court found that home instruction that was unplanned and unscheduled, by a mother who was not certified or accredited, did not satisfy the state compulsory attendance law.[7]

By contrast, the Georgia Supreme Court declared the state compulsory education law "unconstitutionally vague in that it failed to provide fair notice to persons of ordinary intelligence and to establish minimum guidelines to local officials as to what constitutes 'private school.' " This case involved a family who were members of the Worldwide Church of God. The parents began teaching their children at home because they felt the public schools would have a disruptive influence on their children, and that they were of poor quality, unsafe, and immoral. The issue of freedom of religion was not addressed in the case.[8] If, however, a state by statute requires that children attend only public or approved private schools, and if such laws are clear, specific, and unambiguous, courts will sustain them.[9]

Since earlier statutory language often failed due to vagueness, much of recent legislative activity aimed at clarifying statutory language. The State of Arkansas, for example, made its law more clear and specific, requiring that students taught at home be given the same standardized tests as students in public schools. When parents challenged the law, a federal appeals court upheld it in 1988, indicating that this type of monitoring of student achievement was "the least restrictive system to assure its goal of adequately educating its citizens."[10] A similar conflict in Missouri over the vagueness of a state statute requiring "substantially equivalent" education led to a lawsuit, and the court held that a statute is too vague if "persons of common intelligence must necessarily guess at its meaning and differ as to its application."[11] As a consequence of this lawsuit, the Missouri statute was revised to cure the vagueness.[12]

. Parents in Ohio challenged a statutory requirement that they seek approval of the local superintendent for their home education program, but the Ohio Supreme Court upheld the statute as one that "reasonably furthers the state's interest in the education of its citizens." Though some dissenting judges considered the statute vague, in that it gives the superintendent "unbridled discretion to determine if a home-schooling teacher is qualified," the majority found no problem in this and the U.S. Supreme Court declined to review the case, thus tacitly approving the majority's view.[13]

During the recent years, advocates of home schooling have succeeded in influencing many state legislatures to pass laws that accommodate their wishes. While no one has definitive up-to-date statistics on the topic, various surveys have indicated that the numbers of home schoolers have increased, exceeding 120,000 during the 1985–86 school year.[14] Thirty states have revised or adopted laws or regulations concerning home schooling since 1956, and all but three of them in the 1980s.[15] This legislative activity resulted primarily from parents challenging existing laws in court actions or through lobbying. Most of the changes are favorable toward home schooling.

State statutes controlling home schooling can be grouped in four categories: (1) "Explicit Language" statutes, which explicitly permit home instruction; (2) "Equivalency Language" statutes that require attendance in public schools or their "equivalent"; (3) "Qualifies as Private School" statutes, which permit private school attendance and allow home instruction to qualify as a private school; and (4) "Silent Language" statutes, where state laws are silent on the matter, leaving it entirely in the hands of courts, state deparments of education, and local officials.[16]

What about the social development of children schooled at home?

A New Jersey case ruled that "equivalent" instruction requires that standard, approved teaching materials be used, that the parent doing the teaching have the necessary qualifications, and that the children have the full advantages supplied by the public schools including free association with other children.[17] In this case, the home instruction was found not to be "equivalent" because the mother, though certified to teach in secondary schools, had not kept up with educational developments for the past 20 years. Furthermore, the children's home school did not include opportunities for social interaction with others of their age.

The requirement that there be opportunities for social development is a difficult one for home schools to meet. And, in fact, most courts do not impose this requirement, for it effectively eliminates the alternative of home schooling. Courts have said that the inclusion of social development in deciding whether or not home schooling is "equivalent" would in effect eliminate "instruction elsewhere than at school." Group interaction and instruction in groups would constitute a de facto school, and if that is what the legislature intended, it should so specify. With this line of reasoning, most courts do not impose social interaction as a requirement for home schooling, and even a later case in New Jersey refused to follow the requirement imposed by the earlier decision in the state.[18]

What constitutional and statutory grounds are there for home schooling?

A trial court in Massachusetts faced the home schooling issue in 1978 in the light of a state statute on compulsory attendance that exempted children who are "being otherwise instructed in a manner approved in advance by the superintendent or the school committee." The court found both constitutional and statutory grounds to protect the right to home education. The constitutional grounds are derived from the right to privacy, which, though nowhere mentioned explicitly in the Constitution, is nonetheless an important right recognized by various decisions of the Supreme Court.

The Massachusetts court relied on the words of Justice Douglas, who expressed the following as a source of parents' rights: "The Ninth Amendment obviously does not create federally enforceable rights. It merely says, 'the enumeration in the Constitution of certain rights shall not be construed to deny or disparage others retained by the people.' But a catalogue of these rights includes customary, traditional and time honored rights, amenities and privileges. . . . Many of them, in my view, come within the meaning of the term 'liberty' as used in the Fourteenth Amendment . . . [one] is *freedom of choice in the basic decisions of one's life* respecting marriage, divorce, contraception, *and the education and upbringing of children.*"[19]

In addition to the constitutional source of parents' rights, the court also noted that when the Massachusetts legislature revised its compulsory attendance law, it chose to retain the phrase "otherwise instructed." From this, the inference can be drawn that home education was intended to be maintained as an alternative available to parents. The court nonetheless recognized the interest of the state in an educated citizenry and thus wanted to preserve reasonable regulatory powers in the hands of school officials. In search of an appropriate balance between the rights of parents and the interests of the state, the judge ordered the school committee to consider the following in determining the adequacy of home instruction:

1. the competency of the teachers ("and though certification would not be required, the presence or absence of the requirements that would lead to certification may be considered");
2. the teaching of subjects required by law or regulation;
3. the "manner in which the subjects are taught so as to impart comparable knowledge as given in the local schools";
4. the "number of hours and days devoted to teaching";
5. the "adequacy of the texts, materials, methods, and programs being used";
6. the "availability of periodic tests and measurements of the child's educational growth."

School officials were *not* to consider the following factors in judging the adequacy of the home educational plan:

1. the parents' reasons for wanting to educate their child at home;
2. the lack of a curriculum identical to that of the school;
3. the lack of group experience;
4. the possibility that this exemption may become a precedent for other cases.[20]

The more recent case of *Care and Protection of Charles*[21] similarly upheld the state law authorizing local education officials to approve home schooling programs regarding curriculum, length of program, competency of the parent, content of instruction, and processes for the evaluation of progress.

In sum, whether a particular home teaching arrangement satisfies the law depends on the constitution and statutes of the particular state, the courts' interpretation of those state laws, and tends to turn on whether the parent is qualified to teach, whether systematic instruction is given, how well the children are progressing in comparison with their age mates in public schools, and the adequacy of a reporting system supervised by a responsible school official.

OBJECTIONS TO THE CURRICULUM

Can parents object to certain courses or materials?

The answer depends on the grounds of the parental objection, the nature of the course or material to which the parent is objecting, and relevant state and constitutional laws. At the base of all parental objections to curriculum and instruction lie two conflicting propositions. The first asserts that parents have the basic right to guide the upbringing of their children. The second proclaims that states and boards of education have the power to make and enforce reasonable regulations for the efficient and effective conduct of schools.

Every state has some laws prescribing portions of the curriculum, and it is clear that legislatures can require children to study subjects that are "essential to good citizenship." Although what this phrase covers is often controversial, there have not been a large number of cases concerning this question. The most common objections to curriculum and instruction have had a religious basis. Perhaps the best-known issue is parental objection, on religious grounds, to the inclusion of theories of natural evolution in the school curriculum. When the Arkansas legislature forbade the teaching of evolution in the public schools of that state, the Supreme Court declared the state law unconstitutional, as a violation of the establishment clause of the First Amendment.[22]

During recent years, several states enacted laws requiring "equal time" for the teaching of creationism along with theories of evolution. Such laws have been struck down as violations of the Establishment Clause, for they tend to protect or advance particular religious beliefs.[23] (See also Chapter 2.)

Can children be exempt from portions of the curriculum to which their parents object on religious grounds?

Yes, they can, if their parents have bona fide religious or moral objections. A California court so ruled in 1921, when parents objected, on religious grounds, to their children's participation in dancing, which was part of the school's physical education program. The court, ruling in favor of the parents, noted that beyond religious objections, parents may also have moral objections "which may concern the conscience of those who are not affiliated with any particular religious sect."[24]

In recent years, objections have arisen concerning a variety of sex education classes. For example, some New Jersey parents raised objections, on grounds of religion, to their children being required to take a course entitled "Human Sexuality." School board surveys indicated widespread citizen support for the program (70 percent approval), but the court indicated that issues such as this are not decided by majority vote.[25] "If majority vote were to govern in matters of religion and conscience, there would be no need for the First Amendment," wrote the judge. That amendment was adopted precisely to protect the small minority "who is sincere in a conscientious religious conviction." The Supreme Court of Hawaii and a U.S. Court of Appeals also ruled that parents' rights in general, or their religious freedom, are not violated simply by the inclusion in the curriculum of family life or sex education, as long as children of objecting parents may be excused from the instruction.[26]

In 1987 a federal appeals court decided the highly controversial *Mozert* case, that arose in Hawkins County, Tennessee.[27] There, parents objected to the use of the Holt, Rinehart, & Winston reading series, readers widely used throughout the country. Parents claimed the readers violated their constitutional rights "to the free exercise of their religion," because they taught values offensive to their religious beliefs. While the district court ruled in favor of the parents, a divided appeals court reversed the decision. The majority held that, just because the readers contained some ideas objectionable to the parents on religious grounds, "does not create an unconstitutional burden under the free exercise clause" since the students are not required to affirm or deny any religious beliefs. The books were used to teach reading as well as critical thinking, both legitimate purposes of schooling. Although the several judges who made up the majority could not agree on their exact reasoning, they upheld the school's position over parental objections. Crucial to the majority was a perception that accommodation to the parents' religious claim "will leave public education in shreds." Thus, schools may select materials useful to achieve important educational goals even if some parents consider some of the materials objectionable on religious grounds. Courts will consider the importance of the educational goals and the nature of the materials used as well as the grounds of the objections. As long as students are not required to affirm or deny religious beliefs, courts are likely to protect schools' discretion in the use of curricular materials.

Can parents have their children excused from parts of the curriculum for reasons other than religious or moral objections?

Yes, they can, as long as the studies to be missed are not "essential for citizenship." An historic case on this issue arose in Nebraska in 1891 and involved a father's objection to his daughter's studying rhetoric and his desire that she study grammar instead. After his wish was granted, he changed his mind and demanded she not study grammar. When the school board expelled her, the Supreme Court of Nebraska ordered a reinstatement without the requirement that she study grammar.[28] The court protected the parents' preference because the study of neither grammar nor rhetoric was considered to be essential for citizenship.

Similarly, in recent years, the deputy attorney general of California supported the "good citizenship" standard under which "elementary mathematics could be required, although calculus could not; handwriting could be required, creative writing could not." He further wrote that "when the state chooses to override a parent's wish, the burden is on the state to establish that in order to function effectively as a citizen, one must be versed in the subject to which the parents object."[29] Thus parents could withdraw their children from a music class and have them take private music lessons instead. Local schools could not object to such parental decisions unless the state law required instruction in the particular subject.

Can schools require certain courses as prerequisites for graduation?

Yes they can, as long as their requirements are reasonable. Students who meet such requirements are entitled to their diplomas even if they violate a school rule, such as the requirement that they wear a cap and gown and attend graduation ceremonies. At least one court ruled that such a student has a right to the diploma, but the school may exclude the student from participating in the graduating exercises.[30]

Can parents require a local school system to offer certain courses of instruction, use particular books or materials, or exclude books or materials?

No, they cannot. Local school boards must offer courses of study required by state law, and they may not violate state and federal constitutional provisions. Within the boundaries of such laws, however, school boards have discretion to determine what courses will be taught, what books and materials will be used, the selection of personnel, and even the methods of instruction employed. Although the states have basic authority over the provision of public education, significant authority and responsibility have been delegated, in almost all states, to local school districts. Courts are reluctant to interfere with the discretion of local boards in the operation of public schools and will do so only in clear cases of arbitrary and unreasonable exercises of authority or violation of constitutional rights. In a celebrated case in West Virginia, for example, courts upheld the discretion of a local board in its choice of books, since parents could not show that such books were "subversive" or "maliciously written."[31]

SUMMARY

Although the national Constitution and federal laws neither mandate nor provide public schools, each of the 50 states make publicly supported schools available for all children. State laws provide such schools, although the age of compulsory attendance varies somewhat from state to state.

State compulsory education laws generally have been upheld by the courts because important social interests are served by a well-educated citizenry. The state requirement that children attend school can be satisfied by attending public or private schools, and if private, religious or secular schools. Generally speaking, states have the authority to supervise the quality of schooling in both public and private institutions, but states vary in the provision and rigor of such supervision.

State laws requiring children to attend school usually provide for alternative ways of meeting such requirements if the alternatives are "equivalent" to public schools. Home schooling has been ruled to satisfy such "equivalencies" as long as the parents or tutors are qualified, the time spent on instruction is comparable to time spent in schools, and the subjects taught cover the "common branches of knowledge" taught in public schools. In one case involving a traditional Amish religious group, the courts exempted children from attendance beyond the eighth grade when evidence indicated that such attendance would be destructive to their religious beliefs and way of life. This kind of exemption would be very difficult for other groups to achieve.

Where state laws prescribe part of the curriculum, local school systems must follow such prescriptions. Beyond that, local boards have wide discretion over curriculum and instruction as well as book and material selection, personnel, and other aspects of schooling. Parents may exempt their children from parts of the curriculum that clearly conflict with their religious or moral values. They may also exempt their children from elective studies in order to substitute other, out-of-school experiences. Courses of study considered "essential for citizenship" may not be avoided by children, even if their parents object to them. Finally, local school officials may specify requirements for graduation as long as such requirements are reasonable and not arbitrary. Thus courts and the law attempt to maintain an appropriate balance between the needs of society and the rights of parents to guide the upbringing of their children.

NOTES

1. *Concerned Citizens for Neighborhood Schools, Inc. v. Board of Education of Chattanooga*, 379 F.Supp. 1233 (E.D. Tenn. 1974).
2. *Pierce v. Society of Sisters*, 268 U.S. 510 (1925).
3. *Wisconsin v. Yoder*, 406 U.S. 205 (1972).
4. *People v. Levisen*, 90 N.E.2d 213 (Ill. 1950).
5. *In re Shinn*, 195 Cal. App. 2d 683 (1961).
6. *State v. McDonough*, 468 A.2d 977 (Me. 1983).
7. *In re Sawyer*, 672 P.2d 1093 (Kan. 1983).
8. *Roemhild v. State*, 308 S.E.2d 154 (Ga. 1983).
9. See *State v. Edgington*, 663 P.2d 374 (App. 1983), *cert. denied*, 464 U.S. 940 (1983).

10. *Murphy* v. *Arkansas*, 852 F.2d 1039 (8th Cir. 1988).

11. *Ellis* v. *O'Hara*, 612 F. Supp. 379 (D.C. Mo. 1985).

12. Mo. STAT. ANN, § 167 031-167.071 (1988).

13. *State* v. *Schmidt*, 505 N.E. 2d 627 (Ohio 1987).

14. Reported in STATE EDUCATION LEADER, a quarterly publication of the Education Commission of the States, Vol. 7., No. 1 (Spring 1988).

15. Klicka, C. J., HOME SCHOOLING IN THE UNITED STATES: A STATUTORY ANALYSIS, Great Falls, Va., Home School Legal Defense Association, 1988.

16. For a systematic study of this topic, *see* S. Yastrow, "Home Instruction: A National Study of State Law," unpublished doctoral dissertation, Loyola University of Chicago, 1989.

17. *Knox* v. *O'Brien*, 72 A.2d 389 (N.J. 1950).

18. *State* v. *Massa*, 231 A.2d 252 (N.J. 1967).

19. *Roe* v. *Wade*, 410 U.S. 113 (1973). Emphasis added.

20. *Perchemlides* v. *Frizzle*, No. 16641 (Mass. Super. November 13, 1978).

21. 504 N.E.2d 592 (Mass. 1987).

22. *Epperson* v. *State of Arkansas*, 393 U.S. 97 (1968).

23. *Edwards* v. *Aquillard*, 482 U.S. 578 (1987).

24. *Hardwick* v. *Board of Trustees*, 205 P.49 (Cal. 1921).

25. *Valent* v. *New Jersey State Board of Education*, 274 A.2d 832 (N.J. 1971).

26. *Medeiros* v. *Kiyosaki*, 478 P.2d 314 (Hawaii, 1970); *Cornwell* v. *State Board of Education*, 428 F.2d 471 (4th Cir. 1970), *cert. denied*, 400 U.S. 942 (1970).

27. *Mozert* v. *Hawkins County Public Schools*, 827 F.2d 1058 (6th Cir. 1987).

28. *State ex rel. Sheibley* v. *School District No. 1*, 48 N.W. 393 (Neb. 1891).

29. Joel S. Moskowitz, *Parental Rights and Responsibilities*, 50 WASH. L. REV. 623 (1975).

30. *Valentine* v. *Independent School District*, 183 N.W. 434 (Iowa 1921).

31. *Williams* v. *Board of Education of County of Kanawha*, 388 F.Supp. 93 (S.D. W.Va. 1975).

CHAPTER 18

When Can Schools Restrict Personal Appearance?

OVERVIEW

During the 1950s, teachers and students rarely questioned a school's dress and grooming codes. Had students or teachers thought of challenging these codes in court, they would have uniformly lost. Teachers were expected to be adult models of neatness and good taste and to conform to the dress and grooming standards of other professionals in the community. Generally they did. In the late 1960s, however, teachers began to challenge dress and grooming codes, and a great number of school districts abandoned them. As a result many teachers came to believe that such codes were unconstitutional. But this is far from true. An issue that seemed buried in the 1970s is reemerging today.

Controversy over student dress and grooming was especially intense 20 years ago. In fact, long hair and unconventional clothes were among the hottest students' rights issues of the time.* And they were often viewed as important symbols of protest and dissent by teachers as well as students.

Unlike most constitutional controversies that bombard the courts, judges have been deeply divided over the question of grooming in the public schools. Although they are less divided about appropriate school clothing, the law concerning personal appearance still differs among the states. The constitutional and

---

* Grooming controversies did not begin in the 1960s. Disputes about hair length have been taking place on this continent at least since 1649 when the magistrates of Portsmouth decried "the wearing of long hair, after the manner of ruffians" and declared their "dislike and detestation against wearing such long hair, as against a thing uncivil and unmanly."[1]

educational reasons underlying these differences and the current state of the law on the subject are examined in this chapter.

GROOMING STANDARDS FOR TEACHERS

Can teachers be punished without due process for violating a school's grooming code?

No. What constitutes due process in cases such as this was explained by a federal court in a Massachusetts controversy.[2] A teacher named David Lucia grew a beard one winter vacation. This conflicted with an unwritten school policy explained to Lucia by the superintendent after the vacation. When Lucia failed to shave his beard following a meeting with the school committee, he was suspended because of "insubordination and improper example set by a teacher." He was not invited to a subsequent meeting at which the committee voted to dismiss him, and he took his case to court.

The court did not decide whether a teacher had a constitutional right to wear a beard. However, it did rule that Lucia's freedom to wear a beard could not be taken from him without due process. The court noted several deficiencies in the procedure used to dismiss Lucia: Prior to this case, there was no announced policy against teachers wearing beards; and the committee did not indicate that failure to remove his beard would result in the dismissal. After criticizing the committee's lack of due process, the court observed: "The American public school system, which has a basic responsibility for instilling in its students an appreciation of our democratic system, is a peculiarly appropriate place for the use of fundamentally fair procedures."

From this case we can conclude that a teacher cannot be lawfully dismissed for wearing a beard or sideburns unless (1) there is a clear school policy outlawing such grooming, (2) teachers are given adequate notice of the policy and the consequences of not adhering to it, and (3) teachers are given the right to request a hearing if specific facts are in dispute.

Have some courts ruled that teachers have a constitutional right to wear beards and sideburns?

Yes, a few have. In the case of a Pasadena schoolteacher, Paul Finot, a California appeals court explained why.[3] When Finot arrived at school one September wearing a recently grown beard, his principal asked him to shave it off. After he refused, the board of education transferred him to home teaching because he violated the teacher handbook requirement that teachers conform to acceptable standards of dress and grooming and set an example for the students. (The student handbook prohibited beards and mustaches.) The administrators were concerned that Finot's beard might attract undue attention, interfere with education, and make the prohibition of beards for students more difficult to enforce.

The court was not persuaded. It ruled that Finot's right to wear a beard was guarded by two constitutional provisions. It was one of the liberties protected by the Fourteenth Amendment, and it was a form of symbolic expression protected by the First Amendment. The court noted that some people interpret a beard as a symbol of masculinity, authority, or wisdom; others see it as a symbol of nonconformity or rebellion. In either case, the court felt that such symbols "merit constitutional protection." Thus the court ruled that beards on teachers "cannot constitutionally be banned from the classroom" unless the school can show that the beard had an adverse effect on the educational process.

Have some courts ruled that teachers do not have a constitutional right to wear beards and sideburns?

Yes. In the case of an Illinois math teacher, a federal appeals court explained why many judges do not believe teacher grooming is a major constitutional issue.[4] When Max Miller's contract was not renewed because of his beard and sideburns, he alleged that this violated his rights. The judge acknowledged that he personally regarded "dress and hair style as matters of relatively trivial importance on any scale of values in appraising the qualifications of a teacher." He noted that, logically, appearance should not be significant and that "a teacher should be able to explain the pythagorean theorem as well in a T-shirt as in a three-piece suit." But the court doubted whether grooming choices are protected by the Constitution and indicated that school officials may consider an individual's appearance as one of the factors affecting his suitability. Therefore the court concluded that if a school board decided a "teacher's style of dress or plumage" had an adverse educational impact, there was "no doubt that the interest of the teacher is subordinate to the public interest."

In a related case upholding a school's antibeard policy for teachers, the Tennessee Supreme Court wrote: "The grooming of one person is of concern not only to himself but to all others with whom he comes in contact; we have to look at each other whether we like it or not. It is for this reason that society sets certain limits upon the freedom of individuals to choose his own grooming."[5]

Is there a trend of decision in teacher grooming cases?

Yes. Although courts are divided over this issue, the trend of decision is reflected in a 1982 judgment of the Fifth Circuit Court of Appeals.[6] The case involved a Louisiana district that applied their student antibeard rule to teachers. The court upheld the no-beard rule, explaining that grooming "may be regulated" if the regulation is reasonable. "In the high school environment," wrote the court, "a hair-style regulation is a reasonable means in furthering the school board's undeniable interest in teaching hygiene, instilling discipline, asserting authority, and compelling uniformity." On the other hand, a school rule would be unconstitutional if it is irrational and arbitrary.[7] Thus in a related case the Seventh Circuit Court struck down a rule prohibiting schoolbus drivers but not teachers from wearing mustaches.[8] The court concluded that this policy had no reasonable relationship "with a proper school purpose," and was "so irrational as to be arbitrary."

Is grooming a constitutional right if it reflects a teacher's racial or ethnic values and beliefs?

Probably. Booker Peek, a black teacher from Florida, wore a goatee as a matter of racial pride. Although Peek was a superior high school French teacher, he was not rehired because he refused repeated requests to remove his goatee. The principal said the denial of reappointment was based on his discretionary power to ensure appropriate dress and discipline. Peek called the action unconstitutional, and the court agreed.[9] According to the court, when a goatee is worn by a black man as an expression of his heritage, culture, and racial pride, its wearer "enjoys the protection of First Amendment rights." Furthermore, there was no evidence that the goatee disrupted school discipline. Thus it appeared that the decision not to recommend reappointment was racially motivated and tainted with "institutional racism," the effects of which were manifested in "an intolerance of ethnic diversity and racial pride."

TEACHERS' CLOTHING

Do teachers have a right to dress as they wish? Is this right protected by the Constitution?

No. First, courts that do not protect a teacher's grooming choice will not protect clothing choice. Second, even courts that recognize grooming as constitutionally protected may not rule the same way in matters of dress because judges feel that school regulations concerning dress are not as personal and that their impact is not as great. Therefore most teachers who challenge clothing regulations do not argue that they have a right to dress any way they wish; rather, they contend that the dress code is arbitrary, unreasonable, or discriminatory. This was the argument used by Edward Blanchet after he was suspended for violating a Louisiana school board dress policy requiring that male teachers wear neckties.

The state appeals court wrote positively about Blanchet's sincerity, convictions, and character and described him as "a dedicated and effective teacher, an assistant principal at his school, [and] a sober church-going family man." Nevertheless, the court ruled against him.[10] The judge wrote that the court could not overturn school policy and substitute its judgment for that of the board unless the board's action was clearly unreasonable and arbitrary. Since the purpose of the board's rule was to enhance the professional image of its teachers in the eyes of students and parents, and since there was some evidence supporting the rule, the court concluded that it could not find the necktie policy arbitrary or unreasonable.

In a related case, a 25-year-old high school French teacher was not rehired because she insisted on wearing short skirts. A federal appeals court observed that, the teacher was terminated because her "image" was "overexposed." Although the court had recognized grooming as a constitutional right, it refused to extend constitutional protection to clothing regulations, which the court felt involve less personal matters and only affect teachers during school hours.[11]

Would a teacher's refusal to conform to a school dress code be protected as a form of symbolic expression?

Probably not. This was the argument used by Richard Brimley, an English teacher from East Hartford, Connecticut. Since Brimley wanted to present himself to his students as a person not tied to "establishment conformity," he refused to comply with his school's dress code, which required a coat and tie for male teachers. Brimley argued that an individual's appearance was protected by the First Amendment as a form of symbolic expression and academic freedom, which should give teachers wide discretion over teaching methods and style of clothing—especially when they are neat and reasonable. Moreover, he argued that a tie was no longer mandatory or even typical among other young professionals and that the requirement did not promote discipline, respect, or good grooming among students.

Two judges of a federal appeals court were persuaded by these arguments, but the majority was not.[12] On behalf of the majority, Judge Meskill wrote that federal courts should not overturn school rules that "appear foolish or unwise" unless they directly involve "basic constitutional values." If courts decided a dress code controversy, then they could be asked to rule on every insubstantial school policy. Therefore, wrote Judge Meskill, "we are unwilling to expand the First Amendment protection to include a teacher's sartorial choice." If we bring "trivial activities" under constitutional protection, "we trivialize the Constitution."

STUDENTS' GROOMING: A CONSTITUTIONAL RIGHT?

Are students free to wear their hair as they wish?

About half of the U.S. circuit courts of appeals answer yes to this question. A typical case arose in Indiana's Wawasee High School where a committee of students, teachers, and administrators developed a dress code "to insure the best possible overall appearance" of the student body. The code was adopted by a vote of the students, and they and their parents were notified of its provisions. Nevertheless, Greg Carpenter, with his parents' consent, chose to violate the code's "long hair provision" and was punished. As a result Greg's father sued on his behalf to prohibit enforcement of the code's hair length regulations.*

The school board argued that because the code was adopted by a majority of the students, it was not an unreasonable interference with Greg Carpenter's constitutional rights. But the Seventh U.S. Circuit Court of Appeals disagreed.[13] It held that "the right to wear one's hair at any length or in any desired manner is an ingredient of personal freedom protected by the United States Constitution." To limit that right, a school would have to bear a "substantial burden of justification." Here the board did not meet that burden. It presented no evidence that Greg's hair disrupted classroom decorum or interfered with other students, or that the hair provision was related to safety or health. The school showed no reasonable relationship between the code and a significant educational purpose. Therefore the court concluded that the democratic process by which the code was adopted did not justify the denial of Greg's constitutional right to wear his hair as he chose. The U.S. Constitution, said the court, cannot be amended by majority vote.

What other arguments support student grooming rights?

Judges have used a variety of legal, educational, and philosophic arguments to uphold grooming as a constitutional right. Here are a few:

A personal liberty protected by the Fourteenth Amendment. In holding unconstitutional a Marlboro, Massachusetts, school policy forbidding "unusually long hair," the First Circuit Court of Appeals noted that the case involved the constitutional protection of certain "uniquely personal aspects of one's life."[14] The court ruled that grooming was protected by the due process clause of the Fourteenth Amendment, which "establishes a sphere of personal liberty for every individual," subject to restriction only if the exercise of that liberty interferes with the rights of others. The court saw "no inherent reason why decency, decorum, or good conduct" requires a boy to wear his hair short. Nor, it concluded, does "compelled conformity to conventional standards of appearance seem a justifiable part of the educational process."

Symbolic speech protected by the First Amendment. Some courts argue that long hair is a form of symbolic speech by which the wearer conveys his individuality or rejection of conventional values and that it should therefore be protected under the First Amendment. According to one judge: "A person shorn of the freedom to vary the length and style of his hair is forced against his will to hold himself out symbolically as a person holding ideas contrary, perhaps, to ideas he holds most dear. Forced dress, including forced hair style, humiliates the unwilling complier, forces him to submerge his individuality in the 'undis-

---

* The code contained a consent provision that allowed noncompliance if at the beginning of each semester a parent appeared before the principal and gave written consent for the exception of his child. Greg's father decided not to seek an exception but to challenge the constitutionality of the code.

tracting' mass, and in general, smacks of the exaltation of organization over member, unit over component, and state over individual."*[15]

A denial of equal protection. In an Indiana case, a high school principal said his grooming regulations were required for health and safety—that long hair could cause problems in the gym, swimming pool, and laboratories. But the Seventh Circuit Court of Appeals observed that girls engaged in similar activities wore long hair, yet only boys were required to wear short hair. Since the principal offered no reason why health and safety regulations were not equally applicable to girls, the court concluded that the rules constituted "a denial of equal protection to male students" in violation of the Fourteenth Amendment.[17] The court noted that legitimate health and safety objectives could be achieved simply through rules aimed directly at the problems caused by long hair—for example, by requiring swimming caps in pools and hairnets around machinery.

A right to govern one's personal appearance. In striking down a St. Charles, Missouri, dress code that prohibited long hair, the Eighth Circuit Court of Appeals wrote that each student possesses "a constitutionally protected right to govern his personal appearance while attending public high school."[18] According to the court, "The Constitution guarantees rights other than those specifically enumerated, and . . . the right to govern one's personal appearance is one of those guaranteed rights."

In a concurring opinion, one of the judges rejected the arguments given by school officials to defend their grooming regulations in these words:

> The gamut of rationalizations for justifying this restriction fails in light of reasoned analysis. When school authorities complain variously that such hair styles are inspired by a communist conspiracy, that they make boys look like girls, that they promote confusion as to the use of restrooms, and that they destroy the students' moral fiber, then it is little wonder even moderate students complain of "getting up-tight." In final analysis, I am satisfied a comprehensive school restriction on male student hair styles accomplishes little more than to project the prejudices and personal distastes of certain adults in authority on to the impressionable young student.

Can schools restrict student grooming?

In about half the states, they can. A case in El Paso, Texas, illustrates the views of those courts which hold that schools have the authority to restrict student hair

---

* In a related North Carolina case a judge wrote that long hair is simply "a harkening back to the fashion of earlier years. For example, many of the founding fathers, as well as General Grant and General Lee, wore their hair . . . in a style comparable to that adopted by the [student] plaintiffs. Although there exists no depiction of Jesus Christ, either reputedly or historically accurate, he has always been shown with hair at least the length of that of the plaintiffs." Thus the judge noted that none of these great men would have been permitted to attend high school if the disputed hair regulations were enforced.[16]

length. In this case, the Fifth Circuit Court of Appeals considered and rejected the following arguments, which were presented by a high school junior, Chelsey Karr.[19]

Symbolic speech. Although some students wear long hair to convey a message, the court noted that many wear it simply as a matter of personal taste or as a result of peer-group influence. Karr, for example, sued not because his hair symbolized anything but "because I like my hair long." Judge Morgan felt that it would be inappropriate and unworkable to have the Constitution protect students who intend to convey a message by wearing long hair but not other students.

A protected liberty. The court pointed out that individual liberties may be "ranked in a spectrum of importance." At one end are the "great liberties" such as speech and religion specifically guaranteed in the Bill of Rights. At the other end are the "lesser liberties" that may be curtailed if the restrictions are related to a proper state activity. The court concluded that hair regulations are reasonably related to schooling, that they do not restrict any fundamental constitutional liberty, and that their interference is a "temporary and relatively inconsequential one." Judge Morgan observed that administrators "must daily make innumerable decisions which restrict student liberty" including the regulation of student parking, eating, and attendance. Students should not be able to force administrators to defend such restrictions in court when fundamental rights are not involved.

Confusion and burden. The appeals court was disturbed that different trial courts in the circuit reached opposite results based on similar facts. The court was even more disturbed by "the burden which has been placed on the federal courts by suits of this nature" by the number of days spent on trials and appeals. Judge Morgan noted that it was impossible for the courts to protect every citizen against every minor restriction on his liberty. Because of this burden and because these cases do not raise issues of "fundamental" importance, the court ruled that henceforth all such regulations would be presumed valid.

Do the principles that apply to the classroom also apply to sports?

Usually. In a 1984 Alabama case, two black high school athletes challenged their coach's "clean shaven" policy that barred them from varsity football.[20] They argued that there was no rational connection between athletic performance and shaving and that shaving caused skin problems—especially among blacks. However, the judge upheld the shaving rule on the basis of the court's prior decision that "grooming regulations at the high school level do not deprive the plaintiffs of any constitutionally recognized rights," and that this policy was aimed "not at athletic performance, but at presenting the school in a favorable light." On the other hand, the court suggested that its decision might have been different if there was medical evidence that these specific students suffered skin problems from the shaving policy. Moreover, in states where grooming choice is a constitutional right, courts are likely to be critical of team grooming regulations that are *not* clearly related to athletic performance.

Why doesn't the Supreme Court resolve the grooming conflict?

When federal appeals courts differ in their interpretation of the Constitution, the U.S. Supreme Court usually reviews the question, renders a decision, and thus establishes a "uniform law of the land." But despite the sharp differences of opinion among federal courts concerning student grooming, the Supreme Court has on at least nine occasions declined to review the decisions on this issue. This is because most justices of the Court apparently do not believe the cases raise important constitutional questions of national significance. In rejecting an urgent appeal to the Supreme Court in one grooming case, Justice Black wrote: "The only thing about it that borders on the serious to me is the idea that anyone should think the Federal Constitution imposes on the United States courts the burden of supervising the length of hair that public school students should wear."[21] As long as the Supreme Court refuses to hear these cases, the law will continue to vary throughout the United States.

Can I know how the various federal courts are likely to rule on grooming cases?

Yes. Despite the many conflicts over grooming regulations, the law on this subject has become relatively clear, as Figure 1 indicates. Most U.S. circuit courts of appeals have ruled on this issue directly, and the others have indicated how they would probably rule.

What is the law in my state?

The federal appeals courts have decided that grooming is a constitutional right in the First Circuit (Maine, Massachusetts, New Hampshire, Rhode Island), the Fourth Circuit (Maryland, North Carolina, South Carolina, Virginia, West Virginia), the Seventh Circuit (Illinois, Indiana, Wisconsin), the Eighth Circuit (Arkansas, Iowa, Minnesota, Missouri, Nebraska, North Dakota, South Dakota), and probably the Second Circuit (Connecticut, New York, Vermont).* In these states, courts will hold grooming regulations unconstitutional unless school officials present convincing evidence that they are fair, reasonable, and necessary to carry out a legitimate educational purpose.

The law is different in the Fifth Circuit (Louisiana, Mississippi, Texas), the Sixth Circuit (Kentucky, Michigan, Ohio, Tennessee), the Ninth Circuit (Alaska,

---

* In 1973, the Second Circuit clearly ruled that hair-length regulations raised "a substantial constitutional issue."[22] Although the U.S. Supreme Court overruled that decision as it applied to police,[23] the Second Circuit would probably reaffirm its decision as applied to students because of the important differences between regulating the appearance of students and police and the refusal of the Supreme Court to rule on student hair cases.

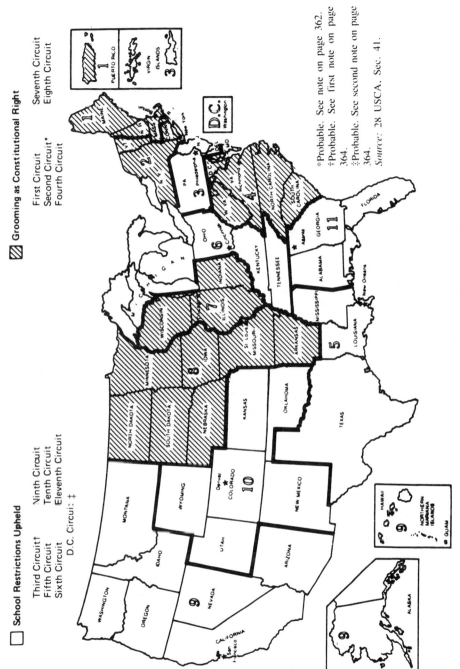

Figure 1. Circuit Court Rulings on Grooming

Arizona, California, Hawaiian Islands, Idaho, Montana, Nevada, Oregon, Washington), the Tenth Circuit (Colorado, Kansas, Oklahoma, New Mexico, Utah, Wyoming), the Eleventh Circuit (Alabama, Florida, Georgia), and probably in the Third Circuit (Delaware, New Jersey, Pennsylvania)* and the District of Columbia Circuit.† In these states, the circuit courts have decided that grooming is not a significant constitutional issue and that federal courts should not judge the wisdom of codes regulating hair length or style. This does not necessarily mean that there is no legal remedy if a student is disciplined for violating school grooming regulations. It only means that federal courts will generally not consider these cases. Such grooming restrictions may still be challenged in state courts.

SCHOOL DRESS CODES

Can school codes regulate student clothing?

Yes. All courts recognize that schools have authority to regulate student clothing. But not all dress codes are constitutional.[27] In New Hampshire, for example, a federal court held that a rule prohibiting the wearing of blue jeans or dungarees was unconstitutional.[28] The court rejected the argument that wearing jeans "detracts from discipline and a proper educational climate" because the school presented no evidence supporting this position. However, the judge wrote that a school "can and must . . . exclude persons who are unsanitary, obscenely or scantily clad." Good hygiene may require that dirty clothing be prohibited. And a school may prohibit scantily clad students "because it is obvious that the lack of proper covering, particularly with female students, might tend to distract other students" and disrupt the educational process.[29] Futhermore, a North Carolina court held that a student was properly excluded from his graduation ceremony for violating a rule requiring men to wear "dress pants, as opposed to jeans" under their graduation gowns.[30]

Can girls be prohibited from wearing slacks?

Probably not. A state court annulled such a prohibition in a New York school district's dress code for secondary schools.[31] School boards have the authority to regulate dress for reasons of safety, order, and discipline, but they have no authority to enforce regulations not related to those factors. According to Judge

---

* Although the Third Circuit held that civilian employees of the National Guard could challenge the Guard's hair-length regulations,[24] this court clearly ruled in 1975 that "the federal courts should not intrude" in the area of school regulation of student hair length and that it would no longer consider school grooming cases.[25]

† The D.C. Court of Appeals has not ruled directly on the issue of school grooming regulations, but in a related case it indicated that it agreed with the U.S. Supreme Court and "sees no federal question in this area."[26]

Meyer, the fact that the no-slacks rule "applies only to female students" and applies to every kind of slacks "makes it evident that what is being enforced is style or taste and not safety, order, or discipline." Similarly, an Idaho court ruled that an absolute prohibition against female students wearing "slacks, pant-suits, and culottes" was "unreasonable, capricious, and arbitrary" and had "no reasonable relationship" to the educational process.[32] However, a Kentucky appeals court refused to strike down a prohibition against girls wearing jeans because the judge felt that school dress code conflicts were not matters of constitutional importance.[33]

What kind of clothing regulations would probably be upheld by the courts?

In the New York "slacks" case, Judge Meyer gave several examples. In the interest of safety, a school board can probably prohibit "the wearing of bell-bottomed slacks by students . . . who ride bikes to school." In the interest of discipline, a regulation against slacks that are "so skintight and, therefore, revealing as to provoke or distract students of the opposite sex" might be valid. And in the interest of order, a rule against slacks "to the bottom of which small bells have been attached" would be upheld. According to the judge, such regulations would be valid because they clearly relate to the school's "authorized concerns"; a flat prohibition against all slacks is invalid "precisely because it does not."[34] Similarly an Arkansas judge indicated that the following dress code provisions would be held valid: prohibitions against girls wearing "excessively tight skirts or pants or dresses more than six inches above the knee" (to prevent immodest clothing), prohibitions against boys wearing shirt-tails outside their pants in "shop" (for safety reasons), or any student wearing clothing displaying obscene pictures.[35]

Will courts rule the same way in clothing cases as in hair controversies?

Sometimes. Courts that do not protect a student's choice of hairstyle will probably not protect his choice of clothing. But courts that *do* protect hairstyle may or may not protect student freedom in matters of dress. Some courts hold that the constitutional liberty that protects a student's grooming choice also protects his clothing choice. Other courts distinguish hair from clothing on the grounds that hair restrictions are more serious invasions of personal freedom. For example, a federal judge in Vermont held a school grooming code unconstitutional but noted that "the cut of one's hair style is more fundamental to personal appearance than the type of clothing he wears."[36] Similarly, a Minnesota judge wrote: "Were a school to prohibit a boy attending school with no shirt," he could take off his shirt as he leaves the school grounds. But a hair regulation "invades private life beyond the school jurisdiction."[37]

Thus, some courts distinguish clothing from grooming on the following grounds: (1) hairstyle is more fundamental to personal appearance, (2) hair restrictions have a long-term effect, and (3) hairstyles today usually do not involve issues of morality and distraction, as do some clothing styles. And even courts that protect both clothing and grooming give schools much wider discretion to regulate clothing in the interests of health, safety, order, or discipline.

FRONTIER ISSUES

During the 1990s new controversies about student dress codes will emerge. Recently, in some large cities such as Baltimore, Detroit, and Los Angeles, students, teachers, and parents have developed stricter dress policies to decrease crime on campus and minimize locker break-ins. Detroit's Mumford High School, for example, prohibited fancy clothing including fur coats, gold jewelry, and certain name-brand trinkets. According to one observer, the goal of these policies is "to ban clothing that made kids look like wealthy drug merchants."[38] A November 1989 article in *Newsweek* reported that stricter student dress codes "have spread from Texas to Alabama, Georgia and North Carolina."[39] Some of these codes cover everything from the length of pants and skirts and the wearing of undergarments to the prohibition of clothing associated with gang membership and the banning of T-shirts with vulgar words or symbols. As one attorney noted, "The pendulum is swinging to conformity."[40] An indication of how courts are likely to respond to these new restrictions may be found in the following recent cases.

Can schools prohibit the wearing of earrings, jewelry, or other symbols of gang membership?

Yes. Because students were intimidated by gang members, Bremen High School banned all gang activities at school and the wearing of gang symbols including earrings, jewelry, and other emblems. But senior Darryl Olesen wore an earring to school because it "expressed his individuality" and was "attractive to young women."[41] As a result, he was suspended, and he challenged the earring ban as a violation of his freedom of expression and his right to equal protection (since the ban only applied to men). However a 1987 court decision supported the school policy. Olesen's earring was not a protected form of expression, the judge wrote, because it did not "convey a particularized message" that "would be understood by those who viewed it." Unlike unconstitutional rules against long hair, there was a clear reason for this rule "directly related to the safety and well-being" of the students. Furthermore, the "gender-based classification" was not unconstitutional because it related to a legitimate government objective (curtailment of gang activity); and it was men, not women, that wore earrings to indicate gang membership.

Can students be prohibited from wearing T-shirts with controversial messages?

It depends on the message. In 1987, Rod Gano, a senior at Twin Falls High School, was sent home several times for wearing a T-shirt with caricatures of three school administrators drinking alcoholic beverages and acting drunk. Gano argued that the school abridged his freedom of speech by disciplining him for wearing the T-shirt. But a federal court disagreed.[42] First, wrote the judge, Gano could not articulate any particular criticism or idea he was trying to convey by wearing the T-shirt. Therefore, banning the shirt would not supress any specific message. Second, the judge wrote that the T-shirt "falsely accuses the three administrators of committing a misdemeanor"—consuming alcohol on school property. Since the Supreme Court has upheld the authority of schools to discipline students for "lewd, indecent or offensive speech and conduct,"* that precedent applies to this case. Therefore, Twin Falls administrators were acting within their authority when they disciplined Rod Gano for wearing his "clearly offensive" T-shirt that falsely depicted the administrators in an alcoholic stupor. Thus schools can prohibit students from wearing clothing with "lewd or indecent" word or gestures. However, this does not mean that administrators can prohibit all messages on clothing, and words or symbols that clearly concern issues of public policy and are not disruptive or indecent are still protected by the First Amendment.

May schools regulate student dress at off-campus, extracurricular activities?

Yes. Warren Harper and his sister Florence attended their high school prom in elegant attire—of the opposite sex. Warren wore earrings, high heels, a dress, and a fur cape. Florence wore a black tuxedo and men's shoes. The principal was not amused and told the Harpers to change their clothes or leave. After they refused, they were escorted out by a police officer and claimed that their constitutional rights were violated. However, the court disagreed since it found that the school's dress code was "reasonably related to the valid educational purpose of teaching community values."[43] According to the judge, the code does not discriminate on the basis of sex (e.g. by allowing females, not males, to wear dresses) but simply "requires all students to dress in conformity with the accepted standards of the community." In addition, the judge indicated that these principles also would apply to transvestites, homosexuals, and others who wished to defy the code because of their nonconventional sexual orientation.

SUMMARY

In the late 1960s and early 1970s, a few courts indicated that teacher grooming was a form of symbolic expression entitled to the protection of the First Amendment. In contrast, other judges held that teacher grooming is not a matter of

---

* This was the holding in *Bethel School District No. 403* v. *Fraser*, 108 S.Ct. 3159 (1986). See Chapter 8 for more on the scope and limits of student freedom of expression.

constitutional importance and should not even be considered by the courts. Now, however, judges tend to hold that teachers have a "constitutional liberty interest" in grooming, but that this right is not fundamental. Therefore, they rule that grooming may be regulated by the schools and will only be struck down if teachers prove that the regulation is unreasonable. While an increasing number of courts are using this "rational basis" test, judges differ about which teacher grooming rules are rationally related to education.

Administrative discretion is even greater regarding teacher attire. Most courts have ruled that teachers do not have a constitutional right to dress as they please. Judges have even upheld the authority of administrators to discipline teachers for violating dress requirements the judges thought unwise or insignificant because it is assumed that all employers can establish some clothing regulations and because such restrictions on teacher freedom are relatively minor. Courts might protect certain nonconforming clothing under special circumstances—for example, a black teacher of African studies who wears a dashiki as a matter of academic freedom or racial pride. But it is doubtful that any court would protect a teacher who insisted on going to class in frayed jeans, sandals, and a T-shirt in violation of school policy.

As far as students are concerned, nine of the thirteen U.S. circuit courts of appeals have clearly ruled on the constitutional right of students to choose the length of their hair.* Some circuits hold that grooming is a constitutional right, and others do not. The arguments used on each side are varied and vigorous, and no final decision establishing a uniform law has been reached because the Supreme Court has refused to rule on the issue.

Most courts hold that student clothing styles are not protected by the Constitution. Moreover, some courts that protect student hair length reject students' claims to wear the clothing of their choice. Judges justify the distinction on the grounds that restrictions on hairstyle are more serious invasions of individual freedom; clothing can be changed after school, but if haircuts are required, the effect is more lasting.

The questions raised by the controversies in this chapter concern more than personal appearance; they concern fundamental legal and educational issues such as: When should schools restrict student and teacher freedom? When should nonconformity be protected or punished? Educators cannot escape these difficult questions as they develop and enforce dress codes for students and teachers and search for an appropriate balance between freedom and conformity in the public schools.

---

* Three other circuits have not ruled directly on this issue, but they have indicated how they probably would vote. (See page 362.)

NOTES

1. Dale Goddy, RIGHTS AND FREEDOMS OF PUBLIC SCHOOL STUDENTS 25 (Topeka: National Organization on Legal Problems in Education, 1971).
2. *Lucia v. Duggan*, 303 F.Supp. 112 (D. Mass 1969).
3. *Finot v. Pasadena City Board of Education*, 58 Cal. Rptr. 520 (1967).
4. *Miller v. School District No. 167, Cook County, Illinois*, 495 F.2d 658 (7th Cir. 1974); *modified, Pence v. Rosenquist*, 573 F.2d 395 (7th Cir. 1978).
5. *Morrison v. Hamilton Board of Education*, 494 S.W.2d 770 (Tenn. 1973).
6. *Domico v. Rapides Parish School Board*, 675 F.2d 100 (5th Cir. 1982).
7. The appeals court based its reasoning on a U.S. Supreme Court decision that upheld grooming restrictions on police but acknowledged a "liberty interest in freedom to choose [one's] own hairstyle." *Kelly v. Johnson*, 425 U.S. 238 (1976).
8. *Pence v. Rosenquist*, 573 F.2d 395 (7th Cir. 1978).
9. *Braxton v. Board of Public Instruction of Duval County, Florida*, 303 F.Supp. 958 (M.D. Fla. 1969).
10. *Blanchet v. Vermilion Parish School Board*, 220 So.2d 534 (La. 1969).
11. *Tardif v. Quinn*, 545 F.2d 761 (1st Cir. 1976).
12. *East Hartford Education Association v. Board of Education of the Town of East Hartford*, 562 F.2d 838 (2d Cir. 1977).
13. *Arnold v. Carpenter*, 459 F.2d 939 (7th Cir. 1972).
14. *Richards v. Thurston*, 424 F.2d 1281 (1st Cir. 1970).
15. Judge Wisdom (dissenting), in *Karr v. Schmidt*, 460 F.2d 609 (5th Cir. 1972).
16. *Massie v. Henry*, 455 F.2d 779 (4th Cir. 1972).
17. *Crews v. Cloncs*, 432 F.2d 1259 (7th Cir. 1970).
18. *Bishop v. Colaw*, 450 F.2d 1069 (8th Cir. 1971).
19. *Karr v. Schmidt*, 460 F.2d 609 (5th Cir. 1972).
20. *Davenport v. Randolph County Board of Education*, 730 F.2d 1395 (11th Cir. 1984).
21. *Karr v. Schmidt*, 401 U.S. 1201 (1971).
22. *Owen v. Barry*, 483 F.2d 1126 (2d Cir. 1973).
23. *Kelley v. Johnson*, 425 U.S. 238 (1976).
24. *Syrek v. Pennsylvania Air National Guard*, 537 F.2d 66 (3d Cir. 1976).
25. *Zeller v. Donegal School District Board of Education*, 517 F.2d 600 (3d Cir. 1975).
26. *Fagan v. National Cash Register Co.*, 481 F.2d 1115 (D.C. Cir. 1973).
27. Students probably would be exempt from a requirement to wear standard gym clothing for religious reasons if they and/or their parents believed such clothing was "immodest" or "improper." But that would probably not exempt them from physical education requirements. *Moody v. Cronin*, 484 F.Supp. 270 (C.D. Ill. 1979).
28. *Bannister v. Paradis*, 316 F.Supp. 185 (D. N.H. 1970).
29. *Id.*
30. *Fowler v. Williamson*, 251 S.E.2d 889 (N.C. 1979).
31. *Scott v. Board of Education, Hicksville*, 305 N.Y.S.2d 601 (1969).
32. *Johnson v. Joint School District No. 60, Bigham County*, 508 P.2d 547 (Idaho 1973).
33. *Dunkerson v. Russell*, 502 S.W.2d 64 (Ky. 1973).
34. *Scott v. Board of Education, Hicksville*, 305 N.Y.S.2d 601 (1969).

35. *Wallace* v. *Ford*, 346 F.Supp. 156 (E.D. Ark. 1972).

36. *Dunham* v. *Pulsifer*, 312 F.Supp. 411 (D. Vt. 1970).

37. *Westley* v. *Rossi*, 305 F.Supp. 706 (D. Minn. 1969).

38. *Newsweek*, November 27, 1989, p. 79.

39. *Id.*

40. *Id.*

41. *Olesen* v. *Board of Education of School District No. 228*, 676 F.Supp. 820 (N.D. Ill.1987).

42. *Gano* v. *School District 411 of Twin Falls County, Idaho*, 674 F.Supp. 796 (D. Idaho 1987).

43. *Harper* v. *Edgewood Board of Education*, 655 F.Supp. 1353 (S.D. Ohio 1987).

APPENDIX A

Selected Provisions
of the U.S. Constitution

ARTICLE I

Section 8. [1] The Congress shall have Power To lay and collect Taxes, Duties, Imposts and Excises, to pay the Debts and provide for the common Defence and general Welfare of the United States; . . .

ARTICLE III

Section 1. The judicial Power of the United States, shall be vested in one supreme Court, and in such inferior Courts as the Congress may from time to time ordain and establish. The Judges, both of the supreme and inferior Courts, shall hold their Offices during good Behaviour, and shall, at stated Times, receive for their Services a Compensation, which shall not be diminished during their Continuance in Office. . . .

Section 2. [1] The judicial Power shall extend to all Cases, in Law and Equity, arising under this Constitution, the Laws of the United States and Treaties made, or which shall be made, under their Authority; . . . to Controversies to which the United States shall be a Party;—to Controversies between two or more States;—between a State and Citizens of another State;—between Citizens of different States;—between Citizens of the same State claiming Lands under the Grants of different States, and between a State, or the Citizens thereof, and foreign States, Citizens or Subjects. . . .

ARTICLE VI

[2] This Constitution, and the Laws of the United States which shall be made in Pursuance thereof; and all Treaties made, or which shall be made, under the Authority of the United States, shall be the supreme Law of the Land; and the Judges in every State shall be bound thereby, any Thing in the Constitution or Laws of any State to the Contrary notwithstanding.

AMENDMENT I [1791]

Congress shall make no law respecting an establishment of religion, or prohibiting the free exercise thereof; or abridging the freedom of speech, or of the press; or the right of the people peaceably to assemble, and to petition the Government for a redress of grievances.

AMENDMENT IV [1791]

The right of the people to be secure in their persons, houses, papers, and effects, against unreasonable searches and seizures, shall not be violated, and no Warrants shall issue, but upon probable cause, supported by Oath or affirmation, and particularly describing the place to be searched, and the persons or things to be seized.

AMENDMENT V [1791]

No person shall be . . . compelled in any criminal case to be a witness against himself, nor be deprived of life, liberty, or property, without due process of law; nor shall private property be taken for public use, without just compensation.

AMENDMENT VIII [1791]

Excessive bail shall not be required, nor excessive fines imposed, nor cruel and unusual punishments inflicted.

AMENDMENT IX [1791]

The enumeration in the Constitution, of certain rights, shall not be construed to deny or disparage others retained by the people.

AMENDMENT X [1791]

The powers not delegated to the United States by the Constitution, nor prohibited by it to the States, are reserved to the States respectively, or to the people.

AMENDMENT XIV [1868]

Section 1. All persons born or naturalized in the United States, and subject to the jurisdiction thereof, are citizens of the United States and of the State wherein they reside. No State shall make or enforce any law which shall abridge the privileges or immunities of citizens of the United States; nor shall any State deprive any person of life, liberty, or property, without due process of law; nor deny to any person within its jurisdiction the equal protection of the laws.

Education and the American Legal System

In this appendix we look first at the role of state governments in education. Then we present the organization of U.S. court systems and indicate the way they relate to educational controversies. In reality the United States has 51 court systems; each of the 50 states has its own system, and there is one federal system. However, there are sufficient similarities in the state systems that a general model can represent them all, and similarly, a general model of the federal system (without all details), will suffice for our purposes.

EDUCATION IS CONTROLLED BY STATE GOVERNMENTS

Unlike most countries, the United States has no national system of education. In fact, the national Constitution is silent on the matter; however, under its Tenth Amendment, education is considered to be among the powers reserved to the states. Courts have accepted this interpretation of the Constitution, and the Supreme Court has repeatedly stated that federal courts may interfere with the actions of state and local school officials only when such actions somehow threaten a personal liberty or property right protected by the Constitution or violate federal law.

All 50 states provide for public education in their constitutions.

State legislatures provide for a state department of education that administers the system for the legislature. The state department of education may have an elected or appointed chief administrative officer and an elected or appointed board of lay citizens. These administrative bodies develop rules and regulations to carry out the laws passed by the legislatures.

With America's historic commitment to decentralized government and local control, states have delegated much power and responsibility over schooling to local governments. Such delegation is a choice made by the people of a state, who could, like the state of Hawaii, choose to have one statewide school district instead. In spite of the existence of local school districts, legally schools remain a responsibility of the state government; school officials, teachers, and staff, are agents of the state when performing their official duties. This is a significant principle because the Constitution only protects individuals against actions by the government. The first ten amendments to the Constitution (more commonly, the Bill of Rights) prohibit certain actions on the part of the federal government. The Fourteenth Amendment applies to actions by the states. Since all actions of school officials and school boards are "state actions," the Fourteenth Amendment prohibits certain arbitrary and discriminatory practices. What makes this all the more important is the historic development whereby all the guarantees of the First Amendment, and many other provisions of the Bill of Rights, have been incorporated into the "liberty clause" of the Fourteenth Amendment and thus made applicable to all the states. While there is a complex and controversial legal history to this incorporation, for our purposes it will suffice to understand that all civil rights protections of the First Amendment, and most civil rights protections of the other Bill of Rights provisions, apply to the actions of public school officials just as much as those of the Fourteenth Amendment.

Thus, while states have the primary power and responsibility for public schools, their power must be exercised at all times consistently with the rights guaranteed in the national Constitution.

THE FEDERAL COURT SYSTEM

The U.S. Supreme Court is the only court that was specifically created by the Constitution (Article III, section 2); all other federal courts were established by Congress. Below the Supreme Court are 13 circuit courts of appeal (see Figure 2), and within each circuit there are trial courts called district courts. Currently, there are about 96 district courts, at least one in each state, though their numbers may change from time to time. Except for special courts, such as the court of claims, tax court, or court of customs and patent appeals, we have a three-tiered hierarchy of federal courts. School-related cases involving federal issues may be brought to trial in a district court; from this court an appeal may be taken to a circuit court of appeals and eventually to the Supreme Court (see Figure 3).

The Constitution specifies what cases the Supreme Court will consider (Article III, section 2, clause 1). For all other federal courts, Congress deter-

376

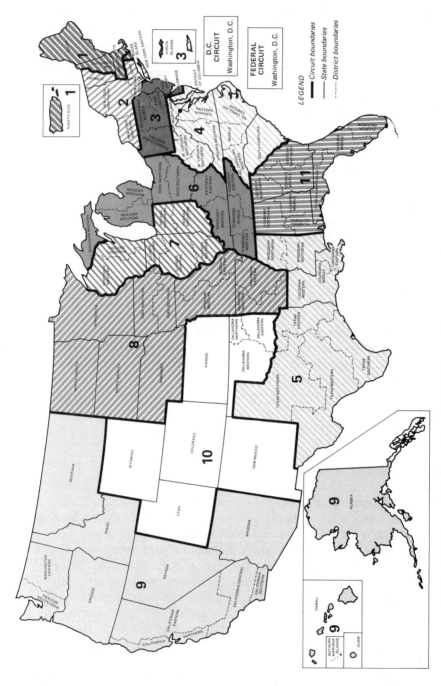

Figure 2. Geographical Boundaries of United States Courts of Appeals and United States District Courts

mines which cases will be tried where, the route appeals will take, and the relationship of courts to the many administrative agencies of government. In general, federal courts take only two kinds of cases: (1) those that present substantial questions under federal laws and the Constitution, and (2) those involving a diversity of jurisdiction (i.e., where suits involve different states or citizens of different states). Many cases present questions involving both federal and state laws and may initially be tried in either federal or state courts. If such a case is brought to trial in a federal court, however, it must decide questions of state law according to the laws of the affected state. Conversely, if the case was initially filed in a state court, it must follow the federal law governing that area.

While decisions of the Supreme Court are applicable to the entire nation, the decisions of circuit courts are binding only within their territories; thus different rules may apply in different regions of the country until the Supreme Court decides the issue. This resolution was illustrated several years ago by a Supreme Court ruling on teacher maternity-leave policies, and the unresolved conflict is illustrated by conflicts in holdings in personal appearance cases in different circuits.

Except for the cases specified by the Constitution, the Supreme Court has great discretion over which cases to accept for review. Literally thousands of petitions are submitted yearly to the Court, urging it to consider particular cases. In these petitions (known as a "petition for *certiorari*") the parties attempt to convince the Court of the significance of the particular issue. Approximately 3000 such petitions are submitted each year, but only a small

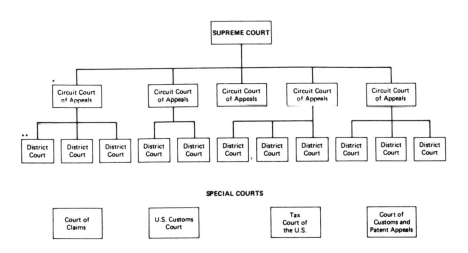

Figure 3. The Federal Court System

* There are currently 13 circuit courts of appeals, including one in the District of Columbia. Several judges may serve on any of these courts as well as other courts.
** There are currently 96 District Courts, including one in the District of Columbia.

number is granted by the Court. (The November 1979 issue of the *Harvard Law Review* presents a statistical summary and analysis of the annual work of the Court.)

THE STATE COURT SYSTEM

Most school-related cases are litigated in state courts. Since these courts are created by state constitutions and legislatures, however, they vary considerably in titles, procedures, and jurisdiction. A general pattern among the states is a three-tiered system, excluding the lower courts of special jurisdiction (see Figure 4).

At the foundation of the state court system, we find the trial courts, often organized along county lines. From these, appeals go to intermediate appeals courts and finally to the highest court of the state, variously named in different states. For example, the highest court is named the Supreme Judicial Court in Massachusetts, the Court of Appeals in Kentucky, the Supreme Court of Errors in Connecticut, and the Supreme Court in California.

THE FUNCTIONS OF TRIAL AND APPEALS COURTS

A school-related controversy that cannot be resolved without a lawsuit first goes to a trial court. Here the facts are established and the relevant legal principles applied to the facts. If the case is appealed, the appellate court will not retry the

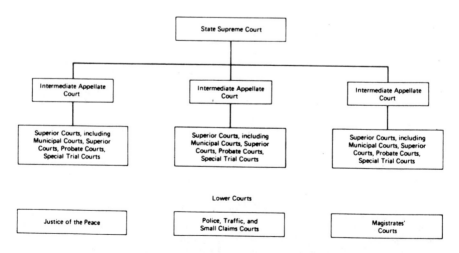

Figure 4. A Typical State Court System

case; it will usually accept the facts as established by the trial court unless it is very clear that evidence to support such facts was inadequate. The main concern of appeals courts is whether correct legal principles were applied to the facts determined by the court below.

For example, a school may want to terminate Teacher X for insubordination. Teacher X would typically fight such a case in a state court unless the claim could be reasonably made that a constitutionally protected activity (e.g., free speech) formed the basis of the dismissal. The trial court would hear evidence from both sides in order to establish whether the alleged behaviors occurred and whether they constituted insubordination. Once the facts were established, the trial court would apply the relevant law and arrive at a decision on the case. The judge would consider all laws, state and federal, applicable to the case, for Article IV of the Constitution provides that the Constitution and the "Laws of the United States" and "Treaties . . . shall be the Supreme Law of the Land" and that "Judges in any state shall be bound thereby." If the case were appealed, the appeals court would consider whether or not the principles of law were properly applied by the trial court.

The highest state court will be the final authority on legal questions related to the law of that state unless there is federal law on the same matter. The U.S. Supreme Court is the final authority on matters arising out of the Constitution, treaties, federal laws, or conflicts among state laws. In matters that involve only state laws, the state courts have the authoritative voice.

ADMINISTRATIVE BODIES

It is generally recognized today that the courts are overburdened and their calendars overcrowded. It is all too true that "justice delayed is justice denied," yet in many cities it takes over a year for a criminal case to come to trial and several years for a civil suit to be tried. This situation would be worse if we did not have administrative agencies acting in quasi-judicial capacities. Without a doubt, the largest and most detailed body of law is created by administrative rules and regulations, by agencies created by statutes to regulate public affairs. Administrative law functions at both federal and state levels, and the lives of educators are heavily influenced by them. (See, for example, Title IX regulations, Special Education regulations, Department of Education regulations, and others.)

HOW TO FIND REPORTS OF COURT CASES

Every county has a courthouse that contains a law library. Every law school has such a library, and most universities and colleges have legal collections. In each of these places a librarian can help one find cases of interest. The following brief comments constitute an introduction to legal research.

Appellate courts almost always publish their decisions. The decisions of the highest appellate court, the U.S. Supreme Court, can be found in the *United States Reports.* For example, the citation *Brown* v. *Board of Education of Topeka, Kansas,* 349 U.S. 294 (1955), indicates that the case, decided in 1955, is reported in volume 349 of the *United States Reports* at page 294. Since Supreme Court cases are reported in several publications, the same case may be followed by the notations 75 S.Ct. 753, 99 L.Ed. 1083. This means that the same case also appears in volume 75 of the *Supreme Court Reporter* at page 753 and in volume 99 of the *Lawyers Edition* at page 1083. (Because most educators will have access to libraries containing only the official reporters, cases mentioned in this book only include citations to the official reporter, such as *United States Reports.* The most recent cases decided by the Supreme Court appear in a looseleaf volume called *United States Law Week,* cited, for example, as *Givhan* v. *Western Line Consolidated School District,* 47 L.W. 4102 (January 9, 1979).

Cases decided by the U.S. Courts of Appeals are reported in the *Federal Reporter, Second Series.* For example, *Clark* v. *Whiting,* 607 F.2d 634 (4th Cir. 1979) would indicate that this case can be found in volume 607 of the *Federal Reporter, Second Series* at page 634 and that the case was decided by the Fourth Circuit Court of Appeals in 1979. Decisions of the federal district courts are reported in the *Federal Supplement* and are similarly cited. For example, *Valencia* v. *Blue Hen Conference,* 476 F.Supp. 809 (D. Del. 1979), indicates that this case was decided by a district court in Delaware in 1979 and is reported in volume 476 of the *Federal Supplement* at page 809.

Again, as in the case of decisions of the U.S. Supreme Court, state supreme court and state appellate court decisions are often published in more than one set of publications. One set is referred to as the "official reporter," and the other publications are referred to as "unofficial reporters." In New Jersey, for example, the official reporter is *New Jersey Reports* and the unofficial reporter is a regional volume known as the *Atlantic Reporter.*

Thus, cases decided by the Supreme Court of New Jersey are reported in both publications. The full citation for a case would look like this: *Tibbs* v. *Board of Education,* 59 N.J. 506, 284 A.2d 179 (1971). The "A.2d" indicates that this is the second series of the *Atlantic Reporter.* The original set of the *Atlantic Reporter* is cited as "A."; when a series becomes too long and the volume numbers too large, a second series is begun and cited as "A.2d." (As was mentioned previously in the discussion of U.S. Supreme Court cases, citations in the footnotes of this book refer to the publications to which teachers are most likely to have access, generally regional reporters.)

In addition to reading cases, teachers interested in a particular topic might go to one of the standard legal encyclopedias to gain an overview of the topic. The best known of these encyclopedias are *Corpus Juris Secundum* (cited as "C.J.S.") and *American Jurisprudence* (cited as "Am. Jur.").

The foregoing should suffice as an introduction to legal research for teachers. Anyone interested in a more thorough understanding of the field should consult with a law librarian and read one of the standard guides on the subject.

APPENDIX C

Major Civil Rights Laws Affecting Schools

OVERVIEW OF MAJOR FEDERAL CIVIL RIGHTS STATUTES RELATED TO ELEMENTARY AND SECONDARY SCHOOLS

Statute	Groups Protected	Interests Protected	Schools Covered
Acts of 1866, 1870 42 U.S.C., Sec. 1981	Race	Right to make and enforce contracts	Public and private if they solicit clients
Acts of 1871, 42 U.S.C. Sec. 1983	All individuals	Constitutional rights	Public and private if they operate "under color of law"
Acts of 1871, 42 U.S.C., Sec. 1985 (prohibits conspiracy)	All groups; general civil rights	Equal protection of law	Any conspiracy by any persons
Equal Pay Act of 1963, 29 U.S.C., Sec. 206(d)	Sex	Salaries and wages	All who are subject to the Fair Labor Standards Act
Civil Rights Act of 1964, 42 U.S.C. Sec. 2000, Title VI	Race, color, or national origin	All benefits under federally aided programs	All, in federally supported activities
Civil Rights Act. of 1964, 42 U.S.C. Sec. 2000, Title VII	Race, color, national origin, religion, sex	Employment benefits	All with 15 or more

Note: For excerpts of the statutes, see *Instructor's Manual*, Sec. 3.

Other Legal Resources for Teachers

1. American Association of
   School Administrators
   1801 N. Moore Street
   Arlington, VA. 22209
   (703) 528-0700

A national organization with state chapters that is a professional association of school administrators. Produces materials including *The School Administrator*.

2. American Civil Liberties Union
   132 W. 43rd Street
   New York, N.Y. 10036
   (212) 944-9800

A national organization with both state and local chapters that "champions individual rights set forth in the United States Constitution." Activities include litigation, lobbying for civil rights legislation, and publication of materials on civil liberties issues. State and local chapters also conduct seminars and take test cases.

3. American Federation of Teachers
   555 New Jersey Avenue, N.W.
   Washington, D.C. 20001
   (202) 879-4400

A national organization with local chapters that works with teachers in the areas of collective bargaining and employment rights. Engages in research and lobbying activities, offers technical assistance, and publishes materials including *American Teacher.*

4. National Association of
     Secondary School Principals
   1904 Association Drive
   Reston, VA. 22091
   (703) 860-0200

A national organization with state chapters that assist school administrators. Sponsors conferences and publishes materials including *Legal Memoranda* (five times a year).

5. National Education Association
   1201 16th Street, N.W.
   Washington, D.C. 20036
   (202) 833-4000

A national organization with state and local chapters that is a professional association of elementary and secondary school teachers and administrators. Provides technical assistance and publishes materials including *NEA Today*

6. National Organization on
     Legal Problems of Education
   3601 W. 29th Street
   Suite 223
   Topeka, Kansas 66614
   (913) 273-3550

An organization that exchanges information on school law among lawyers, school board members, and others. Conducts seminars and publishes materials on school law, including a monthly newsletter and an annual update.

7. State Department of Education

Each state department of education has a legal department that may provide publications or lists of state and local resources concerning education law.

Glossary

Administrative agency. Any branch or division of the government other than the judicial or legislative branches (such as the Social Security Administration, Veterans Administration, or the Department of Agriculture).

Administrative law. Regulations and procedures that govern the operation of administrative agencies.

Adversary system. System of law in America where the truth is thought to be best revealed through a clash in the courtroom between opposite sides to a dispute.

Affidavit. A written statement sworn to before a person officially permitted by law to administer an oath.

Amicus curiae. "Friend of the court"; a person or organization allowed to appear in a lawsuit, to file arguments in the form of a brief supporting one side or the other, even though not party to the dispute.

Answer. The first pleading by the defendant in a lawsuit. This statement sets forth the defendant's responses to the charges contained in the plaintiff's "complaint."

Appeal. Asking a higher court to review the actions of a lower court in order to correct mistakes or injustice.

Appellate court. A court having jurisdiction to review the actions of an inferior court (such as trial court) but not having the power to initially hear a legal action.

Beyond a reasonable doubt. The level of proof required to convict a person of a crime. This is the highest level of proof required in any type of trial, in contrast to *a fair preponderance of the evidence,* the level of proof in civil cases.

Brief. A written summary or condensed statement of a case. Also a written statement prepared by one side in a lawsuit to explain its case to the judge.

384

By a fair preponderance of the evidence. The level of proof required in a civil case. This level is lower than that required in criminal cases.

Cause of action. Facts sufficient to allow a valid lawsuit to proceed.

Certiorari. A request for review of a lower court decision, which the higher court can refuse.

Circumstantial evidence. Evidence which indirectly proves a main fact in question. Such evidence is open to doubt, since it is inferential, for example, a student seen in the vicinity of the locker room at the time of a theft is the thief.

Civil case. Every lawsuit other than a criminal proceeding. Most civil cases involve a lawsuit brought by one person against another and usually concern money damages.

Class action. A lawsuit brought by one person on behalf of himself or herself and all other persons in the same situation; persons bringing such suits must meet certain statutory criteria and must follow certain notice procedures.

Code. A collection of laws. Most states have an education code containing all laws directly relevant to education.

Common law. Law made by judges (as opposed to law made by legislatures).

Compensatory damages. Damages which relate to the actual loss suffered by a plaintiff, such as loss of income.

Complaint. The first main paper filed in a civil lawsuit. It includes, among other things, a statement of the wrong or harm done to the plaintiff by the defendant and a request for specific help from the court. The defendant responds to the complaint by filing an "answer."

Criminal case. Cases involving crimes against the laws of the state; unlike civil cases, the state is the prosecuting party.

De facto. In fact, actual; a situation that exists in fact whether or not it is lawful. *De facto* segregation is that which exists regardless of the law or the actions of civil authorities.

Defamation. Injuring a person's character or reputation by false or malicious statements. This includes both *libel* and *slander.*

Defendant (appellee). The person against whom a legal action is brought. This legal action may be civil or criminal. At the appeal stage, the party against whom an appeal is taken is known as the appellee.

De jure. Of right, legitimate; lawful. *De jure* segregation is that which is sanctioned by law.

De minimus. Small, unimportant; not worthy of concern.

Demurrer. The formal means by which one party to a lawsuit argues against the legal sufficiency of the other party's claim. A demurrer basically contends that even if all the facts which the other party alleges are true they do not constitute a legal cause of action.

De novo. New, completely new from the start; for example: a trial *de novo* is a completely new trial ordered by the trial judge or by an appeals court.

Dictum. A digression; a discussion of side points or unrelated points. Short for *obiter dictum;* plural is *dicta.*

Disclaimer. The refusal to accept certain types of responsibility. For example, a college catalogue may disclaim any responsibility for guaranteeing that the courses contained therein will actually be offered since courses, programs, and instructors are likely to change without notice.

En banc. The full panel of judges assigned to a court sit to hear a case, usually a case of special significance.

Equity. Fairness; the name of a type of court originating in England to handle legal problems when the existing laws did not cover some situations in which a person's rights were violated by another person. In the United States, civil courts have both the powers of law and equity. If only money is represented in a case, the court is acting as a law court and will give only monetary relief. If something other than money is requested—injunction, declaratory judgment, specific performance of a contractual agreement, etc.—then the court takes jurisdiction in equity and will grant a decree ordering acts to be done or not done. There is no jury in an equity case. Actions at law and suits in equity involve civil cases, not criminal.

Et al. "And others." When the words "et al." are used in an opinion, the court is thereby indicating that there are unnamed parties, either plaintiffs or defendants, also before the court in the case.

Ex parte. With only one side present; an *ex parte* judicial proceeding involves only one party without notice to, or contestation by, any person adversely affected.

Ex post facto law. A law which retrospectively changes the legal consequences of an act which has already been performed. Article 1, section 10 of the U.S. Constitution forbids the passage of ex post facto laws.

Expunge. Blot out. For example, a court order requesting that a student's record be expunged of any references to disciplinary action during such and such a time period means that the references are to be "wiped off the books."

Ex rel. On behalf of; when a case is titled *States ex rel. Doe* v. *Roe,* it means that the state is bringing a lawsuit against Roe on behalf of Doe.

Fiduciary. A relationship between persons in which one person acts for another in a position of trust.

Guardian ad litem. A guardian appointed by a court to represent a minor unable to represent him or herself.

Hearing. An oral proceeding before a court or quasi-judicial tribunal. Hearings which describe a process to ascertain facts and provide evidence are labeled "trial-like hearings" or, simply, "trials." Hearings which relate to a presentation of ideas as distinguished from facts and evidence are known as "arguments." The former occur in trial courts and the latter occur in appellate courts. The terms "trial," "trial-like hearing," "quasi-judicial hearing," "evidentiary hearing," and "adjudicatory hearing" are all used by courts and have overlapping meanings. See *trial.*

Hearsay. Secondhand evidence; facts not in the personal knowledge of the witness, but a repetition of what others said that is used to prove the truth of what those others said. Hearsay is generally not allowed as evidence at a trial, although there are many exceptions.

Holding. The rule of law in a case; that part of the judge's written opinion that applies the law to the facts of the case and about which can be said "the case means no more and no less than this." A holding is the opposite of *dictum*.

In camera. "In chambers"; in a judge's private office; a hearing in court with all spectators excluded.

Incriminate. To involve in a crime, to cause to appear guilty.

Informed consent. A person's agreement to allow something to happen (such as being the subject of a research study) that is based on a full disclosure of facts needed to make the decision intelligently.

Injunction. A court order requiring someone to do something or refrain from taking some action.

In loco parentis. In place of the parent; acting as a parent with respect to the care, supervision, and discipline of a child.

In re. In the matter of; this is a prefix to the name of a case often used when a child is involved. For example, *"In re John Jones"* might be the title of a child neglect proceeding though it is really against the parents.

Ipso facto. By the fact itself, by the mere fact that.

Judicial review. The power of a court to declare a statute unconstitutional; also the power to interpret the meaning of laws.

Jurisdiction. A court's authority to hear a case; also the geographical area within which a court has the right and power to operate. Original jurisdiction means that the court will be the first to hear the case; appellate jurisdiction means that the court reviews cases on appeal from lower court rulings.

Law. Basic rules of order as pronounced by a government. Common law refers to laws originating in custom or practice. Statute law refers to laws passed by legislatures and recorded in public documents. Case law are the pronouncements of courts.

Libel. Written defamation; published false and malicious written statements that injure a person's reputation.

Mandamus. A writ issued by a court commanding that some official duty be performed.

Material. Important, going to the heart of the matter; for example, a material fact is one necessary to reach a decision.

Misrepresentation. A false statement; if knowingly done, misrepresentation may be illegal and result in punishment.

Mitigation. The reduction in a fine, penalty, sentence, or damages initially assessed or decreed against a defendant.

Moot. Abstract; not a real case involving a real dispute.

Motion. A request made by a lawyer that a judge take certain action, such as dismissing a case.

Opinion. A judge's statement of the decision reached in a case.

    Concurring opinion. Agrees with the majority opinion, but gives different or added reasons for arriving at that opinion.

    Dissenting opinion. Disagrees with the majority opinion.

    Majority opinion. The opinion agreed on by more than half the judges or justices hearing a case, sometimes called the opinion of the court.

Ordinance. The term applied to a municipal corporation's legislative enactments.

Parens patriae. The historical right of all governments to take care of persons under their jurisdiction, particularly minors and incapacitated persons.

Per curiam. An unsigned decision and opinion of a court, as distinguished from one signed by a judge.

Petitioner. One who initiates a proceeding and requests some relief be granted on his behalf. A plaintiff. When the term "petitioner" is used, the one against whom the petitioner is complaining is referred to as the respondent.

Plaintiff. One who initiates a lawsuit; the party bringing suit.

Pleading. The process of making formal, written statements of each side of a case. First the plaintiff submits a paper with facts and claims; then the defendant submits a paper with facts and counterclaims; then the plaintiff responds; and so on until all issues and questions are clearly posed for a trial.

Political question. A question that the courts will not decide because it concerns a decision more properly made by another branch of government such as the legislature.

Precedent. A court decision on a question of law that gives authority or direction on how to decide a similar question of law in a later case with similar facts.

Prima facie. Clear on the face of it; presumably, a fact that will be considered to be true unless disproved by contrary evidence. For example, a *prima facie* case is a case that will win unless the other side comes forward with evidence to dispute it.

Punitive damages. Money awarded to a person by a court that is over and above the damages actually sustained. Punitive damages are designed to serve as a deterrent to similar acts in the future.

Quasi-judicial. The case-deciding function of an administrative agency.

Redress. To set right, remedy, make up for, remove the cause of a complaint or grievance.

Remand. Send back. A higher court may remand a case to a lower court with instructions to take some action in the case.

Res judicata. A thing decided. Thus, if a court decides a case, the matter is settled and no new lawsuit on the same subject may be brought by the persons involved.

Respondent. One who makes an answer in a legal appellate proceeding. This term is frequently used in appellate and divorce cases, rather than the more customary term, defendant.

Sectarian. Characteristic of a sect.

Secular. Not specifically religious, ecclesiastical or clerical; relating to the worldly or temporal.

Sine qua non. A thing or condition that is indispensable.

Slander. Oral defamation; the speaking of false and malicious words that injure another person's reputation, business, or property rights.

Sovereign immunity. The government's freedom from being sued for money damages without its consent.

Standing. A person's right to bring a lawsuit because he or she is directly affected by the issues raised.

Stare decisis. "Let the decision stand"; a legal rule that when a court has decided a case by applying a legal principle to a set of facts, that court should stick by that principle and apply it to all later cases with clearly similar facts unless there is a good reason not to. This rule helps promote fairness and reliability in judicial decision making and is inherent in the American legal system.

Statute of limitation. A statute which sets forth the time period within which litigation may be commenced in a particular cause of action.

Tort. A civil wrong done by one person to another. For an act to be a tort, there must be: a legal duty owed by one person to another, a breach of that duty, and harm done as a direct result of the action.

Trial. A process occurring in a court whereby opposing parties present evidence, subject to cross-examination and rebuttal, pertaining to the matter in dispute.

Trial court. The court in which a case is originally tried, as distinct from higher courts to which the case might be appealed.

Ultra vires. Going beyond the specifically delegated authority to act; for example, a school board which is by law restricted from punishing students for behavior occurring wholly off-campus acts *ultra vires* in punishing a student for behavior observed at a private weekend party.

Waiver. An intentional or uncoerced release of a known right.

Selected Bibliography

Alexander, Kern, and David M. Alexander. *The Law of Schools, Students and Teachers in a Nutshell* St. Paul, Minn.: West, 1984.

Bosmajian, Haig A., ed. *Academic Freedom.* New York: Neal Schuman Publishers, Inc., 1989.

Education for the Handicapped Law Report. Alexandria, Va: CRR Publishing Company, 1987.

Fellman, David, ed. *The Supreme Court and Education.* 3d ed. New York: Teachers' College Press, 1976.

Fischer, Louis, and Gail Paulus Sorenson. *School Law for Counselors, Psychologists, and Social Workers.* 2d ed. New York: Longman, 1991.

Gee, Gordon E., and David J. Sperry. *Education Law and the Public Schools: A Compendium.* Boston: Allyn and Bacon, 1978.

Goldstein, Stephen R. *Law and Public Education.* Indianapolis: Bobbs-Merrill, 1974.

Hagerty, Robert, and Thomas Howard. *How to Make Federal Mandatory Special Education Work for You: A Handbook for Educators & Consumers.* Springfield: Charles C. Thomas, 1978.

Hazard, William R. *Education and the Law: Cases and Materials on Public Schools.* 2d ed. New York: Free Press, 1978.

Hogan, John C. *The Schools, the Courts and the Public Interest.* 2d ed. Lexington, Mass.: Lexington Books, 1985.

Hull, Kent. *The Rights of Physically Handicapped People.* New York: Avon, 1979.

Journal of Law and Education. Jefferson Law Book Company, 646 Main Street, Cincinnati, Ohio 45201.

Kemerer, Frank R., and Kenneth L. Deutsch. *Constitutional Rights and Student Life.* St. Paul: West, 1979.

Levine, Alan H. *The Rights of Students.* New York: Avon, 1977.

Memin, Samuel. *Law and the Legal System: An Introduction*. Boston: Little, Brown, 1973.

Morris, Arval A. *The Constitution and American Education*. St. Paul: West, 1980.

Nolte, M. Chester. *How to Survive in Teaching: The Legal Dimension*. Chicago: Teach 'em, Inc., 1978.

Nygaard, Gary, and Thomas H. Boone. *Law for Physical Educators and Coaches*. 2d ed. Columbus, Ohio: Publishing Horizons, 1989.

O'Neil, Robert M. *Classrooms in the Crossfire: The Rights and Interests of Students, Parents, Teachers, Administrators, Librarians and the Community*. Bloomington: Indiana University Press, 1981.

Pepe, Thomas J. *A Guide for Understanding School Law*. Danville, Ill.: Interstate Printers and Publishers, 1976.

Peterson, LeRoy J., Richard A. Rossmiller, and Martin M. Volz. *The Law and the Public School Operation*. New York: Harper & Row, 1978.

Rapp, James. *Education Law*. New York: Matthew Bender, 1985.

Reutter, Edmund E., Jr. *The Law of Public Education*. 3d ed. Mineola, N.Y.: The Foundation Press, 1985.

Rothstein, Laura F. *Special Education Law*. New York: Longman, 1990.

Sametz, Lynn, and Caven S. Mcloughlin. *Educators, Children, and the Law*. Springfield, Ill.: C.C. Thomas, 1985.

Schimmel, David, and Louis Fischer. *The Rights of Parents*. Columbia, Md.: National Committee for Citizens in Education, 1987.

School Law News. Capitol Publications, Inc., Suite G-12, 2430 Pennsylvania Avenue, N.W., Washington, D.C. 20037.

Thomas, Stephen B. *The Yearbook of School Law 1987*. Topeka, Kansas: National Organization on Legal Problems of Education, 1987.

Valente, William D. *Education Law: Public and Private*. St. Paul, Minn.: West, 1985.

West's Education Law Reporter. St. Paul, Minn.: West Publishing Company, 1989.

Wong, Glenn M. *Essentials of Amateur Sports Law*. Denver Mass: Auburn House, 1988.

Yudof, Mark G., David L. Kirp, Tyll van Geel, and Betsy Levin. *Educational Policy and The Law*. 2d ed. Berkeley, Cal.: McCutchan Pub. Corp., 1982.

Table of Cases

Index

405